LEGAL
RESEARCH
IN A NUTSHELL

TENTH EDITION
By

MORRIS L. COHEN
Librarian (Retired) and Emeritus Professor of Law
Yale Law School

KENT C. OLSON
Director of Reference, Research and Instruction
University of Virginia Law Library

WEST®

A Thomson Reuters business

Mat #41004035

Thomson Reuters created this publication to provide you with accurate and authoritative information concerning the subject matter covered. However, this publication was not necessarily prepared by persons licensed to practice law in a particular jurisdiction. Thomson Reuters does not render legal or other professional advice, and this publication is not a substitute for the advice of an attorney. If you require legal or other expert advice, you should seek the services of a competent attorney or other professional.

Nutshell Series, In a Nutshell and the Nutshell Logo are
trademarks registered in the U.S. Patent and Trademark Office.

COPYRIGHT © 1968, 1971, 1978, 1985, 1992, 1996 WEST PUBLISHING CO.
© West, a Thomson business, 2003
© 2007 Thomson/West
© 2010 Thomson Reuters
 610 Opperman Drive
 St. Paul, MN 55123
 1–800–313–9378
Printed in the United States of America

ISBN: 978–0–314–26408–4

To my friends and colleagues at the
University of Virginia Law Library

—KO

PREFACE

More than forty years have now passed since the first edition of *Legal Research in a Nutshell* in 1968. Legal research then required access to a law library's extensive sets of digests and reporters, but today most research can be performed just as effectively from anywhere with an Internet connection. For many years Westlaw and Lexis have been among the most important legal information resources, but they have been joined in recent years by a wide range of free and subscription-based websites. Finding an answer to a legal question is easier than ever. Finding a correct and complete answer requires as much skill as it did in the print era.

Although the *Nutshell* focuses predominantly on online research methods, it also continues to devote attention to printed, or "traditional," legal resources. Online research can perform tasks impossible with print materials and can locate information unavailable in any local library, but keyword retrieval and search engines have not fully supplanted the sophisticated editorial tools that form the basis of our legal literature. Many online sources are based on printed works and incorporate their structure and logic. An understanding of their purpose and scope is required for effective research, whether it is done in print or online. An integrated approach to print and electronic sources pervades most of this text and shapes the actual practice of successful legal research.

This book presents legal materials in the order in which they are often consulted by beginning researchers. The first four chapters provide an introductory overview and cover essential secondary and primary sources in American law. General background sources such as legal encyclopedias and law review articles are discussed at the outset, just as they are usually the first sources consulted in research. Case research are discussed next, in keeping with the central place of court decisions in the American legal system and in legal education, followed by a discussion of constitutional and statutory law. The next four chapters cover areas such as legislative history, administrative regulations, court rules, and current awareness resources. While these topics are more specialized than the basic case law and statutory sources, they are just as important in many research situations. The final two chapters provide a brief introduction to research in international and foreign law. These topics may be beyond the scope of many introductory courses in legal research, but no consideration of legal resources is quite complete without recognizing the place of the United States in a larger community. The discussion of international and foreign law resources reflects their increased role in practice and in scholarship.

PREFACE

The book covers a wide range of government and commercial websites in addition to printed resources and Westlaw and LexisNexis databases. The Internet is notoriously fluid, of course, and yesterday's valuable site may be today's dead link. All addresses listed were still valid as of April 2010, and the *Nutshell*'s companion website <www.law. virginia.edu/nutshell> provides a regularly updated set of links to all sites mentioned in the text.

My colleague Amy Wharton was of great help in preparing this edition, spending evenings and weekends finding many of my errors, suggesting changes, and trying to make my prose less stilted. The rest of the team at the University of Virginia Law Library also contributed, if only by allowing me the time and space needed to complete the project. It is my pleasure and privilege to work with them.

KENT C. OLSON

Charlottesville, Virginia
April 2010

ACKNOWLEDGMENTS

The material shown in Exhibits 1–4, 1–5, 3–4, 3–14, 3–15, 4–6, 4–8, 4–14, 4–15, 5–7 and 5–8 is reprinted with permission of LexisNexis. Copyright 2010 LexisNexis, a division of Reed Elsevier Inc. All Rights Reserved. LexisNexis and the Knowledge Burst logo are registered trademarks of Reed Elsevier Properties Inc. and are used with the permission of LexisNexis.

The page shown in Exhibit 2–4 is reprinted from *Restatement of the Law, Torts—Liability for Physical Harm (Basic Principles): Tentative Draft No. 1* (March 28, 2001) with the permission of the American Law Institute.

The page shown in Exhibit 2–5 was previously published in the *Fordham Law Review* and is reprinted by permission.

The screenshot reproduced in Exhibit 4–12 is used with permission of the Legal Information Institute, Cornell Law School.

The page shown in Exhibit 4–16 is reprinted from *Subject Compilations of State Laws 2005–2006* and is reprinted by permission.

The material shown in Exhibit 5–10 is reproduced with permission of Congressional Quarterly Inc. Copyright 2007 by Congressional Quarterly Inc.

ACKNOWLEDGMENTS

The page shown in Exhibit 6–1 is reprinted from *Washington Information Directory* and used with permission of CQ Press, A Division of SAGE Publications Inc.

The material shown in Exhibit 6–2 is reprinted from *Federal Yellow Book* courtesy of Leadership Directories, Inc., http://www.leadershipdirectories.com.

The pages reproduced in Exhibits 8–2 to 8–5 are © 2010 CCH, a Wolters Kluwer Business. All Rights Reserved. Reprinted with permission from the *Standard Federal Tax Reporter*.

The screenshot reproduced in Exhibit 8–6 is used with permission of John Ensminger, author of http://doglawreporter.blogspot.com/ and of *Service and Therapy Dogs in American Society: Science, Law and the Evolution of Canine Caregivers* (Springfield, Ill.: Charles C. Thomas, 2010).

The screenshot reproduced in Exhibit 9–4 is used with permission of the Institute of Advanced Legal Studies, School of Advanced Study, University of London.

The screenshot reproduced in Exhibit 10–1 is used with permission of Foreign Law Guide.

OUTLINE

———

LEGAL RESEARCH
IN A NUTSHELL

TENTH EDITION

CHAPTER 1

THE RESEARCH PROCESS

---

§ 1–1. Introduction

Legal research is an essential component of legal practice. It is the process of identifying the rules that govern an activity and finding materials that explain or analyze those rules. These resources give

1

lawyers the knowledge with which to provide accurate and insightful advice, to draft effective documents, or to defend their clients' rights in court. Ineffective research wastes time and money, and inaccurate research leads to malpractice.

Determining what law applies to a particular situation requires expertise in legal analysis. Lawyers must be able to analyze factual situations, determine the relevant fields of legal doctrine, and apply rules developed by courts, legislatures, and administrative agencies. Finding these rules requires expertise in legal research. Traditionally this meant mastering the print resources housed in a law library. Today much of the law library may be found online, but the need for legal research expertise is no less critical. Not all legal information is equally trustworthy or authoritative, and not all search methods are equally effective. You will know you've become proficient when you feel comfortable with using multiple search techniques and can discern quality resources from an overabundant supply of information.

To best serve your clients, you will need excellent legal research skills both to gain knowledge of the present state of the law and to assess its trajectory for the future. While these skills take time and practice to develop, it is here that your journey toward proficiency begins.

§ 1–2.   The Sources of the Law

The law consists of the recorded rules that society will enforce and the procedures by which they are implemented. These rules and procedures are created in various ways. Statutes are enacted by elected representatives, for example, while common law doctrines are shaped over the course of many years in court decisions. These are just two of the many sources of the law, but the distinction between statutory and common law is one of several dichotomies and classifications that characterize the legal system.

Both federal and state governments have law-making powers, and in each case three branches—legislative, executive, and judicial—share in this responsibility. As the elected voice of the citizens, the legislature raises and spends money, defines crimes, regulates commerce, and generally determines public policy by enacting statutes. Some of these statutes are broadly worded statements of public policy, while others regulate activity in minute detail.

The executive branch is charged with enforcing the law, and in the process it creates legally binding rules. The president and most governors issue executive orders, and administrative agencies provide detailed regulations governing activity within their areas of expertise. Agencies also act in a "quasi-judicial" capacity by conducting hearings and issuing decisions to resolve particular disputes. These *administrative law* sources are less familiar to law students and the public than statutes and court decisions, but they may be just as important in determining legal rights and responsibilities. Attorneys in heavily regulated areas such as securities law or telecommunications may work more frequently with agency pronouncements than with congressional enactments.

The judicial branch plays a complex role in this system. Judges apply the language of constitutions and statutes to court cases, which often involve circumstances that could not have been foreseen when the laws were enacted. In many instances, these judicial interpretations are just as important as the text of the provisions they interpret. The courts have determined, for example, that sexual harassment is a form of employment discrimination under the Civil Rights Act of 1964 even though those words never appear in the statute. Through the power of *judicial review*, asserted by Chief Justice Marshall in *Marbury v. Madison*, the courts also determine the constitutionality of acts of the legislative and executive branches.

Judges also create and shape the *common law*. In a common law system such as ours, the law is expressed in an evolving body of doctrine determined by judges in specific cases, rather than in a group of prescribed abstract principles. As established rules are tested and adapted to meet new situations, the common law grows and changes over time.

An essential element of the common law is the doctrine of precedent, or *stare decisis* ("let the decision stand"), under which courts are bound to follow earlier decisions. These prior cases provide guidance to later courts faced with similar issues, and aid in preventing further disputes. People can study earlier cases, evaluate the legal impact of planned conduct, and modify their behavior to conform to existing rules. Although the law changes with time, precedent is designed to provide both fairness and stability. The important role of judicial decisions as precedent makes them vital to American legal research.

The law school curriculum sorts legal issues another way as well, into distinct areas of doctrine such as contract, tort, and property. In doing so, it provides a framework for analyzing legal situations and applying a particular body of rules. Real life does not always divide so neatly into issues of contract or tort, but legal materials generally follow this paradigm. A lawyer with a case involving injury from a defective product, for example, may need to research breach of warranty issues in texts and articles on contracts as well as strict liability and negligence issues in the tort literature.

Other distinctions that pervade legal thinking include *civil* and *criminal law*, *substance* and *procedure*, and *state* and *federal jurisdiction*. Law students learn how legal issues fit into these dichotomies, not only to solve problems but to know where to look for answers. Classifying a question is necessary, but it is important not to pigeonhole a situation too narrowly. Analysis within a particular doctrinal area can clarify a specific issue, but most situations contain issues from a number of areas. A lawyer who does thorough research on causation issues but forgets about the statute of limitations or service of process is a lawyer who loses cases.

§ 1–3. The Forms of Legal Information

Effective legal research requires not only knowledge of the nature of the legal system, but also an understanding of the ways in which legal information is disseminated. Several characteristics affect the research process. Laws are published chronologically, and meaningful access requires both resources that compile current laws and those that provide access to historical sources. Legal literature is comprised of both official, primary statements of the law and an extensive body of unofficial secondary writings. Information is accessible both in print and electronically, creating a wide range of research choices.

a. Current and Historical Information

The legal system is created over the course of time, and the law in force today is a combination of old and new enactments and decisions. The United States Constitution has been in force for more than two centuries, and many judicial doctrines can be traced back even farther. These laws generally retain their force and effect until they are expressly repealed or overruled. Other laws are just days or weeks old, as legislatures, courts, and executive agencies address issues of current concern. To determine the law that governs a particular situation, you may need access to some sources that are centuries old and others that have just been issued.

This vast body of legal sources has required creation of a complex collection of resources to find relevant information. Today the most widely used research approach is keyword searching in databases that contain the full text of thousands of court decisions or other documents. Other ways to access court opinions include digests with case summaries arranged by subject; texts and reference works summarizing and comparing similar cases; and citators tracing doctrines forward in time. Statutes and regulations in force are arranged by subject in codes, which are accessible online by keyword or in print through detailed indexes. Laws no longer in force may be required to interpret documents or resolve disputes, so historical resources are needed as well. Many older materials have been digitized and are available online, but some can be found only in print.

It is just as important for lawyers and others interested in the legal system to keep up with new developments, and numerous resources exist to provide current information. New statutes, regulations, and court decisions are issued by the government and by commercial publishers, both in print and electronically. Newsletters, looseleaf services, websites, and blogs provide notice and analysis of new developments.

The codes and texts that lawyers use are updated regularly to reflect changes. Many print publications have *pocket parts*, supplements which fit inside the back covers of bound volumes, while others are issued in looseleaf binders and updated with supplementary inserts or replacement pages. Some online resources are updated on the same schedule as their print counterparts, while others are revised on a daily basis.

b. Primary and Secondary Sources

Legal sources differ in the weight they are accorded. Some are binding authority, while others are only persuasive in varying degrees or are useful only as tools for finding other sources. Each source must be used with a sense of its place in the hierarchy of authority. A decision from a state supreme court has much more authority in its jurisdiction than a scholarly article, but rulings from courts in other jurisdictions may have less persuasive value than an influential article.

In evaluating authority, you must distinguish between *primary* and *secondary sources*. Primary sources are the official pronouncements of the government lawmakers: the court decisions, legislation, and regulations that form the basis of the legal doctrine. Not all primary sources have the same force for all purposes. A decision from a state supreme court is mandatory authority in its jurisdiction and must be followed by the lower state courts. A state statute also must be followed within the state. Other primary sources are only persuasive authority; a court in one state may be influenced by decisions in other states faced with similar issues, but it is free to make up its own mind. A statute or regulation from one state is not even persuasive authority in another state.

Works which are not themselves the law, but which discuss or analyze legal doctrine, are considered secondary sources. These include treatises, hornbooks, *Restatements*, and the academic journals known as *law reviews*. Secondary sources serve a number of important functions in legal research. Scholarly commentaries can propose changes in the law, clarify the sometimes bewildering array of statutes and court decisions, and provide current awareness about developing legal doctrines. Their footnotes contain extensive references to primary sources and to other secondary material.

c. Print and Electronic Resources

Most of the resources to be discussed in this book first appeared in printed form and developed as print publications over several decades or even centuries. Detailed editorial systems such as digests, citators, and annotated codes were created to make sense of the jumble of primary sources. Lawyers now do more research online than in print, but books still have some advantages. The astute researcher knows how to take advantage of both media.

Electronic research has dramatically reshaped the legal research process. Online databases can integrate a variety of tasks that are conducted with separate print sources, such as finding cases, checking the current validity of their holdings, and tracking down secondary commentary. You can search the full text of documents for specific combinations of words and are not limited to the choices made by the editors who create indexes and digests. A research situation presents a unique set of factual and legal topics, and an online search can find documents that address each specific confluence of issues. Hypertext links between documents make it possible to pursue leads and ideas as they arise, rather than following one linear research path.

Yet editors have hardly been put out of work. Researchers forced to work only with an uncontrolled mass of electronic data can quickly find themselves drowning in unstructured information. Tools such as digests and indexes, whether used online or in print, continue to provide the invaluable service of presenting material by subject. Basic online keyword searches find only those documents that match terms exactly. A treatise or encyclopedia may point you toward important documents with slightly different terms or facts, or it may confirm your results and boost your confidence.

Computerized research has also blurred the distinctions among different types of information and broadened the scope of legal inquiry. Case law research, for example, was traditionally a process quite distinct from research in secondary commentary or social sciences. When researching online you can switch from one source to another and back again, bringing to legal research more empirical experience and a wider range of scholarly commentary.

Two major commercial database systems, Westlaw <www.westlaw.com> and Lexis <www.lexis.com>, are widely used in law schools and in legal practice as comprehensive legal research tools. Westlaw and Lexis, however, are available only to subscribers and other paying customers. Law students generally have access through their school's subscriptions, but for other researchers these can be expensive tools. (Much of the information in these databases may be available to university faculty and students through LexisNexis Academic <web.lexis-nexis.com/universe/> or Westlaw Campus Research <campus.westlaw.com>.)

Other commercial online research systems provide lower-cost alternatives to Westlaw and Lexis for access to primary sources. These systems generally have reliable access to case law and statutes, but offer a smaller range of secondary sources and other features. Some of these, such as Loislaw <www.loislaw.com> and VersusLaw <www.versuslaw.com>, are available free to law students. Others, such as Casemaker <www.lawriter.net> and Fastcase <www.fastcase.com>, are offered to lawyers as a free or low-cost benefit of state bar membership.

Free Internet sites, particularly those provided by the federal and state governments, can also be valuable sources of legal information. In addition to current statutes and recent case law, government sites also may include previously hard-to-find resources such as legislative documents, administrative agency materials, and court documents. Several websites have directories organizing legal material by jurisdiction and topic. Sites such as FindLaw <lp.findlaw.com> and Cornell Law School's Legal Information Institute <www.law.cornell.edu> provide links to primary sources, blogs, journals, and numerous other sources.

Google <www.google.com> and other Internet search engines can also help you find relevant sites, although it may be difficult to evaluate results and weed out advertisements and misleading information. Search engines focusing on legal materials, such as Westlaw WebPlus (available only to Westlaw subscribers while logged in) and Lexis Web <www.lexisweb.com>, may yield more focused results. The Internet is also an invaluable means of linking scholars and researchers through websites, blogs, and e-mail.

One advantage of major commercial services such as Westlaw or Lexis is that their information is generally (but not always) accurate and up to date. Even government sites can present obsolete information without indicating that it is no longer current, and other websites can be biased, selective in coverage, or dangerously out of date. You must always assess the currency and reliability of information found online before relying on it as an accurate statement of the law.

§ 1–4. Legal Language

One of the tasks law students face is mastering a new way of speaking and writing. The law has developed its own means of expression over the centuries. Latin words and phrases are still prevalent, from the familiar writs of *certiorari* and *habeas corpus* to doctrines such as *res ipsa loquitur*, and even everyday words such as *infant* or *issue* may have specialized meanings in legal documents.

A good law dictionary is needed to understand the language of the law. The leading work, *Black's Law Dictionary* (Bryan A. Garner ed., 9th ed. 2009), provides definitions for more than 45,000 terms, and includes pronunciations and nearly 3,000 quotations from scholarly works. It can be used to find new legal terminology and to define older terms found in historical documents. The eighth edition of the dictionary is available on Westlaw.

Less comprehensive law dictionaries are available as free Internet resources. These include works hosted by FindLaw <dictionary.lp.findlaw.com> and law.com <dictionary.law.com>. Other works found in law libraries or bookstores include *Ballentine's Law Dictionary* (3d ed. 1969, available online through Lexis), which was once the major competitor to *Black's* but it is now considerably out of date; Steven H. Gifis, *Law Dictionary* (5th ed. 2003); and

Daniel Oran, *Oran's Dictionary of the Law* (4th ed. 2000).

Other language reference works are also available. Bryan A. Garner, editor of *Black's Law Dictionary*, is also author of *A Dictionary of Modern Legal Usage* (2d ed. 1995, earlier ed. available on Lexis), which focuses on the way words are used in legal contexts. It is an entertaining guide to legal language's complexities and nuances, with definitions and essays providing guidance for clear and simple writing. William C. Burton, *Burton's Legal Thesaurus* (4th ed. 2006) can aid the research process by identifying alternate search terms for use in indexes or online databases. Several sources reprint the most memorable uses of legal language. Fred R. Shapiro, *Oxford Dictionary of American Legal Quotations* (1993), the most scholarly of these, is arranged topically, with precise citations to original sources and indexes by keyword and author.

§ 1–5. Legal Citations

A second hurdle in understanding legal literature is decoding the telegraphic citation form used in most sources. Before reading *Tarasoff v. Regents of the University of California*, a researcher must be able to decipher "551 P.2d 334 (Cal. 1976)" and understand that "551" is the volume number, "334" the page number, and "P.2d" the abbreviation for the *Pacific Reporter, Second Series*, a source for California Supreme Court opinions. This form may seem obscure at first, but in a very succinct manner it provides the information necessary to find the source and to determine its potential value as precedent. All case citations, for example, identify not only where a case can be found but also the issuing court and the date of decision.

The standard guide to legal citation form is *The Bluebook: A Uniform System of Citation* (19th ed. 2010) <www.legalbluebook.com>, published by the Harvard Law Review Association. *The Bluebook* establishes rules both for proper abbreviations and usage of signals such as "cf." and "But see." The Association of Legal Writing Directors' *ALWD Citation Manual* (3d ed. 2006) is used in numerous law schools and by a few journals as a more straightforward and easier-to-learn alternative to *The Bluebook*. Cornell Law School's Legal Information Institute publishes an online Introduction to Basic Legal Citation <www.law.cornell.edu/citation/>, a concise guide that incorporates both *Bluebook* and *ALWD* rules.

Even though most research is done electronically, *The Bluebook* and other citation systems generally require references to page numbers in printed sources if the material is published in that form. Some electronic resources provide PDF page images that mirror the printed version, while others (including Westlaw and Lexis) indicate the printed page numbers in the text of the electronic documents. In some instances, however, a complete citation may still require tracking down the original print publication in the library.

Citations to legal authorities that do not depend on references to particular volume and page numbers, and thus can be easily used online as well as in print, are called *public domain* or *medium neutral* citations. Under such a system, official numbers are assigned to documents as they are issued, and each paragraph is numbered so that references to specific portions of the text can be identified. This approach has been endorsed by the American Bar Association, and if a public domain citation is available its use is required by *The Bluebook*. Only a few jurisdictions, however, have adopted rules requiring paragraph numbers or other public domain citation features. *Universal Citation Guide* (2d ed. 2004) has guidelines for a uniform public domain format.

No matter what citation rules are followed, part of the puzzle is simply deciphering an abbreviation in order to identify its source. Reference works such as *Black's Law Dictionary* and *The Bluebook* contain tables listing the major abbreviations found in legal literature, but these are hardly comprehensive. Cases and law review articles contain numerous abbreviations and citations that are cryptic even to experienced researchers. The most convenient guide to abbreviations may be the free online Cardiff Index to Legal Abbreviations <www.legalabbrevs.cardiff.ac.uk>, which can be searched by abbreviation or title keyword. Specialized abbreviation dictionaries, such as Mary Miles Prince, *Prince's Bieber Dictionary of Legal Abbreviations* (6th ed. 2009, earlier edition available on Lexis) and

Donald Raistrick, *Index to Legal Citations and Abbreviations* (3d ed. 2008), also have extensive coverage of both common and obscure abbreviations.

§ 1–6. Online Research Basics

The methods of legal research using books depend on factors such as the scope of the work and the nature of its indexing. Approaches to specialized resources such as digests and annotated codes will be discussed in later chapters. Online legal research, on the other hand, has several basic characteristics no matter what type of sources are being explored.

Because legal research often requires identifying relevant documents from the thousands or millions of documents in a database, simple Internet-type searches for keywords or phrases may not always be sufficient. Online databases such as Westlaw and Lexis permit much more powerful and focused searches, allowing the use of features such as synonyms, truncation, proximity connectors, and field restrictions for searching specific parts of documents. They also accommodate natural language searching, provide hyperlinks between documents, and display information on the validity of primary sources.

Which database to use for a particular research problem (if a choice is available) is a decision based in part on personal preference and in part on the features and resources offered. Law students should learn to use more than one online system, if only to be prepared for whatever their employers offer once they enter practice.

a. Westlaw

In February 2010, Westlaw announced a new research platform that can dramatically affect the way online research is conducted. This new platform, called WestlawNext, changes several of the basic features of searching. For a few years, however, it will be offered along with the traditional Westlaw platform and will not even be available to all users immediately. Most of this discussion therefore focuses on traditional research techniques, many of which will carry over to the new platform, with a few major WestlawNext changes noted.

Database Selection. Using the traditional Westlaw platform, one of the first choices confronting an online researcher is the selection of an appropriate database. Westlaw has a wide selection of databases, some limited to particular jurisdictions or specific subject areas and others providing more comprehensive access. Whether to limit research to a particular jurisdiction or topical area depends upon a variety of factors, including cost (searches in large databases are generally more expensive), the purpose of the research, and the value of information from other jurisdictions or in other subjects.

Several means are available for choosing appropriate databases. The introductory Westlaw screen includes a "Search for a database" box, and typing keywords such as "animal torts" in the box will retrieve a list of suggested databases. Westlaw also has an online directory that lists databases by jurisdiction and subject. Exhibit 1–1 on page 38 shows part of the Westlaw directory, indicating some of its federal case law databases. The *i* icon after the name of each database leads to an explanation of its scope of coverage. The directory is also available for free <directory.westlaw.com> so that you can find databases without logging in or incurring search charges.

Perhaps the most significant innovation of WestlawNext is that it does not require choosing a database before searching. You simply identify the jurisdiction in which you are interested, and WestlawNext searches across several types of core legal materials. Once your search is complete, you are presented with a list of document types (e.g., cases, statutes, secondary sources) and choose which to view. A WestlawNext search screen is shown in Exhibit 1–2 on page 39.

Searching. Westlaw offers two basic methods of searching: natural language, and terms and connectors (or Boolean). In the traditional Westlaw, you choose which method to use for each search. WestlawNext has a single search box in which you enter your query, and it recognizes the search method you've chosen. Whichever version of Westlaw you are using, you should understand the strengths of each approach.

A natural language search allows you to enter a phrase, or a combination of words (e.g., *Is an owner without knowledge of her dog's vicious propensity liable for injuries?* or simply *vicious dog liability knowledge*). The computer assigns relative weights to the terms in a query, depending on how often they appear in the database. It then retrieves a specified number of the most relevant documents, giving greater weight to the less common terms. Every search term will not necessarily appear in all documents retrieved, but you can specify "required terms" that *must* appear in every document.

A terms and connectors search can provide greater precision in retrieval, but it requires learning a structured search syntax. Specific terms or phrases are joined by logical connectors such as *and*, or by proximity connectors indicating the maximum number of words that can separate the search terms (e.g., */10*) or specifying that the words appear in the same sentence (*/s*) or the same paragraph (*/p*). In Westlaw, an *or* connector is understood between two adjacent search terms. The search *dangerous dog*, for example, searches for documents containing either the word *dangerous* or the word *dog*. To search for a phrase such as "dangerous dog," you must place the phrase in quotation marks. A terms and connectors search screen is shown in Exhibit 1–3 on page 40.

Another aspect of terms and connectors searching is the use of the truncation symbols *!* and ***. An exclamation point is used to find any word beginning with the specified letters. *Manufactur!*, for example, finds *manufacturer*, *manufactured*, and *manufacturing*. Without the truncation symbol, only the word itself and its plural form are retrieved. *Manufacturer* retrieves *manufacturers*, but not *manufactured* or *manufacturing*. The asterisk is less frequently used, but represents a particular character or a limited number of characters. *Legali*e* retrieves either the American *legalize* or the British *legalise*, and *hand*** retrieves *hand*, *handy* or *handle* but not *handgun*.

Term Frequency is another tool available with terms and connectors searching, and allows you to specify that a particular term appear at least a specified number of times in a document. This makes it more likely that retrieved cases or articles will focus on the term rather than mentioning it in passing. The word "dog" might be used in a saying such as "Every dog has its day," but a search for *atleast10(dog)* will skip such documents and find those more likely to discuss canine-related issues.

Terms and connectors searches can become quite long and complicated, with several groups of terms in parentheses telling the system which terms to combine first. Complex searches can be unnecessarily confusing, however, and it is usually more effective to run a simple search and use its results as a springboard to find other documents.

Whether natural language or terms and connector searching is used, the search terms entered will determine what documents are retrieved. Since most concepts can be expressed in more than one way, it is important to enter synonyms or related terms. One court decision may use the word *ambiguous*, another *vague*, and a third *unclear*. Westlaw has an online thesaurus to help you identify additional terms. For *dog*, for example, it provides such terms as *domestic animal*, *pet*, and *canine*. In a terms and connectors search, these alternates are simply typed one after the other, as in *dangerous /p dog animal canine*; in a natural language search, alternate terms are included in parentheses after the term to which they relate, as in *dangerous dog (animal canine) liability*.

One major difference between the two types of searching is that a natural language search always retrieves the same number of documents, unless it includes required terms. (The number is something you determine on the Preferences–Search screen, and can be anywhere from 1 to 100.) A terms and connectors search, on the other hand, can retrieve anywhere from nothing to thousands of cases, depending on how well the search is written and how often the terms appear in the database. The number of retrieved documents can be a useful indication of whether your search was appropriate. In a natural language search result, which ranks documents by relevance, the first few documents may be right on point but the value of subsequent documents can drop off precipitously. It is important to recognize when relevance declines, and to be aware that reading every document retrieved will usually be a waste of time. The effectiveness of a search depends on the quality of the documents found, not their quantity.

Researchers generally develop a preference for natural language or terms and connectors search methods, but they are best suited for different purposes. Because natural language searching retrieves documents based on how frequently search terms appear, it is ideal for finding documents on issues involving frequently used terms such as "summary judgment." Many cases mention the standards for summary judgment, but the few decisions focusing on it in depth would be presented first as most relevant. Natural language is also useful for finding one highly relevant document as a starting point, especially if drafting an appropriate terms and connectors search seems too daunting a task. Terms and connectors searches, which require documents to match a request exactly, are generally more effective when searching for a particular phrase or a precise combination of terms. Often the best strategy is to perform similar searches using both methods.

Fields and Filters. *Fields* are an important feature of Westlaw searching. These are specific parts of a document, such as the title of an article or the name of the judge writing an opinion. Limiting a search to a particular field can produce much more specific results. A search in a case database for *bell* retrieves every decision mentioning the word *bell* anywhere in the opinion. A title search, *ti(bell)*, retrieves only those cases where one of the parties is named Bell.

Some fields allow research that is virtually impossible by other means. It would be a lengthy and tedious process manually to find all opinions written by a particular judge, but you can easily retrieve a complete list of a judge's opinions with online searches such as *ju(sotomayor)*. You can examine a judge's decisions on a particular topic by combining this request with other search terms. The list of available fields is in a drop-down box on the terms and connectors search screen, below the "Dates" box as shown in Exhibit 1–3.

You can use fields in WestlawNext, but the new platform also offers another way to narrow retrieval after doing a search. The results screen offers several ways to filter documents by topic, author, date, and other characteristics. You can run a more general search and do much of the "field" narrowing once you have results to evaluate.

Results Display. Once you enter a search, Westlaw displays either a list of retrieved documents showing the context in which the search terms appear or the beginning of the first document. Buttons at the bottom of the document display allow you to jump to the portions of the document that match the search query or go to the next document. Natural language search results also include a *Best* button to focus on the part of the document that most closely matches the query. Most documents on Westlaw include *star paging*, which indicates the page breaks in the original printed sources. This allows you to cite to a particular passage in a case, law review article, or other document without having to track down the printed version.

WestlawNext offers three levels of viewing, depending on how closely you need to study retrieved documents. You can begin with "Less Detail" providing only cursory information about each document, and then switch as appropriate to "More Detail" and "Most Detail."

In addition to the documents retrieved by the search, Westlaw displays a "Results Plus" list (simply called "Related Documents" in WestlawNext) suggesting secondary sources and other materials based on the concepts in the search or the terms in a specific document retrieved. These references to legal encyclopedias and other sources may provide helpful background and can lead to additional research resources.

Other Features. If a completed search retrieves a large number of cases, you can narrow your inquiry by using the *Locate* feature, or *Search Within Results* in WestlawNext. This allows you to search within the retrieved set of documents for specific terms, even if those terms were not included in the initial request.

A valuable Westlaw feature which many students overlook is the ability to save a search and have the system automatically run it to check for new material on a daily or weekly basis. This feature, West-Clip, can be accessed by clicking on the "Add Search to WestClip" link at the top of the full screen list of search results, and provides for notification either by e-mail or when you sign onto Westlaw. WestClip is a convenient way to stay abreast of developments in a specific case or in an area of interest.

Locate and WestClip work only with terms and connectors searches, not natural language. Both services identify documents that match specific criteria, rather than finding the most relevant documents as a natural language search does. The ability to take advantage of these services is a good reason to become proficient in terms and connectors searching instead of relying too heavily on natural language.

Most legal documents cite extensively to other documents, such as cases, statutes, and law review articles, and you may find it necessary to examine these cited sources. Westlaw hyperlinks to these other documents if they are available online. A new document may open in a "Link Viewer," making it easy to return to the original source, but clicking the "Maximize" button enables the full array of Westlaw features for the new document and lets you pursue a new line of research from its links.

KeyCite. A Westlaw document has links not only to the resources it cites, but also to later sources that cite it. This is done through the KeyCite feature, which is an integral part of Westlaw's document display. If later citing documents are available, the display includes a small "C" (or one of several other symbols conveying more specific information) at the top of the document and a "Citing References" link to the left. Clicking on either of these links will lead to a list of cases, law review articles, court documents, and other sources that make some reference to the document being viewed. This is an invaluable way to find related materials and to bring research forward in time.

If a document has been frequently cited, KeyCite has several ways to focus retrieval. *Limit KeyCite Display* can be used to see only particular types of documents, references from specific jurisdictions, or documents using specific keywords. In the same way that WestClip provides automatic notification of new documents matching a particular search, KeyCite Alert is a service for receiving notice of any new citations to an important document. You can limit a KeyCite Alert to specific keywords, creating an easy way to learn of new citing documents meeting very specific criteria.

KeyCite plays an important role in case research, where it is used to determine that a decision is still "good law," and will be discussed more fully in Chapter 4.

b. Lexis

Using Lexis is quite similar to using Westlaw, with just enough differences to make either system a challenge for someone familiar only with its competitor. Lexis too is in the process of creating a new platform, but its format and features had not been announced at the time this book was prepared.

Database Selection. The first step in using Lexis is to choose an appropriate database from the menu on the screen. You can browse through the databases listed on the screen, use the "Find a Source" tab to look for a database, or search the free directory <w3.nexis.com/sources/>. Exhibit 1–4 on page 41 shows a Lexis database list, with "i" icons linking to information about the contents and scope of coverage of each database.

Searching. Lexis offers both natural language and terms and connectors searching. Natural language searching is similar to Westlaw's. You can specify the number of documents retrieved, from as few as ten to as many as 250. If you add "mandatory terms" that *must* appear in all documents, you may get a smaller results list.

Lexis terms and connectors searching is slightly different than Westlaw's. Most connectors are similar, although you must include the word *or* between synonyms or related terms. Because an *or* is not understood between adjacent words, phrases in Lexis do not have to be entered in quotations. Proximity connectors begin with *w/* instead of just / (as in *w/10*, *w/s*, or *w/p*), although each system is forgiving enough to understand the other's format. Like Westlaw, Lexis uses the ! and * characters to truncate terms and find word variations. Exhibit 1–5 on page 42 shows a basic terms and connectors search screen.

Lexis includes a "suggest terms for my search" feature that is broader than a thesaurus. It lists not only synonyms and related concepts but terms that regularly appear near the term. *Dog*, for example, leads to such terms as *injury*, *vicious*, *probable cause*, and *propensity*. These may suggest further search terms or other lines of inquiry.

Segments. The Lexis counterparts to Westlaw's *fields* are called *segments*. Segments are added to a terms and connectors search by clicking "Restrict by Segment," and to a natural language search as "mandatory terms." The *atleast* segment, as in *atleast10(dog)*, is used to specify the minimum number of times a term must appear in each document.

Results Display. Lexis has three basic display formats. *Cite* provides a list of citations, including the overview and core terms; you can choose *Show hits* to display the search terms as well. *Full* displays an entire document, and *KWIC*, short for "key words in context," shows an individual case with a window of twenty-five words around each occurrence of the search terms. Lexis includes star paging references for most documents, and links to cases, statutes, law review articles, and other documents available in its databases.

Other Features. Like Westlaw's *Locate*, the *Focus* feature provides a way to examine a retrieved set of documents for specific terms without incurring additional charges. Two Lexis features providing other ways to expand research are *More Like This* and *More Like Selected Text*. *More Like This* finds either cases that cite the same authorities (*Core Cites*) or cases that use similar terms (*Core Terms*).

You may find it useful to begin a research project by searching by topic or headnote. This provides a way to explore legal topics, such as Torts–Harm Caused by Animals–Dangerous Animals. Once a topic is selected, you can either retrieve all relevant cases from a particular jurisdiction or narrow your results by adding specific search terms.

Lexis offers a service, *Alerts*, that automatically runs a search on a daily or weekly basis to monitor new developments. Along with *Focus*, *More Like This*, and *More Like Selected Text*, *Save as Alert* is listed at the top of a document display. Saved searches can be retrieved by clicking on the *Alerts* tab at the top of the screen.

Shepard's. Lexis also provides a way to bring research forward by finding later citations to a given document. The Lexis feature, *Shepard's*, is represented at the top of a document display by a "Shepardize" link and usually by graphic symbols such as red or yellow signs. *Restrictions* on Shepard's can be used to see negative or positive citing references, or to run a *Focus* search within the text of the citing documents to find specific terms. *Shepard's Alerts* are a means to receive automatic notice of new citing documents.

Unlike Westlaw's KeyCite, which exists only electronically, *Shepard's Citations* is also available in a series of printed volumes. The printed version of *Shepard's* will be discussed, along with a fuller explanation of *Shepard's* online features, in Chapter 3.

More in-depth knowledge of Westlaw and Lexis comes from experience, training classes, and guides prepared for specific tools. It is easy to learn the basics of online research, but the expertise gained from practice and study will dramatically improve search effectiveness. Anyone can run an online search, but experience will give you confidence that your results are accurate and complete.

c. Other Databases

Westlaw and Lexis are by no means the only databases in the legal market. Several other companies offer databases of cases and statutes, with some providing selected secondary sources as well. Most of these systems offer terms and connectors searching, including proximity connectors and fields for particular information such as judges' names. Some offer natural language approaches as well. Display generally provides hyperlinks to other documents within the system.

Searching free Internet sites is often the same as using Google, with simple search boxes and relatively few advanced options. Some sites, such as Public Library of Law <www.plol.org>, have more extensive approaches such as word truncation and proximity searching. LexisONE <www.lexisone.com> has a free database of recent case law that accepts the same terms, connectors and segments used in the Lexis database. It always pays to check a site's help screens or user guide to learn its search engine's capabilities.

§ 1–7.　Handling a Research Project

A research project usually requires you to answer a specific question, applying a general legal principle to a particular set of facts. It often involves two distinct steps, first coming up to speed in the law governing a situation, and then searching for the specific rules that apply.

a.　First Steps

The first step in most research projects is to determine the legal issues in a factual situation. Before looking anywhere, step back and study the problem. If possible, determine whether the jurisdictional focus is federal or state. Formulate tentative issues, but be prepared to revise your statement of the issues as research progresses and you learn more about the legal background.

Some preliminary research is usually necessary to understand the context of a particular problem and to get some sense of the terminology and rules of an area of law. Without knowing the parameters of a particular field, you cannot understand the significance of material found and appreciate the nuances.

It is often best to begin research by going to a trustworthy secondary source, such as a legal treatise or a law review article. Primary sources such as statutes and cases can be confusing, ambiguously worded documents. Secondary materials are usually more straightforward and try to explain the law. They summarize the basic rules and the leading authorities and place them in context, allowing you to select the most promising primary sources to pursue.

When researching an issue that fits within a traditional area of legal doctrine, begin by consulting a subject treatise or hornbook in the area. A treatise explains the major issues and terminology, and provides a context in which analogous matters are raised or considered. The names of some of the most famous treatises, such as *Corbin on Contracts* or Wright & Miller's *Federal Practice and Procedure*, are familiar to most law students, and works in other areas can be found by using a law library's online catalog or asking a reference librarian.

If no treatise is available, a legal encyclopedia such as *American Jurisprudence 2d* or *Corpus Juris Secundum* can be a useful first step. Like a treatise, an encyclopedia outlines basic legal rules and has extensive references to court decisions. A treatise or encyclopedia may not address a specific situation, but it provides the general framework in which to place the situation.

Law review articles are particularly useful starting points when researching a new or developing area of law that may not be very well covered in treatises or encyclopedias. Sources such as legal newspapers, newsletters, and blogs are even more current than law reviews.

This early stage of the research process is also a good point at which to use free Internet sites such as search engines or Wikipedia <www.wikipedia.org>. At this point you are looking for background information and not definitive answers or citable authority, so a free and readily accessible website can be a real boon. A general source such as Wikipedia, while not authoritative, can provide basic facts as well as leads to more in-depth resources.

Most researchers begin their research online, but resources such as treatises and encyclopedias may actually be easier to understand in print. Books can make it simpler to scan headings, get an overview of an area, and learn about related issues without incurring online search charges.

The most difficult part of many research projects is finding the first piece of relevant information. Once one document is found, it often leads to a number of other sources. Cases cite earlier cases as authority; a statute's notes provide useful leads to decisions, legislative history documents, and secondary sources; and law review articles cite a wide variety of sources.

b. In–Depth Research

Once you gain background knowledge of an area, you can apply that knowledge to a specific set of facts. This is often a process that requires time and concentration.

Several research tools are designed for in-depth research:

—Annotated codes not only have the texts of current statutes, but also lead directly to most of the other relevant primary sources and may provide references to secondary sources as well. Specialized services in areas such as securities or taxation often combine the statutory text with editorial explanatory notes.

—Key-number digests, whether used in print or on Westlaw, expand on keyword searches by grouping cases together by topic whether or not they use the same terminology. They are a valuable resource for finding situations with different facts but similar legal issues.

—Once you know the contours of a legal issue, you have the background necessary to talk to experts in the area. The most current information is not always available in print or online. Sometimes an e-mail or telephone call can uncover information that couldn't be found through ordinary research methods. Government agencies and professional associations are staffed with experts who can answer questions, provide invaluable references, or send essential documents. Do your homework first, and make sure that the information isn't posted on the organization's website.

In-depth research may require several approaches. At first you may seem to be facing a blank wall, or think you have found everything there is to be found. Try rephrasing the question and running searches using new terminology. Taking a break from the project for a few hours or talking to colleagues may lead you to fresh insights.

c. Providing Current Information

An essential part of legal research is verifying that the information found is current. You must make sure that your sources are still in force and "good law." No research is complete unless you have checked the latest supplements, searched current-awareness sources for new developments, and determined the status of cases and statutes to be relied upon.

There are at least two distinct aspects to making sure that information is current. Tools such as KeyCite (on Westlaw) and Shepard's Citations (on Lexis) check the validity of precedent and lead you to more current information. They provide signals indicating that the precedential value of cases might be affected by subsequent decisions or other developments, and they alert you to recent documents that might provide clarification or new perspectives.

The other aspect of having current information comes with experience in a particular subject area, and is a result of monitoring new developments on a regular basis. When researching in an unfamiliar area, you may only find out about the effect of a new case or regulation by finding it in a keyword search. But keeping up with newsletters, trade magazines, and blogs in a particular area ensures that you won't be blindsided by a new development.

d. Completing a Project

Knowing when to stop researching can be just as difficult as knowing where to begin. In every research situation, however, there comes a time when it is necessary to synthesize the information found and produce the required memorandum, brief, or opinion letter.

Sometimes the limits to research are set by the nature of the project. An assignment may be limited to a specified number of hours or a certain amount of money. If so, the ability to find information quickly and accurately is essential.

If there is no preset limit to the amount of research to be done, it is up to you to determine when you are finished. You must do enough research to be confident that your work is based on information that is comprehensive and current. The surest way to achieve this confidence is to try several different approaches to the research problem. If a review of the secondary literature, a digest search, and online queries produce different conclusions, more research is necessary. When these various approaches lead to the same primary sources and a single conclusion, chances are better that a key piece of information has not eluded you.

As we will see in the following chapters, the law has a voluminous literature and a wide range of highly developed research tools. Many of these are unfamiliar even to experienced scholars in other disciplines. Learning to use these resources requires patience and effort, but in time you should become aware of the different functions they serve, their strengths and weaknesses, and the ways they fit together. Familiarity with legal resources and experience in their use will produce the confidence that you are finding the information you need.

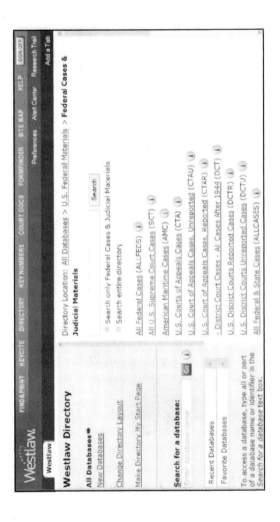

Exhibit 1–1. A Westlaw directory screen

Exhibit 1–2. A WestlawNext search screen

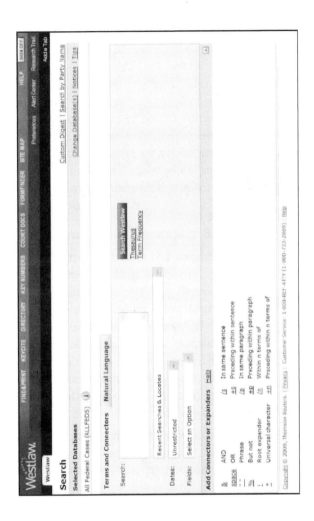

Exhibit 1–3. A Westlaw search screen

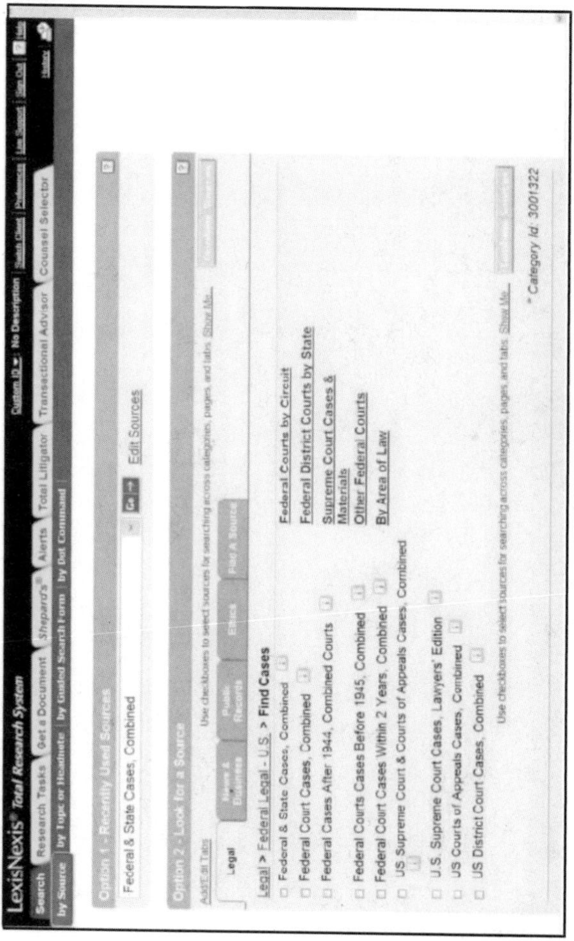

Exhibit 1–4. A Lexis directory screen

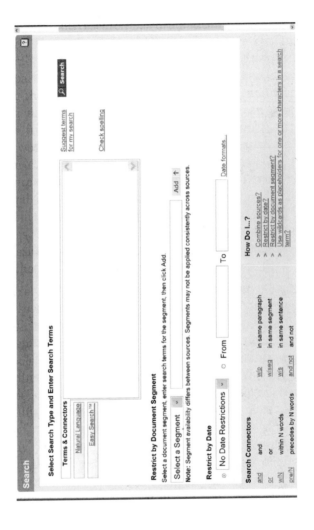

Exhibit 1–5. A Lexis search screen

CHAPTER 2

BACKGROUND AND ANALYSIS

---

§ 2–1. Introduction

Primary sources of law—such as constitutional provisions, legislative enactments, and judicial decisions—determine legal rights and govern procedures. Primary sources, however, can be notoriously difficult places in which to find answers, especially at the beginning of a research project. Secondary sources that explain and analyze governing legal doctrines make primary sources more accessible and should serve as the launching pad for most research projects.

This brief survey of major secondary sources focuses on general resources that are most likely to be helpful to beginning researchers. Encyclopedias, texts, *Restatements*, and law review articles set forth established legal doctrine, explain its nuances, and help you understand how a problem fits into the doctrinal structure. They can serve as an introduction to a new area of law or refresh your recollection of a familiar area.

Some secondary sources, particularly treatises and law review articles, contain influential insights that can shape law reform or stimulate new legislation. Others are more practical and provide a straightforward overview of the law without advocating changes. Some sources are written primarily for law students and spell out basic doctrines, while others are designed for practicing lawyers and provide guidelines and forms to simplify common procedures.

Most secondary sources include references to the primary sources needed for further research. They discuss the leading cases and major statutes, and contain extensive footnotes leading directly to these and numerous other sources. For the reader these footnote references may be among the more mundane aspects of a secondary source, but for the researcher they can be invaluable.

Secondary legal literature is much broader than the basic resources discussed in this chapter, and additional specialized materials will be discussed in later chapters. These general works, however, can provide a solid basis for successful research of most legal issues.

§ 2–2. Overviews

Even introductory materials such as legal encyclopedias can be daunting to someone new to legal literature. Fortunately, resources written for a more general audience are available to help.

Several works explain the nature of the American legal system and provide a broad outline of basic institutions and doctrines. Publications such as William Burnham, *Introduction to the Law and Legal System of the United States* (4th ed. 2006), and *Fundamentals of American Law* (Alan B. Morrison ed., 1996) explain common legal concepts, survey doctrinal areas such as contracts, torts, and family law, and include references to texts providing more extensive coverage of specific subject areas.

A number of encyclopedias have basic coverage of legal issues. One of the broadest and most accessible is *West's Encyclopedia of American Law* (2d ed. 2005), with nearly 5,000 entries on legal doctrines and terminology, major court decisions, government agencies, and influential jurists and lawyers. Its articles are a mix of legal theory, history, and politics.

Other reference works cover more specific topics in greater depth. Some, such as *Encyclopedia of Crime and Justice* (Joshua Dressler ed., 2d ed. 2002), or *Encyclopedia of the American Constitution* (Leonard W. Levy & Kenneth L. Karst eds., 2d ed. 2000), are well-respected interdisciplinary treatments with contributions from legal scholars as well as historians and political scientists. *Oxford Companion to American Law* (Kermit L. Hall ed., 2002) is a one-volume work covering a broad range of major legal concepts, institutions, cases, and historical figures, with most articles accompanied by references for further reading. *The New Oxford Companion to Law* (Peter Cane & Joanne Conaghan eds., 2008) focuses on British institutions and legal history, but it also covers American topics and contains a great deal of useful information on our common law heritage.

Works such as these provide a broad perspective on legal issues and can place these issues in the context of other political or societal concerns. They generally will not answer more specific questions about particular legal situations, however, and they contain references to relatively few primary sources. More detailed coverage is found in works designed specifically for lawyers and law students.

§ 2–3. Legal Encyclopedias

Legal encyclopedias are not simply general encyclopedias about legal topics, but works that attempt to describe systematically the entire body of legal doctrine. Instead of thousands of articles on specific topics, they have a few hundred articles covering broad areas such as constitutional law or criminal law.

Encyclopedias are relatively easy to understand and are often among the first law library resources used by new law students. In most instances, however, their perspective is quite limited. Legal encyclopedias tend to emphasize case law and neglect statutes and regulations, and they rarely examine the historical or societal aspects of the rules they discuss. Encyclopedias are relatively slow to reflect changes in the law or to cover significant trends in developing areas. Unlike law review articles or scholarly treatises, they simply summarize legal doctrine without criticism or suggestions for improvement. They are generally not viewed as persuasive secondary authority, but rather as introductory surveys and as case-finding tools.

a. *American Jurisprudence 2d* **and** *Corpus Juris Secundum*

Two national legal encyclopedias were once competing works but both are now published by West: *American Jurisprudence 2d* (*Am. Jur. 2d*) and *Corpus Juris Secundum* (*C.J.S.*). Each of these sets contains more than 140 volumes, with articles on more than 400 broad legal topics. Some articles, such as "Cemeteries" or "Dead Bodies," are narrowly defined and span just a few dozen pages, but articles on topics as broad as "Corporations" or "Evidence" can occupy several volumes. Each article is divided into numbered sections and begins with a section-by-section outline of its contents and an explanation of its scope.

Am. Jur. 2d and *C.J.S.* are quite similar, but there are differences between these two works. Exhibits 2–1 and 2–2 on pages 71–72 show pages from the *Am. Jur.* and *C.J.S.* Animals articles, discussing the vicious or dangerous propensities of domestic animals. Note that *Am. Jur.*'s discussion is slightly more general, while *C.J.S.* cites cases from many more states than *Am. Jur.* Even though these sections cover the same issues, there is no overlap in the cases they choose to cite.

In *C.J.S.*, but not *Am. Jur. 2d*, each section or subsection begins with a concise statement of the general legal principle. This "black letter" summary is followed by text elaborating on the topic. Generally, the discussion in *Am. Jur. 2d* tends to focus a bit more on federal law, while *C.J.S.* seeks to provide an overall synthesis of state law. The discussion in both works is accompanied by copious footnotes to court decisions and occasional references to federal statutes and uniform laws. Neither work cites state statutes; even when expressly discussing state statutory provisions, the footnotes refer to cases that cite these statutes.

Am. Jur. 2d and *C.J.S.* also contain references to other case-finding materials. Both encyclopedias provide relevant *key numbers*, classifications that can be used to find cases on Westlaw or in West digests. *Am. Jur. 2d* also includes references to

tions. These state encyclopedias often do a better job of tying together statutory and case law than the national encyclopedias. While not generally viewed as authoritative, they can provide both a good general overview of state law and footnotes leading to many primary sources.

Fewer than half of the states have their own legal encyclopedias, but most of the largest jurisdictions are covered. Each of these works is a comprehensive summary of its state's legal doctrine, organized like *Am. Jur. 2d* or *C.J.S.* into several hundred alphabetically arranged articles and regularly updated by annual supplements and revised volumes. Depending on its publisher, each state encyclopedia is available through either Westlaw or Lexis as well as in print.

Many states have other reference works that summarize and explain their law, although not necessarily made up of alphabetically arranged articles like the national encyclopedias. Sets such as *Kentucky Jurisprudence* and *Massachusetts Practice*, for example, contain separate volumes for doctrinal areas such as criminal procedure, domestic relations, and evidence. They may not cover all legal topics comprehensively, but they do address most major areas. The state research guides listed in Appendix A on pages 438–53 can help you identify available resources.

West also publishes, in print and on Westlaw, an encyclopedia focusing specifically on federal law, *Federal Procedure, Lawyers' Edition*. It emphasizes procedural issues in civil, criminal and administrative proceedings, but many of its chapters also discuss matters of substantive federal law. Because it deals exclusively with federal law rather than attempting to generalize about fifty state jurisdictions, it is often more precise and useful than *C.J.S.* or *Am. Jur. 2d* and includes helpful pointers for federal practice.

§ 2–4. Texts and Treatises

Legal scholars and practitioners have written thousands of texts and treatises addressing topics of substantive and procedural law. These range from multivolume sets on broad areas of law to short guides to specific issues in particular jurisdictions.

For centuries, legal treatises have played a vital role in legal research. They analyze the changing common law and also influence its development. By synthesizing decisions and statutes, texts and treatises help to impose order on the chaos of individual precedents. Although they lack legal authority and effect, some are written by scholars of outstanding reputation and are well respected by the courts. Other texts offer convenient overviews by which practitioners can familiarize themselves with specialized fields of law. Often these texts contain practice checklists and sample forms.

While there is no clear demarcation between different types of texts, they can be grouped into several general categories:

• Scholarly treatises (e.g., *Moore's Federal Practice*, *Wigmore on Evidence*) provide exhaustive coverage of specific subjects. A treatise is similar to an encyclopedia in that it methodically outlines the basic aspects of legal doctrine, but its focus on a specific subject means that a treatise usually has greater depth and insight. Many of the original multivolume treatises were written by leading scholars (such as James William Moore or John H. Wigmore), but a number of titles are now produced by editorial staffs at publishing companies. The traditional treatise is a multivolume work covering a broad area of legal doctrine such as contracts or trusts. Modern treatises tend to focus on increasingly narrow areas of law, and many are just one or two volumes.

• Hornbooks and law school texts are written primarily for a student audience but can be of value to anyone seeking an overview of a doctrinal area. These are distinct from *casebooks*, designed as teaching tools, which reprint cases for discussion and tend to provide a less straightforward summary of legal doctrine. There is no clear line distinguishing hornbooks from treatises. Some hornbooks, such as *McCormick on Evidence* or *Wright on Federal Courts*, are highly respected and are frequently cited as authority in court decisions and law review articles. Other works, such as West's Nutshell Series, are meant primarily as law school study guides and are rarely cited by judges or scholars.

• Practitioners' handbooks and manuals, many published by groups such as the American Law

Institute–American Bar Association (ALI–ABA) Joint Committee on Continuing Legal Education or the Practising Law Institute (PLI), are less useful for students but can be invaluable to practicing lawyers. Many have features designed to simplify routine aspects of law practice. Works focusing on the law of a specific state may be particularly useful for quickly determining the rules in force and finding relevant primary sources.

• Scholarly monographs on relatively narrow topics, such as Gary L. Francione, *Animals as Persons: Essays on the Abolition of Animal Exploitation* (2008), can help provide an understanding of the history or policy background of a particular area. They are often published by university presses and are similar to scholarly works in other disciplines. Because they are generally not exhaustive in their coverage of doctrinal issues and are rarely updated on a regular basis, such works are usually not the best sources for current research leads.

• Self-help publications, such as those published by Nolo Press (e.g., Mary Randolph, *Every Dog's Legal Guide*), can be good starting points and often provide clear introductions to areas of law. They may oversimplify complex issues, however, and they tend to include fewer leads to primary sources than works designed specifically for lawyers.

For any of these publications to be reliable for coverage of current legal issues, it must reflect changes in the law promptly and accurately. Some form of updating, whether by looseleaf inserts, pocket parts or periodic revision, is usually essential to preserve a treatise or text's value. An outdated text may be of historical or intellectual interest, but it cannot be relied upon as a statement of today's law.

Although printed texts remain the norm, an increasing number are available online. Westlaw provides access to hundreds of treatises, including major works such as *McCarthy on Trademarks and Unfair Competition*, Rotunda & Nowak's *Treatise on Constitutional Law*, and Wright & Miller's *Federal Practice and Procedure*. Lexis has a number of Matthew Bender treatises, including *Chisum on Patents*, *Collier on Bankruptcy*, *Immigration Law and Procedure*, and *Nimmer on Copyright*. Digital texts are usually not updated more frequently than their print counterparts, but full-text keyword searching and desktop access provide greater flexibility and convenience. Once you have found a relevant treatise section using a keyword search, however, you should generally link to the table of contents to get a sense of context and to explore related material. If you read only a specific section, you'll learn little about the contours of that area of law.

Neither Westlaw nor Lexis has comprehensive access to treatises, as each focuses on works published by its parent company. This is different from other areas such as case law and law reviews, where Westlaw and Lexis offer many of the same resources.

Exhibit 2–3 on page 73 shows a page from a hornbook, *The Law of Torts*, by Professor Dan B. Dobbs of the University of Arizona College of Law, on strict liability for abnormally dangerous domestic animals. The hornbook places this issue in the context of related tort doctrines; like the encyclopedias, it cites numerous cases and other sources to support its text.

There are several ways to find relevant and useful texts and treatises. A law library's online catalog is a basic starting place. A title keyword search can be used initially to find a few relevant works, but you will want to go beyond keywords and use the subject headings for more comprehensive research. Most online catalogs allow you to limit a search to a specific library location, such as a reserve collection, or to find works from a specific date range. These options can be particularly helpful if a general keyword search turns up an unmanageably large number of publications. If a quick way to limit searches isn't apparent from the main catalog screen, look for an "advanced search" or "expanded search" screen.

Treatises are often cited in cases and law review articles, and following leads provided by these sources is usually a reliable way to find works that are considered well-reasoned and reputable. Recommendations from professors or reference librarians may also help you identify the most reliable and influential sources.

Several printed guides list legal publications by subject. Most, unfortunately, do not differentiate between major treatises and obscure monographs, and few are updated regularly. The most extensive and current coverage is found in Kendall Svengalis's annual *Legal Information Buyer's Guide and Reference Manual*. A 300–page chapter on treatises has annotated listings in about sixty subject areas, with useful information about the scope and expense of the works listed. A shorter list of major treatises and hornbooks is included in this volume, as Appendix B on pages 454–69.

Treatises and practice materials focusing on the law of particular jurisdictions are usually listed or described in state legal research guides (listed in Appendix A at pages 438–53), and *State Practice Materials: Annotated Bibliographies* (Frank Houdek ed., 2002–date) covers treatises by subject for more than half of the states.

The subscription service IndexMaster <www. indexmaster.com> has a searchable database of the tables of contents and indexes from more than 8,000 legal texts and treatises. It doesn't provide access to the texts themselves, but its PDFs of the tables of contents and indexes highlight the search terms and may indicate whether a particular title is worth tracking down (in the library online catalog or by other means).

Part of the process of using a text for the first time is deciding whether it is a resource you will want to return to for further research. Even without expertise in a subject area, you can ask several questions when encountering a new work:

—What is its purpose and intended audience? Is it written for experienced specialists or a more general readership?

—How is it organized, and what is its scope? Does it cover too broad an area for your purposes, or does it focus on issues that don't concern you?

—What is the reputation of the author? Has she written other texts or articles in this area?

—How useful are such features as the work's footnotes, tables, bibliography, and index? Do they lead effectively to relevant passages in the work and to other resources?

—Is the work supplemented in an adequate and timely manner?

Ultimately the deciding factor in determining whether you will turn to a text a second time is whether it helped answer your question. Did it clarify matters and provide fruitful research leads? With growing familiarity in a particular area of law comes a sense of which sources are best for background information, for working through a complicated legal issue, or for references to further research sources. Having access to a reliable treatise can allow you to explore an unfamiliar area with the help of an experienced and insightful guide.

§ 2–5. *Restatements of the Law*

Some of the most important commentaries on American law are the series called *Restatements of the Law*. These American Law Institute (ALI) texts attempt to organize and articulate the rules in selected subject fields. The reporters and advisors who have drafted *Restatements* are respected scholars and jurists, and their work is perhaps more persuasive in the courts than any other secondary material. Courts sometimes explicitly adopt *Restatement* provisions as correct statements of the law, and they *are* the law by statute in the Virgin Islands and the Northern Mariana Islands.

The *Restatements* provide excellent summaries of basic doctrines, useful both for students learning an area of law and for lawyers seeking to apply the law to novel issues arising in practice. Each *Restatement* covers a distinct area of law. The first series of nine *Restatements* (covering agency, conflict of laws, contracts, judgments, property, restitution, security, torts, and trusts) was published between 1932 and 1946, and after several years a second series (of all the original topics except restitution and security, as well as foreign relations law) was issued to reflect new developments or later thinking. Several components of the *Restatement of the Law (Third)* have been published, including new areas such as unfair competition and the law governing lawyers. The ALI has also published other works as *Principles* (less firmly based on existing case law than *Restatements*) on issues of corporate governance, family law, and intellectual property. Other *Restatement* and *Principles* projects are in various stages of development.

The *Restatements* and *Principles* are divided into sections, each of which contains a concise "black letter" statement of law, followed by explanatory comments and illustrations of particular examples and variations on the general proposition. The comments and illustrations in recent *Restatements* are followed by Reporter's Notes providing background information on the section's development. Appendices for *Restatements* in the second and third series contain annotations of court decisions that have applied or interpreted each section. Cases and law review articles citing *Restatements* can also be found through KeyCite and Shepard's (on Lexis and in the printed *Shepard's Restatement of the Law Citations*).

The process of drafting a *Restatement* or *Principles* is a long one, usually involving the publication of several preliminary and tentative drafts. The various drafts are distributed to ALI members in paperback pamphlets and are less widely available than the final bound volumes, although larger law libraries generally have copies. Exhibit 2–4 on page 74 shows a page from a *Restatement* tentative draft on tort liability discussing abnormally dangerous animals, showing the standard format of black-letter rule and comment.

The *Restatements* and *Principles* are also available on both Westlaw and Lexis. Lexis has the most

recent final version of each publication, while Westlaw also has the earlier series and recent draft
versions. The subscription site HeinOnline <www.
heinonline.org> offers an American Law Institute
collection, with PDF versions of the *Restatements* as
well as other ALI materials such as annual reports
and proceedings. The American Law Institute website <www.ali.org> has information on publications
and pending projects, but it does not provide free
access to full text.

§ 2–6. Law Reviews

The academic legal journals known as law reviews
contain some of the most important commentary in
American law. The law review is a form of scholarly
publication unknown to most disciplines. It is usually edited by law students rather than established
scholars, and serves as an educational tool for its
editors as well as a forum for discussion of legal
developments and theories.

Most law review articles have two features that
make them an invaluable part of the research process. They generally begin with an introductory
overview of the area of law, summarizing the relevant doctrine and literature, and they are usually
replete with footnotes citing to primary sources and
to other secondary sources.

A law review issue usually follows a fairly standard format, containing lengthy *articles* and shorter
essays by professors and lawyers followed by *comments* or *notes* by students. The articles and essays

are more influential, but the student contributions can also be very useful in research. Law review articles differ from more general works such as legal encyclopedias and treatises in several ways. Articles are often written on recent developments in the law, so they are among the best resources for researching changes in the law. They often advocate changes in the legal system and generally have a less neutral perspective than other sources. Unlike many other secondary sources, law review articles are not updated after they are published.

In addition to general law reviews covering a variety of subjects, an ever growing number of specialized academic journals are published on topics from agricultural law to telecommunications. Some law schools publish a dozen or more general and specialized journals. Most subject-specific journals are student-edited, but a few, such as *Florida Tax Review* and *Supreme Court Review*, are edited by law school faculty members. The term "law review" generally encompasses all of these academic legal journals, whether or not those words appear in the title.

Bar associations and commercial publishers also publish legal journals. Articles in these journals tend to be shorter and more practical than those found in academic law reviews, often focusing on current developments of interest to practicing lawyers. Specialized practice sections of the American Bar Association publish some of the most respected bar journals, and state and local bar association journals have insights into practice concerns in specific jurisdictions.

Exhibit 2–5 on page 75 shows an excerpt from a student comment in a recent law review issue on dangerous-dog issues related to the encyclopedia and treatise pages shown earlier in this chapter. Note that the footnotes, which occupy more than half the page, provide references to cases, statutes, websites, and other law review commentary.

Thousands of law review articles are published every year, and effective research requires familiarity with several repositories. The full-text databases in Westlaw and Lexis are among the most convenient and most frequently used resources, and PDF-based databases such as HeinOnline and JSTOR are particularly good for historical and cross-disciplinary research. Indexes available online and in print can expand retrieval beyond full-text sources and focus it more accurately on a specific topic. You can also use tools such as KeyCite and Shepard's Citations to find articles discussing particular cases, statutes or other authorities.

a. Westlaw and Lexis

Both Westlaw and Lexis have the full text of several hundred law reviews, with coverage for some reviews extending from the early 1980s or earlier and many more beginning in the 1990s. Lexis law review coverage is available both through lexis.com (for most legal professionals and law students) and through LexisNexis Academic <web.

lexis-nexis.com/universe/> (for university faculty and students).

Both major search methods, natural language and Boolean, can be effective for locating law review articles. A natural language search finds articles that use keywords most frequently and are therefore most likely to be relevant. Because it lists search results by relevance rather than by date, however, you must be careful not to rely on outdated articles or miss important recent contributions. A Boolean keyword search allows greater precision and can be used to pinpoint discussion or footnotes using any particular combination of words, including phrases, case names, or titles of other articles or books. Even an article that is not directly on point may have references to more relevant sources, including treatises or journal volumes that are not themselves online.

Because the databases contain thousands of lengthy articles, a search limited to the *ti* field (in Westlaw) or *title* segment (in Lexis) may lead to a smaller but more relevant group of documents. You can also focus retrieval in terms and connectors searches by using proximity connectors and the *Term Frequency* or *Atleast* features. You can use the *au* field in Westlaw and the *name* segment in Lexis to find articles by particular authors.

There is another way to find law review articles on Westlaw or Lexis that can be used once one relevant article is found. The display of the article indicates whether the system includes any later articles or other documents that cite it. Clicking on the KeyCite "citing references" symbol or "Shepardize" produces a list of subsequent articles. (In print, *Shepard's Law Review Citations* performs this same function.) Even if the first article you find is several years old, KeyCite and Shepard's give you an easy way to find related articles and bring your research up to date.

b. HeinOnline

Westlaw and Lexis have the full text of articles, but the footnotes are generally grouped together at the end of the article. Scrolling or clicking back and forth between the text and the notes looking for research leads can be time-consuming. Another electronic service, HeinOnline <www.heinonline. org>, has digitized images from the printed journal issues, with the footnotes at the bottom of each page for convenient access. Its PDFs also include tables and graphics that the other databases may be unable to display.

HeinOnline covers more than a thousand journals, and its retrospective coverage extends back in most instances to the very first volumes of the journals in its database. The *University of Pennsylvania Law Review*, for example, is included back to 1852, when it began publication as the *American Law Register*. This full-text access to older law reviews makes HeinOnline particularly valuable in legal history research, but for many titles its range also extends to the most recently published issue.

HeinOnline offers full-text searching of its journals, but its search mechanism is not as flexible or sophisticated as those of Westlaw and Lexis. A "Field Search" screen provides options to search for words or phrases in author, title or text fields and to limit a search to specific subjects, journals or dates. The Boolean connectors AND, OR and NOT can be used, but not proximity connectors. HeinOnline also has a Citation Navigator, allowing you to retrieve a document if you know its citation. Westlaw and Lexis generally have more powerful search options to find recent law review articles, and HeinOnline is most effective for historical research or document retrieval.

c. Periodical Indexes

Full-text searching is a powerful tool, but it does have limitations. Searching for keywords can retrieve extraneous articles that only mention these terms in passing, not just those that focus specifically on a particular subject. An index is a way to narrow retrieval to articles more specifically on point. In addition, thousands of articles are not available electronically and might never be found through full-text searches. Periodical indexes remain valuable resources, especially when you can follow links directly from index entries to the full text of articles.

Two general indexes to English-language legal periodical literature are available. Both are issued in printed volumes with monthly updating pamphlets, but online searching is usually the most convenient form of access. *Index to Legal Periodicals and Books* (*ILP*) is available through Wilson-Web <www.hwwilson.com>, and to some subscribers through Westlaw, Lexis, and other database systems. *LegalTrac* is available as part of the Gale Group's InfoTrac system <infotrac.galegroup.com>, and is known as *Legal Resource Index* (*LRI*) on Westlaw and Lexis.

Each of these indexes covers more than a thousand law reviews and periodicals, with more than twenty-five years of online coverage. *LegalTrac* coverage begins in 1980, and *ILP* in 1981. WilsonWeb also offers an *Index to Legal Periodicals Retrospective* database, cumulating entries from older index volumes from 1908 to 1981, and allows the historical and modern indexes to be combined for comprehensive research.

Both *LegalTrac* and *ILP* offer keyword and natural language searching as well as subject indexing, making it easy to find articles on related topics. *LegalTrac* uses detailed Library of Congress subject headings with extensive subheadings and cross-references, while *ILP* generally has fewer, broader headings. Articles on vicious dogs, for example, might be indexed under "Dangerous animals–Litigation" in *LegalTrac* and "Animals" in *ILP*. Each approach has advantages; sometimes your research may have a very specific focus, while at other times a broader survey is appropriate. Once you find one relevant article, clicking on its subject headings links you to other articles on related topics.

Both indexes include the full text of some of the articles they index, and many libraries also offer "link resolvers" that lead directly from an index entry to the full text in HeinOnline or other databases. This method combines the best of both research worlds: expert indexing to ensure that relevant articles aren't missed, and immediate online access to the text.

The printed version of *Index to Legal Periodicals and Books* (*ILP*), which began publication in 1908, indexes articles by subject and author, with a book review section and tables listing cases and statutes that are the focus of articles. (Earlier articles are covered by the Jones–Chipman *Index to Legal Periodical Literature*, with indexing back to 1770.) The printed counterpart to LegalTrac, known as the *Current Law Index* (*CLI*), has been published since 1980. It has separate subject and author indexes, as well as case and statute tables. *CLI* is somewhat narrower in scope than *LegalTrac* and *LRI* because it omits their coverage of legal newspapers and relevant articles in non-law periodicals.

d. Other Sources

Law review literature is also available in several more general research databases. JSTOR <www. jstor.org>, for example, includes more than three dozen legal journals in its interdisciplinary, retrospective coverage of more than 600 scholarly journals. Articles can be found through keyword searches and downloaded or printed as PDFs. JSTOR coverage generally excludes the most recent four to six years for most journals, but it includes some titles not available through HeinOnline such as *Journal of Law and Economics* and *Law and Human Behavior.*

Google Scholar <scholar.google.com> provides full-text access to thousands of law review articles. Access to the full text of some articles is free, but for others it depends on whether your institution subscribes to databases such as HeinOnline or JSTOR. Google Scholar listings also have ways to expand research with links to more recent works citing the listed article ("Cited by") and articles with similar terms ("Related Articles").

Other free Internet sites also provide some access to recent law review literature. Some law review websites feature only tables of contents or abstracts, but a growing number make the full text of recent articles available. The University of Southern California Law Library maintains a list of links to law review websites <weblaw.usc.edu/library/resources/journals.cfm>, noting which sites have full text. In addition, many articles and working papers are available through scholarship repositories such as Berkeley Electronic Press <www.bepress.com> and Social Science Research Network (SSRN) <www.ssrn.com>.

References to law review articles are also found in the process of researching primary sources such as case law or statutes. The KeyCite and Shepard's displays for cases and statutes include references to any citing law review articles, and annotated statutory codes often contain article citations. These approaches will be discussed, along with other aspects of case and statutory research, in Chapters 3 and 4.

Law reviews and journals are not the only types of legal periodicals. More specialized and practice-oriented sources such as legal newspapers and newsletters, as well as resources for notice of recent articles and new scholarship, are considered in Chapter 8.

§ 69   What constitutes vicious or dangerous propensity

Research References

West's Key Number Digest, Animals ⊙66.2

A vicious or dangerous disposition or propensity may consist of mere mischievousness or playfulness of the animal, which, because of its size or nature, might lead to injury, for it is the act of the animal, rather than its state of mind, which charges the owner or keeper with liability.[1] Consequently, a plaintiff need not show that the animal actually injured someone to prove that the animal had a vicious propensity.[2] "Vicious propensities" of a domestic animal, which will result in the animal owner's liability if the animal causes harm as a result of those propensities, include the propensity to do any act that might endanger the safety of the persons and property of others in a given situation.[3]

A known dangerous propensity does not arise from an animal injuring others under circumstances where the animal has been provoked to do so.[4]

In deciding whether an animal has dangerous propensities, a jury may take into consideration the nature of the assault on the plaintiff.[5] In an action to recover damages for personal injuries resulting from a dog bite, evidence that the dog constantly barked, exposed his teeth, and strained his leash, was sufficient to establish the dog possessed vicious propensities, since he habitually tended to do acts which might endanger persons.[6]

§ 70   What constitutes knowledge of dangerous or vicious propensities

Research References

West's Key Number Digest, Animals ⊙66.2
Knowledge of Animal's Vicious Propensities, 13 Am. Jur. Proof of Facts 2d 473

In order to impose liability upon the owner of an animal which is not naturally dangerous to humanity on the basis that the owner had

---

[Section 69]

[1]Groner v. Hedrick, 403 Pa. 148, 169 A.2d 302 (1961).

[2]Hunt v. Hunt, 86 N.C. App. 323, 357 S.E.2d 444 (1987), decision aff'd, 321 N.C. 294, 362 S.E.2d 161 (1987).

[3]Collier v. Zambito, 1 N.Y.3d 444, 775 N.Y.S.2d 205, 807 N.E.2d 254 (2004).

[4]Wignes v. Bottger, 136 Misc. 2d 490, 518 N.Y.S.2d 936 (Sup 1987).

[5]Lynch by Lynch v. Nacewicz, 126 A.D.2d 708, 511 N.Y.S.2d 121 (2d Dep't 1987).

[6]Fontecchio v. Esposito, 108 A.D.2d 780, 485 N.Y.S.2d 113 (2d Dep't 1985).

For a detailed discussion of liability for injury caused by a dog, see §§ 75 to 79.

Exhibit 2–1.   A page from *American Jurisprudence 2d*

invitee, the invitee had no such knowledge, and the invitor failed to warn the invitee;[14] and where the invitee knows all the facts actually known to the invitor, superior knowledge on the invitor's part with respect to the dangerous character of the animal which attacked the invitee is necessary to make the invitor liable.[15]

§ 323 Viciousness

Generally, if the injury results from the exercise of a vicious propensity which is not natural or usual in the class of animals to which the offending animal belongs, the owner or keeper is not liable, unless he had knowledge or notice of the vicious propensity; and this rule applies, at least, where there has been no negligence or the animal was not wrongfully in the place where the injury was inflicted.

Research References

West's Key Number Digest, Animals ⇐67, 70

Generally the owner of a domestic animal is under no obligation to guard against injuries which he has no reason to expect on account of some disposition of the individual animal different from the species generally if he has no notice of such disposition.[1] Hence, if the injury has resulted from the exercise of a vicious propensity, which is not natural to the class of animals to which the offending animal belongs, the owner or keeper of the animal is usually not liable if he did not have previous knowledge or scienter of the vicious propensity,[2] or could not have ascertained the same by the exercise of reasonable care,[3] unless there has been negligence or, the animal was wrongfully in the place where the injury was inflicted.

Knowledge of an animal's viciousness or dangerous propensities toward humans must be accompanied by a showing the animal was inclined to cause the class of injury inflicted, to establish owners' or rider's liability for injuries.[4] On the other hand, if the animal, to the knowledge of the owner, is vicious, he must keep it safely or respond in damages for injuries resulting from a display of its known propensities;[5] and, it is often held that the liability thus imposed is in no way dependent

[14]Mo.—Maisch v. Kansas City Stock Yards Co. of Mo., 241 S.W.2d 487 (Mo. Ct. App. 1951); Alexander v. Crotchett, 233 Mo. App. 674, 124 S.W.2d 534 (1939).

[15]Mo.—Alexander v. Crotchett, 233 Mo. App. 674, 124 S.W.2d 534 (1939).

[Section 323]

[1]Ill.—Domm v. Hollenbeck, 259 Ill. 382, 102 N.E. 782 (1913); Ciaglo v. Ciaglo, 20 Ill. App. 2d 360, 156 N.E.2d 376 (1st Dist. 1959).

Mo.—Humes v. Salerno, 351 S.W.2d 749 (Mo. 1961); Gardner v. Anderson, 417 S.W.2d 130 (Mo. Ct. App. 1967).

Or.—Schnell v. Howitt, 158 Or. 586, 76 P.2d 1130 (1938).

[2]Cal.—Mann v. Stanley, 141 Cal. App. 2d 438, 296 P.2d 921 (3d Dist. 1956).

Ga.—Starling v. Davis, 121 Ga. App. 428, 174 S.E.2d 214 (1970).

Ill.—Ciaglo v. Ciaglo, 20 Ill. App. 2d 360, 156 N.E.2d 376 (1st Dist. 1959).

Ind.—Williams v. Pohlman, 146 Ind. App. 523, 257 N.E.2d 329 (Div. 2 1970).

Ky.—True v. Shelton, 314 Ky. 446, 235 S.W.2d 1009 (1951).

La.—Moore v. Smith, 6 So. 2d 803 (La. Ct. App., Orleans 1942).

Mass.—Greeley v. Jameson, 265 Mass. 465, 164 N.E. 385 (1929).

Me.—Young v. Proctor, 495 A.2d 828 (Me. 1985).

Mo.—Gardner v. Anderson, 417 S.W.2d 130 (Mo. Ct. App. 1967).

Neb.—Huber v. Timmons, 184 Neb. 718, 171 N.W.2d 794 (1969).

N.J.—Barber v. Hochstrasser, 136 N.J.L. 76, 54 A.2d 458 (N.J. Sup. Ct. 1947).

N.Y.—Hosmer v. Carney, 228 N.Y. 73, 126 N.E. 650 (1920).

N.C.—Patterson v. Reid, 10 N.C. App. 22, 178 S.E.2d 1 (1970).

Or.—Schnell v. Howitt, 158 Or. 586, 76 P.2d 1130 (1938).

Pa.—Andrews v. Smith, 324 Pa. 455, 188 A. 146 (1936).

S.C.—Mungo v. Bennett, 238 S.C. 79, 119 S.E.2d 522, 85 A.L.R.2d 1155 (1961).

Tenn.—Henry v. Roach, 41 Tenn. App. 289, 293 S.W.2d 480 (1956).

[3]Ind.—Williams v. Pohlman, 146 Ind. App. 523, 257 N.E.2d 329 (Div. 2 1970).

N.Y.—Hosmer v. Carney, 228 N.Y. 73, 126 N.E. 650 (1920).

Or.—Schnell v. Howitt, 158 Or. 586, 76 P.2d 1130 (1938).

[4]Ky.—Ewing v. Prince, 425 S.W.2d 732 (Ky. 1968).

[5]U.S.—Zarek v. Fredericks, 138 F.2d 689 (C.C.A. 3d Cir. 1943).

Ala.—McCullar v. Williams, 217 Ala. 278, 116 So.

Exhibit 2–2. A page from *Corpus Juris Secundum*

to graze animals on open range.[18] Some courts, however, have taken the position that the animal owner owes no duty at all to those on the highway and hence is not liable, even for negligence.[19]

§ 344.　Strict Liability for Abnormally Dangerous Domestic Animals

Strict liability for personal injury caused by domestic animals. The common law rule already discussed made owners of livestock strictly liable for the trespasses of such animals, but that rule did not impose strict liability for personal injuries inflicted by livestock except as injury might be a direct result of trespass. Domestic animals like dogs and cats were treated differently; their owners or keepers[1] were not strictly liable for the animals' trespasses at all but under limited conditions could be strictly liable for personal injuries inflicted by such animals. Strict liability is imposed when the keeper of the animal knows or has reason to know that his animal is abnormally dangerous in some way and injury results from that danger.[2]

For example, if a dog owner knows that his dog has an abnormal or vicious propensity to attack and bite,[3] or his horse to kick,[4] he is liable for the dog's biting and the horse's kicking. The owner would be liable for ordinary negligence or an intentional tort,[5] but strict liability based upon the owner's knowledge of a dangerous propensity differs from ordinary negligence. Although the knowledge or scienter requirement necessarily means that harm is foreseeable in light of the animal's known propensity, liability is imposed even if the defendant exercised reasonable care to keep the dog penned and horse stabled.[6]

18. Carrow Co. v. Lusby, 167 Ariz. 18, 804 P.2d 747 (1990); contra: Kendall v. Curl, 222 Or. 329, 353 P.2d 227 (1960).

19. Douglass v. Dolan, 286 Ill.App.3d 181, 675 N.E.2d 1012, 221 Ill.Dec. 588 (1997) (no common law duty, but recovery if the plaintiff can bring herself within a statute imposing liability upon those in charge of animal); James L. Rigelhaupt, Jr., Annotation, Liability of Owner of Animal for Damage to Motor Vehicle or Injury to Person Riding Therein Resulting from Collision with Domestic Animal at Large in Street or Highway, 29 A.L.R.4th 431 (1981).

§ 344

1. A temporary caretaker such as a babysitter may not qualify as a keeper or possessor of the animal, but even such a person would be subject to liability for negligent failure to control. See Trager v. Thor, 445 Mich. 95, 516 N.W.2d 69 (1994). Similarly, an employer who merely permits an employee to bring his dog to a job site is not a keeper or harborer of the dog. Falby v. Zarembski, 221 Conn. 14, 602 A.2d 1 (1992).

2. Marshall v. Ranne, 511 S.W.2d 255 (Tex.1974); Jividen v. Law, 194 W.Va. 705, 461 S.E.2d 451 (1995); Restatement § 509. Courts sometimes speak of mischievous or vicious propensities of the animal, but the dog's good faith is not an issue and the plaintiff need only show his dangerous tendency. See Restatement § 509, cmt. c.

3. Moura v. Randall, 119 Md.App. 632, 705 A.2d 334 (1998); cf. Marshall v. Ranne, 511 S.W.2d 255 (Tex.1974) (vicious hog biting plaintiff).

4. Cf. Bauman v. Auch, 539 N.W.2d 320 (S.D.1995) (horse rearing up when plaintiff attempted to mount). Because the question of an animal's vicious propensity is relevant both to strict liability and to negligence, decisions may permit the claim to go to the jury without specifying the basis. E.g., Zboray v. Fessler, 154 A.D.2d 367, 545 N.Y.S.2d 844 (1989).

5. See Restatement § 518.

6. See Van Houten v. Pritchard, 315 Ark. 688, 870 S.W.2d 377 (1994).

Exhibit 2–3.　A page from Dan B. Dobbs, *The Law of Torts* (2000)

§ 23. Abnormally Dangerous Animals

An owner or possessor of an animal that the owner or possessor knows or has reason to know has dangerous tendencies abnormal for the animal's category is subject to strict liability for physical harms caused by the animal which ensue from that dangerous tendency.

Comment:

a. Subject to strict liability. Even in cases covered by this section, various limitations on liability apply and various defenses are available. The most pertinent of these are set forth in §§ 24 and 25.

b. Explanation and rationale. This section supplements §§ 21 and 22. The premise of this section is that, apart from animals that trespass (§ 21) and wild animals that pose an inherent risk of personal injury (§ 22), most animals normally are safe, or at least are not abnormally unsafe in a way that would justify the imposition of strict liability. In addition, such animals provide important benefits to those who own or maintain possession of them. Thus, livestock such as cows, horses, and pigs are of substantial economic value, while pets such as dogs and cats provide essential companionship for households and families. Indeed, dogs and cats are frequently regarded as members of the family. Furthermore, the ownership of animals such as dogs and cats is widespread throughout the public; therefore, the limited risks entailed by ordinary dogs and cats are to a considerable extent reciprocal. Accordingly, the case on behalf of strict liability for physical harms that all such ordinary animals might cause is weak. However, even though animals in such categories generally entail only a modest level of danger, particular animals may present significant and abnormal dangers.

398

Exhibit 2–4. A section of a *Restatement* tentative draft

Currently, Ohio has the only breed-specific state law, imposing dangerous-dog regulations on all pit bulls.[113] Though most states permit local legislatures to regulate dogs in any manner deemed necessary to protect the public, resulting in breed-specific enactments in several cities,[114] eleven states have expressly forbid breed-based local regulations or bans.[115] However, a recent court decision in favor of the City of Denver, which successfully challenged the Colorado state law prohibiting breed-specific legislation, may call into question the ability of a state to proscribe breed-based bans.[116]

---

legislature that would permit breeding restrictions on pit bulls following a fatal attack on a twelve-year old boy); Kory A. Nelson, Denver's Pit Bull Ordinance: A Review of Its History and Judicial Rulings (Apr. 15, 2005), http://www.denvergov.org/City_Attorney/template319853.asp (noting increased community support for pit bull regulations after a fifty-eight-year old reverend was attacked by a pit bull).

113. Ohio Rev. Code Ann. § 955.11(A)(4)(a)(iii) (defining a vicious dog as one that, inter alia, "belongs to a breed that is commonly known as a pit bull dog").

114. There has been an estimated fifty percent increase in the number of communities that have attempted to enact some type of breed-specific legislation over the past several years. Heather K. Pratt, Comment, *Canine Profiling: Does Breed-Specific Legislation Take a Bite Out of Canine Crime?*, 108 Penn. St. L. Rev. 855, 871 (2004) (citing Mike Pulfer & Dave Ferman, *Clamping Down on Vicious Dogs*, Cincinnati Enquirer, Feb. 16, 2001, *available at* http://www.enquirer.com/editions/2001/02/16/tem_clamping_down_on.html).

115. *See* Colo. Rev. Stat. § 18-9-204.5(5) (2004); Fla. Stat. Ann. § 767.14 (West 2005); 510 Ill. Comp. Stat. Ann. 5/24 (West 2004); Me. Rev. Stat. Ann. tit. 7, § 3950 (2002 & Supp. 2005); Minn. Stat. Ann. § 347.51 (West 2004); N.J. Stat. Ann. § 4:19-36 (West 1998); N.Y. Agric. & Mkts. Law § 107 (McKinney 2004); Okla. Stat. Ann. tit. 4, § 46(B) (West 2003); 3 Pa. Cons. Stat. Ann. § 459-507-A(b) (West 1995); Tex. Health & Safety Code Ann. § 822.047 (Vernon 2003); Va. Code Ann. § 3.1-796.93:1(2) (1994 & Supp. 2005). Until recently, California also prohibited local governments from enacting breed-specific regulations. Cal. Food & Agric. Code § 31683 (West 2001) (repealed 2005). The state legislature introduced S.B. 861, which permits local governments to require sterilization of potentially dangerous breeds, such as pit bulls and pit bull mixes, after the fatal mauling of a twelve-year-old San Francisco boy by pit bulls. S.B. 861, 2005-06 Leg., 2005-06 Reg. Sess. (Cal. 2005); *California OKs Forced Sterilization of Pit Bulls*, MSNBC.com, Oct. 7, 2005, http://msnbc.msn.com/id/9624136. On October 7, 2005, California Governor Arnold Schwarzenegger signed that bill into law. *Id.* Some state laws, such as Florida's, permit cities with breed-specific legislation in force at the time of enactment of the state statute to retain the local law. Fla. Stat. Ann. § 767.14.

116. A 2004 Colorado state law proscribing breed-specific enactments by local governments would have invalidated Denver's 1989 law that prohibited ownership and harboring of pit bulls in the City and County of Denver. Nelson, *supra* note 112. Denver challenged the state law and won a judgment that it was an unconstitutional violation of local control. *Id.* The State challenged Denver's local law as unconstitutional, claiming new facts and scientific developments had undermined the rationality of breed-specific legislation. *Id.* On April 7, 2005, a district court judge ruled that the State had failed to provide any new evidence to undermine the 1990 findings regarding differences between pit bulls and other dogs and upheld Denver's law as constitutional. *Id.*; *see* Colo. Dog Fanciers, Inc. v. City of Denver, 820 P.2d 644 (Colo. 1991) (en banc) (making the original finding as to differences between pit bulls and other breeds).

Exhibit 2–5.   A page from a law review student comment

CHAPTER 3

CASE LAW

§ 3–1. Introduction

Reports of judicial decisions are among the most important sources of legal authority in the common law system. Over the course of time, judges shape legal doctrines to address the complex issues of our changing society. Legislative enactments now cover an ever broader range of issues, but case law remains vital. Even a statute that appears straightforward must be read in light of the court decisions that construe and apply its provisions.

Court Systems. To use cases effectively, it is necessary to understand the hierarchical structure of the American judicial system. The precedential value of a decision is determined in large part by a court's place in this hierarchy. Decisions from a higher court in a jurisdiction are binding or *mandatory authority*, and must be followed by a lower court in the same jurisdiction. Decisions from courts in other jurisdictions are not binding, but a court in another state may have considered a situation similar to that in issue and may provide *persuasive authority*.

Litigation usually begins in a *trial court*. The jurisdiction of these courts may be based on geography (the U.S. District Courts in the federal system, or county courts in many states) or subject (the U.S. Tax Court, or state family courts and probate courts). In the trial court, *issues of fact* (e.g., whether a "Beware of Dog" sign was posted) are decided by the fact finder, either the judge or a jury. Factual findings are binding on the parties and cannot be appealed. *Issues of law* (e.g., whether such a sign limits a dog owner's liability for injuries) are decided by the judge, and a party who disagrees with these rulings can appeal them to a higher court.

Appeals from trial court decisions are generally taken to an *intermediate appellate court* (the U.S. Courts of Appeals and similar state tribunals). An appellate court usually consists of a panel of three or more judges, who typically confer and vote on the issues after considering written briefs and oral argument. One of the judges writes a majority opinion summarizing the question and stating the court's holding. In some cases a *per curiam* opinion is issued, one which represents the court without authorship attributed to any individual judge. A judge who agrees with the holding of a case but for reasons that differ from those expressed by the majority may write a separate concurring opinion outlining her views. A judge who disagrees with the holding may write a dissenting opinion. A case report includes all of these opinions, although only a majority opinion is binding authority.

The *court of last resort* in each jurisdiction (called the Supreme Court in the federal system and in most states) usually reviews cases from the intermediate appellate courts, but may take appeals directly from trial courts. Unlike other appellate courts, most courts of last resort have discretion in deciding which cases they will hear. Their role in the judicial system is not to resolve every individual dispute, but rather to establish rules, review legislative and administrative acts, and resolve differences among intermediate appellate courts. A court of last resort's decisions on issues of law are binding on all courts within its jurisdiction.

Numerous works provide more extensive discussions of the role of judges in deciding cases and creating legal doctrine. Daniel John Meador's *American Courts* (2d ed. 2000) is one of the more concise introductory works. Longer treatments designed as course texts but useful for background reading and references to other sources include Lawrence Baum, *American Courts: Process and Policy* (6th ed. 2008) and Robert A. Carp et al., *Judicial Process in America* (7th ed. 2007).

Publication of Cases. Case law generally consists of the decisions of courts of last resort and intermediate appellate courts on issues of law. Very few trial court decisions are published. Trial court decisions on issues of fact have no precedential effect and usually do not even result in written judicial opinions. A jury verdict at the end of a trial, for example, produces no published decision unless the judge rules on a motion challenging the verdict on legal grounds. Some trial court decisions on issues of law are published, but they have less precedential value than appellate court decisions. Selected intermediate appellate court decisions and nearly all decisions from courts of last resort are published both in print and electronically.

A bit of history may help in understanding court reports. The American colonies inherited the English legal system and its common law tradition. Colonial judges and lawyers relied on English precedents, as no decisions of American courts were published until *Kirby's Reports*, in Connecticut, in 1789. Reports from other states and from the new federal courts soon followed. *Official* series of court reports (published pursuant to statutory direction or court authorization) began in several states in the early 1800s. Many of these early reports were cited by the names of their editors and are known as *nominative reports*.

As the country grew in the 19th century, the number of reported decisions increased dramatically. Official reporting systems began to lag further and further behind, and the need for timely access to cases was met by commercial publishers. In 1876, John B. West began publishing selected decisions of the Minnesota Supreme Court in a weekly leaflet, the *Syllabi*. Three years later he launched the *North Western Reporter*, covering five surrounding states as well as Minnesota. By 1887, West published cases from every state and the federal system, in what became known as the National Reporter System. These reporters are now the most widely accepted source for citations to court opinions. Exhibit 3–1 on page 140 shows the beginning of a case in *West's Southern Reporter*.

New decisions are now available electronically much sooner than they are published in print. The most widespread electronic resources are the commercial databases Westlaw and Lexis, but a number of other companies and court websites also provide access to court decisions. Even though most researchers find and read cases online instead of in printed reports, cases are still identified by citations to the published volumes. Generally, only cases unavailable in print are cited to electronic sources.

The first print appearance of a new decision is the official *slip opinion* issued by the court itself, usually an individually paginated copy of a single decision. Slip opinions provide the text of new cases and are often available free from official court websites, but they have two major drawbacks. First, they rarely provide editorial enhancements summarizing the court's decision and facilitating research. Second, because their page numbering is not final they must be cited by docket number and date rather than to a permanent published source. Several jurisdictions have ameliorated this second problem by assigning public domain citations to their recent cases. Opinions are numbered as they are issued, and in some states each paragraph is numbered so that a particular point in an opinion can be identified.

The next forms of printed court reports provide the editorial summaries and page citations that slip opinions lack. Cases usually appear first in weekly or biweekly pamphlets known as *advance sheets*, containing a number of decisions paginated in a continuous sequence, and then in bound volumes consolidating the contents of several advance sheets. Volumes are numbered consecutively, often in more than one successive series. If a reporter is in a second, third, or fourth series, that must be indicated in its citation in order to distinguish it from the same volume number in another series. The case in Exhibit 3–1, for example, is on page 815 of volume 6 of the third series of the *Southern Reporter*, and is cited as 6 So. 3d 815 (La. Ct. App. 2008).

Most court reports include editorial features that make it easier to find and understand the decisions. In West's National Reporter System series, each case is prefaced with a brief summary of its holding, called a *synopsis*, and with numbered editorial abstracts, or *headnotes*, of the specific legal issues. Each headnote is assigned a legal topic and a number indicating a particular subdivision of that topic. This classification plan, known as the *key number system*, consists of over four hundred broad topics and tens of thousands of subtopics. The headnotes are reprinted by subject in *digests*, which allow uniform subject access to the cases of different jurisdictions. *Bradford v. Coody* in Exhibit 3–1 has three numbered headnotes, in the Judgment and Animals topics.

It is important to remember that the synopsis and headnotes are not prepared by the court and should not be cited or relied upon as authoritative.

Headnotes may cover topics discussed in dictum, sometimes even in footnotes, rather than the case's holding. You need to read the opinion to determine the court's holding, and to rely on and cite the text in the opinion rather than a synopsis or headnote.

Exhibit 3–1 includes other standard features of court reports. The right-hand column has a list of the lawyers representing the parties, the names of the judges who heard the case, and the name of the judge writing the opinion for the court.

Case Research. For the doctrine of precedent to operate effectively, lawyers must be able to find cases which control or influence a court's decision-making. This requires locating "cases on point" from courts that have binding or persuasive precedent in your jurisdiction, earlier decisions with factual and legal issues similar to a dispute at hand. You then need to determine that these decisions are valid law and have not been reversed, overruled, or otherwise discredited.

This chapter discusses several major tools that perform these functions, but it is not exhaustive. Much of legal research revolves around finding cases, and several resources discussed elsewhere—such as treatises, law reviews, annotated codes, and looseleaf services—are also valuable in case research.

We start with an overview of electronic case research, the most widely used method in legal practice today. We then introduce printed tools such as West digests and *ALR* annotations. These are complex resources that may at first seem more confusing than helpful, but skill in their use can yield more thorough, accurate results than online searching alone. The assistance of editors who have analyzed and classified related cases can lead to insights and analogies that you might never reach on your own using only keyword searches.

Many law students tend to rely almost exclusively on keyword searching in online databases, only to find when they enter practice that these databases can be very expensive. Yet financial constraints are not the only reason to extend your skills beyond methods that depend on your ability to phrase an effective search request. If the language of a decision does not precisely match your request, it will remain undiscovered unless you use another research method. Full-text keyword searches are most effective as part of a research strategy that integrates a number of different approaches.

§ 3–2. Electronic Research

Chapter 1 provided a brief overview of basic online research techniques that can be applied in any database. This section will focus more specifically on ways to use case databases effectively. It emphasizes Westlaw and Lexis procedures, but for researchers without access to these databases alternatives are available. Several lower-cost and free databases include extensive coverage of case law, with a range of search capabilities. What these services generally lack is the synopses, headnotes, and other editorial materials that Westlaw and Lexis provide.

a. Westlaw

One of your first decisions in online case research is whether to limit a search to a specific jurisdiction. For some issues, it may not matter what courts in other states have decided. The only relevant cases are those from a particular state or within a narrow doctrinal area. For other research questions, however, cases from other jurisdictions may be persuasive authority or may provide useful analogies.

Westlaw's most extensive case databases cover the entire country. For most research questions, however, your best approach may be to limit your search to a specific state. Because federal courts often are required to interpret state laws, another option is to search cases from both the state courts and the relevant federal jurisdictions (the U.S. Supreme Court, the particular U.S. Court of Appeals, and the U.S. District Courts within the state). This approach may yield too many results, as it includes *all* Supreme Court cases and *all* cases from the Court of Appeals, whether or not they arose in that state. It is usually best to start with just that state's courts and then check federal case law once the research issues have been more clearly defined. Finding a small number of cases directly on point is better than finding a large number of vaguely relevant cases.

Simple keyword searches can find cases, but it is important to use features such as proximity connectors, truncation, synonyms, and term frequency. Remember that you are searching through thousands (or millions) of documents. A search may retrieve a case containing your search terms, but those terms may be unconnected to each other or may appear in a peripheral discussion unrelated to the holding. Using proximity connectors and term frequency increases the chances that a case is indeed relevant.

The most effective Westlaw searches take advantage of the editorial synopsis and headnotes that precede each case, as shown in the opening page of *Bradford v. Coody* in Exhibit 3–1. This focuses retrieval to cases that turn on the specific research issues, rather than any and all cases that may only mention the search terms in passing.

There are two basic ways to search the synopsis and headnotes in Westlaw cases. Westlaw considers these parts of the case document as *fields*, or portions of a document to which a search can be limited. Most fields can be entered into a search by using a two-letter abbreviation. The introductory synopsis is the *sy* field. The numbered headnotes make up the *digest (di)* field, which combines the *topic (to)* field, consisting of the subject headings and key numbers, and the *headnote (he)* field, containing the text of the notes. While each of these fields can be searched separately, often the strongest search is one that encompasses the synopsis and

digest by using both fields at once. A search for
sy,di(vicious /3 dog) will retrieve a smaller body of
cases more precisely on point than a simple full-text
search for *vicious /3 dog*.

The other way to search the headnotes on Westlaw is to use the digest topics and key numbers
assigned to each headnote. The West digest system
consists of over 400 topics, arranged alphabetically
from Abandoned and Lost Property to Zoning and
Planning. Each topic is then divided into numbered
sections, called *key numbers*, designating specific
points of law for that topic. Some narrow topics like
Party Walls employ relatively few key numbers,
while broader ones such as Taxation or Trade Regulation have thousands. The second headnote in
Bradford v. Coody, shown in print in Exhibit 3–1
and on Westlaw in Exhibit 3–2 on page 141, is
Animals ☞ 66.4(2), dealing with the liability of
landlords for injuries caused by their tenants' animals.

This classification system serves the same purpose for legal topics that call numbers do for library
books, in that it allows related items to be classed
together whether or not they use the same keywords. Similar legal issues may arise, for example,
in cases involving dogs and other animals, but it
may not occur to you to search for both *cat* and
horse as well as *dog*. The key numbers provide a
way to make sure that all relevant cases on a single
subject are being retrieved.

For use in Westlaw, each of the topics has been assigned a number between 1 and 450. *Animals* is topic 28, for example, and a search for Animals ☞ 66.4(2) is *28k66.4(2)*. This key number can used in combination with other terms to create a very precise and effective search.

Obviously you are not going to begin a research project with a search like *28k66.4(2)*. The trick, though, is to assess the cases you find through a keyword search or a synopsis and digest search; if a retrieved headnote is particularly relevant, then you can use its key number to find other cases. One way to do this is to click on the headnote's hyperlinked key number. This brings up a Custom Digest search screen, on which you specify the courts to search and add keyword search terms if desired. The subsequent search finds similar headnotes, with links to the full text of the cases. Exhibit 3–3 on page 142 shows the search screen for *28k66.4(2)* linked from the *Bradford* headnote.

Key numbers can also be incorporated into searches through the "Key Numbers" link at the top of the Westlaw screen, which allows you to search for terms appearing in relevant key number descriptions or headnotes. The "Key Numbers" link also has a feature called Keysearch, for browsing through a list of broad topics and more detailed subtopics until you reach the specific focus of your inquiry. Clicking on this term leads to a search screen on which Westlaw automatically creates a key number search to match the legal topic. You choose a jurisdiction and can add additional search terms if you wish.

In addition to the synopsis and digest, other fields can be used to search particular parts of case documents. Thus searches can be limited to the names of the parties (*ti* or *title*), the judge writing the opinion (*ju* or *judge*), or a particular court (*co* or *court*). The easiest way to use these fields is to select one from the drop-down menu on the search screen; this enters the field abbreviation into the search with the cursor between the parentheses symbols.

Once a search is entered, Westlaw displays either the first case or a list of cases accompanied by a *ResultsPlus* list of links to other relevant resources such as treatises and encyclopedias. The links in the *Bradford v. Coody* case display in Exhibit 3–2, for example, include sections of *American Jurisprudence 2d* and an *ALR* annotation on liability for dog bites.

Westlaw's KeyCite feature is an integral part of case display. It shows whether a case is still good law, and provides a convenient way to find cases on related topics. KeyCite performs several valuable functions in the research process, and will be discussed later in the chapter with other citators, in § 3–5 beginning on page 108.

b.   Lexis

Lexis has the full text of practically every published federal and state court opinion, as well as Case

Summaries and headnotes that allow its databases to be searched in several ways similar to those used in Westlaw. The Case Summaries and headnotes are accompanied by computer-generated "core terms" listing several of the major keywords found in the opinion. Exhibit 3–4 on page 143 shows these features as part of its display of *Bradford v. Coody*.

A Lexis Case Summary consists of three parts: Procedural Posture, explaining the nature and status of the litigation; Overview, summarizing the facts of the case; and Outcome, providing a brief description of the court's decision. These can be searched as separate segments, but the most effective approach is to use the *LN-Summary* segment combining the three.

Lexis headnotes do not employ a numerical classification system like West's key numbers, but the terms in headnotes can be searched as a distinct segment. Once you find a relevant case, its headnotes can be incorporated into further searching in several ways. Clicking on "More Like This Headnote" runs a natural language search using the terminology of the headnote.

As part of its case display, Lexis also includes a *Related Content* panel on the left side of the screen that includes *Issue Analysis* links to ALR annotations, treatise sections, and law review articles. Like Westlaw's ResultsPlus, these links may lead to secondary sources that can clarify issues or cite other relevant cases.

A feature that you may find useful when beginning a research project is *Search by Topic or Headnote*. You can browse through subject areas or
search for particular terms. Another way to use
Search by Topic or Headnote is to click on a case
headnote's hyperlinked topic heading. This opens
up a window displaying a topical outline of the
subject area, from which you can click on a specific
topic within the subject area and run a search for
cases and other documents assigned to this topic.
The Lexis headnotes are also valuable when expanding research using Shepard's Citations, which
will be discussed separately in § 3–5.

c. Other Resources

Although this section has focused on Westlaw and
Lexis procedures, lower-cost databases such as
Casemaker <www.lawriter.net>, Fastcase <www.
fastcase.com>, Loislaw <www.loislaw.com>, and
VersusLaw <www.versuslaw.com> also include extensive coverage of case law. They also offer sophisticated search approaches, with features such as
truncation, Boolean connectors, and document
fields. They generally lack editorial features similar
to those offered by Westlaw and Lexis, such as
introductory synopses or headnotes to provide research springboards to other cases. They do, however, have the full, searchable text of court opinions.
For many lawyers, access to one of these systems is
a benefit of bar membership.

Until recently, most free Internet sites with case
law were limited to a particular court's opinions

and the most recent few years (or months) of decisions. This changed dramatically in November 2009 when Google Scholar <scholar.google.com> added coverage of federal cases since 1923 and state appellate cases since 1950. You can search these using the standard Google advanced search options such as exact phrases, "all of the words," or "at least one of the words." You can also choose specific jurisdictions to search and limit retrieval to particular dates. A "How cited" link shows excerpts from later decisions citing the displayed case.

LexisONE <www.lexisone.com> provides free access to the most recent ten years of cases from all federal and state appellate courts, and permits the use of the extensive Boolean connectors and segments offered by Lexis. You can search individual jurisdictions, combined state cases, or combined federal cases.

Websites for individual courts or jurisdictions also offer opinions, but some sites are much more accessible and more extensive than others. Some state court sites simply provide chronological access to opinions with no full-text searching, while others have searchable retrospective collections of appellate court decisions. Dramatic differences can be found even among the United States Courts of Appeals. Some have very useful sites, while others have primitive search engines or do not even allow keyword searching.

Free websites are most useful for obtaining copies of new decisions and monitoring recent developments, and they may yield a few cases that can lead to other documents. When using a free resource for case research, it is essential to recognize its limitations and not to overlook important precedent just because it is beyond the scope of coverage.

§ 3–3. West Digests

We have already seen in the discussion of Westlaw the importance of headnote classifications in finding relevant cases. West editors write headnotes for each case and assign each headnote to a legal topic and a specific key number classification within that topic. By using subject access, you can frequently find relevant cases that a keyword or natural language search would miss.

West topics and key numbers can be incorporated into Westlaw searches, as discussed above, or used in print series of volumes known as *digests*. These are tools that reprint in a classified arrangement the headnote summaries of each case's points of law, with citations to the full text.

Whether online or in print, digests are valuable case-finders but have several shortcomings. They consist simply of case headnotes, with no text to explain which decisions are more important or how they fit together. Often a textual discussion of an area of law, such as in a treatise or a law review article, offers a clearer and more selective introduction to relevant case law. Digest entries may reflect dicta and may even misstate points of law in the cases they abstract, and they generally don't indicate that a case may no longer be good law unless it has been directly reversed or modified. It is essential to locate and read the cases themselves to determine whether they are actually pertinent, and then to verify their status using KeyCite or Shepard's Citations.

The West key number system is not the only digest classification system used in legal research. Some looseleaf services and topical reporters use digests for cases in specific subject areas and will be discussed briefly in Chapter 8. *United States Supreme Court Reports, Lawyers' Edition* is accompanied by a digest arranging its cases' headnotes by subject, but the *Lawyers' Edition* classification system does not appear in other reports and is useful only for Supreme Court research.

a. Finding Cases in Digests

To use a print digest, you must identify a topic and key number relevant to the problem. Digest topics and key numbers can be found in several ways: (1) by using a Descriptive–Word Index after analyzing the factual and legal issues involved in a problem; (2) by surveying the outline of a relevant legal topic; or (3) by using the headnotes of a case known to be on point.

Descriptive-Word Method. To find the key number under which relevant cases are digested, it is usually most productive to begin with the Descriptive–Word Index shelved either at the beginning or the end of each digest set. This detailed index lists thousands of factual and legal terms, and provides references to key numbers.

You can approach a Descriptive–Word Index by looking up either legal issues, such as causes of action, defenses, or relief sought, or factual elements in an action, such as parties, places, or objects involved. In a personal injury case involving a dog bite, for example, you would use the index to investigate legal issues such as duty or strict liability, or facts such as animals or landlords. Exhibit 3–5 on page 144 shows a page from a Descriptive–Word Index, including a reference under the Animals ☞ subheading "Landlords–Liability of" to Animals 66.4(2). Besides numerous references to the Animals topic, entries on the page also lead to the Health and Products Liability topics and provide cross-references to other index headings such as Horses and Railroads.

Finding appropriate key numbers in the index can sometimes be a simple step. When using any legal index, however, you should be prepared for some frustration. Even the most thorough index cannot list every possible approach to a legal or factual issue. You'll often need to rethink issues, reframe questions, check synonyms and alternate terms, and follow leads in cross-references.

When turning from the index to the volume of digest abstracts, looking first at the outline of the topic can help you verify that the legal context is indeed appropriate. You may be looking for cases on substantive negligence issues, for example, but find that a key number that appeared relevant actually deals with some other issue such as the standard of review for summary judgment. Exhibit 3–6 on page 145 contains part of the outline for the Animals topic, showing how ☞ 66.4(2) fits with other issues involving liability for injuries by dogs and other animals.

Exhibit 3–7 on page 146 shows a page from a *West's Louisiana Digest 2d* pamphlet reprinting two headnotes from *Bradford v. Coody* and headnotes from other cases on alternative dispute resolution, animals, and antitrust.

Topic Approach. You can also bypass the Descriptive–Word Index and go directly to the West digest topic that seems most relevant to a problem. Each topic begins with a scope note, indicating which subjects it includes and which are covered in related topics. The Animals topic, for example, covers issues such as property rights and cruelty to animals, but it does not incorporate matters such as hunting (covered in the Game topic) or protection of endangered species (covered in Environmental Law).

Once the correct topic is found, analyze the outline to select the appropriate key number for a specific issue. An advantage of this method is that it gives you the context of the individual key numbers; reading through the outline may help clarify issues or raise concerns you had not yet considered. This can be a very time-consuming approach, however, and beginning researchers may not have the legal background to choose the right topic and determine the appropriate issues. In most instances, the index is a faster and more reliable starting point.

Case Headnotes. The easiest and most foolproof way to use a digest is to begin with the headnotes of a case on point. When you already know of a relevant case, you can find it in the National Reporter System volume or on Westlaw, then scan its headnotes for relevant issues and use the key numbers accompanying these headnotes to access the digest. This eliminates the need to search through indexes or to analyze the digest's classification system, and reduces the likelihood of turning to the wrong issue or getting stuck in a dead end. This method, of course, requires that at least one initial case be found through other means, but several other case-finding resources—from legal encyclopedias to on-line full-text searches—have already been discussed.

b. Jurisdictional and Regional Digests

West digests are available for the entire country, for some regions, for individual states, and for a few specific subjects. Choosing the right digest depends on the scope of your inquiry. For some research you may want to find cases from only one jurisdiction, but for other projects you may be interested in developments throughout the country. A more focused digest obviously covers fewer cases but is usually easier to use.

There are digests for every state but Delaware, Nevada, and Utah, and for four of the regional reporter series (*Atlantic*, *North Western*, *Pacific*, and *South Eastern*). The state digests include references to all the cases West publishes from the state's courts, as well as federal cases arising from the U.S. District Courts in that state.

State digests are kept up to date by annual pocket parts in the back of each volume, by quarterly pamphlets between annual supplements, and by occasional replacement volumes incorporating the newer material. A single volume can thus contain headnotes of decisions from the earliest nominative reporters through a few months ago. For about a dozen states, the current digest only provides coverage of cases from recent decades. An earlier digest set must be consulted for complete retrospective coverage of the older court decisions, but the modern cases in the current set are all that is needed for most research projects.

The key number system has been in use for more than a century, but the law of course has not remained static in that time. Old doctrines have faded in significance and new areas of law have developed. West attempts to reflect changes by revising and expanding old topics and by establishing new topics. When new or revised topics are introduced, West editors reclassify the headnotes in thousands of older cases. On Westlaw, the numbers assigned to older cases are updated when the key number system is revised, and the current classification can be used to find relevant cases of any age. The new classifications are also used when state digest volumes are recompiled. Until the recompilation, new or revised topics are accompanied by tables converting older topics and key numbers to those newly adopted and vice versa.

The digest changes slowly, however, and it may take several years for new areas of legal doctrine to be recognized and to receive adequate coverage. Until 2006, for example, cases involving landlord liability for injuries by tenants' animals were under a general "Persons liable for injuries" key number. As the number of cases grew, landlord liability was given its own key number, 66.4(2), within the Animals topic. Because cases in newly developing areas of the law are often assigned to general key numbers, digest research may not be the best way to find cases in these areas.

West also publishes a separate series of digests for federal court decisions. The current set is known as the *Federal Practice Digest 4th*, covering cases from the mid–1980s and occupying several hundred volumes. Supreme Court headnotes are also printed in *United States Supreme Court Digest*, and the specialized federal courts have their own digests as well.

c. *Decennial* and *General Digests*

The most comprehensive series of digests is known as the American Digest System. This covers cases in all of West's federal and state reporters, and is a massive and rather unwieldy finding tool. Its most current component, the *General Digest*, collects and publishes headnotes from all West advance sheets. A *General Digest* volume is published about every three weeks, cumulating headnotes from about twenty reporter volumes from federal and state courts and covering the entire range of more than 400 digest topics.

Every few years, West recompiles the headnotes from the *General Digest* and publishes them in a multivolume set called a *Decennial Digest*. The name *Decennial* comes from the fact that these sets used to be published every ten years. The *Eighth Decennial*, for example, covers cases decided between 1966 and 1976. Due to the increased volume of case law, West now compiles these digests after every sixty volumes of the *General Digest*. The *Eleventh Decennial Digest, Part 3* is the most recent set, covering 2004–07.

Finding cases in the *Decennial* and *General Digests* may require checking the same key number in several volumes. Each *Decennial* covers a set period of years, and fifteen to twenty *General Digest* volumes are published each year. You may have to look through several dozen volumes to search for recent cases. Because some key numbers are infrequently used and only appear in occasional *General Digest* volumes, this process can be eased somewhat by using tables that list the key numbers found in each volume. These tables cumulate in every tenth volume; if twenty-seven *General Digest* volumes have been published, for example, you would need to check the tables in volumes 10, 20, and 27. Even with this short cut, checking the *General Digest* can be a rather time-consuming process.

One problem in using *Decennial Digests* is that older volumes are not revised to reflect changes in topics and classifications. Cases on Westlaw are updated with new key numbers and jurisdictional digest volumes are revised and reissued, but *Decennial Digests* have only conversion tables indicating corresponding key numbers in older and newer classifications.

The first unit of the American Digest System, called the *Century Digest*, covers early cases from 1658 to 1896. It was followed by a *First Decennial Digest* for 1897 to 1906, and subsequent *Decennials* for each decade since. *Decennial Digests* are found in most large law libraries, and they remain the most comprehensive collection of case headnotes available for researchers without Westlaw access.

d. *Words and Phrases*

West reprints some headnote abstracts in a separate multivolume set, *Words and Phrases*. Headnotes are included in *Words and Phrases* if a court defines or interprets a legally significant term. *Words and Phrases* is arranged alphabetically rather than by key number, and it can be a useful tool when the meaning of a specific term is at issue.

The *Words and Phrases* set covers the entire National Reporter System. Shorter "Words and Phrases" lists also appear in many West digests and in West reporter volumes and advance sheets. Exhibit 3–8 on page 147 shows a page from *Words and Phrases* with headnotes from several cases defining terms such as "vicious dog," "vicious nature," and "vicious propensities." Judicial definitions from *Words and Phrases* can also be found on Westlaw by searching the *wp* field.

§ 3–4. *American Law Reports* Annotations

At the same time that West was developing its National Reporter System in the late 19th century, other publishers were attempting a different approach to case reporting. They selected "leading cases" for full-text publication, and added commentaries, or *annotations*, which surveyed the law on the subject of the selected case and described other decisions with similar facts, holdings, or procedures. Selective publication was not a successful alternative to comprehensive reporting, but the annotations have proved to be valuable case research tools.

The modern successor to these early annotated reporters is *American Law Reports (ALR)*, which is now published in three current series: *ALR6th* for general and state legal issues, *ALR Federal 2d* for issues of federal law, and a new *ALR International* comparing the law of U.S. and foreign courts. A few annotations limited to Supreme Court cases are also published in *United States Supreme Court Reports, Lawyers' Edition*.

Annotations summarize the cases on a specific topic and classify decisions that have reached conflicting results. The coverage of *ALR* is not encyclopedic, and not every research issue is covered by its annotations. An annotation directly on point, however, can save you considerable research time. It does the initial time-consuming work of finding relevant cases, and arranges them according to specific fact patterns and holdings. Because it synthesizes the cases into a narrative discussion, rather than simply offering a collection of headnotes, an annotation is usually easier to understand than a digest.

Annotations differ significantly from other narrative resources such as treatises and law review articles. Their purpose is to present in a systematic way the varied judicial decisions from around the country, not to criticize these decisions or to integrate case law into broader concerns. They are best viewed as research tools rather than as secondary authority which may persuade a tribunal. If they are cited, it is as convenient compilations of prevailing judicial doctrine.

ALR annotations are available on both Westlaw and Lexis. Westlaw coverage goes all the way back to the beginning of *ALR1st*, and it includes new annotations that have not yet been released for publication in the print *ALR*. Lexis coverage begins with *ALR2d* and also includes *Lawyers' Edition 2d* annotations.

a.   Format and Content

An *ALR* volume usually contains from ten to twenty annotations, each analyzing decisions on an issue raised in an illustrative recent case, which is printed in full either before the annotation or at the end of the volume. Each annotation begins with a table of contents, a detailed subject index, and a table listing the jurisdictions of the cases discussed. In volumes published since 1992 (the beginning of *ALR5th*), this introductory material has also included a Research References section providing leads to encyclopedias, practice aids, digests, and other sources, as well as sample electronic search queries and relevant West digest key numbers. Exhibits 3–9 and 3–10 on pages 148–49 show pages from the beginning of an *ALR4th* annotation on the liability of landlords for injuries caused by their tenants' animals. Exhibit 3–9 shows the table of contents, organizing the annotation's sections according to theories of liability and whether or not liability was established. Exhibit 3–10 shows part of the index, listing specific factual scenarios and legal issues arising in the cases discussed, and the jurisdictional table, a state-by-state listing of the cases.

The first two sections of an annotation are an introduction describing its scope and a summary providing a general overview and giving practice pointers. For annotations before *ALR6th* and *ALR Fed 2d*, § 1[b] has a list of related *ALR* annotations; these are now included in the Research References section. The remaining sections of the annotation then summarize cases on point from throughout the country, arranged according to their facts and holdings. From the landlord liability annotation, Exhibit 3–11 on page 150 shows the annotation's discussion of cases involving specific relationships between the landlords and tenants.

The annotation in Exhibits 3–9 through 3–11 was originally published in 1991, but the volume's annual supplement provides references to more recent cases. Annotations since *ALR3d* are updated with pocket parts in each volume, but *ALR1st* and *ALR2d* use other methods. These older annotations are not used as often as those in the newer series, but many remain current and continue to be updated. *ALR2d* volumes have no pocket parts, so instead new cases are summarized in a separate set of blue *Later Case Service* volumes, which *do* have annual pocket parts. Annotations in *ALR1st* are updated through a set called *ALR1st Blue Book of Supplemental Decisions*, which simply lists relevant new case citations. The Westlaw and Lexis versions incorporate supplementary material into the appropriate sections of the annotation.

If later cases substantially change the law on a subject covered by an annotation, a new annotation may either supplement or completely supersede the older annotation. The older volume's pocket part or other supplement alerts you to the existence of the newer treatment (another good reason to *always* check the pocket part). Online, a notice and a link to the newer annotation replace the older work. Another way to determine whether an annotation remains current is to check the "Annotation History Table" in the back of each volume of the *ALR*

Index, which lists all superseding and supplementing annotations.

b. Finding Annotations

The online versions of *ALR* annotations are searchable by keyword, just like cases or law review articles. Because annotations describe the facts of the cases discussed, including aspects unrelated to the subject of the annotation, a full-text search often turns up numerous documents on unrelated topics. Annotations have descriptive titles and introductory summaries, so it is often best to limit your search to the *title* or *summary* portions of the document. A natural language search, which automatically ranks documents by relevance, can also focus in on the most useful annotations.

The basic tool for subject access to the printed version of *ALR* is the nine-volume *ALR Index*, which is kept current by quarterly pocket parts. A less comprehensive *ALR Quick Index* covers only *ALR3d-6th*, and a separate *ALR Federal Quick Index* is limited to *ALR Fed* and *ALR Fed 2d* annotations. Exhibit 3–12 on page 151 shows a page from the *ALR Index*, containing references under "Dogs" to a wide range of annotations including the one illustrated.

Remember that in almost all *ALR* annotations, either section 1[b] or the Research References section provides a list of other annotations on related topics. If a quick check of the index does not turn up an annotation directly on point but does lead to one on a similar issue, the most productive next step may be to turn to that annotation and read through its list of related annotations. This list could lead to analogies or concepts you may not have thought to check in the index. The list for the landlord liability annotation, for example, includes more than twenty cross-references to annotations on topics such as restrictions on pets in leases and liability for injuries caused by cats.

Another means of access to annotations is through the *ALR Digest*, a multivolume set classifying *ALR*'s annotations and cases in West's key number system. Older digests using a different classification system may be found in some libraries, but these are no longer being updated.

You can also use a case or statute to find relevant annotations. Westlaw's ResultsPlus and Lexis's Related Content displays that accompany search results often include links to annotations as well as encyclopedias and other sources. KeyCite, to be discussed in the next section, includes coverage of annotations as citing references. In print, the *ALR Index* is accompanied by a volume listing the statutes, rules and regulations cited in annotations. Online or in print, many annotated codes and encyclopedias also provide references to relevant *ALR* annotations.

Annotations can be very useful research tools for many legal problems. If an annotation has been written on a point being researched, that means someone has already examined the issue and collected almost every relevant case. Because each annotation is written about a specific topic, however, coverage in the series is not comprehensive or encyclopedic. There are many issues for which no annotation can be found.

§ 3–5. Citators

Under the doctrine of precedent, the holdings of governing cases determine the resolution of issues in subsequent controversies. A precedential decision continues to have binding effect regardless of its age, but its authority can change either suddenly or through gradual erosion. A decision might be reversed on appeal to a higher court or overruled years later by a decision of the same court. Later cases may also criticize or question the reasoning of a decision, or limit its holding to a specific factual situation. Any of these circumstances can diminish or negate the authority of a case.

Before relying on any case, you must verify its current validity. This process of updating cases was traditionally performed by checking printed volumes known as *Shepard's Citations*, and as a result it is sometimes known as *Shepardizing*. Shepard's information is now available electronically on Lexis as well as in print, and Westlaw has a competing electronic resource, KeyCite, that provides a similar service.

Citators perform three major functions:

• Providing parallel citations for the decision and references to other proceedings in the same case, allowing you to trace its judicial history;

• Indicating if subsequent cases have overruled, limited, or otherwise diminished a case's precedent, providing the information you need to determine whether it remains "good law"; and

• Listing research leads to later citing cases, as well as periodical articles, attorney general opinions, *ALR* annotations, and other resources, enabling you to find related cases and to trace the development of a legal doctrine forward from a known case to the present.

KeyCite and Shepard's are invaluable resources not only because they validate research already done and ensure that cases are still good law. They also serve as powerful links from one document to others on related issues, providing one of the most effective ways to find sources for further research. You can use citators to shape your research and to explore specific issues arising in relevant cases.

KeyCite and Shepard's are not the only citators available. Loislaw has a *GlobalCite* service that lists citing documents and includes case treatment terms such as "Agree," "Disagree," or "Overrule" to indicate the effect of later decisions. Other services such as Casemaker's *Casecheck* or Fastcase's *Authority Check* provide links to subsequent citing cases, but neither has codes or flags indicating the nature of the citations. It is also possible, of course, to find citing references by including a case's name or citation in a full-text search.

a. KeyCite

Westlaw's citator service, KeyCite, is incorporated into its case research system. A case display on Westlaw has several links to KeyCite information. Links on the left side of the screen include *Full History* (decisions which may bear a direct impact on a case's validity) and *Citing References* (the full list of citing documents). In addition, a small symbol at the top of the case display indicates what citator information is available. A red flag generally indicates that a case is not good law on some point, and a yellow flag that there is some negative history. If neither of these flags is applicable, a blue "H" indicates that there is some case history information available or a green "C" shows that there are citing references. Clicking on the displayed symbol leads directly to the case's KeyCite references. Key-Cite information can also be accessed by typing a citation into a form on Westlaw's welcome screen, or by clicking on the KeyCite link at the top of the Westlaw page.

Full History includes prior and subsequent decisions in the same litigation, so that the case can be traced through the appellate process, and "negative indirect history" cases, those decisions involving different litigants that may have an adverse impact on the precedential value of the cited case. Be aware, however, that "negative" history is broadly construed. A lower court decision that declines to extend a Supreme Court precedent to an unrelated area is listed as "distinguishing" its holding. This is considered a negative citation, even though it has no impact on the Supreme Court decision's precedent. Another option, *Direct History (Graphical View)*, shows the course of the litigation through the levels of the court system.

Citing References lists negative citing cases first, and then the remaining cases by the extent to which they discuss the cited case, with rankings from four stars (an extended discussion) to one star (mentioned in a list with other citations). KeyCite also indicates those cases that quote directly from the cited case, by adding quotation marks to the display. Secondary sources such as law review articles and *ALR* annotations are listed next, followed by briefs and other appellate and trial court documents. The court documents, but not the secondary sources, include star rankings and quotation marks. Linked citations lead to the full text of any of these citing documents.

KeyCite offers several ways to focus your retrieval. *Limits* can be used to see only those references from specific jurisdictions, or those that cite the point of law in particular headnotes. KeyCite can also limit by depth of treatment (number of stars) or by type of citing document (e.g., cases, law review articles, treatises and encyclopedias). One of the most powerful KeyCite tools is the ability to use the *Locate* feature to run a keyword search within the citing documents. This can focus immediately on those documents applying a precedent to a particular set of facts.

Another way to move directly from a displayed case to a KeyCite result is to use the *KeyCite Citing References for this Headnote* link preceding each headnote. This takes you to a screen on which you choose what type of citing documents you wish to see (or to a notice that there are not yet any citing references for the headnote), and then to a list of KeyCite references limited to those discussing this particular legal issue.

Exhibit 3–13 on page 152 shows KeyCite results for a U.S. Supreme Court decision, *United States v. Olson*, 546 U.S. 43 (2005). *Olson* has been cited in 376 documents, but the first screen shows the "negative cases," those later decisions that have distinguished its holding or declined to follow it on state law grounds. These are followed by other citing cases, ranked by the extent to which they discuss the cited case.

In the same way that WestClip provides automatic notification of new cases or other documents matching a particular search, KeyCite has an alert service that monitors developments in a case's history or citing references. KeyCite Alert can be set up to send notices for all new citing references or for references meeting specific criteria such as cited headnote number, jurisdiction, or depth of treatment.

b. Shepard's Citations Online

Shepard's Citations is an integral part of Lexis case research. One of the choices at the top of a case display is "Shepardize," and in most instances a signal to the left of the case name indicates the nature of citing documents. A red stop sign indicates strong negative treatment (e.g., the case has been reversed or overruled) and a gold "Q" indicates that a case's validity has been questioned, while a yellow caution sign indicates possible negative treatment (e.g., its holding has been criticized or limited). A green plus sign indicates positive history or treatment, and a blue circle indicates other citing references. Like KeyCite, Shepard's has a broad definition of "negative" treatment.

You can also choose *Shepard's* from the menu at the top of the Lexis screen, and then type in a citation. When using this approach, you have the option of retrieving a list of decisions which may have a direct impact on a case's validity ("Shepard's for Validation," limited to proceedings in the same litigation and any negative citing cases) or the full list of citing documents ("Shepard's for Research").

Shepard's does not rank documents as Westlaw does, but instead provides a broader range of treatment codes. Some, but not all, positive cases are given treatment codes such as "followed" or "explained" to indicate the nature of their citations. Citing cases are displayed by jurisdiction, beginning with cases from the home jurisdiction of the cited case. You can use *Restrictions* in Shepard's to see only those references with particular treatments (negative only, positive only, or your choice of specific codes), as well as cases from specific jurisdictions or those that cite the point of law in particular headnotes. You can also run a *Focus* search within the text of the citing cases to find specific fact patterns or terminology.

Exhibit 3–14 on page 153 shows a Shepard's screen from Lexis, displaying the result for *United States v. Olson*. Note that the display begins with a summary listing the number of cautionary, positive, and neutral citing cases, with links to those using specific treatment codes, as well as other citing sources such as law reviews, treatises, and court documents.

Although their editorial treatment and arrangement differ, KeyCite and Shepard's generally provide coverage of the same citing cases. Both include cases that are designated as unpublished but are available through the online databases, as well as cases published in the official reports, West reporters, and other topical reporters. Occasionally one service includes a reference to an unpublished decision available through its database but not the other, but the differences in case coverage are slight. Both provide thorough coverage and timely notice of new developments.

Coverage of secondary sources in the two services does differ. Both have references to law reviews available online, but otherwise each focuses on materials available on its system. This means that

KeyCite includes *ALR* annotations and West treatises, while Shepard's has treatises and encyclopedias published by LexisNexis or Matthew Bender.

It is important when using either KeyCite or Shepard's Citations to understand that its signals and editorial signposts are not authoritative statements of the law. Relying on a red flag or a stop sign is no substitute for reading a citing document and determining for yourself its scope and effect. A case that has been overruled on one point may still be good law on other issues, but learning this requires reading the overruling case and perhaps examining *its* subsequent history.

c.　*Shepard's Citations* in Print

While the electronic versions of KeyCite and Shepard's compete for online customers, *Shepard's Citations* is the only choice for researchers using print resources. There is no print version of KeyCite, but sets of *Shepard's Citations* are published for the Supreme Court, the lower federal courts, every state, the District of Columbia, Puerto Rico, and each region of the National Reporter System.

In order to convey a large amount of information in a small space, the print versions of *Shepard's* use a system of one-letter symbols to indicate the treatment of citing cases. The letter c, for example, stands for *criticized*; d for *distinguished*, and j for *citing in dissenting opinion*. In addition, the abbreviations that identify citing sources are usually shorter than the citations commonly used in the

Bluebook and other sources. *California Reporter 3d* becomes *CaR3d* in a *Shepard's* volume. These symbols and abbreviations may be confusing at first, but they are listed in tables at the front of each volume.

Printed *Shepard's Citations* can never be as current as the electronic resources, but most sets are supplemented biweekly or monthly. Each set contains one or more maroon bound volumes, and supplementary pamphlets of varying colors. To help you know which volumes or supplements you need to use, the cover of each supplement includes a list, "What Your Library Should Contain," of the current volumes and pamphlets for the set.

Exhibit 3–15 on page 154 shows a page from *Shepard's United States Citations* containing references to *United States v. Olson*. After the page number (the large bold "43") and the name and date of the case, the rest of the column lists citations to *Olson*, including a Supreme Court case at the beginning of the list, several federal cases, and one state court case. Several of the citing cases follow (*f*) the *Olson* holding.

Shepardizing state cases in print adds one wrinkle not apparent from the *Olson* exhibit. References in law review articles are noted in the state *Shepard's* set, but not in the regional *Shepard's*. On the other hand, citing cases from other states appear only in the regional series and not in the state *Shepard's*. Both state citators and regional citators list citing cases from the home jurisdiction and in federal courts, but neither provides a complete list of all citing documents.

Some recent citing cases in supplementary *Shepard's* pamphlets are listed by Lexis citations (e.g., 2005 U.S. LEXIS 8372) if reporter citations are not yet available. Lexis subscribers can use these citations to find the cases online, while other *Shepard's* users can learn the names of the cases by entering the citation in lexisONE or calling a toll-free customer service number.

Electronic citators have numerous advantages over printed *Shepard's Citations*. References to new cases are added within hours or days. Coverage is not divided into separate state and regional citators, with each displaying only some of the citing documents. Citing entries are compiled into a single online listing, eliminating the need to search through multiple volumes and pamphlets. Because page space is not a concern, case treatments and names of publications are spelled out rather than abbreviated. You can easily narrow retrieval to specific treatments or headnote numbers, without scanning a lengthy list of citations. Finally, hypertext links make it possible to go directly from the online citator to the text of citing cases. For some researchers, however, the printed version of *Shepard's Citations* remains the primary means to verify the validity of decisions and to find research leads.

§ 3–6. Sources for Federal Court Cases

Cases are available from a variety of printed and online sources. Even if you do most of your research online, knowing about the major series of court reports can help you understand citations and assess the precedential value of decisions. It also allows you to make informed choices about retrieving cases. There may be official and unofficial versions, some with headnotes and some with the page numbers needed for pinpoint citations. In some situations any version of a case will work fine, but in others you may need to find and cite a specific source.

a. Supreme Court of the United States

The Supreme Court of the United States stands at the head of the judicial branch of government, and provides the definitive interpretation of the U.S. Constitution and federal statutes. Its decisions are studied not only by lawyers but by political scientists, historians, and citizens interested in the development of social and legal policy.

The Supreme Court is the court of last resort in the federal court system. It also has the final word on federal issues raised in state courts, and it hears cases arising between states. The Court exercises a tight control over its docket and has wide discretion to decline review, or to *deny a writ of certiorari* as it is called in almost all cases. The Supreme Court usually accepts for consideration only those cases that raise significant policy issues. In recent years it has issued opinions in fewer than ninety cases during its annual term, which begins on the first Monday of October and ends in late June or early July.

Numerous reference works explain the history and role of the Supreme Court in the American political and legal system. Three works with encyclopedic coverage of the Court, including articles on major cases, doctrinal areas, and specific justices, are *Encyclopedia of the American Constitution* (Leonard W. Levy et al. eds., 2d ed. 2000), *Encyclopedia of the Supreme Court of the United States* (David S. Tanenhaus ed., 2008), and *Oxford Companion to the Supreme Court of the United States* (Kermit L. Hall ed., 2d ed. 2005). David G. Savage, *Guide to the U.S. Supreme Court* (4th ed. 2004) is arranged thematically rather than alphabetically, but it too explains major doctrines and provides historical background. A wide range of statistical and historical information is available in *The Supreme Court Compendium: Data, Decisions, and Developments* (Lee Epstein et al. eds., 4th ed. 2007). The major practical guide for lawyers bringing a case before the Court is Eugene Gressman et al., *Supreme Court Practice* (9th ed. 2007).

The Court's website <www.supremecourtus.gov> includes a variety of information in its "About the Supreme Court" section. Numerous other websites provide background information on the Court. The Supreme Court Historical Society <www.supreme courthistory.org> has sections on the Court's history and how it works, as well as a guide to research-

ing various Supreme Court topics. SCOTUSblog
<www.scotusblog.com> is the leading website for
the most current information on new decisions and
developments in pending cases.

Reference sources are useful for historical and
general background, but they are no substitute for
reading the Supreme Court's opinions. These are
published in three permanent bound reporters and
in a weekly newsletter, and they can be searched
and retrieved through several commercial databases
and free Internet sites.

1. The *United States Reports*

Begun in 1790 as a private venture, the *United
States Reports* (cited as U.S.) became official in 1817
and continues today as the official edition of Supreme Court decisions. The government publishes
several volumes of *U.S. Reports* every year. The
decisions appear first in slip opinion form the day
they are announced, then in official advance sheets
(called the "preliminary print"), and finally in the
bound *U.S. Reports* volume. Unfortunately, as with
many government publications, the *U.S. Reports*
tends to be published rather slowly. More than a
year passes before a decision appears in the preliminary print, and another year before its inclusion in
a bound volume.

The early volumes of Supreme Court decisions
are now numbered sequentially as part of the *U.S.
Reports* series, but for many years they were cited
only by the names of the individual reporters. *Blue-*

book citations to these early cases include a parenthetical reference to the nominative reporter volume, as in *Marbury v. Madison*, 5 U.S. (1 Cranch)
137 (1803), while *ALWD* rules use the *U.S. Reports*
citation only. Older cases and articles, however,
tended to cite only the nominative reports, so a
familiarity with the early reporters' names and
their periods of coverage will make it easier to read
and understand these citations:

1–4 Dallas (Dall.)	1–4 U.S. (1790–1800)
1–9 Cranch	5–13 U.S. (1801–15)
1–12 Wheaton (Wheat.)	14–25 U.S. (1816–27)
1–16 Peters (Pet.)	26–41 U.S. (1828–42)
1–24 Howard (How.)	42–65 U.S. (1843–61)
1–2 Black	66–67 U.S. (1861–63)
1–23 Wallace (Wall.)	68–90 U.S. (1863–75)

Beginning with volume 91 (October Term 1875),
U.S. Reports volumes are cited only by number and
not by the name of the reporter. The opening pages
of the Supreme Court decision KeyCited and Shepardized in the previous section, *United States v.
Olson*, appear in Exhibits 3–16 and 3–17 on pages
155–56. This version does not include numbered
headnotes, but the Court's reporter of decisions
prefaces the text of each decision with a *syllabus*
summarizing the case and the Court's holding. Following the syllabus, Exhibit 3–17 indicates that the

opinion was unanimous, identifies the attorneys in the case, and shows the beginning of the Court's opinion by Justice Breyer.

The Supreme Court website <www.supreme courtus.gov> has new opinions in PDF as soon as they are announced. Slip opinions from several terms are available, although these lack the pagination necessary for citing purposes. Under the heading "Opinions—Bound Volumes," the site also has PDF files containing the final versions of *U.S. Reports* beginning with volume 502 (October Term 1991).

More extensive online coverage is provided by the subscription site HeinOnline <www.heinonline. org>, which has searchable PDF access to the *U.S. Reports* all the way from volume one to the most recent slip opinions. Cornell Law School's Legal Information Institute (LII) <supct.law.cornell.edu/ supct/> is a free source for PDF images of current and recent slip opinions. Image files begin in 1997, although LII also has all cases since 1990 and several hundred historic decisions. LII offers a notification service for new decisions, providing the official syllabus by e-mail with links to the full text.

2. *Supreme Court Reporter* and *Lawyers' Edition*

Supreme Court opinions are also printed in two commercially published series, West's *Supreme Court Reporter* (cited as S. Ct.) and LexisNexis's *United States Supreme Court Reports, Lawyers' Edition* (known simply as *Lawyers' Edition*, and cited as L. Ed.). These reporters contain editorial features not available in the official *U.S. Reports*, and they are the versions found in Westlaw and Lexis respectively.

Because the *U.S. Reports* are published so slowly, the *Bluebook* and the *ALWD Citation Manual* specify that a recent opinion that does not yet have a *U.S.* citation should be cited to the *Supreme Court Reporter* or *Lawyers' Edition*. Both of these sources are published in paperback advance sheets within a few weeks of decision. The permanent bound volumes are not published until the cases appear in the *U.S. Reports* volumes, so that the commercial editions can include *star paging* references to the official *U.S. Reports* text.

The *Supreme Court Reporter* began in 1882, with cases from volume 106 of the *U.S. Reports*. As a component of West's National Reporter System, it includes its publisher's editorial synopses and headnotes. The opening page of *United States v. Olson* as it appears in the *Supreme Court Reporter* at 126 S. Ct. 510 is shown in Exhibit 3–18 on page 157, including the synopsis and two West headnotes. At the beginning of the official syllabus, note the star paging reference to the *U.S. Reports* pagination.

Westlaw's database of Supreme Court cases has complete historical coverage of decisions since 1790 as well as new decisions available within minutes of their release. For cases since 1882 that have been published in bound *Supreme Court Reporter* volumes, Westlaw includes an option to view and print a PDF file of the printed version.

Lawyers' Edition contains all Supreme Court decisions since the Court's inception in 1790. It is now in a second series, and its version of *Olson* appears at 163 L. Ed. 2d 306. Like the *Supreme Court Reporter*, *Lawyers' Edition* contains editorial summaries and headnotes for each case. The early *Lawyers' Edition* volumes are particularly valuable, because the editors worked from the original manuscripts rather than the sometimes erroneous versions in the *U.S. Reports*. For some cases they include information, such as the exact date of decision, not found in the official reports.

Like Westlaw, Lexis has Supreme Court cases since the Court's inception in 1790 as well as the most recent decisions the morning that they are announced. The online cases have two sets of summaries and headnotes, including those printed in *Lawyers' Edition*, as well as star paging references to the official *U.S. Reports*. For many cases, Lexis also has expanded "Case in Brief" summaries with links to related cases and secondary sources.

3. Other Sources

While *Supreme Court Reporter* and *Lawyers' Edition* are published much sooner than the official *U.S. Reports*, there is still a lag of several weeks while editors prepare their synopses and headnotes. Another publication provides access to Supreme Court cases much sooner in a newsletter format, reproducing the official slip opinions the week they are announced. This service, *The United States Law Week* (cited as U.S.L.W.), published by the Bureau of National Affairs, Inc., is the preferred *Bluebook* and *ALWD* citation for very recent Supreme Court decisions. As will be discussed in Chapter 8, *U.S. Law Week* also has extensive information about the Supreme Court's docket, arguments, and other developments.

You can also find Supreme Court opinions at several free Internet sites, in addition to the Court's own website and the Legal Information Institute. Several sites provide free access to the entire retrospective Supreme Court collection back to 1790, including Google Scholar <scholar.google.com>, Justia <supreme.justia.com>, lexisONE, and Public Library of Law <www.plol.org>. These sites offer a variety of search approaches, and several provide hypertext links in opinions to other Supreme Court cases cited. Subscription sites such as Loislaw and VersusLaw also have more than a century of older decisions.

b. Lower Federal Courts

The federal court system has grown dramatically from the thirteen District Courts and three Circuit Courts created by the Judiciary Act of 1789. The intermediate appellate courts in the federal system, the United States Courts of Appeals, are divided into thirteen circuits, consisting of the First through Eleventh Circuits (each covering several states), the District of Columbia Circuit, and the

Federal Circuit. The general trial courts, the United States District Courts, are divided into ninety-four districts, with one or more in each state. In addition, there are several specialized trial courts, such as the Bankruptcy Courts, the Court of Federal Claims, and the Court of International Trade. The map in Exhibit 3–19 on page 158 shows the boundaries of the circuits and districts. The U.S. Courts website has a map with links to individual court sites <www.uscourts.gov/courtlinks/>.

The most comprehensive sources for federal court opinions are the databases of Westlaw and Lexis, which have complete coverage back to the beginning of the court system in 1789. The *Bluebook* and *ALWD Citation Manual*, however, require that cases be cited to printed reporters if available there.

There is no counterpart to the *U.S. Reports* for the decisions of the U.S. Courts of Appeals and District Courts. The only officially published sources are the individual slip decisions the courts issue and post on their websites. The Court of Appeals sites generally only include cases since the mid–1990s and have rudimentary searching options. District Court sites vary widely; some require login to the PACER case management system for access to opinions and have no full-text search capabilities.

The most extensive printed sources for lower federal court decisions are reporters published by West. In 1880 its *Federal Reporter* began covering decisions of both circuit and district courts. More than 1,800 volumes later it is now in its third series (cited as F.3d). In 1932, with the increasing volume of litigation in the federal courts, West began another series called *Federal Supplement* (F. Supp.) for selected U.S. District Court decisions, leaving the *Federal Reporter* to cover the U.S. Courts of Appeals. *Federal Supplement* is now in its second series (F. Supp. 2d), and also includes decisions of the U.S. Court of International Trade and rulings from the Judicial Panel on Multidistrict Litigation. Like the *Supreme Court Reporter*, both of these reporters contain editorial synopses and headnotes with key numbers, which are reprinted in West's series of digest publications.

Because these reporters cover so many different courts (unlike the *U.S. Reports*), citations to the *Federal Reporter* or *Federal Supplement* must identify the specific circuit or district in parentheses. The lower court's ruling in the *Olson* case (the Supreme Court decision shown earlier), for example, is cited as *Olson v. United States*, 362 F.3d 1236 (9th Cir. 2004). Knowing the jurisdiction is vital in evaluating the scope and precedential value of a decision, but beginning researchers sometimes forget to include this information.

The *Federal Reporter* and *Federal Supplement* publish thousands of new decisions each year, but not every case the lower federal courts consider is represented by a decision in one of these reporter series. Some matters are settled or tried to a jury verdict and do not result in any written opinions.

Decisions in many cases are issued as slip opinions but are not published in the reporters. In an attempt to limit the proliferation of reported cases, each circuit has local court rules establishing criteria to determine whether decisions are published (e.g., establishing a new rule of law, resolving a conflict in the law, or involving issues of continuing public interest). Under a recently adopted Federal Rule of Appellate Procedure, "unpublished" or "non-precedential" decisions issued after January 1, 2007, can be cited as persuasive authority, but the handling of earlier decisions varies from circuit to circuit. Some courts prohibit citation of these decisions; some allow citation, but with restrictions; and some simply limit their precedential value.

Some "unpublished" decisions are available in printed sources. In 2001, West began publishing *Federal Appendix*, a series limited to Court of Appeals decisions "not selected for publication in the *Federal Reporter*." These decisions are published with headnotes and are indexed in West's digests, but you'll need to determine the extent to which they can be cited as precedent before you rely on them. More unreported decisions can be found online from Westlaw, Lexis, and court websites. For some unreported decisions, particularly in older cases, it may be necessary to contact the clerk of the court.

Before the inception of the *Federal Reporter* in 1880, federal court decisions were issued in more than a hundred different series of nominative reports. West gathered these cases in the 1890s into a thirty-volume series called *Federal Cases*. This set incorporates over 20,000 early decisions, arranged alphabetically by case name.

Another West series, *Federal Rules Decisions* (F.R.D.), began publication in 1940 and contains a limited number of U.S. District Court decisions dealing with procedural issues under the Federal Rules of Civil Procedure and the Federal Rules of Criminal Procedure. *Federal Rules Decisions* also includes judicial conference proceedings and occasional speeches or articles dealing with procedural law in the federal courts.

West also issues a number of other reporters in specialized subject fields of federal law. These selective reporters include: *Military Justice Reporter* (1978–date), containing decisions of the U.S. Court of Appeals for the Armed Forces (formerly the U.S. Court of Military Appeals), as well as selected decisions of the Court of Criminal Appeals for each military branch; *Bankruptcy Reporter* (1980–date), containing Bankruptcy Court decisions and bankruptcy decisions from the U.S. District Courts; *Federal Claims Reporter* (1982–date), containing U.S. Court of Federal Claims (formerly U.S. Claims Court) decisions; and *Veterans Appeals Reporter* (1991–date), containing U.S. Court of Veterans Appeals decisions. West's National Reporter System does not include decisions from the U.S. Tax Court, which are published by the government in *Reports*

of the United States Tax Court (1942–date) and by
the major commercial tax publishers.

Federal court decisions are also printed in a variety of other sources, including commercial topical
reporters designed for practitioners in specialized
subject areas. Some cases appearing in these
sources are not available in the *Federal Reporter* or
Federal Supplement, although there is extensive
duplication. In addition to *Federal Rules Decisions*,
West publishes two more series of cases on procedural issues which are *not* part of its National
Reporter System, *Federal Rules Service* (1939–date)
and *Federal Rules of Evidence Service* (1979–date).
Other reporters in specialized areas include *American Maritime Cases* (1923–date), *Environment Reporter Cases* (1970–date), and *U.S. Patents Quarterly* (1929–date). Several topical reporters, such as
BNA's *Fair Employment Practice Cases* (1969–date)
and CCH's *Trade Cases* (1948–date), are published
as adjuncts to looseleaf services on those topics.

Westlaw and Lexis have full-text coverage of all
federal court cases that appear in print in these
various reporters, back to the earliest decisions in
Federal Cases, and new decisions are available online well before they are published. In addition, the
electronic services also provide access to many decisions which never appear in the reporters and are
otherwise available only as slip opinions. As a result, many recent cases are cited by docket number
and online database source rather than to a printed
reporter. *United States v. 8,800 Pounds of Powdered*

Egg White, No. 1:04CV76, 2007 WL 2955571 (E.D. Mo. Oct. 5, 2007), is an example of a case available on Westlaw but not in print. The same case is also available on Lexis, where its citation is 2007 U.S. Dist. LEXIS 74999.

Federal court decisions are also available from several other online sources. Subscription databases such as Casemaker, Fastcase, Loislaw, and Versus-Law all have more than sixty years of Court of Appeals cases as well as extensive coverage of District Court decisions. Google Scholar <scholar.google.com> has free access to Court of Appeals and District Court cases since 1923, and appellate cases since 1950 are also available through several other websites including Justia <www.justia.com> and Public Library of Law.

Individual Court of Appeals websites have access to recent opinions, in most instances going back to about 1995. District and bankruptcy courts are also represented on the Internet, but most of these sites focus on local rules and procedures rather than the text of decisions. The U.S. Courts website has a Court Locator <www.uscourts.gov/courtlinks/> with links to each court's homepage, and FindLaw has a list of websites <www.findlaw.com/10fedgov/judicial/district_courts.html> with brief descriptions of their contents.

§ 3–7. Sources for State Court Cases

Although federal law governs an increasing range of activities, state courts have a vital lawmaking role in many important areas such as family law, contracts, insurance, and substantive criminal law. A state's court of last resort has the final say in interpreting the state's constitution and statutes.

The structure of most state court systems roughly follows the federal paradigm, with various trial courts, intermediate appellate courts, and a court of last resort. There are, however, wide variations. A few states have no intermediate appellate courts, with appeals going directly from the trial court to the state supreme court. Other states have more complicated systems, with more than one appellate court for different subject areas. Oklahoma and Texas have separate courts of last resort for civil and criminal matters.

A good way to develop a quick familiarity with a state court system is to examine a chart of its structure, indicating the jurisdiction of the various courts and the routes of appeal within the court hierarchy. The U.S. Bureau of Justice Statistics (BJS) publishes these charts in *State Court Organization 2004*, available online in PDF <bjs.ojp.usdoj. gov/content/pub/pdf/sco04.pdf>. The National Center for State Courts (NCSC) website has a clickable map <www.ncsconline.org/D_Research/Ct_Struct/> linking to the chart for each individual state. The tables are reprinted in several other sources, including *BNA's Directory of State and Federal Courts, Judges, and Clerks*, CQ Press's *Federal-State Court Directory*, and *State Court Caseload Statistics*. More detailed information can usually be found on a state court system's website.

Just as Supreme Court decisions are published both in the official *U.S. Reports* and in commercial reporters, so decisions from state appellate courts are traditionally published both in official reports, issued by or under the auspices of the courts themselves, and in West's series of National Reporter System volumes.

Westlaw and Lexis are virtually comprehensive sources for state court decisions, lacking only a very few early reports from some states. They include some opinions not available in print, but coverage is generally limited to the same courts for which reports are published. Relatively few state trial court decisions are available either in print or online, although Westlaw has "Trial Court Orders" collections of selected recent decisions from most states.

a. Official Reports

Like the *U.S. Reports*, state official reports are the authoritative version of a court's decisions and must be cited in briefs before that court. They are generally less widely available than commercial reporters, which are usually published more quickly and are more useful in research. In fact, twenty-one states have ceased publishing official reports series and have designated a West reporter as the authoritative source of state case law.

Forms of publication vary from state to state. Some states publish just one series of reports, containing decisions of the state supreme court and in some instances of intermediate appellate courts as well. More than a dozen states issue two or more series of reports, with separate series for decisions of the supreme court, for intermediate appellate decisions, and in a few states for selected trial court decisions. New York, for example, has three official series: *New York Reports*, covering the Court of Appeals, the state's court of last resort; *Appellate Division Reports*, covering the Appellate Divisions of the Supreme Court; and *Miscellaneous Reports*, with decisions of various lower courts.

Even though official reports do not generally include links to a comprehensive digest system like West's, they can still provide a valuable perspective on a state's appellate court decisions. If the summaries or headnotes are written by court staff or by lawyers practicing in that state, they may be more attuned to local judicial developments than headnotes written by commercial editors. Some official reports include research leads not found in the West reporters, and others provide their own classification and digest systems. Although official reports are less widely used than West's, in some jurisdictions they maintain an important research role.

As with the early *U.S. Reports* volumes, the early reports of several of the older states were once cited as nominative reports (identified by the names of their reporters). Many of these volumes have now been incorporated into the numbered series, but you may still need to use an abbreviations dictionary or other reference work to understand some case citations. Westlaw and Lexis generally recognize the nominative reporter citations, so you may not need to decipher the citation before retrieving a case online.

b. National Reporter System

West's National Reporter System includes a series of *regional reporters* publishing the decisions of the appellate courts of the fifty states and the District of Columbia. The National Reporter System divides the country into seven regions, and publishes the decisions of the appellate courts of the states in each region together in one series of volumes. The reporters and the states each cover are:

Atlantic Reporter: Connecticut, Delaware, the District of Columbia, Maine, Maryland, New Hampshire, New Jersey, Pennsylvania, Rhode Island, Vermont

North Eastern Reporter: Illinois, Indiana, Massachusetts, New York, Ohio

North Western Reporter: Iowa, Michigan, Minnesota, Nebraska, North Dakota, South Dakota, Wisconsin

Pacific Reporter: Alaska, Arizona, California, Colorado, Hawai'i, Idaho, Kansas, Montana, Nevada, New Mexico, Oklahoma, Oregon, Utah, Washington, Wyoming

South Eastern Reporter: Georgia, North Carolina, South Carolina, Virginia, West Virginia

South Western Reporter: Arkansas, Kentucky, Missouri, Tennessee, Texas

Southern Reporter: Alabama, Florida, Louisiana, Mississippi

Four of these sets are now in their second series (*Atlantic* (A.2d), *North Eastern* (N.E.2d), *North Western* (N.W.2d), *South Eastern* (S.E.2d)); and three have started their third series (*Pacific* (P.3d), *Southern* (So. 3d), and *South Western* (S.W.3d).

These sets are supplemented by separate reporters for two of the most populous states, *California Reporter* (Cal. Rptr. 3d) and *New York Supplement* (N.Y.S.2d). (Cases from the highest courts of California and New York appear in both the regional and the state reporter, while lower court cases are not published in the *Pacific* or *North Eastern Reporter*.) These nine reporters, together with West's federal court reporters, comprise a uniform system tied together by the key number headnote and digest scheme.

In most states, cases appear in both official and National Reporter System editions. Cases are traditionally cited to both of these sources, with the official reports cited first. Extensive tables in *The Bluebook* and *ALWD Citation Manual* indicate the scope of coverage for each state appellate court in official and regional reporters.

The citation manuals require parallel citations *only* for cases cited in documents submitted to that state's courts; in other documents such as law review articles and memoranda, only the National

Reporter System citation is used. If citing to a regional reporter, remember to identify the deciding court in parentheses with the date.

If you have a citation to only one report of a case, there are several ways to find its parallel citation. The simplest is usually to retrieve the case in an online database, which will generally provide both citations. The parallel citation is sometimes, but not always, printed at the beginning of the case. West publishes a series of volumes called the *National Reporter Blue Book*, which is updated annually and lists the starting page of each case in the official reports with cross-references to National Reporter System citations.

Not all cases have parallel citations. Only the official reports exist for older state cases, before West created the National Reporter System in the 1880s. On the other hand, for those states that have discontinued their official reports and have not institute public domain citation systems, the West reporter citation may be the only citation for recent cases.

c. Other Sources

In addition to Westlaw and Lexis, other commercial online databases also provide access to state court decisions. Loislaw, for example, has more than eighty years of case law for most states, and other databases generally have coverage back to the mid–20th century. This may not be sufficient for comprehensive historical research, but it is more than adequate for most contemporary case law research.

Free Internet sites generally have access to court decisions beginning in the mid- to late–1990s, although some states maintain only the most recent three months of decisions on their official websites. A few states lead the way with much more extensive databases; the Oklahoma State Courts Network <www.oscn.net> has the entire history of the state's appellate courts, back to 1890, and the North Dakota Supreme Court <www.ndcourts. gov> has cases back to 1965.

Several commercial sites also have free access to recent state court opinions, and permit combined searches of all state jurisdictions. The most extensive is Google Scholar, which has appellate cases going back to 1950. Public Library of Law has cases back to 1997, and lexisONE has a ten-year collection of state appellate decisions.

Websites for state court decisions can be found through search engines or by starting with a directory of online legal resources. FindLaw's State Resources page <www.findlaw.com/11stategov/> has links to official and commercial sites for each state under "Primary Materials." One advantage of using a directory rather than a search is that for many states there are two or more sites with opinions, and these may have different dates of coverage or search capabilities.

Decisions from Indian tribal courts can be difficult to find, although West's *American Tribal Law*

Reporter has coverage back to 1997 of about a dozen courts. VersusLaw has the most extensive online coverage, with free searchable access to its databases available through the National Tribal Justice Resource Center <www.ntjrc.org> and the Tribal Court Clearinghouse <www.tribal-institute.org>.

2008-1059 (La.App. 1 Cir. 12/23/08)

Audrey BRADFORD

v.

Evelyn S. COODY, Robert Sanford Simon, Lawrence Randall Simon, Debra Dixon and Stan Karusee.

No. 2008 CA 1059.

Court of Appeal of Louisiana, First Circuit.

Dec. 23, 2008.

Background: Dog-bite victim brought action against dog owner and landlords of property where dog owner resided, seeking damages for her injuries. The District Court, East Baton Rouge Parish, No. 556,-932, William A. Morvant, J., entered summary judgment for landlords, and victim appealed.

Holding: The Court of Appeal, Whipple, J., held that genuine issue of material fact existed as to whether one of landlords knew of dog's vicious propensities, precluding summary judgment.

Affirmed in part, reversed in part, and remanded.

1. Judgment ⚖181(24)

Genuine issue of material fact existed as to whether one of landlords of property where dog owner resided knew of dog's vicious propensities, precluding summary judgment in dog-bite victim's action against landlord seeking damages for her injuries.

2. Animals ⚖66.4(2)

Although a landlord is strictly liable for vices or defects of his building, he is not strictly liable to a third person for injuries caused by his tenant's animal.

3. Animals ⚖66.4(1)

The strict liability of an animal owner pursuant to the statute governing damage caused by an animal cannot be imputed to a non-owner. LSA–C.C. art. 2321.

_____

John F. McKay, Baton Rouge, LA, for Plaintiff/Appellant, Audrey Bradford.

Peter T. Dudley, Baton Rouge, LA, for Defendant, Debra Dixon.

Keith L. Richardson Baton Rouge, LA, for Defendants/Appellees, Evelyn S. Coody, Robert Sanford Simon, and Lawrence Randall Simon.

Before CARTER, C.J., WHIPPLE, and DOWNING, JJ.

WHIPPLE, J.

⎰This is an appeal from a judgment in a dog-bite case granting the motion for summary judgment filed by the owners of the property leased by the dog owner and dismissing plaintiff's claims against the homeowners with prejudice. For the following reasons, we affirm in part, reverse in part, and remand for further proceedings.

FACTS AND PROCEDURAL HISTORY

On August 1, 2006, plaintiff, Audrey Bradford, an employee of United Broadband, was installing cable in a home located on North 5th Street in Baton Rouge. Upon completing the work, Bradford returned to her truck, which was parked in front of a house located at 504 Lakeland Drive, which was adjacent to the house where she had been working. At that time, a man, later identified as Stan Karusee, exited the house at 504 Lakeland Drive with two dogs, a pit bull and a

Exhibit 3–1. The first page of a case in *West's Southern Reporter*

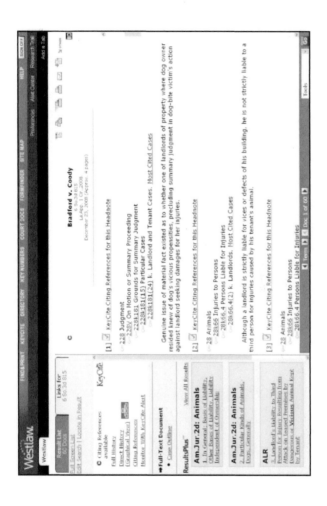

Exhibit 3–2. Headnotes from a case display on Westlaw

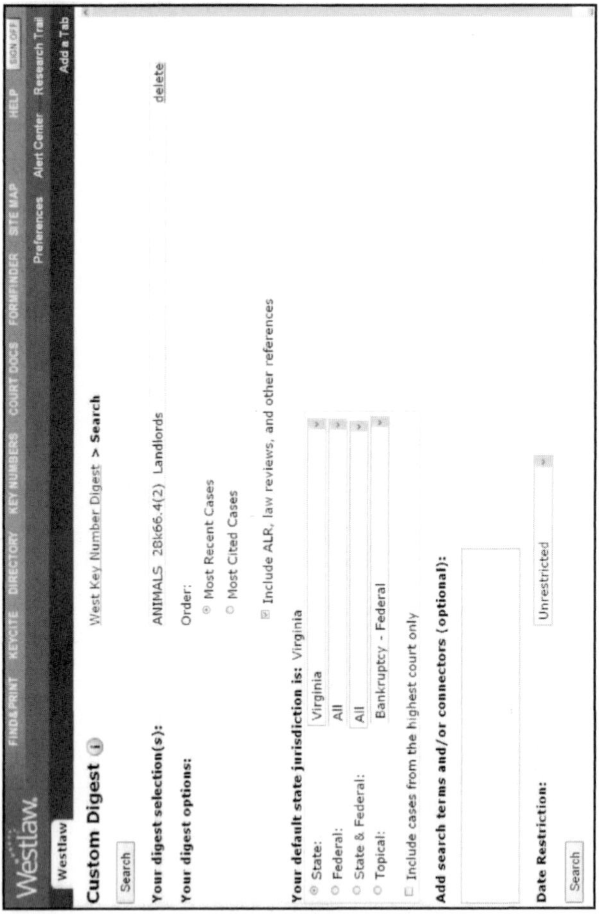

Exhibit 3–3. A Westlaw Custom Digest search screen

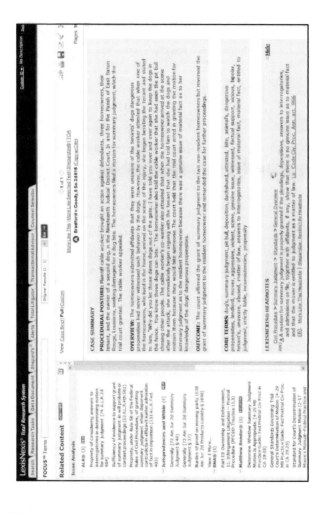

Exhibit 3–4. A Lexis case display, showing the Case Summary, Core Terms and a headnote

1 Va D–35 **ANIMALS**

References are to Digest Topics and Key Numbers

ANIMALS—Cont'd

DISTRESS,
Distraining trespassing animals, Anim ⇐ 95, 100(5)

DOGFIGHTING, Anim ⇐ 3.5(7)

DOMESTICATED animals,
Status as property, Anim ⇐ 1.5(3)

DRUGS,
Generally, Health ⇐ 324
Products liability, Prod Liab ⇐ 232

DUE process. See heading DUE PROCESS, ANIMALS.

ELEPHANTS,
Injuries by, Anim ⇐ 66.9

EQUAL protection. See heading EQUAL PROTECTION, ANIMALS.

EQUINES. See heading HORSES, generally.

EVIDENCE,
Ownership, Anim ⇐ 1.5(9), 10

FEDERAL preemption, Anim ⇐ 3.5(2)

FEES, Anim ⇐ 2.5(4)

FIGHTING, regulation of, Anim ⇐ 3.5(7)

FORFEITURES, Anim ⇐ 3.5(8)

FOWL,
Cockfighting, Anim ⇐ 3.5(7)
Status as property, Anim ⇐ 1.5(6)

GOATS,
Injuries by, Anim ⇐ 66.8

HUMANE societies, Anim ⇐ 3.5(11)

IMPORTS,
Privileges and immunities of citizens of the several states, Const Law ⇐ 2963

IMPOUNDING. See heading IMPOUNDING, ANIMALS.

IMPUTED knowledge of vicious propensities,
Personal injuries caused by animals, Anim ⇐ 66.2

INJURIES by or to animals,
Personal injuries caused by animals. See subheading PERSONAL injuries caused by animals, generally, under this heading.
Railroads injuring animals. See heading RAILROADS, ANIMALS.

INSPECTION,
Generally, Anim ⇐ 3.5(8)
Inspection officers, Inspect ⇐ 4

INSURANCE requirement, Anim ⇐ 3.5(4)

KEEPING and use,
Dangerous animals, Anim ⇐ 3.5(4)

KNOWLEDGE of vicious propensities,
Personal injuries caused by animals, Anim ⇐ 66.2

ANIMALS—Cont'd

LABORATORY animals,
Treatment of, Anim ⇐ 3.5(6)

LANDLORDS,
Liability of, Anim ⇐ 66.4(2), 66.5(8)

LEASH laws, Anim ⇐ 3.5(4)

LICENSES,
Generally, Anim ⇐ 2.5(1), 2.5(3)
Constitutional law in general, Anim ⇐ 2.5(2)
Ordinances, Anim ⇐ 2.5(2)
Statutes, Anim ⇐ 2.5(2)

LIVESTOCK,
Injuries by, Anim ⇐ 66.8
Status as property, Anim ⇐ 1.5(5)

MARKS. See heading BRANDS, ANIMALS.

MEDICINE,
Generally, Health ⇐ 324
Products liability, Prod Liab ⇐ 232

MORTGAGE of animals. See heading CHATTEL MORTGAGES, ANIMALS.

MULES,
Injuries by, Anim ⇐ 66.7

NOTICE of,
Vicious propensities, Anim ⇐ 66.2, 82

NUMBER of animals allowed, Anim ⇐ 3.5(4)

OFFENSES,
Cruelty. See heading CRUELTY TO ANIMALS, generally.
Violation of regulations, Anim ⇐ 3.5(9)

OWNERSHIP,
Duties,
Preventing injuries to other animals, Anim ⇐ 78
Preventing injuries to persons, Anim ⇐ 66.1
Trespassing animals, relating to, Anim ⇐ 90
Evidence of, Anim ⇐ 1.5(9)
Subjects of. See subheading PROPERTY in animals, generally, under this heading.

PENALTIES,
Cruelty to animals, Anim ⇐ 3.5(10)
Regulations, violations of, Anim ⇐ 3.5(10)
Violations of regulations, Anim ⇐ 3.5(10)

PERMITS, Anim ⇐ 2.5(3)

PERSONAL injuries caused by animals,
Generally, Anim ⇐ 66.1, 66.9
Bears, Anim ⇐ 66.9
Bees, Anim ⇐ 66.9
Boars, Anim ⇐ 66.8
Bulls, Anim ⇐ 66.8
Burros, Anim ⇐ 66.7
Cats, Anim ⇐ 66.6
Cattle, Anim ⇐ 66.8
Constructive knowledge of vicious propensities, Anim ⇐ 66.2
Defenses, Anim ⇐ 66.3

Exhibit 3–5. A page from a Descriptive–Word Index

ANIMALS

33. —— Liabilities for communication of disease.
34. —— Offenses.
35. —— Penalties for violations of regulations.
36. —— Criminal prosecutions.
37. —— Liabilities of officers, state or municipalities.
43. Injuring or killing animals in general.
43.1. —— In general.
44. —— Civil liability.
45. —— Criminal responsibility.
46. Conversion.
47. Running at large.
47.1. —— In general.
48. —— Rights and duties of owners.
49. —— Statutory regulations in general.
50. —— Stock laws.
    (1). In general.
    (2). Adoption of stock laws.
    (3). Duties of owners.
    (4). What constitutes running at large.
    (5). Restraint of animals used for breeding.
51. —— Impounding animals at large.
52. —— Killing or injuring animals at large.
53. —— Injuries by animals at large.
54. —— Persons liable for injuries.
55. —— Actions.
56. —— Penalties for violations of regulations.
57. —— Criminal prosecutions.
58. Estrays.
58.1. —— In general.
59. —— Rights of owners.
60. —— Statutory regulations.
61. —— Impounding or taking up.
62. —— Injuries by stray animals.
63. —— Actions and other proceedings for damages.
64. —— Penalties for violations of regulations.
65. —— Criminal prosecutions.
66. Injuries to persons.
66.1. —— Duties and liabilities in general.
66.2. —— Vicious propensities and knowledge thereof.
66.3. —— Defenses in general.
66.4. —— Persons liable for injuries.
    (1). In general.
    (2). Landlords.
66.5. —— Dogs.
    (1). Duties and liabilities in general.
    (2). Vicious propensities and knowledge thereof.
    (3). Defenses in general.
    (4). Contributory and comparative negligence.
    (5). Provocation.
    (6). Assumption of risk.

Exhibit 3–6. A portion of the outline for the Animals topic

⚫374(3). Merits.

La.App. 3 Cir. 2009. Absent the existence of any of the statutory or jurisprudential grounds for vacating or modifying an arbitration award, a reviewing court is prohibited from reviewing the merits of the arbitration judge's decision. LSA-R.S. 9:4210, 9:4211.—Young v. Peaslee Capital Group, LLC, 7 So.3d 1258, 2008-1298 (La.App. 3 Cir. 4/1/09).

La.App. 3 Cir. 2009. Absent the existence of one of the grounds specified in statute, a reviewing court is prohibited from reviewing the merits of an arbitrator's decision. LSA-R.S. 9:4210.—NCO Portfolio Management, Inc. v. Walker, 3 So.3d 628, 2008-1011 (La.App. 3 Cir. 2/4/09).

⚫374(5). Presumptions.

La.App. 3 Cir. 2009. As a general rule, there is a presumption that the arbitrator's award is correct in the absence of a record. LSA-R.S. 9:4210, 9:4211.—Young v. Peaslee Capital Group, LLC, 7 So.3d 1258, 2008-1298 (La.App. 3 Cir. 4/1/09).

Limited liability company (LLC) failed to overcome presumption that arbitrator's award to retiring members, on their claim of breach of contract and fiduciary duty, was correct in absence of record of arbitration proceedings.—Id.

⚫380. Merger and bar of causes of action and defenses.

La.App. 3 Cir. 2009. An arbitration award is res judicata.—Young v. Peaslee Capital Group, LLC, 7 So.3d 1258, 2008-1298 (La.App. 3 Cir. 4/1/09).

La.App. 3 Cir. 2009. Arbitration is favored, and an arbitration award is res judicata.—NCO Portfolio Management, Inc. v. Walker, 3 So.3d 628, 2008-1011 (La.App. 3 Cir. 2/4/09).

(I) EXCHANGES AND DEALER ASSOCIATIONS.

⚫416. —— Award.

La.App. 1 Cir. 2008. Arbitration panel acted improperly and violated fundamental fairness by dismissing with prejudice investor's breach of contract, breach of fiduciary duty and negligence claims against brokerage and its registered representative on the ground that investor's claims were time-barred without providing investor with an opportunity to present evidence or amend her pleadings, as evidence was necessary to establish the precise nature of investor's various claims and to determine the applicable prescriptive periods thereto. U.S.C.A. Const.Amend. 14; LSA-R.S. 9:4210.—Pennington v. Cuna Brokerage Securities, Inc., 5 So.3d 172, 2008-0589 (La.App. 1 Cir. 10/1/08), writ denied 998 So.2d 723, 2008-2600 (La. 1/9/09).

⚫417. —— Review, conclusiveness, and enforcement of award.

La.App. 1 Cir. 2008. Motion by brokerage and its registered representative to supplement the record, in investor's appeal of trial court decision denying investor's motion to vacate arbitration award, with exhibits which allegedly established that a bear market and investor's own conduct were responsible for investor's losses, would be denied, where the exhibits were not introduced in or considered by the trial court.—Pennington v. Cuna Brokerage Securities, Inc., 5 So.3d 172, 2008-0589 (La.App. 1 Cir. 10/1/08), writ denied 998 So.2d 723, 2008-2600 (La. 1/9/09).

ANIMALS

⚫66.4(1). In general.

La.App. 1 Cir. 2008. The strict liability of an animal owner pursuant to the statute governing damage caused by an animal cannot be imputed to a non-owner. LSA-C.C. art. 2321.—Bradford v. Coody, 6 So.3d 815, 2008-1059 (La.App. 1 Cir. 12/23/08).

⚫66.4(2). Landlords.

La.App. 1 Cir. 2008. Although a landlord is strictly liable for vices or defects of his building, he is not strictly liable to a third person for injuries caused by his tenant's animal.—Bradford v. Coody, 6 So.3d 815, 2008-1059 (La.App. 1 Cir. 12/23/08).

⚫66.7. —— Horses and other equines.

La.App. 4 Cir. 2009. Racehorse was a "farm animal" for purposes of statute barring liability for injury resulting from any of the inherent risks of farm animal activities. LSA-R.S. 9:2795.1.—Westmoreland v. Strander, 7 So.3d 1224, 2008-0948 (La.App. 4 Cir. 3/11/09).

Horse rider, who was employed to exercise a racehorse, and who was injured when the horse flipped over and threw him at the end of a ride, was a "participant" in a "farm animal activity" for purposes of statute barring liability for injury to a participant resulting from any of the inherent risks of farm animal activities, and therefore, the rider's negligence claim was precluded as against owner of forklift that allegedly startled the horse while moving feed in the vicinity; although a horse race on a flat course was not set forth as an example of a type of farm animal activity, other horse competitions, such as steeplechase, were included in the examples, and statute also indicated that training activities and daily care related to board a horse were encompassed by the definitions. LSA-R.S. 9:2795.1.—Id.

ANTITRUST AND TRADE REGULATION

III. STATUTORY UNFAIR TRADE PRACTICES AND CONSUMER PROTECTION.

(C) PARTICULAR SUBJECTS AND REGULATIONS.

⚫208. —— Other particular subjects.

La.App. 1 Cir. 2009. The required warranties in the New Home Warranty Act (NHWA) are mandatory and cannot be waived by the owner or reduced by the builder. LSA-R.S. 9:3144(C)(1998).—Hutcherson v. Harvey Smith Const., Inc., 7 So.3d 775, 2008-1046 (La.App. 1 Cir. 2/13/09), rehearing denied in part.

⚫213. —— Practices prohibited or required in general.

M.D.La. 2009. Filing of proof of claim to collect a debt, recovery on which was allegedly time-barred, did not violate provision of the Fair Debt Collection Practices Act (FDCPA) prohibiting harassing, oppressive or abusive debt collection practices, the making of false representation as to legal status of debt, the use of false or deceptive means to collect debt, or attempts to collect any debt not permitted by law; because the Bankruptcy Code, in providing that running of prescriptive period was grounds for disallowance of claim, specifically contemplated filing of time-barred claims, debtor's sole remedy for creditor's filing of allegedly time-

† This Case was not selected for publication in the National Reporter System

Exhibit 3–7. Headnotes from the case in Exhibit 3–1 in a West digest

sioning domestic broils.—Shutt v. Shutt, 17 A. 1024, 71 Md. 193, 17 Am.St.Rep. 519.

VICIOUS DISPOSITION

Del.Super. 1899. A horse is of "vicious disposition" when it is possessed of those habits and propensities which are dangerous in their character to persons coming in contact with it.—Brown v. Green, 42 A. 991, 17 Del. 535, 1 Penne. 535.

VICIOUS DOG

Mont. 1998. Hunting dog, which had never bitten or attempted to bite a human being, was not a "vicious dog," within meaning of county ordinance prohibiting keeping, harboring, or maintaining a vicious dog in county unless dog is securely and adequately confined upon its owner's property, even though dog was bred to hunt mountain lions. —Vennes v. Miller, 954 P.2d 736, 287 Mont. 263, 1998 MT 23.—Anim 3.5(4).

Ohio App. 10 Dist. 1991. Statute defining "vicious dog," for purposes of provision prohibiting the failure to restrain a vicious dog, allows defendant to rebut state's prima facie showing that dog is vicious because it is a "pit bull dog"; however, statute conclusively deems the dog vicious if the dog has without provocation killed or injured a person, killed another dog, or caused injury to another person, and does not allow rebuttal of prima facie showing that dog is "vicious" by merely showing that dog has not killed or injured a person or killed a dog. R.C. § 955.11(A)(4)(a), (A)(4)(a)(i-iii).—State v. Ferguson, 603 N.E.2d 345, 76 Ohio App.3d 747.—Anim 57.

VICIOUS NATURE

N.Y.Sup. 2000. A "vicious nature," for purposes of presumption of negligence attaching to person who keeps dog with knowledge of its vicious nature and fails to prevent dog from injuring others, includes biting, jumping on people, and running at large in a roadway.—Ayala v. Hagemann, 714 N.Y.S.2d 633, 186 Misc.2d 122.—Anim 66.5(2), 74(3).

VICIOUS NATURE OR PROPENSITY

N.Y.City Civ.Ct. 2007. Dog owners will be held in strict liability for injuries sustained as a result of harm caused by a dog with a "vicious nature or propensity"; a vicious nature or propensity is defined as the tendency of a dog to do an act which might endanger another. McKinney's Agriculture and Markets Law § 121.—University Towers Associates v. Gibson, 846 N.Y.S.2d 872, 18 Misc.3d 349. —Anim 66.5(2).

VICIOUSNESS

N.Y.City Ct. 1995. Strict liability is imposed upon dog owners, with no proof of negligence necessary, for injuries inflicted by their vicious dogs, when owners have knowledge of dog's viciousness with "viciousness" defined as prior bites and/or mischievous propensity.—Nardi v. Gonzalez, 630 N.Y.S.2d 215, 165 Misc.2d 336.—Anim 66.5(2).

VICIOUS OR DANGEROUS PROPENSITY

La. 1966. Whether the kicking by a colt was playful mischievousness or viciousness, it endangered safety of others and was therefore a "vicious or dangerous propensity" within rule making owner responsible for actions of his animal which is known to have a vicious or dangerous propensity. LSA–C.C. art. 2321.—Tamburello v. Jaeger, 184 So.2d 544, 249 La. 25.—Anim 66.7.

VICIOUS PROPENSITIES

Hawai'i 1977. The terms "vicious propensities" and "dangerous propensities" have been defined as any propensity on part of dog, which is likely to cause injury under circumstances in which person controlling the dog placed it, and a vicious propensity does not mean only the type of malignancy exhibited by a biting dog, that is, a propensity to attack human beings; it includes as well a natural fierceness or disposition to mischief as might occasionally lead him to attack human beings without provocation.—Farrior v. Payton, 562 P.2d 779, 57 Haw. 620.—Anim 66.5(2).

Mo.App. E.D. 1993. In cases involving injuries caused by dogs, dog's "vicious propensities," are not established by evidence of dog's barking, running loose, jumping, and lunging, since these are activities in which all dogs engage.—Brouk v. Brueggeate, 849 S.W.2d 699.—Anim 66.5(2).

Mo.App. 1974. Terms "vicious propensities" and "dangerous propensities" in a dog bite case generally refer to tendency of dog to injure persons, whether dog acted out of anger, viciousness, or playfulness and such terms are not confined to a disposition on part of dog to attack every person he might meet but includes as well a natural fierceness or disposition to mischief as might occasionally lead dog to attack human beings without provocation.—Frazier v. Stone, 515 S.W.2d 766.—Anim 66.5(2).

Mo.App. 1962. "Vicious" and "dangerous," within dog bite case instruction which referred both to "vicious propensities" and "dangerous propensities", connoted quality of dog which could or would cause harm to person, and use of both words was not confusing.—Bush v. Anderson, 360 S.W.2d 251. —Anim 74(7).

N.Y. 2004. "Vicious propensities" of a domestic animal, which will result in the animal owner's liability if the animal causes harm as a result of those propensities, include the propensity to do any act that might endanger the safety of the persons and property of others in a given situation.—Collier v. Zambito, 775 N.Y.S.2d 205, 1 N.Y.3d 444, 807 N.E.2d 254.—Anim 66.2.

N.Y.A.D. 2 Dept. 2008. "Vicious propensities" of an animal, which will result in animal owner's liability if animal causes harm as result of those propensities, include the propensity to do any act that might endanger safety of the persons and property of others in a given situation.—Debellas v. Verrill, 861 N.Y.S.2d 787, 53 A.D.3d 593.—Anim 66.2.

Exhibit 3–8. A page from *Words and Phrases*

87 ALR4th TENANT'S VICIOUS ANIMAL

87 ALR4th 1004

Landlord's liability to third person for injury resulting from attack on leased premises by dangerous or vicious animal kept by tenant

Exhibit 3–9. The first page of the table of contents of an *ALR* annotation

§ 1[a] TENANT'S VICIOUS ANIMAL 87 ALR4th

87 ALR4th 1004

TABLE OF JURISDICTIONS REPRESENTED

Consult POCKET PART in this volume for later cases

US: §§ 2[b], 4[a], 11, 31[b]
Alaska: §§ 2[b], 4[a], 11
Ariz: § 15
Cal: §§ 2[b], 4[a], 9[a, c], 11, 15
Colo: §§ 2[b], 10, 20
Conn: §§ 4[a], 6[a], 11, 12, 19[b], 23
Del: §§ 2[b], 5
DC: §§ 2[b], 4[a], 11
Fla: §§ 2[b], 3[a], 4[a], 7[a], 9[a, b], 11, 13, 17, 19[b], 20, 27[b], 28
Ga: §§ 2[b], 3[a], 6[a], 12, 19[b]
Ill: §§ 19[b], 25[a, b]
Ind: §§ 2[b], 3[a], 4[b], 5, 6[b], 7[b], 17, 18, 19[d], 21
Ky: §§ 6[a], 12
La: §§ 15, 19[b], 27[a], 29
Mass: §§ 7[b], 19[c]
Mich: §§ 8, 14, 16, 19[b], 21
Minn: §§ 24, 26
Mont: §§ 2[b], 4[b]
Neb: §§ 4[b], 18, 27[a]
NJ: §§ 2[b], 6[a], 12
NM: §§ 6[a], 12, 31[a]
NY: §§ 2[b], 3[a], 4[a], 6[a], 10-12, 15, 19[b, c], 20
Ohio: §§ 2[b], 3[a], 4[a], 6[a], 9[a], 11, 12, 17, 19[a], 22, 24, 30
Pa: §§ 2[b], 4[a], 9[a], 11
RI: §§ 4[a], 11, 31[b]
Tex: §§ 8, 14
Wash: §§ 3[a], 19[b]
Wis: §§ 3[b], 15, 19[b, c]

I. Preliminary Matters

§ 1. Introduction

[a] Scope

This annotation[1] collects and analyzes the reported cases in which the courts have discussed or determined whether or under what circumstances a landlord may be liable to a third person[2] for an injury

1. The present annotation supersedes the annotation at 81 ALR3d 638.

1010

Exhibit 3–10. Parts of the index and jurisdictional table in an *ALR* annotation

§ 22. Where on-premises landlord maintains duplex in which dog's owners live rent free

In the following case, the court held that the defendant landlords could be subject to strict liability under statute as the keepers of a dog that attacked the plaintiff and was owned by the landlords' tenants, where the landlords and their tenants lived in separate halves of a duplex which the landlords maintained, and the landlords were allegedly "economically keeping" the dog by allowing the tenants to live in the duplex without paying rent.

In an action to recover from landlords for injuries sustained by an individual on the landlords' property as a result of an attack by a dog belonging to tenants who lived on the property rent free, the court in Dunn v Platt et al. (1988, **Ohio** App) 1988 Ohio App LEXIS 4929, reversed an order granting summary judgment in favor of the landlords as to the claim that they were strictly liable under statute as the owners or keepers of the dog that bit the plaintiff, concluding that there were genuine issues of material fact as to whether the landlords were keepers of the dog, where the plaintiff argued that the landlords gave the dog's owners permission to live in the residence rent free, and were "economically keeping" the dog's owners as well as the dog, while the landlords argued that they never fed or cleaned up after the dog, and were not responsible for its physical care, although they maintained all of the property, and that the gratuitous living arrangements were actually offered and arranged by the dog owner's mother. At the time of the attack, the dog's owners, one

of whom was the landlord's brother, were living in the basement of one-half of a double residence. The mother of one of the dog's owners lived above them, and the landlords lived in the other half of the double. In support of his contention that the landlords were the dog's keeper, the plaintiff also claimed that one landlord chased the dog when it ran from the property, visited its victim in the hospital after the attack, and complained to the health department's veterinarian about their handling of the dog. The court also rejected the contention that the landlords could not be found liable because the injury did not occur in their residence.

§ 23. Where landlord shares common yard with tenant

The court in the following case held that defendant on-premises landlords were liable to a minor who was bitten by their tenants' dog, based on the conclusion that they were subject to liability under a dogbite statute as the dog's keepers, where the landlords and their tenants shared the yard in which the dog was kept.

The court in Bailey v De Santi (1980) 36 **Conn** Supp 156, 414 A2d 1187, held that on-premises landlords were liable for injuries sustained by a minor who was bitten by their tenants' dog, concluding that they were "keepers" of their son-in-law tenant's dog within the meaning of a dogbite statute making a dog's owner or keeper liable for damage done by the dog, and defining "keeper" as a "person, other than the owner, harboring or having it in his possession,"

Exhibit 3–11. Part of the discussion in an *ALR* annotation

ALR INDEX

DOGS—Cont'd

Fear or fright, dog owner's liability for injuries sustained by person frightened by dog, **30 ALR4th 986**

Future disease or condition, or anxiety relating thereto, as element of recovery, **50 ALR4th 13, § 31(a)**

Gambling, validity and construction of statute exempting gambling operations carried on by religious, charitable, or other nonprofit organizations from general prohibitions against gambling, **42 ALR3d 663, § 4**

Highways and streets

liability for damages due to dog interfering with travel in highway, **11 ALR 270**

liability of motorist for collision as affected by attempts to avoid dog or other small animal in road, **41 ALR3d 1124**

owner's liability for damages from motor vehicle accident involving attempt to avoid collision with dog on highway, **41 ALR3d 888**

Homeowners' insurance

automobiles, construction and effect of provision excluding liability for automobile related injuries or damage from coverage of homeowner's or personal liability policy, **6 ALR4th 555, § 5**

personal injuries inflicted by animal as within homeowner's or personal liability policy, **96 ALR3d 891**

Homicide, dog as deadly or dangerous weapon for purposes of statutes aggravating offenses such as assault and robbery, **124 ALR5th 657**

Identification, admissibility and sufficiency of bite mark evidence as basis for identification of accused, **1 ALR6th 657, § 6, 11**

Injuries by dogs

liability for injuries inflicted by rabid dog, **13 ALR 492**

validity, construction, and effect of statute eliminating scienter as condition of liability for injury by dog or other animal, **142 ALR 436**

DOGS—Cont'd

Intentional, willful, and wanton acts

contributory negligence, assumption of risk, or intentional provocation as defense to action for injury by dog, **11 ALR5th 127**

exhibition, liability for injury inflicted by horse, dog, or other domestic animal exhibited at show, **68 ALR5th 599, § 14**

injury by dog or other animal as willful and malicious injury so as to preclude it or judgment procured on it from operations of bankruptcy discharge, **26 ALR2d 1368**

Judicial review of administrative ruling affecting conduct or outcome of publicly regulated motor vehicle race, **36 ALR4th 1169**

Kennels, eminent domain, unity or contiguity of separate properties sufficient to allow damages for diminished value of parcel remaining after taking of other parcel, **59 ALR4th 308, § 54**

Killing of animal. Destruction or killing of animal, in this topic

Landlord and tenant

lease restrictions, effect, as between landlord and tenant, of lease clause restricting keeping of pets, **114 ALR5th 443**

off leased premises, landlord's liability to third person for injury resulting from attack by dangerous or vicious animal kept by tenant, **89 ALR4th 374**

on leased premises, landlord's liability to third person for injury resulting from attack by dangerous or vicious animal kept by tenant, **87 ALR4th 1004**

third persons, landlord's liability to third person for injury resulting from attack by dangerous or vicious animal kept by tenant, **87 ALR4th 1004; 89 ALR4th 374**

Larceny or theft, dogs as subject of larceny, **92 ALR 212**

Libel and slander, criticism and disparagement of veterinarian's or animal trainer's competence, or conduct, as

Exhibit 3–12. A page from the *ALR Index*

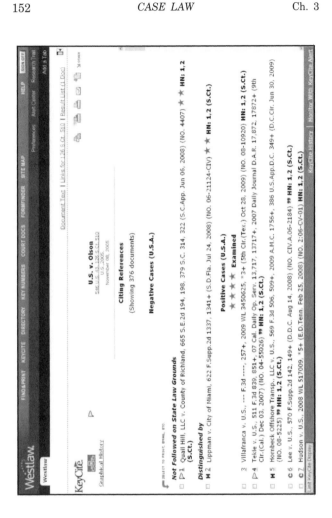

Exhibit 3–13. KeyCite results for a U.S. Supreme Court decision

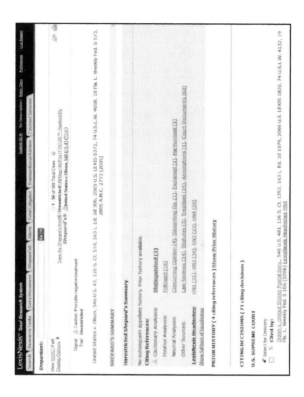

Exhibit 3–14. Shepard's results for a U.S. Supreme Court decision

Exhibit 3–15. A page from *Shepard's United States Citations*

Syllabus

UNITED STATES *v.* OLSON ET AL.

CERTIORARI TO THE UNITED STATES COURT OF APPEALS FOR THE NINTH CIRCUIT

No. 04–759. Argued October 12, 2005—Decided November 8, 2005

Claiming that federal mine inspectors' negligence helped cause a mine accident, two injured workers (and a spouse) sued the United States under the Federal Tort Claims Act (Act), which authorizes private tort actions against the Government "under circumstances where the United States, if a private person, would be liable to the claimant in accordance with the law of the place where the act or omission occurred," 28 U. S. C. § 1346(b)(1). The District Court dismissed in part on the ground that the allegations did not show that Arizona law would impose liability upon a private person in similar circumstances. The Ninth Circuit reversed, reasoning from two premises: (1) Where unique governmental functions are at issue, the Act waives sovereign immunity if a state or municipal entity would be held liable under the law where the activity occurred, and (2) federal mine inspections are such unique governmental functions since there is no private-sector analogue for mine inspections. Because Arizona law would make a state or municipal entity liable in the circumstances alleged, the Circuit concluded that the United States' sovereign immunity was waived.

Held: Under § 1346(b)(1), the United States waives sovereign immunity only where local law would make a "private person" liable in tort, not where local law would make "a state or municipal entity" liable. Pp. 45–48.

(a) The Ninth Circuit's first premise is too broad, reading into the Act something that is not there. Section 1346(b)(1) says that it waives sovereign immunity "under circumstances where the United States, if a *private person*," not "the United States, if a state or municipal entity," would be liable. (Emphasis added.) This Court has consistently adhered to this "private person" standard, even when uniquely governmental functions are at issue. *Indian Towing Co.* v. *United States,* 350 U. S. 61, 64; *Rayonier Inc.* v. *United States,* 352 U. S. 315, 318. Even though both these cases involved Government efforts to *escape* liability by pointing to the *absence* of municipal entity liability, there is no reason for treating differently a plaintiff's effort to *base* liability solely upon the fact that a State would impose liability upon a state governmental entity. Nothing in the Act's context, history, or objectives or in this Court's opinions suggests otherwise. Pp. 45–46.

Exhibit 3–16. The first page of a case in the *United States Reports*

44   UNITED STATES *v.* OLSON

Opinion of the Court

(b) The Ninth Circuit's second premise reads the Act too narrowly. Section 2674 makes the United States liable "in the same manner and to the same extent as a private individual under *like circumstances.*" (Emphasis added.) The words "like circumstances" do not restrict a court's inquiry to the *same circumstances*, but require it to look further afield. See, *e. g., Indian Towing, supra,* at 64. The Government in effect concedes, and other Courts of Appeals' decisions applying *Indian Towing's* logic suggest, that private person analogies exist for the federal mine inspectors' conduct at issue. The Ninth Circuit should have looked for such an analogy. Pp. 46–47.

(c) The lower courts should decide in the first instance precisely which Arizona tort law doctrine applies here. P. 48.

362 F. 3d 1236, vacated and remanded.

BREYER, J., delivered the opinion for a unanimous Court.

Deanne E. Maynard argued the cause for the United States. With her on the briefs were *Solicitor General Clement, Assistant Attorney General Keisler, Deputy Solicitor General Kneedler, Mark B. Stern,* and *Dana J. Martin.*

Thomas G. Cotter argued the cause and filed a brief for respondents.

JUSTICE BREYER delivered the opinion of the Court.

The Federal Tort Claims Act (FTCA or Act) authorizes private tort actions against the United States "under circumstances where the United States, if a private person, would be liable to the claimant in accordance with the law of the place where the act or omission occurred." 28 U. S. C. § 1346(b)(1). We here interpret these words to mean what they say, namely, that the United States waives sovereign immunity "under circumstances" where local law would make a *"private person"* liable in tort. (Emphasis added.) And we reverse a line of Ninth Circuit precedent permitting courts in certain circumstances to base a waiver simply upon a finding that local law would make a "state or municipal entit[y]" liable. See, *e. g., Hines* v. *United States,* 60 F. 3d 1442, 1448 (1995); *Cimo* v. *INS,* 16 F. 3d 1039, 1041 (1994); *Cameron* v. *Janssen Bros. Nurseries, Ltd.,* 7 F. 3d 821, 825

Exhibit 3–17. A case in the *United States Reports*, continued

546 U.S. 43, 163 L.Ed.2d 306

UNITED STATES, Petitioner,

v.

Joseph OLSON, et al.

No. 04–759.

Argued Oct. 12, 2005.

Decided Nov. 8, 2005.

Background: Injured miners sued the Mine Safety and Health Administration (MSHA) pursuant to the Federal Tort Claims Act (FTCA), alleging negligence by federal mine inspectors. The United States District Court for the District of Arizona, William D. Browning, J., granted MSHA's motion to dismiss, and miners appealed. The United States Court of Appeals for the Ninth Circuit, 362 F.3d 1236, reversed and remanded. Certiorari was granted.

Holding: The Supreme Court, Justice Breyer, held that FTCA waives federal government's sovereign immunity only where local law would make private person liable in tort, not where local law would make state or municipal entity liable, even where uniquely governmental functions are at issue; abrogating *Hines v. United States,* 60 F.3d 1442; *Cimo v. INS,* 16 F.3d 1039; *Cameron v. Janssen Bros. Nurseries, Ltd.,* 7 F.3d 821; *Aguilar v. United States,* 920 F.2d 1475; *Doggett v. United States,* 875 F.2d 684.

Vacated and remanded.

1. United States ⟷78(3, 14)

Federal Tort Claims Act (FTCA) waives federal government's sovereign immunity only where local law would make private person liable in tort, not where local law would make state or municipal entity liable, even where uniquely governmental functions are at issue; abrogating

Hines v. United States, 60 F.3d 1442; *Cimo v. INS,* 16 F.3d 1039; *Cameron v. Janssen Bros. Nurseries, Ltd.,* 7 F.3d 821; *Aguilar v. United States,* 920 F.2d 1475; *Doggett v. United States,* 875 F.2d 684. 28 U.S.C.A. § 1346(b)(1).

2. United States ⟷78(3)

Provision of Federal Tort Claims Act imposing liability in same manner and to same extent as private individual under "like circumstances" does not restrict court's inquiry to same circumstances; rather, it is required to look further afield. 28 U.S.C.A. § 2674.

⌐₄₃*Syllabus* *

Claiming that federal mine inspectors' negligence helped cause a mine accident, two injured workers (and a spouse) sued the United States under the Federal Tort Claims Act (Act), which authorizes private tort actions against the Government "under circumstances where the United States, if a private person, would be liable to the claimant in accordance with the law of the place where the act or omission occurred," 28 U.S.C. § 1346(b)(1). The District Court dismissed in part on the ground that the allegations did not show that Arizona law would impose liability upon a private person in similar circumstances. The Ninth Circuit reversed, reasoning from two premises: (1) Where unique governmental functions are at issue, the Act waives sovereign immunity if a state or municipal entity would be held liable under the law where the activity occurred, and (2) federal mine inspections are such unique governmental functions since there is no private-sector analogue for mine inspections. Because Arizona law would make a state or municipal entity

---

* The syllabus constitutes no part of the opinion of the Court but has been prepared by the Reporter of Decisions for the convenience of

the reader. See *United States v. Detroit Timber & Lumber Co.,* 200 U.S. 321, 337, 26 S.Ct. 282, 50 L.Ed. 499.

Exhibit 3–18. The first page of a case in the *Supreme Court Reporter*

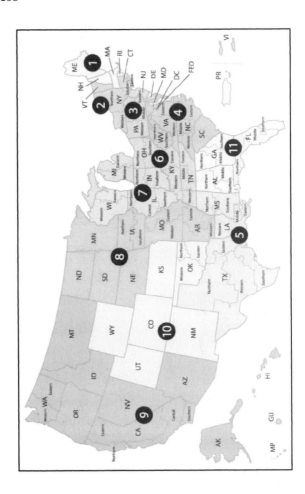

Exhibit 3–19. Jurisdiction of the federal appellate and district courts

CHAPTER 4

STATUTES AND CONSTITUTIONS

---

§ 4–1.　Introduction

The preceding chapter focused on case law because of the importance of appellate decisions in the common law system and in American legal education. The legislature, however, is the branch of government charged with making laws, and legislative enactments play just as vital a role as decisions in today's legal system. Most appellate court decisions, in fact, involve the application or interpretation of statutes rather than the consideration of common law principles.

This chapter considers both legislation and constitutions, which establish the form and limitations of government power. Statutes and constitutions are often published together, and research methods are similar. In considering statutes or constitutional provisions, it is important to find not only the relevant text but also cases that interpret this text and define its terms. The most important research sources for both statutes and constitutions are *annotated codes*, which provide the text of laws in force accompanied by notes of court decisions.

Determining early in the research process whether a problem involves statutory or constitutional provisions can save considerable time, as this significantly affects the direction of your research. Experienced researchers develop a sense of which issues are likely to be governed by statute or constitution, and whether these issues are matters of federal or state law. Substantive criminal law, for example, is generally defined by the enactments of a state legislature, while defendants' procedural rights are determined by both federal and state constitutional law. As legislatures continue to enact statutes to govern traditional common law areas such as contract and tort, more and more questions involve some statutory research. Secondary sources and cases generally provide references to the relevant provisions, so it should soon become apparent from your introductory research whether statutory research is warranted.

§ 4–2. Publication of Statutes

American statutes are published in three basic versions, in either print or electronic form. The first version of a newly enacted statute is the *slip law*. Each law is issued by itself on a single sheet or as a pamphlet with separate pagination. Neither federal nor state slip laws are widely distributed in print, but legislative websites and online databases such as Westlaw and Lexis generally provide convenient access to the texts of new laws. (Instead of slip laws, some sites have only *enrolled bills*, or the final versions of bills as they were passed by the legislature and presented to the executive for approval.)

Next are the *session laws*. The statutes are arranged by date of passage and published in separate volumes for each legislative term. Official session laws are generally published only in bound volumes after a session has ended, but commercial *advance legislative services* or *advance session law services* provide the texts of new laws in pamphlet form on a more timely basis. For most jurisdictions the *Bluebook* and the *ALWD Citation Manual* require citation to session law volume and page numbers, but this information is not always available online. Exhibit 4–1 on page 199 shows the beginning of an Act of Congress in the federal session law publication *United States Statutes at Large*.

In most jurisdictions, the session laws constitute the *positive law* form of legislation, and are the authoritative, binding text of the laws. Codes and other forms are only *prima facie* evidence of statutory language. This means that the session law controls, unless the legislature has enacted the code as positive law.

Although the chronologically arranged session laws contain the official text of legislative enactments, they have limited use as research tools. Researchers usually need the laws currently in force, rather than the laws passed during a specific legislative term. They also need convenient access to amendments and related legislation. For this they turn to the third and most useful form of statutory publication, the *statutory compilation* or *code*.

Codes collect current statutes of general and permanent application and arrange them by subject. The statutes are grouped into broad subject topics, usually called *titles*, and within each title they are divided into chapters and then numbered sections. The parts of a single legislative act may be printed together or may be scattered by subject through several different titles. Exhibit 4–2 on page 200 shows a section from the *United States Code*, incorporating the amendment in section 102 of the session law shown in Exhibit 4–1.

Some jurisdictions have official code publications containing the text of the statutes in force. If an official edition is published, it is usually the authoritative text and should be cited in briefs and pleadings. Almost every jurisdiction provides free online access to the text of its code, usually through the legislature's website. All of the sites can be searched by keyword, although only a few permit natural language or proximity searching. Some sites include warnings that the online version is unofficial and that only the printed volumes have the official text.

Most official codes, whether in print or online, are *unannotated*; that is, they do not include references to judicial decisions which have applied or construed the statutes. Finding relevant cases is such an important part of statutory research that the most useful sources are annotated codes which, though unofficial, include notes of these decisions. Some statutory sections have been construed in thousands of court cases, and are accompanied by dozens or hundreds of pages of notes arranged by subject. Other sections may have no annotations at all, if they are uncontroversial and have not led to litigation or are too new to have been considered in any published court decisions. Exhibits 4–3 and 4–4 on pages 201–02 show a section from the *United States Code Annotated*, illustrating its display of code text and historical notes (Exhibit 4–3) followed by library references and notes of decisions (Exhibit 4–4).

Westlaw and Lexis have annotated codes for federal law and for all fifty states. These databases are among the most thorough and up-to-date resources for statutory research, incorporating new legislation within days of enactment and providing a variety of research links from a code section to related cases and secondary sources. Exhibits 4–5 and 4–6 on pages 203–04 show a *United States Code* section as it appears on Westlaw and Lexis. Because most annotated codes are commercial publications, they are generally not available online at free Internet sites.

Remember, however, that annotated codes are usually not authoritative sources of the text of statutes. Most are unofficial, commercial publications, and the official code is controlling if there is any discrepancy between it and an annotated code. Moreover, the language in the session laws generally controls over the official code in case of discrepancies between those two sources.

Codes, whether annotated or unannotated, must be updated regularly to include the numerous statutory changes that occur every time a legislature meets. Some officially published codes are updated only by the issuance of a new edition every few years, and some government websites are not updated very regularly. Most annotated code publications, on the other hand, are supplemented by annual pocket parts and quarterly pamphlets, and their online counterparts may be even more up to date.

§ 4–3. Statutory Research

Even experienced researchers who do most of their work online find that printed resources are particularly well suited for statutory research. Code volumes make it easy to find related provisions and to place a section in its context. Statutory provisions often have multiple subsections and sub-subsections, and you need to understand how these different subsections relate to each other. You also need to see an entire code chapter or title in order to understand the context and purpose of an individual section. Scanning a few pages in a code volume can be easier than going from document to document in an online database. In addition, the vague and technical wording of statutes means that online keyword searches can often be less productive than using the indexes that accompany annotated codes. Despite these difficulties, online resources are now the most common starting points for statutory research.

a. Online Code Databases

This discussion of research procedures focuses primarily on Westlaw and Lexis, which have the highly useful annotated versions of codes and the same search procedures for statutes from all jurisdictions. Search approaches and features in other online resources for statutes may vary from state to state.

Fields and Segments. The comprehensive nature of statutory databases on Westlaw and Lexis can make them difficult to search successfully. A full-text search finds words appearing either in the statutes themselves or in the annotations of cases, and may retrieve far too many irrelevant documents. You can focus searches on the statutory language, rather than the notes of decisions, by using fields and segments. The *sd* (substantive document) field on Westlaw and the *unanno* segment on Lexis contain the headings, the text, and any official notes, but not the annotations. This is often the most effective way to search for language that is likely to appear in the statute itself. You can also search just the words used to identify a title and the section. Westlaw uses the field *prelim* or *pr* for title, subtitle and chapter designations, and *caption* or *ca* for the section number and description. Lexis has an option for searching only the table of contents and then linking to full text. It also uses the segment *heading* for titles, subtitles and chapters, and *section* for individual sections.

Westlaw offers both annotated and unannotated versions of federal and state codes, so another way to search just the statutory text is to use the unannotated database. This approach, however, does not allow ready access to the notes of decisions that can be essential in interpreting the language of the statutes you find.

Establishing Context. Be aware that a code search retrieves only those specific *sections* that match the particular query. Westlaw and Lexis treat each code section as a separate document.

Because it is essential in statutory research to understand the context of a specific provision, you usually need to examine nearby sections after finding one that is on point. There are several ways to do this.

Both Westlaw and Lexis allow you to browse the sections immediately preceding and following the document on your screen. Westlaw has *Previous Section* and *Next Section* links, and Lexis has a feature called *Book Browse*. A more comprehensive way to grasp the context of a section is to see the table of contents for its chapter. In Westlaw, this is done by clicking on *Table of Contents* in the left window. In Lexis, you click on the hyperlinked name of the chapter in the *TOC* heading at the top of the screen. By scanning the list of sections, you may find others (perhaps labeled "Definitions" or "Exclusions") that have a very direct impact on whether a particular statute is relevant to your research.

In Westlaw, clicking on the hyperlinked chapter number just above a code section opens a window that shows the text of every section in the chapter. This version has no statutory notes or annotations, but it is one of the quickest ways to scan an entire chapter to find relevant provisions.

Other Free and Subscription Databases. Other statutory databases generally offer fewer options and features than do Westlaw or Lexis. Most free websites do not include any case annotations or other research references, and many have fairly

simple options for keyword searching. They may
nonetheless offer convenient and current access to
the statutory text. No matter what site you use, it is
vital to make sure that your source is up to date
and to browse nearby sections to make sure that
important definitions or cross-references are not
missed.

b. KeyCite and Shepard's

Finding statutes is just the first step of statutory
research. Before relying on a statute as authority,
you must verify that it is still in force and ascertain
how it has been affected by subsequent legislation
and by judicial decisions. Annotated codes are indis-
pensable because they provide regularly updated
information on a statute's validity and treatment.

Even the annotated codes, however, lack the most
recent legislative changes and references to *all* citing decisions. It can take weeks or months for
amendments to be incorporated into the code database, and even longer for case annotations to be
written and assigned to specific code sections. Much
more current research leads can be found by using
KeyCite or Shepard's Citations.

KeyCite's coverage of statutes expands on the
cases summarized in code annotations by listing
other citing cases and articles as well as recent and
pending legislation. The cases in the annotated code
are listed first, followed by additional "Citing
Cases" listed by jurisdiction in reverse chronological
order. This is where the most recent court decisions

can be found. (Another way to find very recent cases is to use the Westlaw display's *Last 60 Days* link, which appears only if decisions within the past two months have cited the statute.) Exhibit 4–7 on page 205 shows a KeyCite display for a federal statute, with cases in the *United States Code Annotated* notes under numbered subject headings followed by additional cases that are not mentioned in the code annotations.

Statutes on Westlaw include signals based on KeyCite information. A red flag appears at the top of the display if a code section has been found invalid or unconstitutional, or if it has been amended by recent legislation not yet incorporated into the text. A yellow flag shows that a section's validity has been called into doubt, or that pending legislation would amend a section if enacted. The section in Exhibit 4–5 has a yellow flag, indicating that legislation to amend the section has been proposed. You can limit a KeyCite display in various ways, including document type, jurisdiction, and specific *Locate* terms.

The Lexis display of code sections does not include flags indicating unconstitutionality or recent amendments, but clicking on the "Shepardize" link provides this information. Shepard's indicates significant judicial and legislative actions affecting a cited statute. Clicking in the Shepard's display on the "All Neg" link will limit a listing to documents such as cases that have found a statute unconstitutional. Clicking on "FOCUS–Restrict By" allows you to pick and choose particular treatments, specific jurisdictions, or certain types of citing documents. Exhibit 4–8 on page 206 shows the beginning of a Shepard's result for a federal statute.

One useful feature available in Shepard's is the option to restrict a listing to cases and other documents that cite a specific subsection of a statute. You do this by clicking on the "Index—*Shepard's* reports by court citation" link, leading to a listing of the exact forms in which courts have cited statutory provisions. This way, you can home in immediately on the two cases citing section 704(b)(2) without having to sort through 93 other cases citing the section as a whole or other subsections. Many code sections have numerous subsections and sub-subsections, and this can be an invaluable time-saver.

KeyCite and Shepard's also have references to any citing law review articles, encyclopedias, and other texts available through Westlaw or Lexis. In some instances these resources are also listed in the annotated code, but for many jurisdictions KeyCite and Shepard's have more extensive leads than the code.

Shepard's, but not KeyCite, is available in print as well as online. One advantage of the printed sets of *Shepard's Citations* is that they include citations to session laws and to older codifications as well as current code provisions. The current code is the only statutory source that can be checked online in either KeyCite or Shepard's.

Another Shepard's publication, *Shepard's Acts and Cases by Popular Names: Federal and State*, lists statutes by title and provides references to code citations. This is most useful when the name of an act is known but not its state, or when similar acts from several states are sought.

c. Indexes and Tables

Even if you normally do all of your other work online, you might find it easier to begin statutory research with a printed code. Many statutes are written in a technical language designed to eliminate ambiguities in interpretation, and the terms used may not be the ones that would occur to you in creating an online search. A subject index provides a more standard and straightforward vocabulary, and can lead more quickly to relevant provisions.

Indexes. Code indexes are complex documents, occupying as many as six volumes and filled with cross-references and long lists of subheadings. If you look under "Birds," for example, you may find nothing but an entry such as "See Migratory birds" or "Migratory birds, this index." Indexes can be unwieldy and confusing, but they remain essential resources in statutory research. Statutes are often easier to find through indexes than through full-text keyword searches, which often yield too many irrelevant results. Exhibit 4–9 on page 207 shows a page from the index to the *United States Code*, with a reference to the code section shown in the earlier exhibits.

Westlaw has online versions of the indexes that accompany West's printed codes. A search in the index may give a more complete picture of the law than a keyword search in the text and may reveal related sections that would otherwise be missed. The indexes can be accessed from the database directory or from links at the top of code search screens.

Popular Name Tables. At times you may have a reference to a particular law by its name, without a citation, and need to find the text of the statute. How do you find the Migratory Bird Treaty Reform Act of 1998? You could look in a subject index under "Migratory birds," but it may be quicker to use a *popular name table*, which lists acts by name and provides references to citations in the session laws and code. Exhibit 4–10 on page 208 shows an example of a popular name table in the *United States Code* listing the Migratory Bird Treaty Reform Act of 1998 shown in Exhibit 4–1.

Popular name tables cover the names by which acts are designated by Congress and state legislatures, but they don't always include the terms by which laws are commonly known. "Title VII" is familiar shorthand for a civil rights law, but the term doesn't appear in the table. In order to find a citation for such a reference, the first step is to find more of the name (in this case, Title VII is part of the Civil Rights Act of 1964). It may be simplest to do an online search for the phrase in order to identify the act and ideally its code citation.

Parallel Reference Tables and Parenthetical Notes. At times you may have a citation to a statute, but not the one that immediately directs you to its place in a code. Some references are to session laws, while others are to outdated codifications. In either instance you will need to determine whether a law is currently in force and, if so, where it is codified. For this, most codes include *parallel reference tables* providing cross-references to the current code sections. In most instances, these tables also indicate which sections of session laws have been repealed or were of a temporary nature. Exhibit 4–11 on page 209 shows an excerpt from a parallel reference table mapping the federal session laws to where each section is found in the *United States Code*.

Just as parallel reference tables provide access to current code provisions from session laws or older code citations, the parenthetical notes that follow the text of a code section allow you to reconstruct the language of a statute at any given point in the past. The terms of a repealed statute may still be of value in interpreting related provisions still in force, and older laws are needed to determine the law in effect and the meaning of terms when instruments such as wills or deeds were drafted. The parenthetical notes provide leads to earlier codifications and to all session laws that have amended the section. These references are also the keys to finding legislative history information for a particular enactment.

Some codes make it easier to reconstruct past versions of a statute by indicating the exact changes made. Others merely present a list of citations, making it necessary to check the session laws to determine the changes. Some codes indicate only recent changes or (particularly in the case of many free Internet sites) have no notes at all.

Westlaw and Lexis have statutes from most jurisdictions going back to the late 1980s or early 1990s, and reconstructing the law as of a date during that period may simply require a search in the appropriate archived database. For some jurisdictions, including federal law back to 1996, Westlaw's Past-Stat Locator feature lets you view an older version in force on a specific date of your choice.

§ 4–4. Sources for Federal Statutes

The United States Congress meets in two-year terms, consisting of two annual sessions, and enacts several hundred statutes each term. These statutes range from simple designations of commemorative days to complex environmental or tax legislation spanning hundreds of pages. Each act is designated as either a *public law* or a *private law*, and assigned a number indicating the order in which it was passed. Pub. L. 111–1, for example, was the first public law passed during the 111th Congress (2009–10). Private laws, passed to meet special needs of an individual or small group, are little used in the modern era and do not become part of the statutory code.

a. Slip Laws and Session Laws

The first official text of a new federal law is the slip law, an individually paginated pamphlet. The Government Printing Office's Federal Digital System (FDSys) <www.gpo.gov/fdsys/> has PDF files of slip laws beginning with the 104th Congress in 1995. For current legislation this is one of the quickest and most effective sources, with new laws appearing online within a few days or weeks of enactment. If the public law is not yet available, you can check the legislative site THOMAS <thomas. loc.gov> for the enrolled bill that was passed by both houses and sent to the President.

In print, the first appearance of federal statutes after the slip laws is in the monthly pamphlets of two advance session law services, West's *United States Code Congressional and Administrative News* (*USCCAN*) and LexisNexis's *Advance* pamphlets to the *United States Code Service* (*USCS*). After the end of each session of Congress, the slip laws are cumulated, corrected, and issued in bound volumes as the official *United States Statutes at Large* for the session. These are cited by volume and page number. The Migratory Bird Treaty Reform Act of 1998, Pub. L. 105–312, 112 Stat. 2956 (1998), shown in Exhibit 4–1 on page 199, begins on page 2956 of volume 112 of the *Statutes at Large*. There is a delay of about two years before *Statutes at Large* volumes are published, but the slip laws on the Government Printing Office (GPO) website include the *Statutes at Large* pagination within weeks of enactment.

Public laws are also available online, with *Statutes at Large* citations, from Westlaw and Lexis. Searchable files extend on Westlaw back to 1973, and Lexis back to 1988. Both systems also have retrospective coverage of the *Statutes at Large* back to 1789, but earlier acts are available as image-based PDFs and only citations, dates, and summary information are searchable.

The subscription site HeinOnline <www.hein online.org> has complete retrospective coverage of the *Statutes at Large* in PDF, with the text of all acts back to 1789 searchable by keyword or title. The Library of Congress provides free access to the first eighteen volumes of the *Statutes at Large*, through 1875, as part of its "A Century of Law-making for a New Nation: U.S. Congressional Documents and Debates, 1774–1875" collection <memory.loc.gov/ammem/amlaw/lwsl.html>. Only the index is searchable, but acts can be retrieved by citation.

The easiest way to find court decisions citing acts in the *Statutes at Large* is to do a full-text search for the citation in a case law database. Neither KeyCite nor Shepard's online covers citations to session laws, but two other resources are available in print. The *United States Code Service* includes case summaries by *Statutes at Large* citation in one of its "Annotations to Uncodified Laws and Treaties" volumes, and more citing references can be found using *Shepard's Citations* in print. *Shepard's Federal Statute Citations* covers citations in federal court decisions to acts in the *Statutes at Large*, with references in state court decisions and journal articles available in Shepard's individual state citators and in *Shepard's Federal Law Citations in Selected Law Reviews*. References to *Statutes at Large* citations are one of the few features in print Shepard's that are not available online.

Although the *Statutes at Large* is not the most convenient source for federal legislation, its role in legal research is vital. In most instances it is the official statement of the law, and it is a necessary source for determining the specific language Congress enacted at any given time. This is a key step in legislative history research, as will be discussed in the next chapter.

b. The *United States Code*

The first official subject compilations of federal legislation were the *Revised Statutes of the United States* of 1873, and its second edition of 1878. Congress enacted the first edition of the *Revised Statutes* as positive law in its entirety, expressly repealing the original *Statutes at Large* versions of its contents. It is therefore the authoritative text for most laws enacted before 1873, and is still needed occasionally in modern research. The *Revised Statutes* is online in PDF form from several sources, including the Library of Congress, as part of their coverage of the *Statutes at Large*.

Although the *Revised Statutes* rapidly became outdated, no other official compilation was prepared for almost fifty years. Finally, in 1926, the first edition of the *United States Code* was published, arranging the laws by subject into fifty titles. The *U.S. Code* is published in a completely revised edition of about thirty-five volumes every six years, with an annual supplement of one or more bound volumes. These supplements are cumulative, so you only need to consult the main set and its latest supplement.

The *U.S. Code* is arranged in fifty subject titles, generally in alphabetical order. Titles are divided into chapters and then into sections, with a continuous sequence of section numbers for each title. Citations to the *Code* indicate the title, section number, and year. 16 U.S.C. § 704 (2006), for example, is part of title 16 (Conservation), chapter 7 (Protection of Migratory Game and Insectivorous Birds). The chapter number does not appear in the citation.

You should keep in mind that that not every federal law is published as a section of the *United States Code*. Some laws appear only in the *Statutes at Large*, and others are published as notes following sections of the code. The validity of a statute is unaffected by whether it is published as a code section or a note, or is omitted entirely from the *U.S. Code*.

The *U.S. Code* is available free online from several sources. The most important of these sites are the House of Representatives Office of the Law Revision Counsel <uscode.house.gov> and the Legal Information Institute (LII) <www.law.cornell.edu/uscode/>.

The Office of Law Revision Counsel site has search boxes for convenient access by title and section number, and allows several search options including keywords using proximity connectors and truncation. The site also provides access to PDF files for entire code titles, incorporating the material in the supplements to the printed edition of the code. This makes them more convenient than the printed supplements, but because they do not mirror the published source they cannot be used for citation purposes.

The sections displayed on the Office of Law Revision Counsel site are only as current as the latest printed *U.S. Code* version, and updating a section to determine if it has been amended is a bit laborious. If you run a search by title and section number, you will see an "UPDATE" link if a code section has been amended since the most recent published edition or supplement. The update lists the sections of any public laws that have amended the code section, and you then need to retrieve the public law using a site such as FDSys or THOMAS. The absence of an "UPDATE" link, however, is an easy way to verify that there have been no recent amendments.

LII's version of the *U.S. Code* is much more user-friendly. Like the official site, it has a fill-in-the-blank form for citation searches and allows simple keyword searches with phrases and basic connectors (*and*, *or*, or *not*), in either the entire code or individual titles. "Update(s)" notes are included as part of the display of a code section, and include links to any new public laws amending the section. A note that there is no update confirms that a section has not been amended recently. Exhibit 4–12 on page 210 shows 16 U.S.C. § 704 as it appears on the LII site, including the "Notes" link and a "No Pending Update(s)" notation.

Another online source for the *U.S. Code* is the subscription site HeinOnline, which reproduces every printed edition from 1926 through the most recent supplement in searchable PDF. The older editions can be useful for tracking the history of a provision, and may be needed for a citation to a statute that is no longer in force.

For most federal legislation, the *Statutes at Large* is authoritative and the *U.S. Code* is *prima facie* evidence of the law. A number of *U.S. Code* titles, however, have been reenacted as positive law, and for them the code is the authoritative text. A list of all code titles, indicating which titles have been reenacted, appears in the front of each *U.S. Code* volume and is reproduced as Exhibit 4–13 on page 211.

In addition to the text of statutes, the *U.S. Code* also includes historical notes, cross references, and other research aids. Parenthetical references indicate the *Statutes at Large* or *Revised Statutes* sources of each section, including any amendments. These references lead to the version that is usually the authoritative text, and from there to legislative history documents relating to the law's enactment.

The *U.S. Code* in print features a number of research aids, including an extensive general index and several tables. An "Acts Cited by Popular Name" table lists laws alphabetically under either short titles assigned by Congress or popular names by which they have become known, and parallel reference tables provide links from earlier revisions and from the *Statutes at Large* to *U.S. Code* sections. The index and tables are updated in each annual supplement.

c. Annotated Codes

The *United States Code* is the preferred source for citing federal laws, but two major shortcomings limit its value in research: (1) it is not updated on a very timely basis, and (2) it has no information about court decisions applying or interpreting code sections. These decisions are so important that most researchers rely on one of two commercially published, annotated editions of the code, *United States Code Annotated* (*USCA*), published by West and available on Westlaw, or *United States Code Service* (*USCS*), published by LexisNexis and available on Lexis. Beyond the text of the law and notes of court decisions, these commercial editions also provide references to legislative history, administrative regulations, and various secondary sources.

Unlike the official *U.S. Code*, which is published in a new edition every six years, *USCA* and *USCS* consist of volumes of varying ages, all updated with annual pocket parts or pamphlet supplements. Replacement volumes are published when supplements get too unwieldy. In the case of the portion of Title 16 covering migratory birds, the *USCA* volume was published in 2000 and the *USCS* volume in 1994. For other provisions, the *USCS* volume may well be the more current of the two.

Thorough research involving a particular statute may require checking both *USCA* and *USCS*. Each provides selective annotations of court decisions, and specific cases may be included in one but not the other. *USCA*'s annotations are generally more extensive, but some court decisions appear only in *USCS*—which is also the only source for references to administrative decisions.

Bear in mind that notes of decisions do not follow every code section. Many sections of the *U.S. Code* have not been the subject of judicial interpretation. Some are uncontroversial and have not led to litigation, while others may be too new for any reported cases. If there are no annotations, you will need to interpret a section without the assistance of court decisions directly on point.

As noted, both annotated editions of the code are available online (*USCA* on Westlaw and *USCS* on Lexis). The online code databases are updated to include laws from the current session of Congress; notes above the heading on Lexis and at the bottom of the Westlaw display indicate the latest public law included in code coverage. If a section has been amended by a public law too recent to be incorporated, both services provide notices to check for more current legislative action.

Specialized online and looseleaf services are another source for current, annotated statutes in some subject fields. Most services include federal statutes affecting their fields, accompanied by abstracts of judicial and administrative decisions, relevant administrative regulations, and explanatory text. Major tax services such as the *Standard Federal Tax Reporter* (CCH) and *United States Tax Reporter* (RIA) are basically heavily annotated editions of 26 U.S.C., also known as the Internal Revenue Code.

§ 4–5. Sources for State Statutes

State statutes appear in many of the same forms as their federal counterparts, with slip laws, session laws, codes, and annotated codes. Current session laws and codes are available from government websites, and annotated codes are published both electronically and in print.

a. Slip Laws and Session Laws

State slip laws are rarely distributed widely in paper, but every state legislature provides Internet access to recently enacted laws. Two easy ways to find legislative websites are to search for "[state] legislature" or to check a site with multistate links such as the National Conference of State Legislatures <www.ncsl.org/?tabid=17173>.

Every state has a session law publication similar to the *U.S. Statutes at Large*, containing the laws enacted at each sitting of its legislature. The names of these publications vary (*e.g.*, *Acts of Alabama*, *Statutes of California*, *Laws of Delaware*). In most states the session laws are the authoritative positive law text of the statutes, and you may need them to examine legislative changes or to reconstruct the language in force at a particular date.

Westlaw and Lexis have the texts of new legislation from every state, with retrospective files going back to at least 1991. These are known on Westlaw as "Legislative Services" and on Lexis as "Advance Legislative Services" or ALS. The major difference between the two systems is that Westlaw separates each state's current legislative session from "historical" session laws back to the late 1980s or early 1990s, while Lexis has one database for each state combining older and newer sessions.

In print, commercially published session law services for most states contain laws from a current legislative session, very much as *USCCAN* and *USCS Advance* do for congressional enactments.

HeinOnline has a Session Laws Library that is in the process of providing retrospective coverage of state session laws in PDF. For most states it currently has volumes from 1990 or 1995 to date, with older sessions available for several of the larger jurisdictions. Most larger law libraries also have older state session laws in microform.

b. Codes

All states have subject compilations of their statutes similar to the *U.S. Code*. Some states publish unannotated official codes, regularly revised on an annual or biennial basis. In the states with regularly published official codes, this is usually the authoritative text which should be cited according to *The Bluebook* and *ALWD Citation Manual*.

Every state makes its code available through its state website, although these free online codes vary widely in their currency, official status, and features. Only a handful of state codes available free of charge include annotations of court decisions, and some online codes bear prominent disclaimers that they are unofficial versions for convenience only. All of the codes, however, can be searched by keyword and browsed through tables of contents. Several convenient compilations of links are available, including lists of state legal materials at the Legal Information Institute <www.law.cornell.edu/states/listing.html> and FindLaw <www.findlaw.com/11 stategov/>.

Most researchers rely on annotated codes containing summaries of relevant court decisions and other references, published in most instances by either West or LexisNexis. Several states have competing codes from both publishers. The authority of annotated codes varies from state to state, but they are usually accepted as at least *prima facie* evidence of the statutory law.

Westlaw and Lexis have annotated codes from all fifty states, as well as the District of Columbia, Guam, Puerto Rico, and the Virgin Islands. Westlaw users can choose between annotated and unannotated versions, and in several states between competing editions of the annotated code. Both systems add notices to statutes that have been amended by slip laws not yet incorporated into the code database. The Westlaw display has a red flag linking to legislative action, and Lexis has a "Legislative Alert" with links to new acts.

The outline and arrangement of code material vary from state to state. While most codes are divided into titles and sections, in a format similar to the *U.S. Code*, several states have individual codes designated by name rather than title number (e.g., commercial code, penal code, tax code). Exhibit 4–14 on page 212 shows Indiana statutes as published in *Burns Indiana Statutes Annotated*. Note that it provides not only the text of the code sections, but historical notes indicating when they were enacted, annotations about one section's constitutionality and construction, and a reference to an *ALR* annotation.

State codes usually have references to the original session laws in parenthetical notes following each section, as shown in Exhibit 4–14, but only some include notes indicating the changes made by each amendment. Most also include tables with cross references from session law citations and earlier codifications to the current code.

The Bluebook and *ALWD Citation Manual* have listings by state of the names and citations of current official and commercially published codes. State legal research guides (listed in Appendix A on pages 438–53) provide information about earlier codes and statutory revisions for individual states.

c. Multistate Research Sources

Most state statutory research situations require finding the law in one particular state, for which that state's code is the primary research tool. Sometimes, however, you may want to compare statutory provisions among states or survey legislation throughout the country. Multistate surveys of state laws can be frustrating and time-consuming, since different state codes do not necessarily use the same terminology for similar issues.

Several resources can help to make multistate statutory research a bit easier. Both Westlaw and Lexis have combined databases containing the codes of all fifty states. These databases can save considerable time, although you should remember that any single search may not retrieve all relevant laws. You may also need to search individual codes or check the printed state code indexes.

The Internet provides convenient multistate access to code provisions in some subject areas. One of the most comprehensive sites is the Legal Information Institute's topical index to state statutes

<www.law.cornell.edu/topics/state_statutes.html>,
with links to code sites in several dozen broad
categories. Sites collecting statutes on specific topics
are also available, but it is important that verify
that any site you use is regularly and reliably updated.

Topical looseleaf services often collect state laws
in their subject areas, making it easy to compare
state provisions in areas such as taxation or employment law. More general coverage is provided by two
sources, the Martindale–Hubbell Law Digests (available on Lexis) and Richard A. Leiter, *National
Survey of State Laws* (5th ed. 2005) (available on
Westlaw). These works are organized in very different ways.

The Martindale–Hubbell Law Digests are arranged by state and cover more than a hundred
legal topics, with a focus on commercial and procedural information most likely to be needed by lawyers in other states. Citations to both code sections
and court decisions are included. Formerly published in print as a companion to the *Martindale-
Hubbell Law Directory*, the Law Digests are now
available in the "Reference" folder on Lexis with
other Martindale–Hubbell material. For multistate
research, a search for a topic name retrieves the
relevant section for every state. Exhibit 4–15 on
page 213 shows the Lexis version of the South
Carolina environmental law digest, one of 54 documents retrieved (50 states, the District of Columbia,
Puerto Rico, Virgin Islands, and U.S. federal law)

with the search *section(environmental regulation)*. Links to cases and statutes cited in the digest entry are provided. The Law Digests are also available free online in PDF from Martindale.com <www. martindale.com>, in its "Search Legal Topics" section.

The *National Survey of State Laws* is arranged by topic rather than by state, with tables summarizing state laws in forty-six areas and providing citations to codes. Its "Gun Control" section, for example, includes information on illegal arms, waiting periods, ownership restrictions, and laws prohibiting firearms on or near school grounds. The *National Survey* focuses more on social and political issues than does *Martindale-Hubbell*, with sections on topics such as capital punishment, prayer in public schools, right to die, and stalking.

The *National Survey of State Laws* is part of Westlaw's 50 State Surveys database, which also includes several hundred surveys prepared by West editors consisting of an introductory summary followed by links to states code provisions. A topical listing of Westlaw's surveys is available by clicking on the *50 State Surveys* link at the top of any state statute search screen. Lexis has similar sets of fifty-state surveys providing spreadsheet listings or descriptions of state code sections on hundreds of topics.

Numerous other online and print resources reprint or summarize state laws on specific topics. A valuable series of bibliographies called *Subject Com-*

pilations of State Laws (1981–date) describes these collections and lists of state statutes. This set does not itself summarize or cite the statutes, but it provides annotated descriptions of sources that do so. These include books, compendia, websites, and law review articles, which often have footnotes with extensive listings of state code citations. Exhibit 4–16 on page 214 shows a page from this publication, with entries under the heading "Animals" for a website, an interest group publication, and two law review articles. *Subject Compilations of State Laws* is available by subscription through HeinOnline, cumulative and with links to law review articles in HeinOnline's database as well as to publicly available Internet sites.

d. Uniform Laws

Most multistate research requires finding a wide variety of legislative approaches to a particular topic. In a growing number of areas, however, states have adopted virtually identical acts. This can dramatically reduce the confusion caused by the application of conflicting state statutes. The National Conference of Commissioners on Uniform State Laws (NCCUSL), created in 1892 to prepare legislation which would decrease unnecessary conflicts, has drafted more than two hundred laws. Most of these are in force in at least one state, and some (such as the Uniform Commercial Code or Uniform Child Custody Jurisdiction Act) have been enacted in virtually every jurisdiction.

Uniform Laws Annotated, a multivolume set published by West and available online from Westlaw, contains every uniform law approved by the NCCUSL, lists of adopting states, Commissioners' notes, and annotations to court decisions from adopting jurisdictions. These annotations allow researchers in one state to study the case law developed in other states with the same uniform law. A decision from another state is not binding authority, but its interpretation of similar language may be persuasive. The set is supplemented annually by pocket parts and by the pamphlet *Directory of Uniform Acts and Codes; Tables–Index*, which lists the acts alphabetically and includes a table of jurisdictions indicating the acts adopted in each state. Lexis has several dozen uniform laws, unannotated, in the Model Acts and Uniform Laws section of its Secondary Legal folder.

The text of a uniform law can also be found, of course, in the statutory code of each adopting state, accompanied by annotations from that state's courts. The state code contains the law as actually adopted and in force, which may not be identical to the text as proposed by the Commissioners. The NCCUSL version is merely a proposal, but the state code version is the law.

Uniform acts, and drafts of current projects, are available online from the NCCUSL Archives at the University of Pennsylvania Law Library <www.law.upenn.edu/bll/ulc/ulc.htm>. The Legal Information Institute has "Uniform Law Locators" <www.law.

cornell.edu/uniform/>, listing links to official sites where the text as adopted in particular states can be found.

Model acts are drafted for fields where individual states are expected to modify a proposed law to meet their needs, rather than adopt it *in toto.* The American Law Institute has produced the Model Penal Code and other model acts; the American Bar Association has promulgated and revised the Model Business Corporation Act. Research resources for these acts include *Model Penal Code and Commentaries* (1980–85), and *Model Business Corporation Act Annotated* (4th ed. 2008–date).

e. Interstate Compacts

An interstate compact is an agreement between two or more states, which under the Constitution requires approval by Congress. Compacts generally appear in the *U.S. Statutes at Large* and in the session laws and codes for the states that are parties. The National Center for Interstate Compacts <www.csg.org/programs/policyprograms/NCIC/> has a variety of useful resources on the subject, including background information and a searchable database of more than 1,500 compacts in state codes.

§ 4–6. The U.S. Constitution

The United States Constitution is the basic law of the country, defining political relationships, enumerating the rights and liberties of citizens, and creating the framework of national government. Unlike statutes, which are often written in extreme detail and specificity, the Constitution contains concise statements of broad principles. It entered into force in March 1789, and in more than two centuries it has been amended only twenty-seven times. Among the most important of these amendments are the Bill of Rights, guaranteeing personal liberties, and the Fourteenth Amendment, applying these protections to the states.

Although its text has changed little, courts have applied the Constitution to numerous situations which its drafters could not have foreseen. In interpreting constitutional provisions, it is particularly important to examine relevant Supreme Court decisions and those of the lower federal courts. Judicial interpretations of constitutional principles can be just as significant as the express language of the Constitution.

The text of the Constitution appears in numerous publications ranging from simple pamphlets to standard reference works such as *Black's Law Dictionary*, and it is available at dozens of Internet sites. The Constitution Society has an annotated listing of several online sources <www.constitution.org/cs_found.htm>.

The Constitution is also printed at the beginning of the *United States Code*, the official publication of federal statutes. As with statutes, however, the two annotated publications, *United States Code Annotated* (*USCA*) and *United States Code Service* (*USCS*), are far more useful in legal research. (*USCA* and *USCS* are the versions of the Constitution available through Westlaw and Lexis, respectively.) These publications have much more than just the text of the Constitution. Each clause is accompanied by notes of decisions, arranged by subject and thoroughly indexed. Some major provisions have thousands of notes in several hundred subject divisions. The Constitution is so heavily annotated that it occupies twenty-eight volumes in *USCA* and ten volumes in *USCS*. These exhaustive annotations make *USCA* and *USCS* essential resources in determining how the Constitution's broad principles have been applied to specific circumstances.

Of the many commentaries on the Constitution, one of the most extensive and widely available is *The Constitution of the United States of America: Analysis and Interpretation* (Johnny H. Killian et al. eds., 2002 ed.). Prepared by the Congressional Research Service of the Library of Congress, this work is published as a Senate Document every ten years and is available free on the Internet from the GPO <www.gpoaccess.gov/constitution/>. It is a useful starting point for constitutional research, with a thorough analysis of Supreme Court decisions applying each provision of the Constitution. The most recent edition was published in 2004, covering cases through June 2002, and is updated by a biennial pocket part. Exhibit 4–17 on page 215 shows the beginning of this work's discussion of the Second Amendment, with footnotes citing several scholarly monographs, law review articles, and Supreme Court decisions.

Other helpful background sources include *Encyclopedia of the American Constitution* (Leonard W. Levy & Kenneth L. Karst eds., 2d ed. 2000) and *Encyclopedia of the Supreme Court of the United States* (David S. Tanenhaus ed., 2008), both of which include articles on constitutional doctrines as well as on specific court decisions, people, and historical periods. Shorter works providing similar treatment of constitutional issues include *The Oxford Companion to the Supreme Court of the United States* (Kermit Hall ed., 2d ed. 2005), and Jethro K. Lieberman, *A Practical Companion to the Constitution* (1999).

For further historical research, you can turn to the documents prepared by those who drafted, adopted, and ratified the Constitution. There was no official record of the debates in the constitutional convention, but Max Farrand's *The Records of the Federal Convention of 1787* (1911–87) is considered the most authoritative source. The traditional source for the state ratification debates is Jonathan Elliot, *The Debates in the Several State Conventions on the Adoption of the Federal Constitution* (2d ed., 1836–45). The Library of Congress website provides full-text access to both Farrand's *Records* and Elliot's *Debates* <memory.loc.gov/ammem/amlaw/>. A much more comprehensive modern treatment, *The Documentary History of the Ratification of the Constitution* (Merrill Jensen et al. eds., 20 vols. to date,

1976–date), contains debates, commentaries and other documents. *The Founders' Constitution* (Philip B. Kurland & Ralph Lerner eds., 1987) <press-pubs.uchicago.edu/founders/> and *The Complete Bill of Rights: The Drafts, Debates, Sources, and Origins* (Neil H. Cogan ed., 1997) are useful collections of excerpts from source documents arranged by the constitutional provision to which they apply.

§ 4–7. State Constitutions

Each state is governed by its own constitution, which establishes the structure of government and guarantees fundamental rights. While state constitutions are roughly comparable to their federal counterpart, they tend to be much more detailed and generally are amended far more frequently. Some states have adopted new constitutions several times.

State constitutions can be important sources in cases involving individual rights. While a state cannot deprive citizens of federal constitutional rights, its constitution can guarantee rights beyond those provided under the U.S. Constitution. Just as the U.S. Supreme Court is the arbiter of the scope of protections offered by the federal constitution, the state court of last resort determines the scope of its constitution.

The best source for a state constitution is usually the annotated state code, which provides both the latest text and notes of court decisions interpreting and construing constitutional provisions. Pamphlet texts are also published in many states, and constitutions are available online from state government sites.

Current state constitutions are compiled in *Constitutions of the United States: National and State* (7 vols., 2d ed. 1974–date; available by subscription online <www.oceanalaw.com>). Historical state constitutions are published in a seven-volume "Constitutional Documents of the Unites States of America 1776–1860" component of *Constitutions of the World from the Late 18th Century to the Middle of the 19th Century* (Horst Dippel ed., 2005–date), and available online as The Rise of Modern Constitutionalism, 1776–1849 <www.modern-constitutions. de>. The NBER/Maryland State Constitutions Project <www.stateconstitutions.umd.edu> is another online source for historic and current state constitutions.

Robert L. Maddex, *State Constitutions of the United States* (2d ed. 2006) may be a useful source for surveying constitutional provisions in several states. It has a brief summary of each state's constitutional history and its current constitution, as well as tables comparing provisions in each state. The Council of State Governments' annual *Book of the States* also has tables on topics such as the length of each constitution, dates of adoption, and amendment procedures.

For research into a particular state's constitution, one of the best starting places may be *Reference*

Guides to the State Constitutions of the United States. This series of monographs began with Robert F. Williams, *The New Jersey State Constitution: A Reference Guide* (1990), and now covers more than forty states. Each volume includes a summary of the state's constitutional history, a detailed section-by-section analysis of the constitution with background information and discussion of judicial interpretations, and a brief bibliographical essay providing references for further research.

Journals and proceedings of state constitutional conventions can provide insight into framers' intent, although the lack of indexing in many older volumes can make for difficult research. These documents are available on microfiche in *State Constitutional Conventions, Commissions, and Amendments*, covering all fifty states from 1776 through 1988, and are listed in a series of bibliographies beginning with Cynthia E. Browne's *State Constitutional Conventions from Independence to the Completion of the Present Union, 1776–1959: A Bibliography* (1973). You can find information on resources for territorial and initial state constitutions in *Prestatehood Legal Materials: A Fifty–State Research Guide* (Michael Chiorazzi & Marguerite Most eds., 2005).

112 STAT. 2956   PUBLIC LAW 105–312—OCT. 30, 1998

Public Law 105–312
105th Congress

An Act

Oct. 30, 1998
[H.R. 2807]

To clarify restrictions under the Migratory Bird Treaty Act on baiting and to facilitate acquisition of migratory bird habitat, and for other purposes.

Be it enacted by the Senate and House of Representatives of the United States of America in Congress assembled,

Migratory Bird
Reform Act of
1998.

TITLE I—MIGRATORY BIRD TREATY REFORM

16 USC 710 note.

SEC. 101. SHORT TITLE.

This title may be cited as the "Migratory Bird Treaty Reform Act of 1998".

SEC. 102. ELIMINATING STRICT LIABILITY FOR BAITING.

Section 3 of the Migratory Bird Treaty Act (16 U.S.C. 704) is amended—

(1) by inserting "(a)" after "SEC. 3."; and
(2) by adding at the end the following:
"(b) It shall be unlawful for any person to—
"(1) take any migratory game bird by the aid of baiting, or on or over any baited area, if the person knows or reasonably should know that the area is a baited area; or
"(2) place or direct the placement of bait on or adjacent to an area for the purpose of causing, inducing, or allowing any person to take or attempt to take any migratory game bird by the aid of baiting on or over the baited area.".

SEC. 103. CRIMINAL PENALTIES.

Section 6 of the Migratory Bird Treaty Act (16 U.S.C. 707) is amended—

(1) in subsection (a), by striking "$500" and inserting "$15,000";
(2) by redesignating subsection (c) as subsection (d); and
(3) by inserting after subsection (b) the following:
"(c) Whoever violates section 3(b)(2) shall be fined under title 18, United States Code, imprisoned not more than 1 year, or both.".

Deadline.
16 USC 704 note.

SEC. 104. REPORT.

Not later than 5 years after the date of enactment of this Act, the Secretary of the Interior shall submit to the Committee on Environment and Public Works of the Senate and the Committee on Resources of the House of Representatives a report analyzing the effect of the amendments made by section 2, and the general

Exhibit 4–1.   An Act of Congress in the *United States Statutes at Large*

"(K) Yellow Rail.

"(6) It is essential that the current population of mid-continent light geese be reduced by 50 percent by the year 2005 to ensure that the fragile Arctic tundra is not irreversibly damaged.

"(b) PURPOSES.—The purposes of this Act are the following:

"(1) To reduce the population of mid-continent light geese.

"(2) To assure the long-term conservation of mid-continent light geese and the biological diversity of the ecosystem upon which many North American migratory birds depend.

"SEC. 3. FORCE AND EFFECT OF RULES TO CONTROL OVERABUNDANT MID-CONTINENT LIGHT GEESE POPULATIONS.

"(a) FORCE AND EFFECT.—

"(1) IN GENERAL.—The rules published by the Service on February 16, 1999, relating to use of additional hunting methods to increase the harvest of mid-continent light geese (64 Fed. Reg. 7507-7517) and the establishment of a conservation order for the reduction of mid-continent light goose populations (64 Fed. Reg. 7517-7529), shall have the force and effect of law.

"(2) PUBLIC NOTICE.—The Secretary, acting through the Director of the Service, shall take such action as is necessary to appropriately notify the public of the force and effect of the rules referred to in paragraph (1).

"(b) APPLICATION.—Subsection (a) shall apply only during the period that—

"(1) begins on the date of the enactment of this Act [Nov. 24, 1999]; and

"(2) ends on the latest of—

"(A) the effective date of rules issued by the Service after such date of the enactment to control overabundant mid-continent light geese populations;

"(B) the date of the publication of a final environmental impact statement for such rules under section 102(2)(C) of the National Environmental Policy Act of 1969 (42 U.S.C. 4332(2)(C)); and

"(C) May 15, 2001.

"(c) RULE OF CONSTRUCTION.—This section shall not be construed to limit the authority of the Secretary or the Service to issue rules, under another law, to regulate the taking of mid-continent light geese.

"SEC. 4. COMPREHENSIVE MANAGEMENT PLAN.

"(a) IN GENERAL.—Not later than the end of the period described in section 103(b) [probably means section 3(b)], the Secretary shall prepare, and as appropriate implement, a comprehensive, long-term plan for the management of mid-continent light geese and the conservation of their habitat.

"(b) REQUIRED ELEMENTS.—The plan shall apply principles of adaptive resource management and shall include—

"(1) a description of methods for monitoring the levels of populations and the levels of harvest of mid-continent light geese, and recommendations concerning long-term harvest levels;

"(2) recommendations concerning other means for the management of mid-continent light goose populations, taking into account the reasons for the population growth specified in section 2(a)(3)[;]

"(3) an assessment of, and recommendations relating to, conservation of the breeding habitat of mid-continent light geese;

"(4) an assessment of, and recommendations relating to, conservation of native species of wildlife adversely affected by the overabundance of mid-continent light geese, including the species specified in section 102(a)(5) [probably means section 2(a)(5)]; and

"(5) an identification of methods for promoting collaboration with the Government of Canada, States, and other interested persons.

"(c) AUTHORIZATION OF APPROPRIATIONS.—There is authorized to be appropriated to carry out this section $1,000,000 for each of fiscal years 2000 through 2002."

"SEC. 5. DEFINITIONS.

"In this Act:

"(1) MID-CONTINENT LIGHT GEESE.—The term 'mid-continent light geese' means Lesser snow geese (Anser caerulescens caerulescens) and Ross' geese (Anser rossii) that primarily migrate between Canada and the States of Alabama, Arkansas, Colorado, Illinois, Indiana, Iowa, Kansas, Kentucky, Louisiana, Michigan, Minnesota, Mississippi, Missouri, Montana, Nebraska, New Mexico, North Dakota, Ohio, Oklahoma, South Dakota, Tennessee, Texas, Wisconsin, and Wyoming.

"(2) SECRETARY.—The term 'Secretary' means the Secretary of the Interior.

"(3) SERVICE.—The term 'Service' means the United States Fish and Wildlife Service."

§ 704. Determination as to when and how migratory birds may be taken, killed, or possessed

(a) Subject to the provisions and in order to carry out the purposes of the conventions, as referred to in section 703 of this title, the Secretary of the Interior is authorized and directed, from time to time, having due regard to the zones of temperature and to the distribution, abundance, economic value, breeding habits, and times and lines of migratory flight of such birds, to determine when, to what extent, if at all, and by what means, it is compatible with the terms of the conventions to allow hunting, taking, capture, killing, possession, sale, purchase, shipment, transportation, carriage, or export of any such bird, or any part, nest, or egg thereof, and to adopt suitable regulations permitting and governing the same, in accordance with such determinations, which regulations shall become effective when approved by the President.

(b) It shall be unlawful for any person to—

(1) take any migratory game bird by the aid of baiting, or on or over any baited area, if the person knows or reasonably should know that the area is a baited area; or

(2) place or direct the placement of bait on or adjacent to an area for the purpose of causing, inducing, or allowing any person to take or attempt to take any migratory game bird by the aid of baiting on or over the baited area.

(July 3, 1918, ch. 128, §3, 40 Stat. 755; June 20, 1936, ch. 634, §2, 49 Stat. 1556; 1939 Reorg. Plan No. II, §4(f), eff. July 1, 1939, 4 F.R. 2731, 53 Stat. 1433; Pub. L. 105–312, title I, §102, Oct. 30, 1998, 112 Stat. 2956.)

AMENDMENTS

1998—Pub. L. 105–312 designated existing provisions as subsec. (a) and added subsec. (b).

1936—Act June 20, 1936, substituted "conventions" for "convention" wherever appearing.

EFFECTIVE DATE OF 1936 AMENDMENT

Section effective June 30, 1937, see section 1 of act of June 20, 1936, set out as a note under section 703 of this title.

TRANSFER OF FUNCTIONS

Transfer of functions of Secretary of Agriculture to Secretary of the Interior by Reorg. Plan. No. II of 1939, see Transfer of Functions note set out under section 701 of this title.

DELEGATION OF FUNCTIONS

For delegation to Secretary of the Interior of authority vested in President, see Ex. Ord. No. 10752, Feb. 12,

Exhibit 4–2. A *United States Code* section

16 § 704　　　　　　　　　　　　　CONSERVATION　Ch. 7

§ 704. Determination as to when and how migratory birds may be taken, killed, or possessed

(a) Subject to the provisions and in order to carry out the purposes of the conventions, referred to in section 703 of this title, the Secretary of the Interior is authorized and directed, from time to time, having due regard to the zones of temperature and to the distribution, abundance, economic value, breeding habits, and times and lines of migratory flight of such birds, to determine when, to what extent, if at all, and by what means, it is compatible with the terms of the conventions to allow hunting, taking, capture, killing, possession, sale, purchase, shipment, transportation, carriage, or export of any such bird, or any part, nest, or egg thereof, and to adopt suitable regulations permitting and governing the same, in accordance with such determinations, which regulations shall become effective when approved by the President.

(b) It shall be unlawful for any person to—

(1) take any migratory game bird by the aid of baiting, or on or over any baited area, if the person knows or reasonably should know that the area is a baited area; or

(2) place or direct the placement of bait on or adjacent to an area for the purpose of causing, inducing, or allowing any person to take or attempt to take any migratory game bird by the aid of baiting on or over the baited area.

(July 3, 1918, c. 128, § 3, 40 Stat. 755; June 20, 1936, c. 634, § 2, 49 Stat. 1556; 1939 Reorg. Plan No. II, § 4(f), eff. July 1, 1939, 4 F.R. 2731, 53 Stat. 1433; Oct. 30, 1998, Pub.L. 105–312, Title I, § 102, 112 Stat. 2956.)

HISTORICAL AND STATUTORY NOTES

Amendments

1998 Amendments. Subsec. (a). Pub.L. 105–312, § 102(1), designated subsec. (a).

Subsec. (b). Pub.L. 105–312, § 102(2), added subsec. (b).

1936 Amendments. Act June 20, 1936 substituted "conventions" for "convention" wherever appearing.

Effective and Applicability Provisions

1936 Amendments. Amendment by Act June 20, 1936, effective June 30, 1937, see Act June 20, 1936, § 1, set out as a note under section 703 of this title.

Transfer of Functions

Transfer of functions of Secretary of Agriculture to Secretary of the Interior by Reorg. Plan No. II of 1939, see Transfer of Functions note under section 701 of this title.

Delegation of Functions

For delegation to the Secretary of the Interior of authority vested in the President, see Ex. Ord. No. 10752, Feb. 12, 1958, 23 F.R. 973, set out as a note following section 715j of Title 15, Commerce and Trade.

Secretary of the Interior empowered to promulgate regulations under this section without the approval, ratification, or other action of the President, see section 2(b) of Ex. Ord. No. 10250, June 5, 1951, 16 F.R. 5385, set out as a note under section 301 of Title 3, The President.

Report on Effects of Legislative Amendments and General Practice of Baiting on Migratory Bird Conservation and Law Enforcement Efforts

Pub.L. 105–312, § 104, Oct. 30, 1998, 112 Stat. 2956, provided that: "Not later

Exhibit 4–3.　A section in the *United States Code Annotated*

Ch. 7   MIGRATORY BIRDS

than 5 years after the date of enactment of this Act [Oct. 30, 1998], the Secretary of the Interior shall submit to the Committee on Environment and Public Works of the Senate and the Committee on Resources of the House of Representatives a report analyzing the effect of the amend-

ments made by section 2 [sic; probably should be "section 102", which amended this section], and the general practice of baiting, on migratory bird conservation and law enforcement efforts under the Migratory Bird Treaty Act (16 U.S.C. 701 et seq.)."

LIBRARY REFERENCES

Administrative Law
General permit procedures, see 50 CFR § 13.1 et seq.
Hunting, generally, see 50 CFR § 32.1 et seq.
Importation, exportation, and transportation of wildlife, see 50 CFR § 14.1 et seq.
Migratory bird hunting, see 50 CFR § 20.1 et seq.
Migratory bird permits, see 50 CFR § 21.1 ét seq.
Seizure and forfeiture procedures, see 50 CFR § 12.1 et seq.

American Digest System
Game ⊂=3, 3.5.
Key Number System Topic No. 187.
Woods and Forests ⊂=5.
Key Number System Topic No. 411.

Encyclopedias
Game, see C.J.S. § 3 to 8, 11 to 23, 26 to 37, 39 to 40, 44 to 49, 51, 55, 59.
Woods and Forests, see C.J.S. § 5.

WESTLAW ELECTRONIC RESEARCH

See WESTLAW guide following the Explanation pages of this volume.

Notes of Decisions

Bag or kill limitations 9
Baiting or luring, prohibitions against 10
Construction 1
Construction with other laws 2
Delegation, power of congress 4
Discretion of Secretary 5
Duty of Secretary 6
Gun restrictions 11
Injunction 21
Issues reviewable by appellate court 22
Judicial notice 19
Jurisdiction 18
Power of Congress 3, 4
    Generally 3
    Delegation 4
Powerboat prohibitions 12
Presidential proclamation, scope of district court review 17
Presumptions 20
Privilege to hunt 7
Requisites and validity of regulations 8
Scope of district court review 16, 17
    Generally 16
    Presidential proclamation 17
Seasonal or time restrictions 13
Tagging requirements 14
Territorial limitations 15

1. Construction
The regulatory authority conferred upon the Secretary of the Interior by this section is liberally construed. Bailey v. Holland, C.C.A.4 (Va.) 1942, 126 F.2d 317.

2. Construction with other laws
The Migratory Bird Conservation Act, section 715 et seq. of this title, does not deprive the Secretary of the Interior of his regulatory authority under this section. Bailey v. Holland, C.C.A.4 (Va.) 1942, 126 F.2d 317.

3. Power of Congress—Generally
Regulation promulgated under this section prohibiting the hunting of migratory wildfowl on land and water adjacent to federally owned Back Bay Migratory Waterfowl Refuge in Virginia is not invalid on ground that the regulation extends the boundaries of government owned reservation and thereby confiscates valuable property right without payment of com-

Exhibit 4–4. Library references and notes of decisions in the *United States Code Annotated*

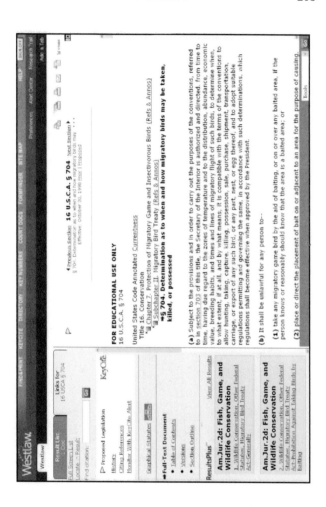

Exhibit 4-5. A *United States Code* section on Westlaw

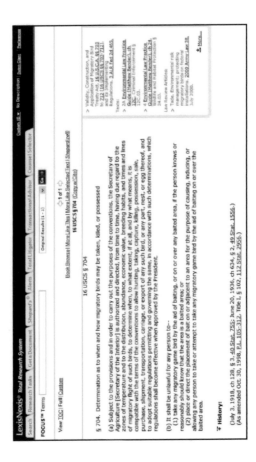

Exhibit 4–6. A *United States Code* section on Lexis

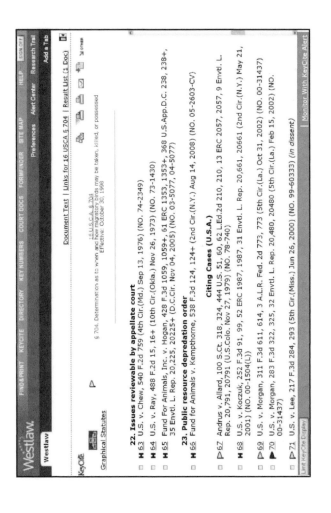

Exhibit 4–7. A KeyCite display for a federal statute

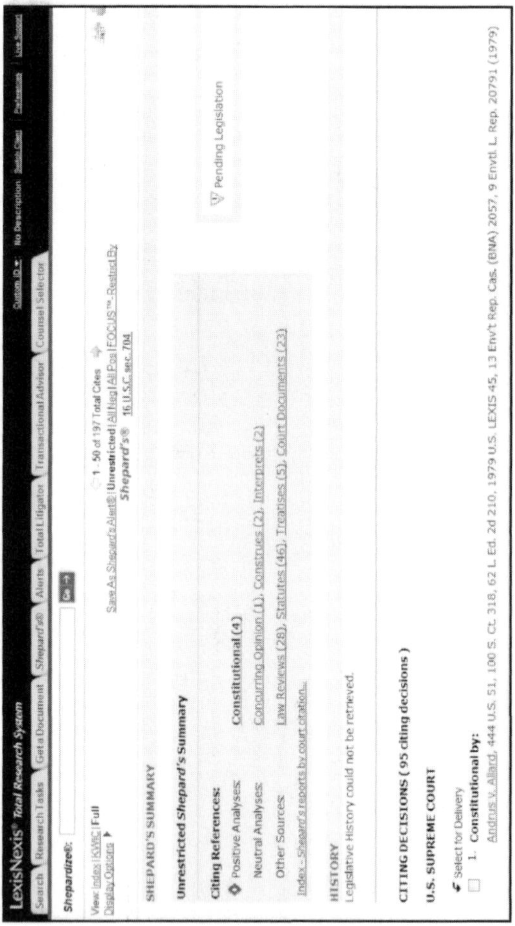

Exhibit 4–8. A Shepard's display for a federal statute

MIGRATORY BIRDS—Continued
Stamps—Continued
  Klamath Marsh, 25 § 564w-1
  Loans, 16 § 718e
  Migratory Bird Conservation Fund, 16 § 718b et seq.
  Military installations, 16 § 670b
  National conservation recreational areas, 16 § 460k-1
  Postal Service, 16 § 718b et seq.
  Production areas, 16 § 718d
  Redemption, 16 § 718b
  Reports, electronic duck stamps, 16 § 718 note
  Retail dealer, definitions, 16 § 718b
  Sales, 16 § 718b et seq.
  Signatures, 16 § 718a
  States, 16 § 718a et seq.
  Time, 16 § 718b
  Transfers, 16 § 718e
  Unused stamps, 16 §§ 718b, 718b-1
  Validity, 16 § 718b
States, 16 § 708
  Acquisitions, 16 § 715k-5
  Cooperation, 16 § 715p
  Sanctuaries, 16 § 715h
  Stamps, 16 § 718a et seq.
~~Take, definitions, conservation, 16 § 715n~~
Taking,
  Indigenous inhabitants of Alaska, 16 § 712
  Killing, possessing, 16 §§ 703, 704
~~Taxation, hunting and conservation stamp,~~ 16 § 718a et seq.
Termination, wetlands, drainage assistance, farms, 16 § 590p-1
Territorial laws permitted, 16 § 708
Time, stamps, 16 § 718b
Transfers,
  Real estate, 16 § 667b et seq.
  Stamps, 16 § 718e
Transportation, 16 § 705
Treaties, 16 § 703 et seq.
Tule Lake National Wildlife Refuge, sump levels, 16 § 695p
Union of Soviet Socialist Republics, 16 § 703
United Mexican States, conventions, 16 § 703
Upper Mississippi River National Wildlife and Fish Refuge, generally, this index
Washington, management, 16 § 666e
Water bank, wetlands, preservation, 16 § 1302
Water supply, 16 § 460l-20
Wetlands and Wetlands Resources, this index

MIGRATORY FISH

Fish and Game, this index

MIKE MANSFIELD FELLOWSHIP ACT

Generally, 22 § 6101 et seq.

MIKEVEH ISRAEL CEMETERY

Independence National Historical Park, 16 § 407m note

MILEAGE

Traveling Expenses, generally, this index

MILES CITY, MT

Fish and game, hatcheries, 16 § 760-2

MILITARY ACADEMIES

Air Force Academy, generally, this index

Coast Guard Academy, generally, this index
Naval Academy, generally, this index
West Point Military Academy, generally, this index

MILITARY AIRLIFT COMMAND

Air Mobility Command, generally, this index

MILITARY APPEALS COURT

Court of Appeals for the Armed Forces, generally, this index

MILITARY ASSISTANCE AND SALES

Generally, 22 § 2301 et seq.
Accounts and accounting, 22 § 2392
  International military education and training, 22 § 2392
  Special accounts, 22 § 2344
Administrative expenses, 22 § 2396
Advisory groups, 22 § 2321i
Afghanistan, 22 § 7531 et seq.
Agents and agencies,
  Discrimination, labor and employment, 22 §§ 2314, 2755
  Drawdowns, 22 § 2318
  Gifts, 22 § 2779
  Reimbursement, 22 §§ 2403, 2770
Agriculture, 22 § 2344 note
Aircraft,
  Civil aircraft equipment, 50 App. § 2416
  Jet aircraft, 22 § 2754
Angola, 50 § 1701 note
Antiterrorism assistance, 22 § 2349aa-2
Appeal and review, exports and imports, lists, 22 § 2778
Application of law, 22 § 2353
Applications, exports and imports, licenses and permits, 22 § 2776
Appointments, special ambassadorial commission for Cyprus and the Aegean, 22 § 2373 note
Appropriations, 22 § 2311 et seq.
  Continuing appropriations, 22 § 2413
  Credits, 22 §§ 2344, 2392
  Economic Support Fund, 22 § 2346a
  International military education and training, 22 §§ 2347 note, 2347a
  Nuclear enrichment equipment, 22 § 2799aa
  Nuclear reprocessing equipment, 22 § 2799aa-1
  Pakistan, 22 § 2375 note
  Peacekeeping operations, 22 § 2348a
  Reimbursement, 22 § 2318
  Supplemental appropriations, 22 § 2312
Approved Force Acquisition Objective, 22 § 2403
Approved Force Retention Stock, 22 § 2403
Argentina, this index
Arms race, 22 §§ 2321d, 2344 note, 2791
Assistant Secretary of State for Democracy, human rights, and labor,
  Discrimination, 22 § 2314
  Reports, 22 § 2304
Atomic energy, 22 § 2793
  Depleted uranium, 22 § 2778a
Australia, this index
Baltic States, nonlethal materials, 22 § 2753 note
Bilateral arms control arrangements, 22 § 2791
Boards and commissions, National Commission on the Use of Offsets in Defense Trade, 50 App. § 2099 note; 50 App. § 2099 note, Ex. Ord. No. 13177
Budget, 22 § 2312
Cannons, large-caliber cannons, 10 § 4542

Exhibit 4–9. A page from the *United States Code* index

871 **POPULAR NAME TABLE**

Migratory Bird Hunting and Conservation Stamp Act (Migratory Bird Hunting Stamp Act) (Duck Stamp Act)—Continued
Nov. 7, 1986, Pub.L. 99–625, § 3, 100 Stat. 3502 (16 § 718b)
Nov. 14, 1988, Pub.L. 100–653, Title III, § 302, 102 Stat. 3827 (16 § 718e)
Oct. 19, 1998, Pub.L. 105–269, § 2, 112 Stat. 2381 (16 § 718d)
Aug. 3, 2006, Pub.L. 109–266, § 10(a) to (h), 120 Stat. 674 (16 §§ 718, 718a, 718b, 718c to 718j)

Migratory Bird Hunting and Conservation Stamp Promotion Act
Short title, see 16 USCA § 718 note
Pub.L. 105–269, Oct. 19, 1998, 112 Stat. 1281 (16 §§ 718 note, 718d)

Migratory Bird Hunting Stamp Act
See Migratory Bird Hunting and Conservation Stamp Act

Migratory Bird Treaty Act (MBTA)
Short title, see 16 USCA § 710
July 3, 1918, ch. 128, 40 Stat. 755 (16 §§ 703 to 708, 709a, 710, 711)
Sept. 8, 1960, Pub.L. 86–732, 74 Stat. 866 (16 § 707)
Dec. 5, 1969, Pub.L. 91–135, § 10, 83 Stat. 282 (16 § 705)
June 1, 1974, Pub.L. 93–300, § 1, 88 Stat. 190 (16 § 703)
Nov. 8, 1978, Pub.L. 95–616, § 3(h), 92 Stat. 3111 (16 § 706)
Dec. 13, 1989, Pub.L. 101–233, § 15, 103 Stat. 1977 (16 § 703)
Oct. 30, 1998, Pub.L. 105–312, Title I, §§ 102, 103, 112 Stat. 2956 (16 §§ 704, 707)

Migratory Bird Treaty Reform Act of 1998
Short title, see 16 USCA § 710 note
Pub.L. 105–312, Title I, Oct. 30, 1998, 112 Stat. 2956 (16 §§ 704, 707, 710 note)

Exhibit 4–10. Excerpt from the *United States Code Annotated* popular name table

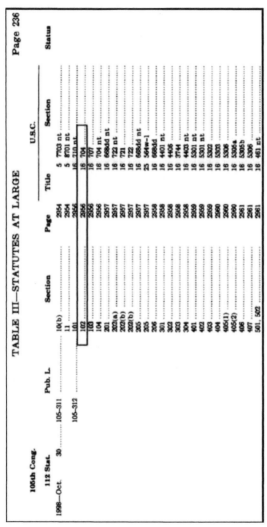

Exhibit 4–11. Excerpt from a parallel reference table in the *United States Code*

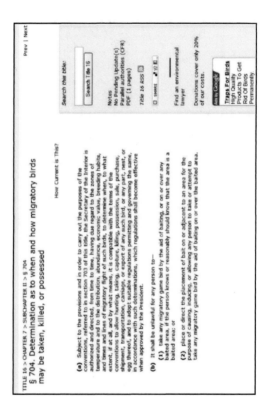

TITLE 16 > CHAPTER 7 > SUBCHAPTER II > § 704.

§ 704. Determination as to when and how migratory birds may be taken, killed, or possessed

How Current Is This?

Prev | Next

(a) Subject to the provisions and in order to carry out the purposes of the conventions, referred to in section 703 of this title, the Secretary of the Interior is authorized and directed, from time to time, having due regard to the zones of temperature and to the distribution, abundance, economic value, breeding habits, and times and lines of migratory flight of such birds, to determine when, to what extent, if at all, and by what means, it is compatible with the terms of the conventions to allow hunting, taking, capture, killing, possession, sale, purchase, shipment, transportation, carriage, or export of any such bird, or any part, nest, or egg thereof, and to adopt suitable regulations permitting and governing the same, in accordance with such determinations, which regulations shall become effective when approved by the President.

(b) It shall be unlawful for any person to—

  (1) take any migratory game bird by the aid of baiting, or on or over any baited area, if the person knows or reasonably should know that the area is a baited area; or

  (2) place or direct the placement of bait on or adjacent to an area for the purpose of causing, inducing, or allowing any person to take or attempt to take any migratory game bird by the aid of baiting on or over the baited area.

Search this title:

Search Title 16

Notes
No Pending Update(s)
Parallel authorities (CFR)
PDF (1 pages)
Title 16 RSS

Share

Find an environmental lawyer

Donations cover only 20% of our costs.

Ads by Google

Traps For Birds
High Quality Products To Get Rid Of Birds Permanently

Exhibit 4–12. A *United States Code* section on the Legal Information Institute website

TITLES OF UNITED STATES CODE

*1. General Provisions.

2. The Congress.

*3. The President.

*4. Flag and Seal, Seat of Government, and the States.

*5. Government Organization and Employees; and Appendix.

6. Domestic Security.

7. Agriculture.

8. Aliens and Nationality.

*9. Arbitration.

*10. Armed Forces.

*11. Bankruptcy; and Appendix.

12. Banks and Banking.

*13. Census.

*14. Coast Guard.

15. Commerce and Trade.

16. Conservation.

*17. Copyrights.

*18. Crimes and Criminal Procedure; and Appendix.

19. Customs Duties.

20. Education.

21. Food and Drugs.

22. Foreign Relations and Intercourse.

*23. Highways.

24. Hospitals and Asylums.

25. Indians.

26. Internal Revenue Code.

27. Intoxicating Liquors.

*28. Judiciary and Judicial Procedure; and Appendix.

29. Labor.

30. Mineral Lands and Mining.

*31. Money and Finance.

*32. National Guard.

33. Navigation and Navigable Waters.

†34. [Navy.]

*35. Patents.

*36. Patriotic and National Observances, Ceremonies, and Organizations.

*37. Pay and Allowances of the Uniformed Services.

*38. Veterans' Benefits.

*39. Postal Service.

*40. Public Buildings, Property, and Works.

41. Public Contracts.

42. The Public Health and Welfare.

43. Public Lands.

*44. Public Printing and Documents.

45. Railroads.

*46. Shipping.

47. Telegraphs, Telephones, and Radiotelegraphs.

48. Territories and Insular Possessions.

*49. Transportation.

50. War and National Defense; and Appendix.

*This title has been enacted as positive law. However, any Appendix to this title has not been enacted as positive law.
†This title was eliminated by the enactment of Title 10.

Exhibit 4–13. *United States Code* titles, indicating those enacted into positive law

CHAPTER 6

REGULATION OF BIRDS AND MAMMALS

14-22-6-1. Unlawful acts regarding wild animals. — A person may not take, chase, or possess a wild animal, except as provided by:

(1) A statute; or

(2) A rule adopted under IC 4-22-2 to implement this article.

[P.L.1-1995, § 15.]

14-22-6-2. Unlawful acts regarding migratory birds. — A person may not:

(1) Take, possess, sell, offer for sale, purchase, or offer to purchase;

(2) Ship, transport, or carry; or

(3) Deliver or receive for shipment, transportation, or carriage in any manner outside Indiana;

a migratory bird designated in this article or a part, nest, or egg of a migratory bird, except as otherwise permitted by this article.

[P.L.1-1995, § 15.]

NOTES TO DECISIONS

ANALYSIS

Constitutionality.
Construction.

Constitutionality.

An individual of ordinary intelligence would have comprehended former IC 14-2-4-1(1) (see now this section) to fairly inform him that the illegal taking or possession of a migratory bird within the state of Indiana constituted an offense under the statute, and the statute itself did not render a charging information inadequate because the statute was vague. Boushehry v. State, 648 N.E.2d 1174 (Ind. App. 1995).

Construction.

The logical construction of the phrase in former IC 14-2-4-1 (see now this section), "beyond the limits of the state of Indiana" modified only the verbs "to ship, transport, or carry, or to deliver or receive for shipment, transportation, or carriage in any manner." Boushehry v. State, 648 N.E.2d 1174 (Ind. App. 1995).

Collateral References. Applicability, to domesticated or captive game, of game laws relating to closed season and the like. 74 A.L.R.2d 974.

Exhibit 4–14. A page from *Burns Indiana Statutes Annotated*

Exhibit 4–15.   Martindale-Hubbell Law Digest on Lexis

LexisNexis® *Total Research System*

Custom ID ▾ : No Description | Switch Client | Preferences | Live Support | Sign Out | Help

Search | Research Tasks | Get a Document | Shepard's | Alerts | Total Litigator | Transactional Advisor | Counsel Selector

History

FOCUS™ Terms [section(environmental regulation)]   Search Within [Original Results (1 - 54)] ▾ Go → Advanced...

View: TOC | Cite | KWIC | Full | Custom   ⇑ 42 of 54 ⇓

Book Browse | Save As Alert | More Like This | More Like Selected Text

1-1 SC - Martindale-Hubbell(R) Law Digest 12.01 (Copy w/ Cite)   Pages: 3

1 SOUTH CAROLINA LAW DIGEST
12 ENVIRONMENT

1-1 SC - Martindale-Hubbell(R) Law Digest 12.01

12.01 ENVIRONMENTAL REGULATION:

General Supervision.

Department of Health and Environmental Control has jurisdiction over quality of air and waters with authority to abate, control, and prevent pollution under Pollution Control Act. (S.C. Code Ann. § 48-1-10 to -350). Act gives department authority to set standards for air and water quality, and makes it unlawful to discharge organic or inorganic matter into air or water, without permit from department. Evidence of violation of air pollution regulations is sufficient to submit question of punitive damages to jury. (289 S.C. 325, 345 S.E.2d 495).

Highways subject to advertising and junkyard control by Department of Transportation. (S.C. Code Ann. § 57-25-110 to -710 and S.C. Code Ann. § 57-27-10 to -100). http://www.dot.state.sc.us/doing/odas.shtml.

Enforcement.

Department is empowered to hold hearings, compel attendance of witnesses, make findings of fact, issue orders and assess penalties. It may institute legal proceedings to compel compliance with Pollution Control Act or determinations and orders of department. (S.C. Code Ann. § 48-1-50).

▲ Outline   Page [Selector Reporter]   ◀ Doc 42 of 54 ▶ ◀ Term of 1 ▶

Animals	Subject Compilations

Table. Cites to codes. Covers felony or misdemeanor status of cock-fighting, possessing cocks for fighting, attending a cockfight, or possessing cockfighting implements. Current as of Sept. 2005.

5161.03 "Dogfighting: State Laws." *Humane Society of the United States* http://www.hsus.org/web-files/PDF/Dogfighting_StateLaws_citation s_June05.pdf.

Table. Cites to codes. Covers felony or misdemeanor status of attending a dogfight, dogfighting, or possessing dogs for fighting. Includes Guam, Puerto Rico, and the Virgin Islands. Current as of July 2005.

5161.04 Fox, Camilla H.; Papouchis, Christopher M. *Coyotes in Our Midst: Coexisting with an Adaptable and Resilient Carnivore*. Sacramento: Animal Protection Institute, 2005. 64 pp. OCLC 61912322.

Pp. 44-64, "Appendix: State Classification and Management of Coyotes." Table. Cites to codes and regulations. Covers depredation, hunting, and trapping. Includes forty-eight states.

Note: Available at http://www.api4animals.org. Free registration required.

5161.05 Gerwin, Kara. "There's (Almost) No Place Like Home: Kansas Remains in the Minority on Protecting Animals from Cruelty." *Kansas Journal of Law & Public Policy* 15 (2005):125-57.

Pp. 149-50, fn. 10. Citations only. Cites to codes. Covers the forty-five states that have laws on "felony prosecution of animal cruelty."

P. 155, fns. 161 and 162. Citations only. Cites to codes. Covers the forty-two states that have animal cruelty laws with felony provisions for first-time offenders (fn. 161) and the twenty-five states that "either allow or require courts to order psychological counseling or anger management upon conviction of animal cruelty" (fn. 162).

5161.06 Hussain, Safia Gray. "Attacking the Dog-Bite Epidemic: Why Breed-Specific Legislation Won't Solve the Dangerous-Dog Dilemma." *Fordham Law Review* 74 (2006):2847-87.

P. 2855, fn. 71. Citations only. Cites to codes. Covers the thirty-four states that have laws on dangerous dogs or vicious animals.

Exhibit 4–16. A page from *Subject Compilations of State Laws*

EXECUTIVE DEPARTMENT

ARTICLE II

SECTION 1. Clause 1. The executive Power shall be vested in a President of the United States of America. He shall hold his Office during the Term of four Years and, together with the Vice President, chosen for the same Term, be elected, as follows:

NATURE AND SCOPE OF PRESIDENTIAL POWER

Creation of the Presidency

Of all the issues confronting the members of the Philadelphia Convention, the nature of the presidency ranks among the most important and the resolution of the question one of the most significant steps taken.[1] The immediate source of Article II was the New York constitution, in which the governor was elected by the people and thus independent of the legislature, his term was three years and he was indefinitely re-eligible, his decisions except with regard to appointments and vetoes were unencumbered with a council, he was in charge of the militia, he possessed the pardoning power, and he was charged to take care that the laws were faithfully executed.[2] But when the Convention assembled and almost to its closing days, there was no assurance that the executive department would not be headed by plural administrators, would not be unalterably tied to the legislature, and would not be devoid of many of the powers normally associated with an executive.

Debate in the Convention proceeded against a background of many things, but most certainly uppermost in the delegates' minds was the experience of the States and of the national government under the Articles of Confederation. Reacting to the exercise of powers by the royal governors, the framers of the state constitu-

---

[1] The background and the action of the Convention is comprehensively examined in C. THACH, THE CREATION OF THE PRESIDENCY 1775-1789 (1923). A review of the Constitution's provisions being put into operation is J. HART, THE AMERICAN PRESIDENCY IN ACTION 1789 (1948).

[2] Hamilton observed the similarities and differences between the President and the New York Governor in THE FEDERALIST, No. 69 (J. Cooke ed. 1961), 462-470. On the text, *see* New York Constitution of 1777, Articles XVII-XIX, in 5 F. Thorpe, *The Federal and State Constitutions*, H. DOC. NO. 357, 59th Congress, 2d sess. (1909), 2632-2633.

433

Exhibit 4–17. A page from *The Constitution of the United States of America: Analysis and Interpretation*

CHAPTER 5

LEGISLATIVE INFORMATION

―――――――

―――――――

§ 5–1. Introduction

Statutory language is often ambiguous, and lawyers and scholars frequently try to discern the intended purpose of an act or the meaning of particular terminology through the legislative documents created during its enactment. Researchers also need to investigate the current progress of proposed laws under consideration by the legislature. These processes—determining the meaning or intent of an enacted law, and ascertaining the status of a pending bill—comprise legislative history research.

The use of legislative history in statutory construction is controversial, with strong disagreement within the Supreme Court and among commentators. Judges have traditionally used congressional materials to interpret ambiguous statutory language, but textualist critics insist that meaning must be determined from the statutory language alone. Despite this criticism, most judges rely on legislative history sources to correct drafting errors, to provide information on specialized meanings of terms, or to identify the purpose of a statutory phrase.

There can be striking differences between federal and state legislative history research. Federal legislative history is thoroughly documented with numerous sources, while the lack of available information often makes state legislative history research quite frustrating. On both federal and state levels, the status of pending legislation and documents relating to recently passed acts are available from government websites. Research into the background of older acts of Congress, however, still requires access to printed sources, and resources on older state laws, if they exist at all, may be found only on tape recordings or in archives at the state capitol.

§ 5–2. Federal Legislative History Sources

Consideration of legislative history begins with the legislative process itself—how a bill wends its way through Congress or a state legislature. The documents of legislative history must be understood in the context of the parliamentary practices that produce them. The federal process is often long and complicated, beginning formally with the introduction of a bill and ending with passage by both houses of Congress of either an act or a joint resolution, and its approval by the President (or repassage over a presidential veto).

Overviews of federal lawmaking procedures can be found in two brief congressional guides prepared by the House and Senate parliamentarians, *How Our Laws Are Made* and *Enactment of a Law*, available from the Library of Congress' THOMAS system <thomas.loc.gov>, under the heading "The Legislative Process." More extensive guides include Charles Tiefer, *Congressional Practice and Procedure: A Reference, Research, and Legislative Guide* (1989), and Walter J. Oleszek, *Congressional Procedures and the Policy Process* (7th ed. 2007). Congressional Quarterly's *Guide to Congress* (6th ed. 2008) has a wide range of political, historical, and statistical information; Part III, Congressional Procedures, is particularly useful in understanding committee and floor action.

Each stage in the enactment of a federal law may result in a significant legislative history document.

The most important potential steps in the legislative process and their related documents are:

Action	Document
Preliminary inquiry	Transcripts of hearings on the general subject of the proposed legislation
Executive recommendation	Presidential message proposing an administration bill
Introduction of bill and referral to committee	Slip bill as introduced
Hearings on bill	Transcript of testimony and exhibits
Approval by committee	Committee report, including committee's version of bill
Legislative debates	*Congressional Record*, sometimes including texts of bill in amended forms
Passage by first house	Final House or Senate version of the proposed legislation
Consideration by other house	Generally same procedure and documents as above
Referral to conference committee (if texts passed by houses differ)	Conference committee version of bill; conference committee report
Passage of identical bill by both houses	Enrolled bill sent to President

Action	**Document**
Approval by President	Presidential signing statement; slip law, subsequently published in *Statutes at Large* and classified by subject in the *U.S. Code*

Of the many types of documents issued by Congress, a few are particularly important for legislative history research. *Bills* are the major source for the texts of pending or unenacted legislation. *Committee reports* analyze and describe bills and are usually considered the most authoritative sources of congressional intent. *Floor debates* may contain a sponsor's interpretation of a bill or the only explanation of last-minute amendments. *Hearings* can provide useful background on the purpose of an act.

This section introduces these various documents, with a brief explanation of how they are published and their availability in electronic sources including THOMAS <thomas.loc.gov>, the Library of Congress website for legislative information, and the Government Printing Office's Federal Digital System (FDSys) <www.gpo.gov/fdsys/>, as well as Westlaw and Lexis. Section 5–3 then looks in greater depth at using these and other sources for legislative history research.

a. Bills

The texts of bills are needed by researchers interested in pending or failed legislation, and may also help in interpreting enacted laws. Variations among the bills and amendments can aid in determining the intended meaning of an act, as each deletion or addition made during the legislative process implies a deliberate choice of language by the legislators.

Bills are numbered in separate series for each chamber, and retain their identifying numbers through both sessions of a Congress. Pending bills lapse at the end of the two-year term, and a new bill must be reintroduced the following term if it is to be considered.

Some public laws arise from *joint resolutions* rather than bills. These usually, but not always, deal with matters of a limited or temporary nature. Joint resolutions and bills differ in form but have the same legal effect. Two other forms of resolution do not have the force of law: *concurrent resolutions* expressing the opinion of both chambers of Congress, and *simple resolutions* concerning the procedures or expressions of just one chamber.

Often bills with similar or identical language, known as *companion bills*, are introduced in both the House and Senate. If each chamber passes its own bill, however, there is no single *enrolled bill* that has passed both chambers and can be presented to the President. Congress frequently employs a procedure known as an *amendment in the nature of a substitute*, which deletes everything after the enacting clause ("Be it enacted by the Senate and House of Representatives of the United States of America in Congress assembled") and inserts new text in its place. Sometimes this is done simply because it is more convenient to replace an entire bill than to make specific changes, but it also permits the House and Senate to pass the same bill so that it can go to the President and become law. The significance of this for researchers is that the number of the bill that becomes law may be different from the number of the version that was the subject of congressional hearings, committee reports, or perhaps even floor debates. The key language in an enacted law may have come from a bill with a different number and a different set of legislative history documents.

Bills are available electronically from several sources. THOMAS has the text of bills since 1989, and FDSys begins coverage in 1993 with PDF files replicating the printed bills. Texts of bills are also available online from commercial electronic services, including Lexis (1989–date) and Westlaw (1995–date). Older bills are available in microform in many larger law libraries.

Exhibit 5–1 on page 251 shows the bill H.R. 137 as introduced in the House in 2007, printed from the FDSys website. This is the bill that would become the Animal Fighting Prohibition Enforcement Act of 2007, Pub. L. 110–22, 121 Stat. 88.

b. Committee Reports

Reports are generally considered the most important sources of legislative history. They are issued by the committees of each chamber on bills they approve and send to the floor for consideration, and by conference committees of the two chambers to reconcile differences between bills passed by the House and Senate. (Committees also issue reports on investigations, nominations, and other matters not related to pending legislation.) Reports usually include the text of the bill, describe its contents and purposes, and give reasons for the committee's recommendations, sometimes with minority views. One of the most informative portions of a committee report is the section-by-section analysis of the bill, explaining the purpose and meaning of each provision.

Committee reports are identified by chamber, Congress, and report number, with conference committee reports included in the series of House reports. Exhibit 5–2 on page 252 shows the first page of H.R. Rep. No. 110–27, pt. 1 (2007), reporting the House Committee on the Judiciary's views on the Animal Fighting Prohibition Enforcement Act.

The committee reports for a session are collected, along with House and Senate Documents, in an official compilation called the *Serial Set*. (Bound *Serial Set* volumes after 1996 are not widely distributed, but some libraries bind their own sets of individual reports.) THOMAS and FDSys coverage begins in 1995, and Westlaw and Lexis have all committee reports beginning in 1990 as well as selected earlier reports. LexisNexis U.S. Serial Set Digital Collection, covering 1789–date, and Readex's U.S. Congressional Serial Set (1817–1994) have retrospective, full-text digital coverage, and selected reports are also reprinted in *United States Code*

Congressional   and   Administrative   News (*USCCAN*).

Reports are the final product of committee deliberation. Committees reach consensus through *markup sessions*, but the transcripts of these sessions are rarely published and only sometimes available online. Newspapers and wire services reporting on Capitol Hill often provide coverage of markup sessions, in articles available through online services including Westlaw and Lexis.

c. Debates

As sources of legislative intent, debates in the House and Senate are generally not as influential as committee reports. While reports represent the considered opinion of those legislators who have studied a bill most closely, floor statements are often political hyperbole and may not even represent the views of the proposed legislation's supporters. The most influential statements are those from a bill's sponsor or its floor managers (the committee members responsible for steering the bill through consideration). These may even correct errors in a committee report or explain aspects of a bill not discussed in the report.

In a few instances, floor debates are the best available legislative history source. Bills can be amended on the floor, sometimes with language that was not considered in committee and thus was not discussed in a committee report. If so, the record of floor debate may be the only available explanation of the intended purpose of an amendment.

The source for debates is the *Congressional Record*, published each day that either chamber is in session. Each daily issue has separately paginated "S" and "H" sections for Senate and House proceedings. The *Record* provides a more or less verbatim transcript of the legislative debates and proceedings, but legislators have the opportunity to revise their remarks and to insert material that was not actually spoken. Material that was not spoken is generally indicated in the House proceedings by a different typeface. Some inserted text in the Senate proceedings is indicated by the use of bullet symbols, but extended colloquies can be added with no indication that they were never heard on the floor of the Senate.

The *Congressional Record* includes the text of conference committee reports, but it rarely reprints other committee reports and never contains hearings. Bills are sometimes printed in the *Record*, particularly if they have been amended on the floor or in conference committee. The *Congressional Record*'s primary role, however, is as a report of debates and actions taken. An excerpt from the *Record*, with House consideration of the Animal Fighting Prohibition Enforcement Act, is shown in Exhibit 5–3 on page 253.

Each *Congressional Record* issue contains a Daily Digest summarizing the day's activities. The digest lists the bills introduced, reports filed, measures debated or passed, and committee meetings held. A cumulative index to the *Record*, by subject, name of legislator, and title of legislation, is available on the FDSys website. A History of Bills and Resolutions table has status information and page references by bill number for the session. A printed version of the index and table is published every two weeks but does not cumulate over the course of the session.

The daily edition of the *Congressional Record* is available electronically through several online sources. Coverage begins in 1989 on THOMAS, and in 1994 from FDSys. THOMAS's version has links from the index and Daily Digest to *Record* pages and to bill texts, while FDSys has the *Record* in PDF format replicating the printed version. Westlaw and Lexis coverage extends back to 1985.

A bound permanent edition of the *Congressional Record* is published several years after the end of each session. Once the permanent edition is published, it becomes the standard source to be cited for congressional debates. The daily and permanent editions have the same volume numbers, but the permanent edition renumbers the separate House and Senate pages into one sequence.

Neither Westlaw nor Lexis has the permanent edition of the *Congressional Record*, but it is available electronically from three other sources. FDSys is adding the permanent edition to its database, but thus far only three volumes are available (volume 145–147, 1999–2001). Two commercial databases, HeinOnline and the LexisNexis Congressional Record Permanent Digital Collection, have retrospective coverage back to the first volume in 1873. HeinOnline is in the process of adding a date-matching tool to convert a daily edition citation to a permanent edition citation, easing what has in the past been an onerous process, and LexisNexis has plans to provide a similar feature. To find the permanent edition citation without these databases, you will usually need to start in the index or the Daily Digest by looking for references to the topic or speaker, or you can browse through the pages looking for a specific passage.

The predecessors of the *Congressional Record* were the *Annals of Congress* (1789–1824); the *Register of Debates* (1824–37); and the *Congressional Globe* (1833–73). All of these earlier publications, as well as the *Congressional Record* for 1873–77, are available online through the Library of Congress "A Century of Lawmaking for a New Nation" site <memory.loc.gov/ammem/amlaw/>.

House and *Senate Journals* are also published (and are, in fact, the only congressional publications required by the Constitution). Unlike the *Congressional Record*, however, these do not include the verbatim debates. The journals merely record the proceedings and report the resulting action and votes taken. The *House Journal* is more voluminous and includes the texts of bills and amendments given floor consideration. Both journals include History of Bills and Resolutions tables and indexes.

d. Hearings

Senate and House committees hold hearings on proposed legislation and on other subjects under congressional investigation such as nominations or impeachments. Government officials, scholars, and interest group representatives deliver prepared statements and answer questions from committee members. The transcripts of most hearings are published, accompanied by submitted material such as letters and article reprints. Hearings are not required for every bill, and legislation is frequently enacted without hearings in one or both chambers.

Hearings provide useful background information, but they are not generally considered persuasive sources of legislative history on the meaning of an enacted bill. Their importance as evidence of legislative intent is limited because they focus more on the views of interested parties rather than those of the lawmakers themselves.

Unlike committee reports, hearings are not issued in one numbered series for each chamber. Instead they are generally identified by the title on the cover, the name of the subcommittee and committee, the term of Congress, and the year. Exhibit 5–4 on page 254 shows the first page of *Animal Fighting Prohibition Enforcement Act of 2005: Hearing Before the Subcomm. on Crime, Terrorism, and Homeland Security of the H. Comm. on the Judiciary*, 109th Cong. (2005), on an earlier version of the bill eventually passed in 2007.

Most committee websites (linked from the Senate <www.senate.gov> and House <www.house.gov> sites) provide access to material from current hearings, including prepared statements of legislators and witnesses, and selected hearings beginning in 1995 are available online from FDSys. Westlaw and Lexis usually have witnesses' prepared statements and commercially prepared transcripts well before the official versions are published. The major retrospective online source for hearings is the LexisNexis Congressional Hearings Digital Collection, with approximately 120,000 hearings back to 1824.

e. Other Congressional Publications

Congress also produces a variety of other publications which are less frequently consulted in legislative history research. These can be important sources of information, however, on statutes, legislative policies, and the workings of the federal government.

Committee Prints. These contain a variety of material prepared for committee use, ranging from studies by its staff or outside experts to compilations of earlier legislative history documents. Some prints contain statements by committee members on pending bills. Others can be useful analyses of laws under the jurisdiction of a committee, such as the House's biennial *Green Book: Background Material and Data on Major Programs Within the Jurisdiction of the Committee on Ways and Means*. Committee prints are not as widely available online as reports or hearings. Selective coverage through Lexis begins in 1994, and FDSys has a limited number of prints beginning in 1997. The most comprehensive subscription source is the LexisNexis Congressional Research Digital Collection, which includes thousands of committee prints dating back to 1830.

House and Senate Documents. These include material such as the *Budget of the United States Government*, special studies or exhibits prepared for Congress, presidential messages, and communications from executive agencies. They are issued in a numbered series for each chamber as part of the official *Serial Set*, and are available starting in 1995 through FDSys and Lexis. Older documents are available through the LexisNexis U.S. Serial Set Digital Collection and Readex's U.S. Congressional Serial Set (1817–1994).

Treaty Documents and Senate Executive Reports. The Senate issues two series of publications in the process of treaty ratification. *Treaty documents* contain the texts of treaties before the Senate for its advice and consent, and *Senate executive reports* from the Foreign Relations Committee contain its recommendations on pending treaties. These publications are discussed more fully in Chapter 9.

Legislative Agencies. Congress also supervises three major investigative and research agencies that produce a range of important analyses and reports. The Congressional Budget Office (CBO) <www.cbo. gov> produces cost estimates for bills reported out of committee as well as a variety of budget reports, analytical studies, and background papers. The Government Accountability Office (GAO) <www.gao.gov> (formerly the General Accounting Office) studies the programs and expenditures of the federal government, and frequently recommends specific congressional actions. The CBO and GAO websites have reports and other documents, and GAO reports back to 1994 are also available through FDSys, Westlaw, and Lexis.

The third and most wide-ranging research arm of Congress is the Congressional Research Service (CRS). Each year it produces several thousand reports, including legal and policy analyses, economic studies, bibliographies, statistical reviews, and issue briefs with background information on major legislative issues. The CRS has no publicly accessible website and does not publish its reports, but they are regularly made available by others. Several sites have links to thousands of CRS reports available online, including Open CRS <www.opencrs.com> and the University of North Texas Libraries' Congressional Research Service Reports site <digital.library.unt.edu/govdocs/crs/>. CRS reports back to 1916 are available through the subscription-based LexisNexis Congressional Research Digital Collection, and LexisNexis publishes a microform edition of these reports as *Major Studies and Issue Briefs of the Congressional Research Service*. An online guide to CRS reports <www.llrx.com/features/crsreports.htm> has links to numerous other sources.

§ 5–3. Congressional Research Resources

While researchers are interested in Congress for numerous reasons, this discussion focuses on tools useful for two basic legal research tasks: investigating the meaning of an enacted law, and tracking the status of pending legislation. You can use a number of approaches for these purposes. For recently enacted laws and pending legislation, several electronic resources are available. For older bills, the choices dwindle to a few tools with retrospective coverage.

Compiling a legislative history can be a time-consuming and ultimately frustrating endeavor. Even after finding all the relevant legislative materials on a statute, you may learn that Congress never explained or discussed the particular language at issue. The increasing use of omnibus legislation and unorthodox procedures creates further frustration. Numerous bills are often combined into mammoth enactments of several hundred pages, and materials addressing a particular provision within a huge omnibus bill can be far more difficult to locate than those on a bill with one discrete subject. In other instances bills bypass the committee process and go directly to the floor for consideration, meaning that there may be no relevant committee reports or hearings.

The bill number is usually the key to finding congressional documents or tracing legislative action. It appears on an enacted law both in its slip form and in the *Statutes at Large*. In the enacted

Animal Fighting Prohibition Enforcement Act of 2007, shown in Exhibit 5–5 on page 255, note that the bill number (H.R. 137) is included in brackets in the left margin. Bill numbers have been included in *Statutes at Large* since 1903; earlier numbers can be found in Eugene Nabors, *Legislative Reference Checklist* (1982), available in HeinOnline's U.S. Federal Legislative History Library. Bill numbers do not appear, unfortunately, in the *United States Code* or in either of its annotated editions.

A quick head start in legislative history research can come from the Public Law itself. At the end of each act, in either slip law or *Statutes at Large*, a brief legislative history summary has dates of consideration and passage in each chamber, and citations of committee reports and presidential signing statements. References to hearings or to reports from earlier Congresses are not included. Summaries have appeared at the end of each law passed since 1975, and in "Guide to Legislative History" tables in *Statutes at Large* volumes from 1963 to 1974.

One of the most useful resources in legislative history research is the Law Librarians' Society of Washington, D.C.'s Legislative Source Book <www.llsdc.org/sourcebook/>. This site includes features such as links to congressional committee publications, questions and answers on legislative research, and a practitioner's guide to compiling a federal legislative history.

Which legislative history research resources to use in any particular circumstance depends on the date of the law and the scope of information you need. A compiled legislative history, if available, may have done most of your work for you. The most up-to-date information on current legislation is found in THOMAS or one of the other online bill-tracking services. The most comprehensive coverage of documents relating to enacted laws is usually found in CIS materials. The quickest way to find and read a committee report may be to see what is reprinted in *USCCAN*. For legislative history information on older laws, the *Congressional Record*'s History of Bills and Resolutions, which dates back to the nineteenth century, may be the only available resource.

a. Compiled Legislative Histories

The documents making up a legislative history can be scattered among many publications and may be difficult to obtain. For some major enactments, however, compiled legislative histories reprint the important bills, debates, committee reports, and hearings.

Online compiled legislative histories, including bills and committee reports, are available on Westlaw and Lexis for several dozen major acts in areas such as bankruptcy, tax, and environmental law. Westlaw has several thousand compilations prepared by the General Accounting Office from 1915 to 1995, listing reports, *Congressional Record* excerpts, and hearings, with links to most documents in PDF. HeinOnline's Legislative History Library has searchable PDFs of documents for dozens of acts, including major legislation in areas such as environmental law, immigration, intellectual property, labor law, and taxation.

You can determine what legislative histories are available on Westlaw, Lexis, and HeinOnline through the Legislative Source Book's "Commercial Legislative Histories of U.S. Laws on the Internet" page <www.llsdc.org/leg-hist-commercial>, which includes links to the sources it lists. Nancy P. Johnson, *Sources of Compiled Legislative Histories* (1979–date), available in print and as part of HeinOnline's U.S. Federal Legislative History Library, provides a checklist of print and online sources for acts as far back as 1789. It covers not only collections that reprint the documents but also law review articles and other sources that list and discuss the relevant materials.

b.   THOMAS and Other Congressional Websites

For current legislation or laws enacted since 1973, one of the easiest places to begin research is THOMAS <thomas.loc.gov>, the official congressional site for legislative information. THOMAS has both the text of bills and summaries of their status or legislative history. You can search either bill text or bill summaries by keyword or bill number. Legislative history summaries are available in THOMAS for laws enacted since 1973, but summaries for older laws lack some of the features included for more recent legislation. Links to the text of legislation, for example, are available beginning in 1989, and *Congressional Record* page references and links begin in 1993. A portion of the THOMAS summary for H.R. 137, the bill that became the Animal Fighting Prohibition Enforcement Act of 2007, is shown in Exhibit 5–6 on page 256. This excerpt shows the "Major Actions" section, with links to the House report, a record of the House vote, and the public law.

THOMAS has the text of many congressional documents, and it also includes links to the Government Printing Office's FDSys website <www.gpo.gov/fdsys/>, which provides these documents as PDF files. FDSys is the more comprehensive source for documents, but it has no links between its congressional documents and does not provide bill summaries or status information.

THOMAS and FDSys are the major comprehensive websites for congressional information. In addition, each chamber maintains a website with general information as well as links to pages for individual members and committees. Most committee homepages have summaries of major pending legislation, background information, hearing statements, and schedules of upcoming meetings.

c. LexisNexis Congressional and CIS

Congressional Information Service, Inc. (CIS), a subsidiary of LexisNexis, indexes virtually all congressional publications since 1789 and publishes full-text copies of these publications either online or in microform. CIS speeds legislative history research by providing a list of all documents related to an enactment, as well as access to the documents themselves.

CIS indexing is available through Lexis, and universities, colleges and law schools have access to more extensive resources through LexisNexis Congressional <web.lexis-nexis.com/congcomp/>. LexisNexis Congressional and the print *CIS Index* contain abstracts of reports, hearings, prints, and documents. Exhibit 5–7 on page 257 shows the CIS abstract for the hearing shown in Exhibit 5–4 on page 254, indicating the names and affiliations of the witnesses and the focus of their testimony. Abstracts provide both the Superintendent of Documents classification (e.g., Y 4.J 89/1:109–115) used in most libraries for locating government publications and the CIS number (e.g., H521–73) used to find documents in CIS's online and microfiche collections.

CIS legislative history coverage varies, depending on the date of enactment. For laws passed since 1984, LexisNexis Congressional and *CIS Index Legislative Histories* volumes have summaries of relevant bills, hearings, reports, debates, presidential documents and any other legislative actions. Rather than limiting coverage to a single term of Congress, these summaries also include references to bills, reports, and hearings from prior terms. A summary for a complex and lengthy act can span several years and list hundreds of items. CIS legislative histories are generally considered the most complete and descriptive compilations available for Acts of Congress. Exhibit 5–8 on page 258 shows the beginning of the CIS legislative history for the Animal Fighting Prohibition Enforcement Act. The page shown includes references to reports, bills and debate from the 108th, 109th and 110th Congresses.

From 1970 to 1983, LexisNexis Congressional and *CIS Index Abstracts* volumes include legislative histories of enacted laws, but these are less convenient to use because they simply list the CIS numbers for the reports, hearings and other materials listed. You need to retrieve the abstracts for more information, but these summaries nonetheless span multiple terms of Congress and are among the most thorough sources available for their period.

Acts before 1970 are not covered by compiled legislative histories, but CIS's thorough retrospective indexing means that reports and hearings on a particular bill are linked to that bill. In LexisNexis Congressional you can search for any documents associated with a particular bill or public law by using the "Search by Number–Find Congressional publications related to a bill or law" feature. This doesn't cover bills in earlier terms of Congress, so it should be supplemented by keyword searching or other approaches. The pre–1970 indexes are available on Lexis as the CIS/Historical Index file. LexisNexis Congressional's digital collections have the full text of most of the material listed.

Other features of LexisNexis Congressional include bill-tracking summaries; transcripts of hearing testimony; and information on committees and legislators. Besides its CIS files, Lexis has other resources for legislative history research such as the full text of bills, committee reports, and the *Congressional Record* as well as bill-tracking databases.

d.   *USCCAN* and Westlaw

United States Code Congressional and Administrative News (*USCCAN*) was mentioned in Chapter 4 as a source for the texts of enacted laws. For major acts it also reprints one or more committee reports, making it a convenient source for basic legislative research. *USCCAN* generally prints either a House or Senate report and the conference committee report, if one was issued. It also lists the citations of some reports it does not reprint and the dates of consideration in the *Congressional Record*. The major benefit of *USCCAN* is its ready availability in many smaller libraries that do not have very extensive collections of congressional materials.

The public laws and committee reports are published in separate "Laws" and "Legislative History" sections of *USCCAN*. Each section prints material in order by public law number, with cross-references between the sections. Exhibit 5–9 on page 259 shows the beginning of the House report on the Animal Fighting Prohibition Enforcement Act, as set out in *USCCAN*. The report is preceded by references to dates of consideration and passage in each chamber, but it does not include *Congressional Record* page citations.

USCCAN has been printing committee reports since 1941. Westlaw has the reports reprinted in *USCCAN* beginning in 1948, and all congressional commitee reports since 1990, including reports on bills that did not become law.

One reason that *USCCAN* legislative histories are convenient is that references to them are included in the notes in the *United States Code Annotated*. Westlaw's online version of *USCA* has links from the statutory notes to the *USCCAN* summary and reports, making it easy to get from a code section to the committee reports. Note, however, that a reference after a specific section means only that legislative history on the act as a whole is available, not that pertinent material on that specific section will be found.

USCCAN has only selective coverage of committee reports, and further research is often required. There are no references to hearings, prints, documents, or materials from previous Congresses, so anyone preparing a complete legislative history will need to use other resources. But it is a handy starting point, and the material in *USCCAN* may be sufficient if all you need is general background or a quick section-by-section analysis.

As noted earlier, Westlaw also has resources such as bills, committee reports, the *Congressional Record*, and compiled legislative histories. One means of access to these resources is through the Westlaw

Tab for "Legislative History—Fed," which shows the congressional lawmaking process in graphical format. Clicking on any of the twelve steps in the diagram leads to a menu of possible resources to search for information and may suggest some useful leads.

e.   CQ and Other News Sources

Newspapers and services that cover Congress and politics are often good sources on topics of congressional action, providing information that may not be available from official documentation. Even if a bill appears to be stalled in committee, news stories and press releases can provide leads to what is happening behind the scenes.

Congressional Quarterly (CQ) is a news service and publisher of several sources of information on congressional activity including *CQ Weekly* (formerly *Congressional Quarterly Weekly Report*), which provides background information on pending legislation and news of current developments. *CQ Weekly* does not include the texts of documents or comprehensive bill-tracking, but it does have useful analysis and background discussion of laws and legislative issues. Exhibit 5–10 on page 260 shows an article from a 2007 issue discussing the Animal Fighting Prohibition Enforcement Act.

CQ Weekly contains tables of House and Senate votes and a status table for major legislation. An annual *CQ Almanac Plus* cumulates much of the information in the *Weekly* into a useful summary of the congressional session. More frequent publications for current congressional news include *CQ Today* and CQ Midday Update, which is available free by e-mail.

Westlaw has *CQ Weekly* and *CQ Today*, with coverage beginning in 2005. CQ publications are available through Lexis in the legal, government and business markets. For academic and public libraries, CQ Library <library.cqpress.com> has a subscription-based Web version of *CQ Weekly* and free access to its index. CQ's more extensive online service CQ.com <www.cq.com> provides customized bill-tracking information, with a Bill Comparison feature for identifying changes between two versions of proposed legislation. It also has the text of documents, including bills, committee reports, and the *Congressional Record*, as well as extensive information about committee meetings and floor activity.

Numerous other newspapers and magazines also focus on developments in Washington. In addition to general news sources, specialized publications include *CongressDaily*, *National Journal*, and *Roll Call*. Westlaw has *CongressDaily* and *Roll Call*, and all three publications are available through Lexis. Some sources, such as *The Hill* <www.thehill.com>, are available on the Internet without charge.

Online subscription services such as GalleryWatch.com <www.gallerywatch.com> also provide information on Congress, including bill tracking and committee markup reports. Designed for specialists in current congressional information, these services may offer a range of sophisticated tracking and notification services unavailable from free government sites and more general database systems.

f. Printed Status Tables

For the purpose of tracking current legislation and researching recently enacted laws, online resources have advantages of convenience and speed that are unmatched in print. For earlier bills and laws, however, printed resources may still be the best available sources of information.

***Congressional Index* (CCH) (1937–date).** This looseleaf service's coverage of pending legislation indexes bills by subject and author and has a status table of actions taken on each bill. *Congressional Index*, published since 1938, is one of the most extensive sources of information on bills predating the coverage of electronic bill-tracking services. Its status table contains references to hearings, a feature lacking in many other resources.

Congressional Index does not contain the texts of bills or reports, but it has a wide range of other information on Congress, including lists of members and committee assignments; an index of enactments and vetoes; lists of pending treaties, reorganization plans, and nominations; a table of voting records; and a weekly newsletter.

***Congressional Record* and Earlier Status Tables (1789–date).** As noted earlier, the *Congressional Record* includes status tables that can be useful for both current and retrospective research. A History of Bills and Resolutions table, online on FDSys back to 1983 (but with page references beginning in 1993), includes references to committee reports and is one of the best sources for citations to debates. The entries have dates and *Congressional Record* daily edition page numbers, but the online version does not include links from these references to the documents.

The final cumulative History of Bills and Resolutions, published in the index volume of the bound *Congressional Record* set, is a valuable resource because it uses the pagination of the bound volumes instead of the separate "S" and "H" pages in the daily edition. This makes it an easy way to locate the bound volume pagination if needed for a citation. Although the History of Bills and Resolutions is less comprehensive than some commercial sources, it remains one of the best sources available for older laws. These tables have been published annually since the 1867 volume of the *Congressional Globe*, long before the earliest coverage of most commercial publications.

For even earlier acts, the House and Senate Journals all the way back to the First Congress (1789–91) include tables or lists of bills indicating when they were reported, passed, or received other floor action. Most of these are found in the subject index under "Bills." The early journals are available online through the Library of Congress's "A Century of Lawmaking for a New Nation" site <memory.loc.gov/ammem/amlaw/>.

g. **Directories**

In some instances, one of the fastest ways to find out about the status of pending legislation is to call congressional staff members responsible for drafting or monitoring the bill. They may be able to provide information or insights that would never appear in published status tables or reports. The best sources for detailed information on staff members are two competing commercial directories, *Congressional Staff Directory* and *Congressional Yellow Book*. Both have addresses, telephone numbers, and (for some staff members) brief biographical information. Internet versions of both directories (<library.cqpress.com/csd/>, <www.leadership directories.com/products/cyb.htm>) are updated daily but are available to subscribers only.

The *Official Congressional Directory* is not as detailed as the commercial directories, but it has information about individuals, offices and the organizational structure of Congress. The online version of this directory, available through FDSys, is modified during the term to reflect changes.

Two useful sources for background information on members of Congress, both published biennially, are National Journal's *Almanac of American Politics* and *CQ's Politics in America*. These have indepth biographical portraits with information on voting records and ratings from interest groups, as well as a brief narrative and statistical overview of each congressional district.

A retrospective Biographical Directory of the United States Congress, 1774–Present (including coverage of the Continental Congress) is available online <bioguide.congress.gov>, and provides basic information on the more than 13,000 persons who have served in Congress. A printed version of the same resource, under the title *Biographical Directory of the American Congress, 1774–1996* (1997), covers the 1st through 104th Congresses. Although it is not as current as the online version, it includes useful Congress-by-Congress directories of congressional leaders and state delegations. These include extensive footnotes indicating deaths, resignations, and other changes.

§ 5–4. State Legislative Information

Legislative history on the state level is a research area of sharp contrasts. Information on current legislation is widely available on the Internet, but documents that might aid in the interpretation of enacted laws can be difficult to find or unavailable.

First the good news: Most state legislatures provide convenient online access to current status information and to the text of pending bills. The better websites have several means of searching for bills, and some offer e-mail notification services when particular bills are acted upon. Some states offer other features such as bill summaries, committee minutes, and staff analyses.

Legislative websites can be found by using a search engine to find "[state] legislature," from state homepages, or from one of several general starting points. The National Conference of State Legislatures has a "State Legislatures Internet Links" page <www.ncsl.org/?tabid=17173> from which you can either go directly to a specific site or create a customized list of links for specific content such as bill information or legislator biographies.

Many legislative websites include an introductory guide to the state's lawmaking process. State legislatures generally follow the federal paradigm, but there can be significant differences from state to state and an important first step in studying legislative action in a particular state is to learn about its procedures. Guides and resources such as charts showing how bills become law can save you considerable time and confusion.

The commercial databases also have bill texts and status information for pending legislation. Both Westlaw and Lexis have databases for each state, as well as multistate resources useful for monitoring developments in legislatures throughout the country. Coverage extends on both systems back to the early 1990s.

For most states, Westlaw and Lexis also have legislative history documents such as reports, bill analyses, legislative journals, and committee reports. Contents vary from state to state depending on the materials available. In Westlaw's statutory display, *Reports and Related Materials* appears as one of the links on the left of the screen if a code section is derived from an act for which documents are available. As with federal statutes, however, a link does not necessarily mean that there is relevant information on the particular section. Dates of coverage vary between states but generally begin in the late 1990s or early 2000s.

Researchers needing to interpret statutes enacted before the late 1990s face a more difficult task. Bills from older sessions can be hard to locate. Almost every state has a legislative journal, but very few of these actually include transcripts of the debates. Only a few states publish committee reports, and even fewer publish hearings.

In some states, reports and hearings are only available, if at all, at the state capitol. Some states have "bill jackets" with legislative information, and some have microform records or tape recordings of sessions. In many instances, contemporary newspaper accounts may be the best available source of information about proceedings or legislators' statements.

Several guides identify the resources available for each state. LLSDC's Legislative Source Book includes a "State Legislatures, State Laws, and State Regulations: Website Links and Telephone Numbers" page <www.llsdc.org/state-leg/>, useful for quick links. The annual *State Legislative Sourcebook: A Resource Guide to Legislative Information in the Fifty States* has information on legislative processes and lists available published and online sources, including a "best initial contact" for each state, introductory guides, and bill tracking services. William H. Manz, *Guide to State Legislation, Legislative History, and Administrative Materials* (7th ed. 2008) lists printed and online sources for bills and for legislative history materials, if available, such as hearings, reports, floor debates, and journals.

A guide to legislative research processes in a specific state can be invaluable. Most of the published state legal research guides listed in Appendix A on pages 438–53 include discussion of available legislative history resources for their states, and state bar journals frequently publish articles on legislative history research. Law library websites in the jurisdiction you are researching, particularly the state legislative library if there is one, may have posted guides to doing legislative history research in their state. The Indiana University School of Law's "State Legislative History Research Guides on the Web" <www.law.indiana.edu/lawlibrary/research/guides/statelegislative/> has links to more than a hundred of these online guides.

A state research guide can also provide leads to official agencies responsible for recommending and drafting new legislation. These groups, including law revision commissions, judicial councils, and legislative councils, often publish annual or topical reports summarizing their work. For recommendations enacted into law, these reports may be valuable legislative history documentation.

Directory information on state legislatures, including organization, members, committees, and staffs, is contained in official state manuals (sometimes called *Bluebooks* or *Redbooks*), published annually or biennially by most states. Several multistate directories are also published, including *State Yellow Book* and the Council of State Governments' *CSG State Directory*.

In almost half of the states, statutes or constitutional amendments can bypass the legislature and be submitted directly to voters through the initiative process. Many states also permit popular referendums, or ballot measures to reject measures enacted by the legislature. Information on the enactment and intent of these measures may not appear in the standard legislative history sources. The Initiative & Referendum Institute at the University of Southern California <www.iandr institute.org> has state-by-state information on the history and procedures of popular ballot measures, with links to state-specific sites. *Exploring Initiative and Referendum Law: Selected State Research Guides* (Beth Williams ed., 2007) explains the initiative processes and research procedures in specific states.

110TH CONGRESS
1ST SESSION
H. R. 137

To amend title 18, United States Code, to strengthen prohibitions against animal fighting, and for other purposes.

IN THE HOUSE OF REPRESENTATIVES

JANUARY 4, 2007

Mr. GALLEGLY (for himself, Mr. BLUMENAUER, and Mr. BARTLETT of Maryland) introduced the following bill; which was referred to the Committee on the Judiciary, and in addition to the Committee on Agriculture, for a period to be subsequently determined by the Speaker, in each case for consideration of such provisions as fall within the jurisdiction of the committee concerned

---

A BILL

To amend title 18, United States Code, to strengthen prohibitions against animal fighting, and for other purposes.

1   *Be it enacted by the Senate and House of Representa-*

2 *tives of the United States of America in Congress assembled,*

3 **SECTION 1. SHORT TITLE.**

4   This Act may be cited as the "Animal Fighting Pro-

5 hibition Enforcement Act of 2007".

Exhibit 5–1. The first page of a House bill

110TH CONGRESS *1st Session*	HOUSE OF REPRESENTATIVES	REPT. 110–27 Part 1

ANIMAL FIGHTING PROHIBITION ENFORCEMENT ACT OF 2007

MARCH 1, 2007.—Committed to the Committee of the Whole House on the State of the Union and ordered to be printed

Mr. CONYERS, from the Committee on the Judiciary, submitted the following

R E P O R T

together with

DISSENTING VIEWS

[To accompany H.R. 137]

[Including cost estimate of the Congressional Budget Office]

The Committee on the Judiciary, to whom was referred the bill (H.R. 137) to amend title 18, United States Code, to strengthen prohibitions against animal fighting, and for other purposes, having considered the same, report favorably thereon with an amendment and recommend that the bill as amended do pass.

CONTENTS

59–006

Exhibit 5–2. The first page of a House committee report

through a series of events far beyond their control. It is only right and fair that we extend the period of eligibility so that the affected disadvantaged businesses are allowed to grow and flourish and enjoy the full 9 years of the program.

Nineteen months since Katrina struck, most of our Gulf coast are still struggling to return.

This bill is about equity and fairness at a time when the road to recovery has been anything but fair for disadvantaged firms in the region. For example, in the time just following the storm, 90 percent of the $2 billion in initial contracts were awarded to companies based outside of the three primary affected States and to large concerns. Minority businesses received just 1.5 percent of the first $1.6 billion spent there. Women-owned businesses received even less. This was the outcome in spite of laws such as the Stafford Act, which require contracting officials to prioritize awards to local businesses and to reach a goal of 5 percent of contracts to minority-owned businesses.

The continued recovery from Katrina is made up of many interconnected issues, and we cannot fully recover without addressing all of them. Helping small businesses, as this and other bills such as the RECOVER Act do, restores jobs that our citizens can return home to and puts our businesses back on track. It broadens the tax base of our region and helps with our recovery.

I look forward to continuing to work on the Small Business Committee with Ms. VELÁZQUEZ and Mr. CHABOT to address the needs of small businesses in the gulf region.

Mr. CHABOT. Mr. Speaker, I have no further requests for time, and I yield back the balance of my time.

Ms. VELÁZQUEZ. Mr. Speaker, I would like to thank the gentleman from Ohio (Mr. CHABOT) for his support and cooperation in helping expedite this legislation.

Mr. Speaker, I yield back the balance of my time.

The SPEAKER pro tempore. The question is on the motion offered by the gentlewoman from New York (Ms. VELÁZQUEZ) that the House suspend the rules and pass the bill, H.R. 1968, as amended.

The question was taken; and (two-thirds being in the affirmative) the rules were suspended and the bill, as amended, was passed.

A motion to reconsider was laid on the table.

RECESS

The SPEAKER pro tempore. Pursuant to clause 12(a) of rule I, the Chair declares the House in recess subject to the call of the Chair.

Accordingly (at 3 o'clock and 13 minutes p.m.), the House stood in recess subject to the call of the Chair.

□ 1700

AFTER RECESS

The recess having expired, the House was called to order by the Speaker pro tempore (Mr. SALAZAR) at 5 p.m.

ANIMAL FIGHTING PROHIBITION
ENFORCEMENT ACT OF 2007

Mr. SCOTT of Virginia. Mr. Speaker, I move to suspend the rules and pass the bill (H.R. 137) to amend title 18, United States Code, to strengthen prohibitions against animal fighting, and for other purposes, as amended.

The Clerk read the title of the bill.

The text of the bill is as follows:

H.R. 137

Be it enacted by the Senate and House of Representatives of the United States of America in Congress assembled,

SECTION 1. SHORT TITLE.

This Act may be cited as the "Animal Fighting Prohibition Enforcement Act of 2007".

SEC. 2. ENFORCEMENT OF ANIMAL FIGHTING PROHIBITIONS.

(a) IN GENERAL.—Chapter 3 of title 18, United States Code, is amended by adding at the end the following:

"§ 49. Enforcement of animal fighting prohibitions

"Whoever violates subsection (a), (b), (c), or (e) of section 26 of the Animal Welfare Act shall be fined under this title, imprisoned for not more than 3 years, or both, for each violation.".

(b) CLERICAL AMENDMENT.—The table of contents for such chapter is amended by inserting after the item relating to section 48 the following:

"49. Enforcement of animal fighting prohibitions.".

SEC. 3. AMENDMENTS TO THE ANIMAL WELFARE ACT.

Section 26 of the Animal Welfare Act (7 U.S.C. 2156) is amended—

(1) in subsection (c), by striking "interstate instrumentality" and inserting "instrumentality of interstate commerce for commercial speech";

(2) in subsection (d), by striking "such subsections" and inserting "such subsection";

(3) by striking subsection (e) and inserting the following:

"(e) It shall be unlawful for any person to knowingly sell, buy, transport, or deliver in interstate or foreign commerce a knife, a gaff, or any other sharp instrument attached, or designed or intended to be attached, to the leg of a bird for use in an animal fighting venture.";

(4) in subsection (g)—

(A) in paragraph (1), by striking "or animals, such as waterfowl, bird, raccoon, or fox hunting"; and

(B) by striking paragraph (3) and inserting the following:

"(3) the term 'instrumentality of interstate commerce' means any written, wire, radio, television or other form of communication in, or using a facility of, interstate commerce"; and

(5) by adding at the end the following new subsection:

"(i) The criminal penalties for violations of subsection (a), (b), (c), or (e) are provided in section 49 of title 18, United States Code.".

The SPEAKER pro tempore. Pursuant to the rule, the gentleman from Virginia (Mr. SCOTT) and the gen-

tleman from North Carolina (Mr. COBLE) each will control 20 minutes.

The Chair recognizes the gentleman from Virginia.

GENERAL LEAVE

Mr. SCOTT of Virginia. Mr. Speaker, I ask unanimous consent that all Members have 5 legislative days to revise and extend their remarks and include extraneous material on the bill under consideration.

The SPEAKER pro tempore. Is there objection to the request of the gentleman from Virginia?

There was no objection.

Mr. SCOTT of Virginia. Mr. Speaker, I yield myself such time as I may consume.

Mr. Speaker, H.R. 137 is a bipartisan effort by the Judiciary Committee, led by the gentleman from California (Mr. GALLEGLY) as the chief sponsor and the gentleman from Oregon (Mr. BLUMENAUER) as the lead Democratic sponsor. Both have worked long and hard on this issue. I would also like to express my appreciation to Chairman CONYERS, Ranking Member SMITH, and Subcommittee Ranking Member FORBES for their leadership and support in moving this matter forward, and also the former chairman of the committee, Mr. COBLE, who is with us today.

The Animal Fighting Prohibition Enforcement Act of 2007 addresses the growing problem of staged animal fighting in this country. It increases the penalties under the current Federal law for transporting animals in interstate commerce for the purpose of fighting and for interstate and foreign commerce in knives and gaffs designed for use in cockfighting.

Specifically, H.R. 137 makes violations of the law a felony punishable by up to 3 years in prison. Currently, these offenses are limited to misdemeanor treatment with the possibility of a fine and up to 1 year of imprisonment. Most States make all staged animal fighting illegal. Just one State currently allows cockfighting to occur legally.

The transport of game birds for the purpose of animal fighting and the implements of cockfighting are already prohibited by Federal law, though the current law only allows, as I have indicated, the misdemeanor treatment. In 1976 Congress amended title 7, U.S. Code, section 2156, the Animal Welfare Act, to make it illegal to knowingly sell, buy, transport, deliver, or receive a dog or other animal in interstate or foreign commerce for the purpose of participation in an animal fighting venture or knowingly sponsoring or exhibiting an animal in a fighting venture if any animal in the venture was moved in interstate or foreign commerce. Amendments to the Animal Welfare Act contained a loophole, however, that allowed shipments of birds across State lines for fighting purposes if the destination State allowed cockfighting.

While Congress did amend section 26 of the Animal Welfare Act to close this

Exhibit 5–3.　A page from the *Congressional Record*

ANIMAL FIGHTING PROHIBITION ENFORCEMENT ACT OF 2005

THURSDAY, MAY 18, 2006

HOUSE OF REPRESENTATIVES,
SUBCOMMITTEE ON CRIME, TERRORISM,
AND HOMELAND SECURITY
COMMITTEE ON THE JUDICIARY,
Washington, DC.

The Subcommittee met, pursuant to notice, at 11:31 a.m., in Room 2141, Rayburn House Office Building, the Honorable Howard Coble (Chairman of the Subcommittee) presiding.

Mr. COBLE. Good morning, ladies and gentlemen. We will convene the hearing. There will be a floor vote imminently, I am told, and we don't have a reporting quorum present, so Mr. Scott and I are going to give our opening statements, and then perhaps we'll be able to move along after that.

This hearing is to examine the issue of animal fighting in this country and whether Congress should take additional steps to address the issue. Animal fighting is not restricted to cockfighting, but also includes pitting dog against dog, or dogs against other animals, such as bears or wild hogs. Often small knives are attached to the animal for use in the fight.

In 1976 Congress passed a law to ban the sponsor or exhibit of animals that were moved to interstate or foreign commerce in an animal fighting venue. The law also made it illegal to transport an animal in interstate or foreign commerce for participation in an animal fighting venue.

On May 13th, 2002, Congress enacted amendments to the Animal Welfare Act. The changes made it a crime, regardless of State law, for exhibiting, sponsoring, selling, buying, transporting, delivering or receiving a bird or other animal in interstate or foreign commerce for the purpose of participation in an animal fighting venue such as cockfighting or dogfighting. For States where fighting among live birds is allowed under the law, the act only prohibited the sponsor or exhibit of a bird for fighting purposes if the person knew that that bird was moved in interstate or foreign commerce.

Currently dogfighting is prohibited in all 50 States and cockfighting is outlawed in most States under specific laws prohibiting it or general prohibitions against animal fighting. In a few States the practice is not specifically outlawed. However, general animal cruelty statutes may be interpreted to outlaw such activities. In two States cockfighting is legal. Dogfighting and cockfighting are legal in some United States territories. Although the possible fines

(1)

Exhibit 5–4.   The first page of a House hearing

121 STAT. 88 PUBLIC LAW 110–22—MAY 3, 2007

Public Law 110–22
110th Congress

An Act

May 3, 2007
[H.R. 137]

To amend title 18, United States Code, to strengthen prohibitions against animal fighting, and for other purposes.

Be it enacted by the Senate and House of Representatives of the United States of America in Congress assembled,

Animal Fighting
Prohibition
Enforcement Act
of 2007.
18 USC 1 note.

SECTION 1. SHORT TITLE.

This Act may be cited as the "Animal Fighting Prohibition Enforcement Act of 2007".

SEC. 2. ENFORCEMENT OF ANIMAL FIGHTING PROHIBITIONS.

(a) IN GENERAL.—Chapter 3 of title 18, United States Code, is amended by adding at the end the following:

"§ 49. Enforcement of animal fighting prohibitions

"Whoever violates subsection (a), (b), (c), or (e) of section 26 of the Animal Welfare Act shall be fined under this title, imprisoned for not more than 3 years, or both, for each violation.".

(b) CLERICAL AMENDMENT.—The table of contents for such chapter is amended by inserting after the item relating to section 48 the following:

"49. Enforcement of animal fighting prohibitions.".

SEC. 3. AMENDMENTS TO THE ANIMAL WELFARE ACT.

Section 26 of the Animal Welfare Act (7 U.S.C. 2156) is amended—

(1) in subsection (c), by striking "interstate instrumentality" and inserting "instrumentality of interstate commerce for commercial speech";

(2) in subsection (d), by striking "such subsections" and inserting "such subsection";

(3) by striking subsection (e) and inserting the following:

"(e) It shall be unlawful for any person to knowingly sell, buy, transport, or deliver in interstate or foreign commerce a knife, a gaff, or any other sharp instrument attached, or designed or intended to be attached, to the leg of a bird for use in an animal fighting venture.";

(4) in subsection (g)—

(A) in paragraph (1), by striking "or animals, such as waterfowl, bird, raccoon, or fox hunting"; and

(B) by striking paragraph (3) and inserting the following:

"(3) the term 'instrumentality of interstate commerce' means any written, wire, radio, television or other form of

Exhibit 5–5. An Act of Congress, showing the bill number

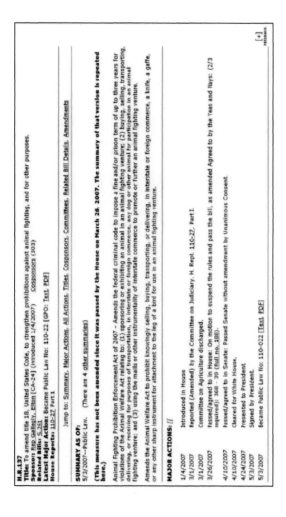

H.R.137

Title: To amend title 18, United States Code, to strengthen prohibitions against animal fighting, and for other purposes.

Sponsor: Rep Gallegly, Elton [CA-24] (introduced 1/4/2007)   Cosponsors (303)

Related Bills: S.261

Latest Major Action: Became Public Law No: 110-22 [GPO: Text, PDF]

House Reports: 110-27 Part 1

Jump to: Summary, Major Actions, All Actions, Titles, Cosponsors, Committees, Related Bill Details, Amendments

SUMMARY AS OF:
5/3/2007--Public Law.   (There are 4 other summaries)

(This measure has not been amended since it was passed by the House on March 26. 2007. The summary of that version is repeated here.)

Animal Fighting Prohibition Enforcement Act of 2007 - Amends the federal criminal code to impose a fine and/or prison term of up to three years for violations of the Animal Welfare Act relating to: (1) sponsoring or exhibiting an animal in an animal fighting venture; (2) buying, selling, transporting, delivering, or receiving for purposes of transportation, in interstate or foreign commerce, any dog or other animal for participation in an animal fighting venture; and (3) using the mails or other instrumentality of interstate commerce to promote or further an animal fighting venture.

Amends the Animal Welfare Act to prohibit knowingly selling, buying, transporting, or delivering, in interstate or foreign commerce, a knife, a gaffe, or any other sharp instrument for attachment to the leg of a bird for use in an animal fighting venture.

MAJOR ACTIONS: ///

1/4/2007	Introduced in House
3/1/2007	Reported (Amended) by the Committee on Judiciary. H. Rept. 110-27. Part I.
3/1/2007	Committee on Agriculture discharged.
3/26/2007	Passed/agreed to in House: On motion to suspend the rules and pass the bill, as amended Agreed to by the Yeas and Nays: (2/3 required): 368 - 39 (Roll no. 186).
4/10/2007	Passed/agreed to in Senate: Passed Senate without amendment by Unanimous Consent.
4/10/2007	Cleared for White House.
4/24/2007	Presented to President.
5/3/2007	Signed by President.
5/3/2007	Became Public Law No: 110-022 [Text, PDF]

[+]

Exhibit 5–6.   THOMAS summary for an enacted House bill

H521-73   **ANIMAL FIGHTING PROHIBITION ENFORCEMENT ACT OF 2005.**
May 18, 2006. 109-2. 64 p.
• Item 1020-A (Paper).
• Item 1020-B (Microfiche).
°Y4.J89/1:109-115.
Committee Serial No. 109-115.

Hearing before the *Subcom on Crime, Terrorism, and Homeland Security* to consider H.R. 817, the Animal Fighting Prohibition Enforcement Act of 2005, to amend the Animal Welfare Act to increase criminal penalties for the purchase, sale, or interstate or foreign transport of animals for the purposes of animal fighting.

Supplementary material (p. 51-60) includes submitted statements, a witness's written statement, and correspondence.

H521-73.1: May 18, 2006. p. 4-49.

Witnesses: **PACELLE, Wayne,** President and CEO, Humane Society.

POLLOT, Mark L., Executive Director, Foundation for Constitutional Law; representing United Gamefowl Breeders Association.

HUNT, David R., Deputy, Franklin County, Ohio, Sheriff's Office.

BRADLEY, Francine A., Extension Poultry Specialist, Department of Animal Science, University of California, Davis.

Statements and Discussion: Differing views on H.R. 817; perspectives on public health and other concerns associated with animal fighting, including cockfighting; review of constitutionality issues related to Federal animal fighting legislation; elaboration on animal cruelty and constitutional issues related to H.R. 817.

Exhibit 5–7. CIS abstract for a House committee hearing

Public Law 110-22   **121 Stat. 88**

Animal Fighting Prohibition Enforcement Act of 2007

May 3, 2007

Public Law

1.1   Public Law 110-22, approved May 3, 2007. (H.R. 137)

(CIS07:PL110-22   2 p.)

"To amend title 18, United States Code, to strengthen prohibitions against animal fighting, and for other purposes."

Amends the Federal criminal code and Animal Welfare Act to revise prohibitions against, and increase criminal penalties relating to the purchase, sale, or transport of animals for the purposes of animal fighting.

P.L. 110-22 Reports

108th Congress

2.1   H. Rpt. 108-756 on H.R. 4264, "Animal Fighting Prohibition Enforcement Act of 2004," Oct. 7, 2004.

(CIS04:H523-56   21 p.)
(Y1.1/8:108-756.)

Recommends passage, with an amendment in the nature of a substitute, of H.R. 4264, the Animal Fighting Prohibition Enforcement Act of 2004, to amend the Animal Welfare Act to increase criminal penalties for the purchase, sale, or interstate or foreign transport of animals for the purposes of animal fighting.
Includes transcript (p. 8-21) of Committee Sept. 30, 2004 markup session on H.R. 4264 (text, p. 10-13).

110th Congress

2.2   H. Rpt. 110-27, pt. 1 on H.R. 137, "Animal Fighting Prohibition Enforcement Act of 2007," Mar. 1, 2007.

(CIS07:H523-2   9 p.)
(Y1.1/8:110-27/PT.1.)

Recommends passage with an amendment of H.R. 137, the Animal Fighting Prohibition Enforcement Act of 2007, to amend the Animal Welfare Act to increase criminal penalties for the purchase, sale, or interstate or foreign transport of animals for the purposes of animal fighting.
Includes dissenting views (p. 8-9).

P.L. 110-22 Bills

108th Congress

HOUSE BILLS

3.1   H.R. 4264 as introduced May 4, 2004; as reported by the House Judiciary Committee Oct. 7, 2004.

SENATE BILLS

3.2   S. 2908 as introduced.

109th Congress

HOUSE BILLS

3.3   H.R. 817 as introduced.

SENATE BILLS

3.4   S. 382 as introduced Feb. 15, 2005; as passed by the Senate Apr. 28, 2005.

110th Congress

ENACTED BILL

3.5   H.R. 137 as introduced Jan. 4, 2007; as reported by the House Judiciary Committee Mar. 1, 2007; as passed by the House Mar. 26, 2007.

COMPANION BILL

3.6   S. 261 as introduced Jan. 11, 2007; as reported by the Senate Judiciary Committee Mar. 26, 2007.

P.L. 110-22 Debate

151 Congressional Record
109th Congress, 1st Session - 2005

4.1   Apr. 28, Senate consideration and passage of S. 382, p. S4605.

153 Congressional Record
110th Congress, 1st Session - 2007

4.2   Mar. 26, House consideration and passage of H.R. 137, p. H3031, H3053.

4.3   Apr. 10, Senate consideration and passage of H.R. 137, p. S4317.

Exhibit 5–8.   The first page of a CIS legislative history

ANIMAL FIGHTING PROHIBITION ENFORCEMENT ACT OF 2007

PUBLIC LAW 110–22, see page 121 Stat. 88

DATES OF CONSIDERATION AND PASSAGE

House: March 26, 2007

Senate: April 10, 2007

Cong. Record Vol. 153 (2007)

House Report (Judiciary Committee) No. 110–27 (Part 1), March 1, 2007 [To accompany H.R. 137]

The House Report is set out below.

HOUSE REPORT 110–27 (Part 1)

[page 1]

The Committee on the Judiciary, to whom was referred the bill (H.R. 137) to amend title 18, United States Code, to strengthen prohibitions against animal fighting, and for other purposes, having considered the same, report favorably thereon with an amendment and recommend that the bill as amended do pass.

CONTENTS

Exhibit 5–9. A House report as reprinted in *USCCAN*

[REGULATORY POLICY]

New Penalties To Aid Ban on Animal Fights

BY CQ STAFF

THE SENATE CLEARED legislation last week that would increase federal penalties for transporting animals across state lines for the purpose of staging fights.

The bill (HR 137) cleared by voice vote April 10. The House had passed it in March.

The legislation, cosponsored by more than 300 lawmakers, would make it a crime to buy or sell animals for fighting. It also would make it unlawful to use the U.S. Postal Service to promote animal fighting in the United States.

Animal fights are illegal in every state except Louisiana and subject to misdemeanor federal penalties. Even so, "the animal fighting industry continues to thrive in the United States," said Robert C. Scott, D-Va., who chairs the House Judiciary Subcommittee on Crime, Terrorism and Homeland Security.

The Senate passed a similar bill last year, but F. James Sensenbrenner Jr., R-Wis., who chaired the House Judiciary Committee at the time, blocked House action on it. Sensenbrenner argued that boosting the animal-fighting penalties to felonies would put an undue strain on federal prosecutors.

The Humane Society of the United States worked for years to get animal fights banned, while the United Gamefowl Breeders Association lobbied against the measure. *(Background, CQ Weekly, p. 631)*

"The Humane Society wants to impose their values and their beliefs on the entire country," said Jerry L. Leber, head of the 15,000-member breeders' association. He said a general ban would hurt breeders of show birds and harm the rural economy.

House passage came March 26 under suspension of the rules. The measure had been pulled once before because critics argued that the lack of review by the Agriculture Committee would set a dangerous precedent.

The legislation alters Title VII, the portion of the U.S. Code related to agriculture, rather than the portion of the code that deals with criminal law. ∎

Exhibit 5–10.   An article from *CQ Weekly*

CHAPTER 6

ADMINISTRATIVE LAW

---

§ 6–1. Introduction

The executive is one of the three coordinate branches of government, but historically its law-making role was limited to orders and regulations needed to carry out the legislature's mandates. With the modern growth of government bureaucracy, however, the rules created by executive agencies are primary legal sources with pervasive impact. In many areas, administrative law can be more immediately relevant to day-to-day legal practice than either statutory or judge-made law.

Administrative law takes several forms, as agencies can act both somewhat like legislatures and somewhat like courts. They may promulgate binding regulations governing activities within their jurisdiction, or they may decide matters involving particular litigants on a case-by-case basis. Approaches vary from agency to agency.

Although executive agencies have existed in this country since its creation, the real growth of administrative law began in the late nineteenth century as the government sought to deal with the increasingly complex problems of industrialized society. In the 1930s, Congress created new regulatory agencies such as the Federal Communications Commission and the Securities and Exchange Commission to administer its New Deal programs. A third boom in administrative law occurred around 1970, as agencies such as the Environmental Protection Agency, the Consumer Product Safety Commission, and the Occupational Safety and Health Administration were created to address growing environmental and health concerns. The regulatory landscape continues to evolve, as the Homeland Security

Act of 2002 created a new cabinet department and several new agencies.

Most of this chapter focuses on federal administrative law, but state agencies play an important role in many areas of activity. States also delegate lawmaking responsibilities to counties and cities, which enact ordinances and have their own local agencies. While federal administrative law is relatively easy to research, state and local sources may be difficult to locate and even harder to update.

§ 6–2.   Background Reference Sources

When researching administrative law, you need to determine what agency has jurisdiction and develop a preliminary understanding of its structure and functions. This may require background analysis or a close reading of statutory and judicial sources to determine an agency's role. Most agencies are formed by legislation that defines their purpose and limits their parameters. You need to understand an agency's organizational structure, legal mandates and information sources before delving into the documents it produces.

a.   Agency Websites

An agency's website is often a convenient source of information on its history and current activities. Here, depending on the agency, you can usually find resources such as introductory overviews, organization charts, speeches, press releases, policy documents, and directories. Much of this online information has never been available in print.

Under the Electronic Freedom of Information Act Amendments of 1996, agency websites are required to include policy statements, interpretations, and administrative staff instructions that affect the public. The E–Government Act of 2002 further mandated that websites describe the agency's mission and organizational structure, and that they include a search function.

Partly as a result of this legislation, agency websites are increasingly the first place to look for information and documents. Ease of access, however, varies considerably from agency to agency. Some have well-organized "Reference Rooms" clearly accessible from their homepages, while others may hide documents under obscure Freedom of Information Act links. Some agency search engines are rather rudimentary, and you may achieve better results by using a general search engine such as Google and limiting results to a particular agency's site.

Most agency websites are easily found through web searches or by using an acronym and the domain *.gov* as a URL. Several lists of government websites are also available. One of the most thorough is Louisiana State University's Federal Agencies Directory <www.lib.lsu.edu/gov/>, which lists more than a thousand sites. Washburn School of Law's WashLaw site has a Federal Agencies page <www.washlaw.edu/doclaw/executive5m.html> covering about seventy major agencies; for each it provides direct links (if available) to publications, organization charts, forms, opinions, manuals, libraries, and directories. USA.gov <www.usa.gov>, the federal government's public portal, also provides an A–Z Agency Index with links to websites.

b.   Guides and Directories

In order to decide which agency website to explore, you may need to do a bit of background research to determine which agency has jurisdiction over a particular area. In other instances, you may want information that is unavailable from the agency site, such as contact information for specific personnel. For purposes such as these, federal government guides and directories can be valuable resources.

You can identify appropriate agencies in several ways. Cases or secondary sources may discuss administrative actions, or an annotated code may cite relevant regulations or decisions. A useful source for identifying federal agencies by subject is CQ Press's annual *Washington Information Directory* (also available online by subscription <library.cqpress.com>). In about a hundred topical areas, it has descriptions and access information for federal agencies as well as congressional committees and nongovernmental organizations. Exhibit 6–1 on page 298 shows a page from this directory for the topic "Animals and Plants," with information about the Animal and Plant Health Inspection Service

(APHIS) as well as offices within the National Institutes of Health and several professional organizations and interest groups.

Once an agency is identified, general information about its structure, authority, and functions can be found in the *United States Government Manual*. This annual federal government directory, available both in print and online through the Government Printing Office's Federal Digital System (FDSys) <www.gpo.gov/fdsys/>, cites the statutes under which an agency operates and explains its functions and major operating units. It includes sources of information (including publications, telephone numbers, and websites) and organizational charts for most major agencies.

CQ Press's *Federal Regulatory Directory* (14th ed. 2010) has a more extensive analysis of twelve major regulatory agencies, with shorter treatment of more than a hundred other agencies and offices. Its coverage of APHIS, for example, has a narrative introduction with historical background and a description of the agency's programs, followed by several pages listing key personnel, information sources, and the major acts that APHIS administers.

To learn about the status of a particular regulation or enforcement activity, you may need to contact an agency directly by phone or e-mail. You should direct your inquiries as specifically as possible to the responsible division and official. Agency websites and resources such as the *U.S. Government Manual* and the *Federal Regulatory Directory* have the names of major agency officials, but not extensive listings of other staffers. Several directories have more detailed information about personnel, including telephone numbers and e-mail addresses. These include *Carroll's Federal Directory*, CQ Press's *Federal Staff Directory* and Leadership Directories' *Federal Yellow Book*. Carroll Publishing and Leadership Directories also produce companion volumes covering federal regional offices outside the Washington, D.C. area. All of these directories are available through their publishers' subscription websites (<www.govsearch.com>, <library.cq.com>, and <www.leadershipdirectories.com>). Exhibit 6–2 on page 299 shows a portion of the Animal and Plant Health Inspection Service entry in the *Federal Yellow Book*, with contact information for key personnel in its Animal Care program.

§ 6–3. Federal Regulations

The basic mechanism by which most agencies govern is the *regulation*, a detailed administrative order similar in form to a statute. Regulations are also known as *rules*, and these terms are used interchangeably in U.S. administrative law. The publication of regulations follows a standard procedure: they are first issued chronologically in a daily gazette, the *Federal Register*; and then the rules in force are arranged by subject in the *Code of Federal Regulations* (*CFR*). This publication of regulations, first chronologically and then by topic, mirrors the way statutes are published in the *Statutes at Large* and the *United States Code*.

a. *Federal Register*

As the federal government promulgated more and more executive and administrative orders and regulations in the early New Deal period, locating regulations and determining which were in force became increasingly difficult. There was no requirement that regulations be published or centrally filed, and two cases reached the U.S. Supreme Court before it was discovered that the administrative orders on which they were based were no longer in effect. The resulting criticism led Congress to establish a daily publication of executive and administrative promulgations, the *Federal Register*, the first issue of which appeared in March 1936.

The Administrative Procedure Act in 1946 expanded the scope of the *Federal Register* by creating a rulemaking system requiring the publication of proposed regulations for public comment. Judicial decisions in the 1960s and 1970s, overturning regulations seen as arbitrary or capricious, led to fuller explanations of agency actions and greater evidence of public involvement in the decision-making process. Since 1973 agencies have been required to preface final rules with an explanatory preamble, and since 1976 this preamble has included summaries of comments submitted and the agency's responses to these comments.

The introductory preambles appear only in the *Federal Register* and are not reprinted with the text of regulations in the *Code of Federal Regulations*. A *Federal Register* preamble can be invaluable in interpreting the scope and meaning of a regulation in the same way that committee reports and other legislative materials help explain the purpose of a statute. The *Register* may also be the only available source for temporary changes occurring between annual *CFR* revisions.

Exhibits 6–3 and 6–4 on pages 300–01 show excerpts from a proposed rule on animal transportation as published in the *Federal Register*. Exhibit 6–3 shows the first page of the proposal, including a summary, contact information, and the beginning of the explanatory background in the preamble. Exhibit 6–4 shows the text of proposed amendments to several *CFR* sections including 9 C.F.R. § 2.131 on handling of animals.

The *Federal Register* is published in print, but the most convenient access is usually through the Internet. Issues since volume 59 (1994) are available free on FDSys, with each new issue added the morning of its publication. The Office of the Federal Register website <www.federalregister.gov> is even more current, and has a Public Inspection Desk with documents scheduled to be published in the very near future.

The *Federal Register* is also available online through several commercial services. Westlaw has coverage extending all the way back to 1936, but documents before 1981 display only in PDF form. Lexis begins coverage in the summer of 1980, and CQ.com in 1990. These services also generally have new issues online the day they are published. Hein-Online has all issues in PDF, with retrospective coverage back to the first volume in 1936. Most large law libraries also have complete runs of the *Federal Register* back to 1936 in microform.

Each daily *Federal Register* begins with a table of contents and a list of the *Code of Federal Regulations* parts affected by new or proposed regulations in the issue. The table of contents is organized alphabetically by agency, so you can easily monitor a particular agency's activity. Skimming the *Register*'s table of contents is part of many lawyers' daily routine, and from the FDSys Federal Register page you can sign up to have it delivered each morning by e-mail.

Readers' aids in the back of each issue include a table of pages and dates for each *Federal Register* issue published during the month, which can be helpful in tracking down a citation; and a cumulative list of *CFR* parts affected during the current month. Exhibit 6–5 on page 302 shows the monthly list of *CFR* parts affected in the *Federal Register* issue in which the proposed animal handling regulations were published, and includes a reference to these proposed regulations at 9 C.F.R. Parts 2 and 3.

An index to the *Federal Register* is published monthly and cumulates over the course of the year.

The index is arranged like the daily table of contents, with entries by agency rather than by subject. The index is available back to 1994 on the Office of the Federal Register's website <www.federal register.gov>, and back to 1936 on HeinOnline.

The Office of the Federal Register website has additional information, including a tutorial "The Federal Register: What It Is and How to Use It" with a detailed explanation of the publication of federal regulations.

The Unified Agenda is a useful feature published twice a year in the *Federal Register*. It lists regulatory actions under development and provides information on their status and projected dates of completion. This can be a way to learn about areas of agency activity that have not yet reached the proposed rulemaking stage.

Further information on pending regulations is available from Reginfo.gov, the General Services Administration's regulatory information website <www.reginfo.gov>, which includes an extensive subject index to entries in the Unified Agenda. Westlaw also has regulatory tracking information on the status of proposed and recently adopted regulations.

Dockets for some regulatory decision-making are available online, providing access to agency analyses, public comments, and other documents involved in the rulemaking process. Regulations.gov <www.regulations.gov> is a centralized site for commenting on proposed regulations and viewing submitted comments, and the commercial site OpenRegs.com <openregs.com> is a more user-friendly portal to information on new and proposed rules.

b. *Code of Federal Regulations*

As with statutes, chronological publication of regulations is insufficient for most legal research. You must know what regulations are currently in force regardless of when they were first promulgated. The *Code of Federal Regulations* was first published in 1938 to meet this need, and it now consists of more than 220 paperback volumes revised on an annual basis.

The regulations in the *CFR* are collected from the *Federal Register* and arranged in a subject scheme of fifty titles, similar to that of the *U.S. Code*. (Some *CFR* titles cover the same topics as the *U.S. Code* title with the same number, but others focus on completely different subjects.) Titles are divided into chapters, each containing the regulations of a specific agency. The back of every *CFR* volume contains an alphabetical list of federal agencies indicating the title and chapter (or chapters) of each agency's regulations.

CFR chapters are divided into parts, each of which covers a particular topic, and finally parts are divided into sections. Exhibits 6–6 and 6–7 on pages 303–04 show sample pages of the *CFR* from Title 9 (Animals and Animal Products), Chapter I (Animal and Plant Health Inspection Service), Part 2 (Regulations). A citation to the *CFR* provides the title, part, section, and year of publication. The section on handling of animals in Exhibit 6–7, for example, is cited as 9 C.F.R. § 2.131 (2009). (The section is a distinct number, not a decimal; § 2.131 follows § 2.130 and does not fall between § 2.13 and § 2.14.)

At the beginning of each *CFR* part is an *authority note* showing the statutory authority under which the regulations have been issued. After this note is a *source note* providing the citation and date of the *Federal Register* in which the regulations were published. This reference is the key to finding the preamble with background information and comments explaining the regulations. If an individual section was added or amended more recently than the other sections in a part, it is followed by a separate source note. In Exhibit 6–6, the regulations in Part 2 were issued under the authority of several sections of the *United States Code* and the *CFR*, and the source was 54 Fed. Reg. 36,147 (1989) unless otherwise noted. The source note for § 2.131, as shown in Exhibit 6–7, indicates that it has been amended twice since 1989.

The Bluebook mandates citation to the official, annually revised edition of the *CFR*. (The *ALWD Citation Manual* permits citation to an online source, if that information is noted parenthetically.) The official volumes are updated and replaced on a rotating cycle throughout the year. Titles 1–16 have regulations in force as of January 1; titles 17–27 as of April 1; titles 28–41 as of July 1; and titles 42–50 as of October 1. The volumes usually come out two to four months after these cutoff dates.

The *CFR* is available in several electronic formats. The official version on FDSys replicates the paper edition and is updated on the same basis. You can retrieve a section by citation or search either individual titles or the entire *CFR*. As with the *Federal Register*, documents can be viewed and printed as the PDF images that may be required for a *Bluebook* citation.

FDSys also offers a much more current Electronic Code of Federal Regulations, or e-CFR. This edition incorporates new amendments from the *Federal Register* within a day or two. While the site explains that this is not an official legal edition of the *CFR* and is subject to correction, it represents a significant improvement in the government's timely delivery of regulatory information.

Regularly updated versions of the *CFR* are also available online from Westlaw and Lexis. Like the e-CFR, these files are updated on an ongoing basis to reflect changes published in the *Federal Register*. Both incorporate amendments within a few days of their appearance in the *Register*. Westlaw's *CFR* provides notice of even newer developments, because it includes red flags indicating "Regulatory Action" and linking to *Federal Register* documents the same day they are published.

Older editions of the *CFR* are sometimes needed to identify regulations in force at a particular time.

FDSys retains older editions as new versions are added, with coverage starting with selected 1996 volumes. Westlaw and Lexis have more extensive historical access, with older editions of the *CFR* back to the early 1980s. HeinOnline fills the rest of the gap, covering from the original 1938 edition through the current version. Many law libraries also have microform collections of the *CFR* back to 1938.

c. Finding and Updating Regulations

You can find federal regulations in several ways. The *Federal Register* and the *Code of Federal Regulations* have indexes, and both publications can be searched through FDSys or other databases, including Westlaw and Lexis. Both annotated editions of federal statutes include citations to regulations after code sections. Agency websites have links to regulations, and references are often found in cases, texts, and articles. One relevant regulation provides leads to other versions, through cross-references in *Federal Register* preambles and *CFR* notes.

Most research into the regulations of a federal agency begins with the *Code of Federal Regulations*, rather than the daily *Federal Register*. The *CFR* includes an annually revised *Index and Finding Aids* volume, but its coverage is far less detailed than most statutory indexes. It has only broad references to *CFR* parts, not specific references to individual sections. Much more detailed subject access is provided in the four-volume *West's Code of Federal Regulations General Index*. This index, available on Westlaw as the *RegulationsPlus Index*, has a reference to the Exhibit 6–7 regulation under "Animals–Handlers and handling–Standards," as well as several dozen entries under both "Cats" and "Dogs."

You can find regulations through online keyword searches, but if you can narrow your search it is often most effective to search within a particular title or a topical file. FDSys offers options of searching the entire *CFR* or specific titles, while Westlaw and Lexis have files for regulations in topical areas such as banking, environmental law, and securities. Another approach is to check an agency's website. Most agency sites have their current body of regulations and information on any current proposed rules, as well as the texts of the statutes under which they operate.

If you have a statute and need to find regulations promulgated under its authority or related to it, the simplest method is to check the *United States Code Annotated* (in print or on Westlaw) or *United States Code Service* (in print or on Lexis). Cross-references or links to relevant *CFR* parts or sections follow individual sections in both codes.

For some agencies, regulations are reprinted in treatises and looseleaf services covering their topical area. Looseleaf services focusing on the work of particular agencies (such as the Internal Revenue Service or the Securities and Exchange Commission) provide regularly updated and well-annotated texts of both statutes and regulations.

Finding relevant regulations, however, is only the first step of research. You also need to verify that those regulations remain current and find cases and other documents that apply and interpret the regulations.

For users of the e-CFR, commercial databases, or looseleaf services, obtaining the current text is relatively simple because the *CFR* versions available through these sources are regularly updated. For researchers using the *CFR* in its print format or in its official version on FDSys, it is necessary to update a regulation from the most recent annual *CFR* edition. Obviously the simplest course is to check a section in the e-CFR or a commercial database to see if it lists among its sources any *Federal Register* issues more recent than the latest annual *CFR* revision.

Another tool for updating regulations is a monthly pamphlet accompanying the *CFR* entitled *LSA: List of CFR Sections Affected* (also available through FDSys), which lists the *Federal Register* pages of any rule changes affecting *CFR* sections since the most recent annual revision. *LSA* usually brings a search for current regulations up to date within a month or so, and more recent changes can then be found by using the cumulative "List of CFR Parts Affected" in the latest *Federal Register* issue (as well as in the last issue of any month not yet covered by *LSA*).

Until recently, this somewhat cumbersome process was the standard *CFR* updating procedure.

LSA remains a convenient resource for scanning an entire *CFR* chapter or part to identify recent regulatory changes. You can also use it to track down an older *CFR* reference cited in a case or article. A cited regulation may have been repealed or transferred to another *CFR* location, but *LSA* tables in the back of each *CFR* volume indicate all sections that have been repealed, transferred, or amended since 2001. Earlier changes from 1949 to 2000 are listed in a separate series of *List of CFR Sections Affected* volumes (included in HeinOnline's *Federal Register* collection).

The official *CFR*, whether used in print or online (including the e-CFR), contains no annotations of court decisions like those in *United States Code Annotated* or *United States Code Service*. Yet a court may invalidate a regulation or provide an important interpretation of key provisions, and identifying relevant cases is an essential part of regulatory research.

The most convenient way to find court decisions is to use Westlaw's version of the *CFR*, which includes notes of decisions similar to those in *United States Code Annotated* as well as references to relevant agency decisions, statutes, and secondary sources. The Westlaw display also includes KeyCite symbols such as red flags for sections that have been amended, repealed, or adversely affected by court decisions. Westlaw in effect gives regulations the same treatment that it does statutes, providing a springboard from the text to a wide range of research references. West also publishes print *West's Code of Federal Regulations Annotated* editions of eight selected *CFR* titles.

Lexis has an unannotated *CFR*, but a "Shepardize" link at the top of the display allows you to find citing cases and law review articles. Comparable coverage in print is provided by *Shepard's Code of Federal Regulations Citations*. As with its coverage of statutes, Shepard's on Lexis offers the "Index— *Shepard's* reports by court citation" option that lists references under the particular subsection cited. This can be a great time-saver if you are looking for references to a specific subsection of a long, detailed *CFR* section.

Research in federal regulations has simplified dramatically in recent years, and users of e-CFR, Westlaw or Lexis no longer need to find updates using the *LSA* and "List of CFR Parts Affected" process. No matter what approach is used, however, you should always verify that the regulation is current and search for court decisions that may affect its scope or validity.

§ 6–4. Guidance Documents

Regulations published in the *Federal Register* and *CFR* are the most authoritative sources of agency law, but in recent years the creation of regulations has become increasingly time-consuming and complicated. As a result of this "ossification" of the rulemaking process, agencies now are just as likely to create policy through guidance documents, statements, or manuals that do not require notice-and-comment procedures and publication in the *Federal Register*. Guidance documents do not have the same binding force as regulations, but they can be important indicators of how an agency perceives its mandate and how it will respond in a specific situation.

Most guidance documents do not appear in the *Federal Register*, the *CFR*, or any other widely available published source, but many are available through agency websites. The Electronic Freedom of Information Act Amendments of 1996 mandates that agencies make policy statements, manuals, and frequently requested information available to the public electronically. Under a 2007 Office of Management and Budget bulletin, agency websites are now required to maintain current lists of significant guidance documents in effect with links to each document listed.

Guidance documents are essential statements of agency policy, but what sets them apart from regulations for the researcher is that there is little consistency in their form and function between agencies. Regulations take basically the same form from all agencies and are published in the *Federal Register* and *CFR*, but an understanding of guidance documents requires a familiarity with an agency's website and the ways in which the agency informs interested parties of its policies and interpretations.

Website organization and ease of access vary considerably from agency to agency. The Animal and

Plant Health Inspection Service site <www.aphis. usda.gov> has information by subject as well as a "Regulations and Assessments" link that leads to a page with links to the *CFR*, APHIS rulemaking dockets, and significant guidance documents. One of these guidance documents, the Animal Care Policy Manual, consists of specific instructions for field inspectors such as the policy on identification of puppies less than 16 weeks of age shown in Exhibit 6–8 on page 305.

Even though agency websites have greatly increased access to government information, a vast store of additional unpublished documentation such as internal records, correspondence, and staff studies still exists. Under the Freedom of Information Act, individuals can request copies of most documents (although it may take weeks or months to receive a reply and there are broad exceptions of material that agencies need not disclose). The first place to check for policies and procedures is the department or agency's website, which should have a Freedom of Information or FOIA link on its front page.

Several more general resources are available for assistance in filing FOIA requests. The Reporters Committee for Freedom of the Press <www.rcfp. org/foia/> has a useful guide and a fill-in-the-blank FOI Letter Generator. The House Committee on Government Reform publishes a concise handbook with sample request forms, *A Citizen's Guide on Using the Freedom of Information Act and the Pri-*

vacy Act of 1974 to Request Government Records,
H.R. Rep. 109–226 (2005) (available online from
GPO Access and through the Federation of Ameri-
can Scientists <www.fas.org/sgp/foia/citizen.pdf>).
Procedures and sample forms for filing requests and
suing to compel disclosure are also available in
Stephen P. Gidiere, *The Federal Information Manu-
al: How the Government Collects, Manages, and
Discloses Information Under FOIA and Other Stat-
utes* (2006).

§ 6–5. Administrative Decisions and Rulings

While regulations and guidance documents are
the primary means by which most agencies create
legal rules within their areas of expertise, administrative agencies also have quasi-judicial functions in
which they hold hearings and issue decisions involving specific parties. Although in most instances
decisions and rulings do not have binding authority
in later cases, they have considerable precedential
value for attorneys practicing before an agency or
appealing an agency decision.

Formal Adjudications. Agency hearings are
usually conducted by an administrative law judge,
whose decision can be appealed to a higher authority within the agency. Review of a final agency
decision can generally be sought in federal court.

About fifteen regulatory commissions and other
agencies publish their decisions in a form similar to
official reports of court decisions. According to *The
Bluebook*, these reports are the source to which

decisions should be cited if they appear therein. Retrospective PDF collections of published reports are available from both HeinOnline <www.hein online.org> and LLMC Digital <www.llmcdigital. org>. Exhibit 6–9 shows the beginning of a Department of Agriculture decision on Animal Welfare Act issues from the publication *Agriculture Decisions*.

Recent decisions are also available from agency websites, but there is little consistency in how agencies provide access to these documents. Because they can be hard to find, a directory of websites with agency decisions, such as the one from the University of Virginia Library <www.lib.virginia. edu/govdocs/fed_decisions_agency.html>, can be a useful resource. Even when a site with decisions is found, its search engine may be ineffective and it may lack retrospective coverage.

Westlaw and Lexis include decisions of more than seventy agencies and offices in topical databases. Their coverage includes many administrative decisions not published in official reports, and generally extends much earlier than official websites.

Many administrative decisions are also published, along with other documents such as statutes, regulations, and court decisions, in topical looseleaf services. These services, which usually combine access to primary sources with commentary and current information, will be discussed in Chapter 8.

A researcher specializing in a particular area must be familiar with decisions of relevant agencies. For nonspecialists, the annotations in *United*

States Code Service may be the easiest way to learn of administrative decisions. *USCS* notes of decisions include coverage of more than fifty commissions and boards. The notes for 7 U.S.C.S. § 2149, dealing with the transportation and handling of animals, summarize more than forty cases from *Agriculture Decisions* (including the one shown in Exhibit 6–9) along with a much smaller number of court cases.

KeyCite and Shepard's both have coverage of selected administrative decisions. They list these decisions among other citing references to court decisions, statutes, and other sources, and they also provide references to later documents that affect or cite administrative decisions. Even though Westlaw's *United States Code Annotated* doesn't include notes of administrative decisions, KeyCiting 7 U.S.C.A. § 2149 retrieves a long list of *Agriculture Decisions* documents.

Advice Letters and Other Rulings. Agencies also provide advice to individuals or businesses seeking clarification of policies or regulations as applied to particular factual situations. This advice is usually accompanied by a disclaimer that the reply has no precedential value in future instances, but it is nonetheless a strong indication of how an agency interprets its mandate.

Internal Revenue Service private letter rulings and Securities and Exchange Commission no-action letters are leading examples of this type of agency document. These communications were originally sent only to the recipients and not made public, but changing views of the value of informal rulings led to their availability in print and online.

Materials like private letter rulings and no-action letters are generally available from agency websites and in printed looseleaf services, as well as from commercial databases. Westlaw and Lexis offer sophisticated search options and combine these materials in databases with other relevant materials from the agencies and courts.

The difficult first step is identifying what informal documentation is available from a particular agency. This can be done by perusing its website, by noting the sources cited in the case law and secondary literature, or by studying a guide to the resources in a particular area of law.

Attorney General Opinions. As the federal government's law firm, the Department of Justice provides legal advice to the president and to other departments. These opinions are advisory and not binding, but they are usually given some persuasive authority. Until 1977, opinions were signed by the U.S. Attorney General and published in a series entitled *Opinions of the Attorneys General of the United States*. This function is now delegated to the Office of Legal Counsel (OLC), which has published *Opinions of the Office of Legal Counsel* since 1977. Opinions of the Attorney General and OLC are available online through Westlaw, Lexis, and HeinOnline, with coverage back to 1791, and OLC opinions since 1992 are on its website <www.usdoj.gov/olc/opinions.htm>.

§ 6–6. Presidential Lawmaking

The president has the power to veto legislation passed by Congress and the duty to enforce enacted laws, and supervises the workings of the departments and administrative agencies. The president also has a wide-ranging lawmaking authority in his or her own right, as the nation's agent of foreign relations and its military commander. In fulfilling these roles and functions, the president issues executive orders, proclamations, and other documents of legal effect.

Background information on the presidency is available in numerous sources. Two of the more comprehensive reference works are *Encyclopedia of the American Presidency* (Leonard W. Levy & Louis Fisher eds., 1993) and *Guide to the Presidency* (Michael Nelson ed., 4th ed. 2008). Presidential lawmaking power more specifically is discussed in Harold J. Krent, *Presidential Powers* (2005).

a. Executive Orders and Proclamations

The major legal documents issued by the president are *executive orders* and *proclamations*. Executive orders usually involve an exercise of presidential authority related to government business, while proclamations are announcements of policy or of matters requiring public notice. Proclamations are often ceremonial or commemorative, but some have important legal effects such as implementing trade agreements or declaring treaties to be in force.

Executive orders and proclamations are issued in separate numbered series and published in the *Federal Register*. They are available, with other *Federal Register* materials, from FDSys since 1994. Westlaw has executive orders since 1936 and other presidential documents since 1984, and Lexis has executive orders since 1980. The American Presidency Project at the University of California, Santa Barbara <www.presidency.ucsb.edu> has free online access to executive orders dating back to 1826 and proclamations back to 1789, as well as a wide range of other documents.

Executive orders and proclamations are reprinted in a number of locations, including an annual compilation of Title 3 of the *Code of Federal Regulations*. Because each annual edition of Title 3 is a unique set of documents rather than an updated codification, older volumes remain part of the current *CFR* set. Documents from the years 1936 to 1975 have been recompiled into multiyear hardcover editions, and all volumes since 1936 are available online through HeinOnline. The *CFR* is the preferred *Bluebook* and *ALWD Citation Manual* source for the presidential documents it contains.

Proclamations, but not executive orders, are printed in the annual *Statutes at Large* volumes. Major orders and proclamations are also reprinted in the notes following related statutory provisions in the *U.S. Code*, *USCA*, and *USCS*. The *U.S. Code* is an important source, if only because *The Blue-book* requires a parallel U.S.C. citation "whenever possible." Tables in each version of the code list presidential documents by number and indicate where they can be found.

Coverage of proclamations and executive orders is included in KeyCite and Shepard's (in print in *Shepard's Code of Federal Regulations Citations*). Shepard's has references to citing court decisions and law review articles, while KeyCite's coverage also includes subsequent amendments and citations in administrative materials and court documents. Amendments and revocations are also noted in *LSA: List of CFR Sections Affected*, and the Office of the Federal Register website <www.federal register.gov> maintains a disposition table of executive orders since 1937 with information on amendment, revocation, and current status.

b. Other Presidential Documents

The president issues several other documents with legal significance. These include various memoranda, reports, speeches, and messages to Congress.

Memoranda and Directives. A variety of other documents are printed in the *Federal Register* along with executive orders and proclamations, but not included as part of either series. Presidential determinations pursuant to specific statutory mandates are issued in a numbered series, and unnumbered documents include memoranda and notices. Many of these documents deal with foreign affairs. They are reprinted in the annual cumulation of 3 C.F.R. in a separate section following executive orders.

Reorganization Plans. A reorganization plan consisting of a presidential proposal to transfer or abolish agency functions was a mechanism used from 1946 to 1979. Several major agencies, including the Environmental Protection Agency and the Department of Health, Education and Welfare, were initially created by reorganization plans. A reorganization plan became law automatically unless either chamber of Congress passed a resolution disapproving it. These plans were published in the *Federal Register*, *CFR*, and *Statutes at Large*, and many are reprinted in all three versions of the code (in appendices to Title 5 in the *U.S. Code* and *USCA*, and following 5 U.S.C.S. § 903).

Messages to Congress. Communications to Congress by the president may propose new legislation, explain vetoes, transmit reports or other documents, or convey information about the state of national affairs or some other matter of concern. Messages are published in the *Congressional Record* and as House Documents. Messages proposing legislation may have some value in determining the intent of laws that are enacted as a result.

The messages or statements issued when the President signs or vetoes particular enactments can also shed light on legislative history. Presidents sometimes use signing statements to convey interpretations of ambiguous or controversial provisions.

These statements have been included in *USCCAN*'s legislative history section beginning in 1986, although their importance in interpreting statutory language has been subject to dispute.

Compilations of Presidential Papers. The most comprehensive source for current presidential material is the *Daily Compilation of Presidential Documents*, which succeeded the *Weekly Compilation of Presidential Documents* in January 2009. The *Daily Compilation* includes nominations, announcements, and transcripts of speeches and press conferences, as well as executive orders, proclamations, signing statements, and other legally significant documents. *Daily Compilation* and *Weekly Compilation* issues are available in PDF on FDSys back to 1993, and HeinOnline has comprehensive coverage back to the first *Weekly Compilation* volume in 1965. Westlaw coverage begins in 2000.

Public Papers of the Presidents is an official series of annual volumes compiling presidential documents. Volumes have been published for Herbert Hoover and for all presidents after Franklin D. Roosevelt, and the papers of Roosevelt and most earlier presidents are generally available in commercially published editions. FDSys provides access to *Public Papers* volumes beginning with 1991, and searchable retrospective collections of the entire set and earlier compilations are available from HeinOnline and the American Presidency Project.

§ 6–7. State Administrative Law

Like the federal government, the states have experienced a dramatic increase in the number and activity of their administrative agencies. In most states, however, publication of agency rules and decisions is far less systematic than it is on the federal level.

a. Websites and Directories

State websites are often the best starting point to determine the jurisdiction of relevant agencies and their publications, and many have directories with contact information for government officials. If a search engine does not quickly lead you to the state homepage, the Library of Congress's State Government Information page <www.loc.gov/rr/news/stategov/> provides links for each state.

Nearly all states publish official manuals paralleling the *United States Government Manual* and providing quick access to information about government agencies and officials. Some of these directories describe state agency functions and publications, while others simply serve as government phone directories. They are described in the "General State Government Information" sections of the annual *State Legislative Sourcebook*, along with information about reference works, statistical abstracts, and other sources. The American Library Association's "State Blue Books" <wikis.ala.org/godort/index.php/State_Blue_Books> links to online versions.

In addition, a number of directories have multi-state access to officials' names and contact information. Extensive listings are provided by *Carroll's State Directory* and Leadership Directories' *State Yellow Book*; both of which are also available online by subscription. The Council of State Governments' *CSG State Directory* lists officials by function, rather than by state, and may be most convenient for someone needing to contact similar officials in several states. CSG's biennial *Book of the States* supplements these directories with more than 170 tables presenting a broad range of information on government operations in each of the fifty states.

b. Regulations and Executive Orders

Almost every state issues a subject compilation of its administrative regulations, and most supplement these with weekly, biweekly or monthly registers. While the states generally follow the paradigm established by the *CFR* and *Federal Register*, few state administrative codes and registers are as readily accessible as their federal counterparts. Some simply compile a variety of material submitted by individual agencies, and some have incomplete coverage. Indexing is often inadequate, sometimes even nonexistent.

The Bluebook and *ALWD Citation Manual* identify administrative codes and registers in their lists of basic primary sources for each state. More detailed information is available in William H. Manz, *Guide to State Legislation, Legislative History, and Administrative Materials* (7th ed. 2008), which lists print and online sources for each state's administrative code. The annual two-volume *CAL INFO Guide to the Administrative Regulations of the States & Territories* provides the tables of contents for each administrative code, making it easier to identify relevant regulations in order to know which title or code volume is needed.

Almost every state makes its administrative code and register available on its government website. One of the easiest ways to find these sources is through the National Association of Secretaries of State's list of administrative code and register links <www.administrativerules.org>. Westlaw and Lexis also have administrative codes from most of the states, and Westlaw has "50 State Regulatory Surveys" with citations and links for each state's administrative code provisions on several hundred topics.

Some of the administrative codes and registers include executive orders or similar legal pronouncements from governors. Several governors include executive orders on their websites, which can be accessed through state government homepages or by links from the National Governors Association <www.nga.org>. Sources for executive orders are also listed in *Guide to State Legislation, Legislative History, and Administrative Materials*.

c. Decisions, Rulings, and Other Documents

Decisions of some state agencies, especially those dealing with banking, insurance, public utilities, taxation, and workers' compensation, may be published in official form in chronological series. A few looseleaf services and topical reporters also include state administrative decisions, and a growing number of state agency decisions are included in the online databases and on agency websites. *Guide to State Legislation, Legislative History, and Administrative Materials* lists publications and online sources for agency rulings, decisions, and orders.

The opinions of state attorneys general, issued in response to questions from government officials, can have considerable significance in legal research. Although attorney general opinions are advisory and have no binding authority, they are given considerable weight by the courts in interpreting statutes and regulations. Most states publish attorney general opinions in bound volumes. Many attorney generals also have recent opinions on their websites, which can be found through links at the National Association of Attorneys General website <www.naag.org>. State attorney general opinions are available online in Westlaw and Lexis, with coverage in most states beginning in 1977 or earlier. Some attorney general opinions are included in the annotations in state codes, but coverage varies from state to state. KeyCite (but not Shepard's) includes attorney general opinions as citing sources in its coverage of cases, statutes, and other sources. It does not, however, provide the option to KeyCite these opinions themselves to find later references.

As with federal agencies, guidance documents and other publications from agencies can also be important in interpreting state law. Materials such as guidelines and manuals are increasingly available from agency websites.

Like the federal government, each state has open records laws under which unpublished information can be obtained upon request. Information on each state's laws and procedures is available from the National Freedom of Information Coalition <www. nfoic.org/states/> and the Reporters Committee for Freedom of the Press's Open Government Guide <www.rcfp.org/ogg/>.

§ 6–8. Local Law

Legal problems and issues are governed not only by federal and state law, but also by the laws of counties, cities, and other local units. Housing, transportation, social welfare, education, municipal services, zoning, and environmental conditions are all heavily regulated at the local level of government.

Cities and counties are administrative units of the states, with lawmaking powers determined by state constitution or by legislative delegation of authority. They create a variety of legal documents that can be important in legal research. *Charters* are the basic laws creating the structure of local government, and *ordinances* are local enactments governing specific issues. In addition many localities have administrative agencies that issue rules or decisions.

Most county and city codes, especially in larger jurisdictions, are available on the Internet. State and Local Government on the Net <www.state localgov.net> can lead you to county and city home-pages, which provide background and contact information if not the text of ordinances. Two of the leading publishers of local codes, both of which permit free online access, are American Legal Publishing Corp. <www.amlegal.com/library/> and the Municipal Code Corporation <www.municode. com>. The Seattle Public Library's Municipal Codes Online <www.spl.org/default.asp?pageID= collection_municodes> has links to other collections.

State and local law often incorporates industry codes on areas such as construction and fire safety. The International Code Council <www.iccsafe.org> publishes a series of fourteen codes on building standards and related issues, and the Building Code Reference Library <www.reedconstructiondata. com/building-codes/> identifies the codes in force in specific states and major cities. PDF versions of many state and local codes are available free from Public.Resource.org <bulk.resource.org/codes. gov/>.

Because much local law information is not available in print or on the Internet, direct contact by telephone or e-mail may be essential. Directories with information on local governments throughout the country include *Carroll's County Directory*, *Carroll's Municipal Directory*, and *Municipal Yellow*

Book. These directories are all available to subscribers through their publishers' websites.

ANIMALS AND PLANTS · 261

▶CONGRESS

For a listing of relevant congressional committees and subcommittees, please see page 252 or the Appendix.

▶NONGOVERNMENTAL

American Herbal Products Assn., *8630 Fenton St., #918, Silver Spring, MD 20910; (301) 588-1171. Fax, (301) 588-1174. Michael McGuffin, President. Press, (301) 588-1171, ext. 104.*
General e-mail, ahpa@ahpa.org
Web, www.ahpa.org

Membership: U.S. companies and individuals that grow, manufacture, and distribute therapeutic herbs and herbal products; associates in education, law, media, and medicine. Supports research; promotes quality standards, consumer protection, competition, and self-regulation in the industry. Monitors legislation and regulations.

American Veterinary Medical Assn., *Governmental Relations, Washington Office, 1910 Sunderland Pl. N.W. 20036-1642; (202) 789-0007. Fax, (202) 842-4360. Dr. Mark Lutschaunig, Director. Toll-free, (800) 321-1473.*
General e-mail, avmagrd@avma.org
Web, www.avma.org

Monitors legislation and regulations that influence animal and human health and advance the veterinary medical profession. (Headquarters in Schaumburg, Ill.)

Animal Health Institute, *1325 G St. N.W., #700 20005-3104; (202) 637-2440. Fax, (202) 393-1667. Alexander S. Mathews, President.*
Web, www.ahi.org

Membership: manufacturers of drugs and other products (including vaccines, pesticides, and vitamins) for pets and food-producing animals. Monitors legislation and regulations.

Assn. of American Veterinary Medical Colleges (AAVMC), *1101 Vermont Ave. N.W., #301 20005-3536; (202) 371-9195. Fax, (202) 842-0773. Dr. Marguerite Pappaionou, Executive Director.*
Web, www.aavmc.org

Membership: U.S., Canadian, and international schools and colleges of veterinary medicine, departments of comparative medicine, and departments of veterinary science in agricultural colleges. Produces veterinary reports; sponsors continuing education programs and conferences on veterinary medical issues.

Animal Rights and Welfare

▶AGENCIES

Animal and Plant Health Inspection Service (APHIS), *(Agriculture Dept.), Animal Care, 4700 River Rd., Unit 84, Riverdale, MD 20737-1234; (301) 734-1234. Fax, (301) 734-4978. Chester Gipson, Deputy Administrator.*

General e-mail, ace@aphis.usda.gov
Web, www.aphis.usda.gov/animal_welfare/index.shtml

Administers laws for the breeding, exhibition, and care of animals raised for sale and research and transported commercially.

National Agricultural Library (Agriculture Dept.), *Animal Welfare Information Center, 10301 Baltimore Ave., #410, Beltsville, MD 20705; (301) 504-6212. Fax, (301) 504-7125. Jean Larson, Coordinator.*
General e-mail, awic@ars.usda.gov
Web, http://awic.nal.usda.gov

Provides information for improved animal care and use in research, testing, teaching, and exhibition.

National Institutes of Health (NIH), *(Health and Human Services Dept.), Animal Care and Use, 31 Center Drive, Bldg. 31, #B1C37, MSC 2252, Bethesda, MD 20892-2252; (301) 496-5424. Fax, (301) 480-8298. Terri Clark, Director (Acting).*
General e-mail, secoacu@od.nih.gov
Web, http://oacu.od.nih.gov

Provides guidance for the humane care and use of animals in the intramural research program at NIH.

National Institutes of Health (NIH), *(Health and Human Services Dept.), Laboratory Animal Welfare, 6705 Rockledge Dr., RLK1, #360, MSC 7982, Bethesda, MD 20892-7982; (301) 496-7163. Fax, (301) 402-7065. Patricia Brown, Director.*
General e-mail, olaw@od.nih.gov
Web, http://grants.nih.gov/grants/olaw/olaw.htm

Develops and monitors policy on the humane care and use of animals in research conducted by any public health service entity.

▶CONGRESS

For a listing of relevant congressional committees and subcommittees, please see page 252 or the Appendix.

▶NONGOVERNMENTAL

Alley Cat Allies, *7920 Norfolk Avenue, #600, Bethesda, MD 20814-2525; (240) 482-1980. Fax, (240) 482-1990. Donna Wilcox, Director.*
General e-mail, webmaster@alleycat.org
Web, www.alleycat.org

Clearinghouse for information on feral and stray cats. Advocates the trap-neuter-return method to reduce feral cat populations.

American Horse Protection Assn., *1000 29th St. N.W., #T100 20007; (202) 965-0500. Fax, (202) 965-9621. Robin C. Lohnes, Executive Director.*
General e-mail, info@ahpa.us

Membership: individuals, corporations, and foundations interested in protecting wild and domestic horses.

Exhibit 6–1. A page from the *Washington Information Directory*

Animal Care [AC]
APHIS Animal Care, 4700 River Road, Unit 84, Riverdale, MD 20737
Tel: (301) 734-7833 (General Information) Fax: (301) 734-4978
E-mail: ace@usda.gov Internet: www.aphis.usda.gov/animal_welfare
- Deputy Administrator **Chester A. Gipson** USDA,
  APHIS, Animal Care, Unit 97 . . . . (301) 734-4980
  E-mail: chester.a.gipson@aphis.usda.gov   Fax: (301) 734-4993
  Education: Florida A&M BS; Florida MA;
  Tuskegee DVM
  Associate Deputy Administrator **Andrea M. Morgan**
  USDA, APHIS, Unit 97 . . . . (301) 734-4980
  E-mail: andrea.m.morgan@aphis.usda.gov
  Education: Missouri 1982 BS, 1985 PhD;
  George Washington 1990 MEd
  Emergency Management Staff Director
  Allan T. Hogue USDA, APHIS, Animal Care . . . . (301) 734-7833
  E-mail: allan.t.hogue@aphis.usda.gov   Fax: (301) 734-4978
  Information Technology Director **Thay Ly** . . . . (301) 734-5189
  E-mail: thay.ly@aphis.usda.gov   Fax: (301) 734-4993
  Resource Management Staff Director **Yvette D. Joyner** . . (301) 734-0625
  E-mail: yvette.d.joyner@aphis.usda.gov   Fax: (301) 734-4993

Exhibit 6–2. An excerpt from the *Federal Yellow Book*

413

Proposed Rules

Federal Register

Vol. 73, No. 2

Thursday, January 3, 2008

This section of the FEDERAL REGISTER contains notices to the public of the proposed issuance of rules and regulations. The purpose of these notices is to give interested persons an opportunity to participate in the rule making prior to the adoption of the final rules.

DEPARTMENT OF AGRICULTURE

Animal and Plant Health Inspection Service

9 CFR Parts 2 and 3

[Docket No. 99–014–2]

RIN 0579–AC41

Animal Welfare; Climatic and Environmental Conditions for Transportation of Warmblooded Animals Other Than Marine Mammals

AGENCY: Animal and Plant Health Inspection Service, USDA.

ACTION: Proposed rule; withdrawal and reproposal.

SUMMARY: We are proposing to amend the Animal Welfare Act regulations regarding transportation of live animals other than marine mammals by removing the current ambient temperature requirements for various stages in the transportation of those animals. We would replace those requirements with a single performance standard under which the animals would be transported under climatic and environmental conditions that are appropriate for their welfare. The regulations currently require that ambient temperatures be maintained within certain ranges during transportation, but animals may be transported at ambient temperatures below the minimum temperatures if their consignor provides a certificate signed by a veterinarian certifying that the animals are acclimated to temperatures lower than the minimum temperature. This proposal would make acclimation certificates for live animals other than marine mammals unnecessary. This proposal replaces a previously published proposed rule, which we are withdrawing as part of this document, that would have required that the acclimation certificate for a dog or cat be signed by the owner of the dog or cat being transported rather than by a veterinarian. This proposal does not address marine

mammals due to their unique requirements for care and handling. These changes would remove potentially confusing temperature requirements and acclimation certificate provisions from the regulations governing the transportation of animals other than marine mammals and focus those regulations on ensuring that climatic and environmental conditions are maintained appropriately during transportation of those animals.

DATES: We will consider all comments that we receive on or before March 3, 2008.

ADDRESSES: You may submit comments by either of the following methods:

• *Federal eRulemaking Portal:* Go to http://www.regulations.gov/fdmspublic/component/main?main=DocketDetail&d=APHIS–2006–0150 to submit or view comments and to view supporting and related materials available electronically.

• *Postal Mail/Commercial Delivery:* Please send two copies of your comment to Docket No. 99–014–2, Regulatory Analysis and Development, PPD, APHIS, Station 3A–03.8, 4700 River Road Unit 118, Riverdale, MD 20737–1238. Please state that your comment refers to Docket No. 99–014–2.

Reading Room: You may read any comments that we receive on this docket in our reading room. The reading room is located in room 1141 of the USDA South Building, 14th Street and Independence Avenue SW., Washington, DC. Normal reading room hours are 8 a.m. to 4:30 p.m., Monday through Friday, except holidays. To be sure someone is there to help you, please call (202) 690–2817 before coming.

Other Information: Additional information about APHIS and its programs is available on the Internet at http://www.aphis.usda.gov.

FOR FURTHER INFORMATION CONTACT: Dr. Jerry D. DePoyster, Veterinary Medical Officer, Animal Care, APHIS, 4700 River Road Unit 84, Riverdale, MD 20737–1234; (301) 734–7586.

SUPPLEMENTARY INFORMATION:

Background

Under the Animal Welfare Act (AWA) (7 U.S.C. 2131 *et seq.*), the Secretary of Agriculture is authorized to promulgate regulations and standards governing the humane handling, housing, care, treatment, and transportation of certain

animals by dealers, research facilities, exhibitors, and carriers and intermediate handlers. The Secretary has delegated the responsibility for enforcing the AWA to the U.S. Department of Agriculture's (USDA) Animal and Plant Health Inspection Service (APHIS). Regulations and standards established under the AWA are contained in 9 CFR parts 1, 2, and 3 (referred to below as the regulations). Parts 1 and 2 contain definitions and general requirements, and part 3 contains specific standards for the care of animals.

The regulations in part 3 are divided into six subparts, designated as subparts A through F, each of which contains facility and operating standards, animal health and husbandry standards, and transportation standards for a specific category of animals. Respectively, these categories of animals are: Dogs and cats (Subpart A); guinea pigs and hamsters (Subpart B); rabbits (Subpart C); nonhuman primates (Subpart D); marine mammals (Subpart E); and warmblooded animals other than those addressed in the previous subparts (Subpart F).

In each of these subparts, the final seven sections contain standards for the transportation of the type of animals addressed in the subpart. These transportation standards are very similar across the subparts, although some details of their requirements differ.

Each of the subparts specifies a range of ambient temperatures to which live animals may be exposed during transportation. For example, § 3.16 of subpart A contains minimum requirements for terminal facilities used in the transportation of dogs and cats. Among other things, § 3.16 requires that the ambient temperature in an animal holding area containing dogs and cats must not fall below 45 °F (7.2 °C) or rise above 85 °F (29.5 °C) for more than 4 consecutive hours at any time dogs or cats are present. Section 3.19 of subpart A contains minimum requirements for handling dogs and cats when they are moved within, to, or from an animal holding area of a terminal facility or a primary conveyance when being transported. Among other things, § 3.19 requires that dogs or cats must not be exposed to an ambient temperature below 45 °F (7.2 °C) or above 85 °F (29.5 °C) for a period of more than 45 minutes.

Exhibit 6–3. The first page of a proposed rule in the *Federal Register*

Federal Register / Vol. 73, No. 2 / Thursday, January 3, 2008 / Proposed Rules 417

commerce. Consignors and practicing veterinarians would no longer have to provide acclimation certificates, and therefore the rule would relieve them from having to fulfill a requirement. Veterinarians would forego the fees that they might otherwise charge consignor-owners for certifications, but any such fees are likely to be insignificant, when judged against the veterinarians' overall revenues from all sources.

From an economic standpoint, the proposal has the potential to impact carriers and intermediate handlers-large and small-because compliance may require that they modify the climatic conditions to which they currently expose animals. However, based on our experience enforcing the regulations, it appears that, for most carriers and handlers, a modification of existing climatic conditions would not be necessary, since those conditions appear to be appropriate already. In addition, the proposed rule would afford carriers and intermediate handlers some flexibility in providing appropriate climatic conditions for each animal they transport. Within the overall carrier and handler category, the airline and to a lesser extent motor freight line industries are most likely to include entities affected by the proposed rule.

It is likely that the rule may affect an unknown number of small entities. Although we believe that the proposal would not have a significant economic impact on a substantial number of small entities, hard data to support that conclusion is not available. Accordingly, we have prepared this initial regulatory flexibility analysis so that the public may have the opportunity to offer comments on expected effects of the proposed rule on small entities.

Executive Order 12372

This program/activity is listed in the Catalog of Federal Domestic Assistance under No. 10.025 and is subject to Executive Order 12372, which requires intergovernmental consultation with State and local officials. (See 7 CFR part 3015, subpart V.)

Executive Order 12988

This proposed rule has been reviewed under Executive Order 12988, Civil Justice Reform. It is not intended to have retroactive effect. This rule would not preempt any State or local laws, regulations, or policies, unless they present an irreconcilable conflict with this rule. The Act does not provide administrative procedures which must be exhausted prior to a judicial challenge to the provisions of this rule.

Paperwork Reduction Act

This proposed rule contains no new information collection or recordkeeping requirements under the Paperwork Reduction Act of 1995 (44 U.S.C. 3501 *et seq.*). Further, this proposed rule would reduce information collection or recordkeeping requirements in 9 CFR part 3.

Lists of Subjects

9 CFR Part 2

Animal welfare, Pets, Reporting and recordkeeping requirements, Research.

9 CFR Part 3

Animal welfare, Marine mammals, Pets, Reporting and recordkeeping requirements, Research, Transportation.

Accordingly, we are proposing to amend 9 CFR parts 2 and 3 as follows:

PART 2—REGULATIONS

1. The authority citation for part 2 continues to read as follows:

Authority: 7 U.S.C. 2131–2159; 7 CFR 2.22, 2.80, and 371.7.

2. In § 2.131, a new paragraph (f) is added to read as follows:

§ 2.131 Handling of animals.

* * *

(f)(1) Transportation of all live animals shall be done in a manner that does not cause overheating, excessive cooling, or adverse environmental conditions that could cause unnecessary discomfort or stress. When climatic or environmental conditions, including temperature, humidity, exposure, ventilation, pressurization, time, or other environmental conditions, or any combination thereof, present a threat to the health or well-being of a live animal, appropriate measures shall be taken immediately to alleviate the impact of those conditions. The different climatic and environmental factors prevailing during a journey shall be considered when arranging for the transportation of and when transporting live animals. Corrections may include, but would not be limited to:

(i) The temperature and humidity level of any enclosure used during transportation of live animals must be controlled by adequate ventilation or any other means necessary;

(ii) Appropriate care must be taken to ensure that live animals are not subjected to drafts;

(iii) Appropriate care must be taken to ensure that live animals are not exposed to direct heat, such as placement in direct sunlight or near a hot radiator;

(iv) Appropriate care must be taken to ensure that live animals are not exposed to direct sources of cold; and

(v) During prolonged air transit stops in local climatic conditions that could produce excessive heat for live animals held in aircraft compartments, the aircraft doors shall be opened and if necessary ground equipment shall be used to control the condition of the air within compartments containing live animals.

(2) In order to determine what climatic and environmental conditions are appropriate for a live animal, factors such as, but not limited to, the animal's age, type or breed, physiological state, last feeding, and acclimation shall be considered when such information is available.

PART 3—STANDARDS

3. The authority citation for part 3 continues to read as follows:

Authority: 7 U.S.C. 2131–2159; 7 CFR 2.22, 2.80, and 371.7.

4. In § 3.13, paragraph (e) is revised to read as set forth below.

§ 3.13 Consignments to carriers and intermediate handlers.

* * * * *

(e) Carriers and intermediate handlers shall not accept a dog or cat for transport in commerce unless their animal holding area can maintain climatic and environmental conditions in accordance with the requirements of § 2.131(f).

* * * * *

5. Section 3.15 is amended as follows:

a. By revising paragraph (d) to read as set forth below.

b. By removing paragraph (e) and redesignating paragraphs (f), (g), and (h) as paragraphs (e), (f), and (g), respectively.

§ 3.15 Primary conveyances (motor vehicle, rail, air, and marine).

* * * * *

(d) During transportation, the climatic and environmental conditions in the animal cargo area shall be maintained in accordance with § 2.131(f).

* * * * *

§ 3.17 [Amended]

6. Section 3.17 is amended as follows:

a. In paragraph (a), by removing the words "the ambient temperature is within the limits provided in § 3.15(e)" and adding the words "climatic and environmental conditions are being maintained in accordance with the requirements of § 2.131(f)" in their place.

b. In paragraph (b), by removing the words "the animal cargo area meets the heating and cooling requirements of § 3.15(d)" and adding the words

Exhibit 6–4. Text of a proposed rule change in the *Federal Register*

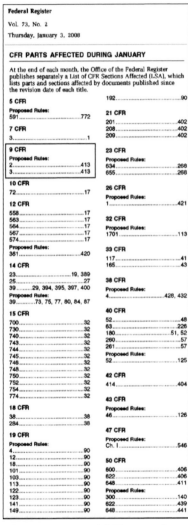

Federal Register

Vol. 73, No. 2

Thursday, January 3, 2008

CFR PARTS AFFECTED DURING JANUARY

At the end of each month, the Office of the Federal Register publishes separately a List of CFR Sections Affected (LSA), which lists parts and sections affected by documents published since the revision date of each title.

5 CFR

Proposed Rules:
591..772

7 CFR

3..1

9 CFR

Proposed Rules:
2..413
3..413

10 CFR

72...17

12 CFR

558.......................................17
563.......................................17
564.......................................17
567.......................................17
574.......................................17
Proposed Rules:
361......................................420

14 CFR

23.............................19, 389
25...27
39.........29, 394, 395, 397, 400
Proposed Rules:
39............73, 75, 77, 80, 84, 87

15 CFR

700.......................................32
730.......................................32
740.......................................32
743.......................................32
744.......................................32
745.......................................32
746.......................................32
748.......................................32
750.......................................32
752.......................................32
754.......................................32
774.......................................32

18 CFR

38...38
284.......................................38

19 CFR

Proposed Rules:
4...90
12.......................................90
18.......................................90
101.....................................90
103.....................................90
113.....................................90
122.....................................90
123.....................................90
141.....................................90
149.....................................90

192.....................................90

21 CFR

201.....................................402
208.....................................402
209.....................................402

23 CFR

Proposed Rules:
634.....................................268
655.....................................268

26 CFR

Proposed Rules:
1...421

32 CFR

Proposed Rules:
1701...................................113

33 CFR

117.......................................41
165.......................................43

38 CFR

Proposed Rules:
4...............................428, 432

40 CFR

52...48
63.......................................226
180...............................51, 52
260.......................................57
261.......................................57
Proposed Rules:
52.......................................125

42 CFR

414.....................................404

43 CFR

Proposed Rules:
46.......................................126

47 CFR

Proposed Rules:
Ch. I...................................546

50 CFR

600.....................................406
622.....................................406
648.....................................411
Proposed Rules:
300.....................................140
622.....................................439
648.....................................441

Exhibit 6–5. The monthly list of *CFR* parts affected in a *Federal Register* issue

Animal and Plant Health Inspection Service, USDA **Pt. 2**

premise in which a live animal or animals are kept for public exhibition or viewing, regardless of compensation.

[54 FR 36119, Aug. 31, 1989, as amended at 55 FR 12631, Apr. 5, 1990; 58 FR 39129, July 22, 1993; 62 FR 43275, Aug. 13, 1997; 63 FR 47148, Sept. 4, 1998; 63 FR 62926, Nov. 10, 1998; 65 FR 6314, Feb. 9, 2000; 68 FR 12285, Mar. 14, 2003; 69 FR 31514, June 4, 2004; 69 FR 42099, July 14, 2004]

EFFECTIVE DATE NOTE: At 64 FR 15920, Apr. 2, 1999, the definitions of *buffer area, interactive area, interactive session, sanctuary area,* and *swim-with-the-dolphin (SWTD) program* were suspended, effective Apr. 2, 1999.

PART 2—REGULATIONS

Subpart A—Licensing

Sec.
2.1 Requirements and application.
2.2 Acknowledgement of regulations and standards.
2.3 Demonstration of compliance with standards and regulations.
2.4 Non-interference with APHIS officials.
2.5 Duration of license and termination of license.
2.6 Annual license fees.
2.7 Annual report by licensees.
2.8 Notification of change of name, address, control, or ownership of business.
2.9 Officers, agents, and employees of licensees whose licenses have been suspended or revoked.
2.10 Licensees whose licenses have been suspended or revoked.
2.11 Denial of initial license application.
2.12 Termination of a license.

Subpart B—Registration

2.25 Requirements and procedures.
2.26 Acknowledgement of regulations and standards.
2.27 Notification of change of operation.

Subpart C—Research Facilities

2.30 Registration.
2.31 Institutional Animal Care and Use Committee (IACUC).
2.32 Personnel qualifications.
2.33 Attending veterinarian and adequate veterinary care.
2.34 [Reserved]
2.35 Recordkeeping requirements.
2.36 Annual report.
2.37 Federal research facilities.
2.38 Miscellaneous.

Subpart D—Attending Veterinarian and Adequate Veterinary Care

2.40 Attending veterinarian and adequate veterinary care (dealers and exhibitors).

Subpart E—Identification of Animals

2.50 Time and method of identification.
2.51 Form of official tag.
2.52 How to obtain tags.
2.53 Use of tags.
2.54 Lost tags.
2.55 Removal and disposal of tags.

Subpart F—Stolen Animals

2.60 Prohibition on the purchase, sale, use, or transportation of stolen animals.

Subpart G—Records

2.75 Records: Dealers and exhibitors.
2.76 Records: Operators of auction sales and brokers.
2.77 Records: Carriers and intermediate handlers.
2.78 Health certification and identification.
2.79 C.O.D. shipments.
2.80 Records, disposition.

Subpart H—Compliance With Standards and Holding Period

2.100 Compliance with standards.
2.101 Holding period.
2.102 Holding facility.

Subpart I—Miscellaneous

2.125 Information as to business; furnishing of same by dealers, exhibitors, operators of auction sales, intermediate handlers, and carriers.
2.126 Access and inspection of records and property.
2.127 Publication of names of persons subject to the provisions of this part.
2.128 Inspection for missing animals.
2.129 Confiscation and destruction of animals.
2.130 Minimum age requirements.
2.131 Handling of animals.
2.132 Procurement of dogs, cats, and other animals; dealers.
2.133 Certification for random source dogs and cats.

AUTHORITY: 7 U.S.C. 2131–2159; 7 CFR 2.22, 2.80, and 371.7.

SOURCE: 54 FR 36147, Aug. 31, 1989, unless otherwise noted.

13

Exhibit 6–6. The first page of 9 *CFR* Part 2

In re: FOR THE BIRDS, INC., AN IDAHO CORPORATION; AND JERRY L. KORN, AN INDIVIDUAL, AND SUSAN F. KORN, AN INDIVIDUAL, d/b/a FOR THE BIRDS; AND BEN KORN, AN INDIVIDUAL.
AWA Docket No. 04-0033.
Decision and Order as to For The Birds, Inc., and Jerry L. Korn.
Filed June 22, 2005.

AWA – Animal Welfare Act – Failure to file timely answer – Default decision – Cease and desist order – License revocation – Civil penalty.

The Judicial Officer concluded that For The Birds, Inc., committed at least 1,545 violations of the regulations and standards issued under the Animal Welfare Act and Jerry L. Korn committed at least 749 violations of the regulations and standards issued under the Animal Welfare Act during the period March 2001 through August 2003. The Judicial Officer stated For The Birds, Inc., and Jerry L. Korn are deemed, by their failures to file timely answers, to have admitted the allegations of the Complaint (7 C.F.R. § 1.136(c)). The Judicial Officer issued a cease and desist order, revoked Jerry L. Korn's Animal Welfare Act license, assessed For The Birds, Inc., a $28,050 civil penalty, and assessed Jerry L. Korn a $20,597 civil penalty.

Colleen A. Carroll, for Complainant.
Respondents For The Birds, Inc., and Jerry L. Korn, Pro se.
Initial Decision issued by Administrative Law Judge Peter M. Davenport.
Decision and Order issued by William G. Jenson, Judicial Officer.

PROCEDURAL HISTORY

Kevin Shea, Administrator, Animal and Plant Health Inspection Service, United States Department of Agriculture [hereinafter Complainant], instituted this disciplinary administrative proceeding by filing a Complaint on September 8, 2004. Complainant instituted the proceeding under the Animal Welfare Act, as amended (7 U.S.C. §§ 2131-2159) [hereinafter the Animal Welfare Act]; the regulations and standards issued under the Animal Welfare Act (9 C.F.R. §§ 1.1-3.142 (2004)) [hereinafter the Regulations and Standards]; and the Rules of Practice Governing Formal Adjudicatory Proceedings Instituted by the Secretary Under Various Statutes (7 C.F.R. §§ 1.130-.151) [hereinafter the Rules of Practice].

Complainant alleges that during the period March 2001 through

Exhibit 6–7. A *CFR* page

Policies	Animal Care Resource Guide
Identification of Puppies	Issue Date: April 14, 1997

Subject:	**Identification of Puppies Less than 16 Weeks of Age**	**Policy #20**
References:	AWA Sections 1 and 12 9CFR, Part 2, Sections 2.50(a)(2) and (b)(3)	
History:	Replaces memorandum dated December 30, 1993, "Identification of Puppies Under 16 Weeks of Age."	
Justification:	The Animal Care staff has been made aware of problems from using plastic collars to identify puppies that are less than 16 weeks of age.	
Policy:	After reviewing the Animal Welfare Act (AWA) and its intent, puppies under 16 weeks of age can be exempt from individual identification if the following requirements are met: 1. The puppies remain housed at the facility where they were whelped and are maintained as a litter. 2. The enclosure containing the puppies is identified with the information required by 9 CFR Section 2.50 until the puppies are sold or moved from the facility where they were whelped or reach the age of 16 weeks, which ever comes first.	

Exhibit 6–8. An Animal and Plant Health Inspection Service guidance document

306   ANIMAL WELFARE ACT

In re: FOR THE BIRDS, INC., AN IDAHO CORPORATION; AND JERRY L. KORN, AN INDIVIDUAL, AND SUSAN F. KORN, AN INDIVIDUAL, d/b/a FOR THE BIRDS; AND BEN KORN, AN INDIVIDUAL.
AWA Docket No. 04-0033.
Decision and Order as to For The Birds, Inc., and Jerry L. Korn.
Filed June 22, 2005.

AWA – Animal Welfare Act – Failure to file timely answer – Default decision – Cease and desist order – License revocation – Civil penalty.

The Judicial Officer concluded that For The Birds, Inc., committed at least 1,545 violations of the regulations and standards issued under the Animal Welfare Act and Jerry L. Korn committed at least 749 violations of the regulations and standards issued under the Animal Welfare Act during the period March 2001 through August 2003. The Judicial Officer stated For The Birds, Inc., and Jerry L. Korn are deemed, by their failures to file timely answers, to have admitted the allegations of the Complaint (7 C.F.R. § 1.136(c)). The Judicial Officer issued a cease and desist order, revoked Jerry L. Korn's Animal Welfare Act license, assessed For The Birds, Inc., a $28,050 civil penalty, and assessed Jerry L. Korn a $20,597 civil penalty.

Colleen A. Carroll, for Complainant.
Respondents For The Birds, Inc., and Jerry L. Korn, Pro se.
Initial Decision issued by Administrative Law Judge Peter M. Davenport.
Decision and Order issued by William G. Jenson, Judicial Officer.

PROCEDURAL HISTORY

Kevin Shea, Administrator, Animal and Plant Health Inspection Service, United States Department of Agriculture [hereinafter Complainant], instituted this disciplinary administrative proceeding by filing a Complaint on September 8, 2004. Complainant instituted the proceeding under the Animal Welfare Act, as amended (7 U.S.C. §§ 2131-2159) [hereinafter the Animal Welfare Act]; the regulations and standards issued under the Animal Welfare Act (9 C.F.R. §§ 1.1-3.142 (2004)) [hereinafter the Regulations and Standards], and the Rules of Practice Governing Formal Adjudicatory Proceedings Instituted by the Secretary Under Various Statutes (7 C.F.R. §§ 1.130-.151) [hereinafter the Rules of Practice].

Complainant alleges that during the period March 2001 through

Exhibit 6-9. The first page of an administrative adjudication, in *Agriculture Decisions*

CHAPTER 7

COURT RULES AND PRACTICE

§ 7–1. Introduction

This chapter discusses a number of resources dealing with court proceedings and legal practice. Some, such as the rules governing trial procedures and lawyer conduct, are primary legal sources. Briefs and docket sheets contain background information on decided cases or pending lawsuits. Directories and formbooks provide practical assistance for anyone who needs to contact courts, draft documents, or transact other legal business.

Litigators need to be familiar with these materials, but their value also extends to other legal research situations. All lawyers, of course, must follow rules of professional conduct, and resources such as briefs and model jury instructions can be useful sources of information about substantive legal issues.

§ 7–2. Court Rules

Rules regulating court proceedings have the force of law, but they generally cannot supersede or conflict with statutes. Most jurisdictions have sets of rules governing trial and appellate procedure, as well as rules for specialized tribunals or for particular actions such as admiralty or habeas corpus. Some of these rules are enacted by statute, but most are promulgated by the courts themselves or by conferences of judges.

a. Federal Rules

Under the Rules Enabling Act, 28 U.S.C. § 2072, federal courts have the power to adopt rules governing their procedures as long as they do not "abridge, enlarge, or modify any substantive right."

Rules of National Scope. Individual federal courts have had rules since the beginning of the judicial system, but the modern era of rulemaking began with the adoption of the Federal Rules of Civil Procedure in 1938. These were prepared by a judicial advisory committee and approved by the Supreme Court, as were subsequent sets of rules governing criminal procedure (1946) and appellate procedure (1968). The Federal Rules of Evidence were originally drafted by judges, but they were enacted by Congress in 1975 due to concerns about their potential impact on substantive rights.

These rules governing federal court proceedings can be found in online and print sources, some unannotated and others accompanied by advisory committee notes, summaries of judicial decisions, and extensive commentaries. Each of the major sets of rules is printed in the *United States Code*, accompanied by its advisory committee's explanatory comments after each section. *United States Code Annotated* (*USCA*) (in print and on Westlaw) and *United States Code Service* (*USCS*) (in print and on Lexis) also include annotations of cases in which the rules have been applied or construed, as well as references to treatises, law review articles, and legal encyclopedias. These annotations can be quite copious; the Federal Rules of Civil Procedure, for example, occupy eighteen volumes in *USCA*.

You will find in-depth scholarly analysis of the federal rules in two major treatises, Wright & Miller's *Federal Practice and Procedure* (1st–4th eds. 1969–date) and *Moore's Federal Practice* (3d ed. 1997–date). These treatises are among the secondary sources most often cited by the federal courts. They are organized rule-by-rule, providing the texts and official comments accompanied by historical background and detailed discussion of cases. Both analyze the civil, criminal, and appellate rules, as well as jurisdictional issues; *Federal Practice and Procedure* also covers the Federal Rules of Evidence. *Federal Practice and Procedure* is available on Westlaw, and *Moore's Federal Practice* is on Lexis. *Weinstein's Federal Evidence* (2d ed. 1997–date), also on Lexis, has similar rule-by-rule treatment of the Federal Rules of Evidence.

Most court rules are available at free websites, but usually without the helpful commentary and annotations found in the treatises or annotated codes. The House Committee on the Judiciary website has committee prints containing each of the major sets of rules <judiciary.house.gov/about/procedural.html>. The Administrative Office of the U.S. Courts website has a section on Federal Rule-making <www.uscourts.gov/rules/>, with links to these sources as well as information on recent and proposed amendments. The Legal Information Institute has searchable versions of the federal rules <www.law.cornell.edu/rules/>.

KeyCite and Shepard's treatment of federal court rules is similar to that for statutes. KeyCite begins with the annotations from *USCA*, followed by additional cases and secondary sources. Shepard's can be accessed online or in print in either *Shepard's Federal Statute Citations* or *Shepard's Federal Rules Citations*.

Local Rules. Individual courts also have local rules to supplement the national sets of rules. Local court rules often govern procedural matters such as the format of documents and the time allowed to file papers. Over the years, however, local rules have proliferated into an extensive array of requirements that has been called a "balkanization" of federal procedure. In addition to rules for each district, individual judges can also promulgate guidelines for the cases they hear. Litigators must be every bit as aware of local and judge-specific rules as they are of more general rules.

The E–Government Act of 2002, 44 U.S.C. § 3501 note, requires that each court's website include its local rules and individual judges' rules. Many court websites also have answers to frequently asked questions about filing requirements and trial procedures. Links to local court homepages are available through the U.S. Courts website <www.uscourts. gov/courtlinks/>, and LLRX Court Rules, Forms and Dockets <www.llrx.com/courtrules> has direct links to the rules for each jurisdiction.

The Supreme Court's rules are available on its website <www.supremecourtus.gov/ctrules/ctrules. aspx> and are also included in the *U.S. Code*, *USCA*, and *USCS*. The rules for each of the Courts of Appeals are also published in *USCA* and *USCS*, with annotations of court decisions applying the rules. Local U.S. District Court rules are usually available in court rules pamphlets published for individual states, some of which include annotations. District Court and Court of Appeals rules from the entire country are published, unannotated, in a seven-volume looseleaf set, *Federal Local Court Rules* (3d ed. 2001–date).

Local court rules are also available on Westlaw and Lexis. It may be easier to focus research on a specific federal court in Lexis, which has separate databases for the U.S. District and Bankruptcy Courts in each state. Westlaw includes local federal rules with its collections of state court rules. Both KeyCite and Shepard's cover local rules.

For each federal district and for some states, West also offers KeyRules (on Westlaw and in print). You select a specific court and type of pleading or motion that you need to file and retrieve a list of the applicable rules governing the filing of that particular document. This list is accompanied by explanation, practice tips, checklists, and links to relevant primary sources, forms, and secondary material. KeyRules are a quick way to come up to speed if filing in an unfamiliar court. Exhibit 7–1 on page 331 shows the KeyRules search form for motions, oppositions, and replies in the U.S. District Court for the Southern District of New York.

Sentencing Guidelines. The Federal Sentencing Guidelines are not court rules, but they occupy a similar position in the hierarchy of legal authorities. Judges must consider the guidelines in determining punishments for criminal convictions. The U.S. Sentencing Commission, an independent agency within the judicial branch, first promulgated the guidelines in 1987 and has revised them several times. The commission publishes its *Guidelines Manual* online <www.ussc.gov/guidelin.htm> and in print.

The sentencing guidelines are not included in the official *U.S. Code*, but both *USCA* and *USCS* have annotated versions of the guidelines accompanied by notes of court decisions and other references. These are available in Westlaw and Lexis, and the guidelines can be KeyCited and Shepardized like code sections. In print, the guidelines are covered in *Shepard's Federal Statute Citations*.

Federal Practice and Procedure and *Moore's Federal Practice* do not discuss sentencing guidelines, but shorter works such as David J. Gottlieb & Phyllis Skloot Bamberger, *Practice Under the Federal Sentencing Guidelines* (4th ed. 2001–date), and Thomas W. Hutchison et al., *Federal Sentencing Law and Practice* (annual), have similar treatment, with commentary and notes of court decisions applying the guidelines. Both of these are available on Westlaw.

b. State Rules

Rules and procedures can differ dramatically from state to state. These distinctions have decreased somewhat in recent decades as many states have adopted provisions modeled on the federal rules, particularly the Federal Rules of Evidence, but they remain significant.

Generally, a combination of statutory provisions and court rules govern procedures. The court rules are usually included in the annotated state codes, accompanied by notes of relevant cases, and are found on Westlaw and Lexis. Treatment of state court rules in KeyCite and Shepard's is similar to that for statutes, with references to citations in court decisions, law reviews, and other sources.

Most states also have annual paperback volumes with rules and procedural statutes. Many of these publications are unannotated, but some include case notes and comments by scholars or drafting committees. More extensive works in larger jurisdictions, such as Witkin's *California Practice* or *Carmody-Wait 2d Cyclopedia of New York Practice* (both available on Westlaw), provide scholarly commentaries on the rules and analysis of relevant case law.

State court websites generally include rules and other procedural information. The National Center for State Courts' "Court Web Sites" <www.ncsconline.org/D_kis/> is one of several directories of trial and appellate state court sites, and LLRX Court Rules, Forms and Dockets <www.llrx.com/courtrules> has links to general and local rules for each state.

§ 7–3. Legal Ethics

The professional activities of lawyers are generally controlled by the courts, although in some states supervision is delegated to bar associations or oversight boards. The primary sources governing legal ethics are found in a distinct body of literature consisting of rules of conduct, ethics opinions, and disciplinary decisions. Ethics opinions are advisory documents, usually issued by bar associations, analyzing how lawyers or judges should handle particular or hypothetical problems. Disciplinary decisions punish specific acts of misconduct.

Rules vary from state to state, but almost all jurisdictions have adopted some form of the American Bar Association's Model Rules of Professional Conduct. The only exceptions are California and Maine, which have developed their own sets of rules, and New York, which continues to follow the older Model Code of Professional Responsibility.

Each jurisdiction's rules of professional conduct are online from either the state court system or the state bar. Links to these sites are available from the ABA Center for Professional Responsibility <www.abanet.org/cpr/links.html> and the Legal Information Institute's American Legal Ethics Library <www.law.cornell.edu/ethics/listing.html>. Westlaw includes professional conduct rules with its more general court rules for each state, and Lexis has them with its state codes.

The rules are also published in the volumes of state court rules, although in some states they are incorporated into larger sets of rules and can be a bit difficult to find. Only a few of these sources are annotated with notes of decisions under the rules. Unannotated versions of the rules for every state are also available in the looseleaf publication *National Reporter on Legal Ethics and Professional Responsibility*.

Annotated Model Rules of Professional Conduct (6th ed. 2007), available on Westlaw, has the text of the ABA rules with comments, legal background, and notes of decisions from various jurisdictions. This is a useful source for comparative analysis and commentary, even though it does not contain the rules as adopted in any specific state. The American Law Institute has also formulated basic rules of legal ethics in its *Restatement of the Law: The Law Governing Lawyers* (2000).

As in other areas of law, you may wish to begin your research by consulting a treatise. The leading modern works are Geoffrey C. Hazard, Jr. & W. William Hodes, *The Law of Lawyering* (3d ed. 2000–date), a two-volume set designed as a workbook "for lawyers faced with immediate practical dilemmas," and Ronald D. Rotunda & John S. Dzienkowski, *Legal Ethics: The Lawyer's Deskbook on Professional Responsibility* (annual, available on Westlaw). The *ABA/BNA Lawyers' Manual on Professional Conduct* (1984–date) can also be a good place to start your research. This looseleaf service includes an extensive commentary with background and practical tips, as well as news of developments and abstracts of new decisions.

Ethics opinions, generally prepared in response to inquiries from attorneys, are issued by the American Bar Association and by state and local bar associations. ABA opinions are available on Westlaw and Lexis, as are opinions from selected state and local bars. Ethics opinions can also be found in the

National Reporter on Legal Ethics and Professional Responsibility, and most state bars have publications either summarizing their opinions or printing them in full. State bar and disciplinary agency websites generally have information about procedures for filing complaints and resolving problems with lawyers, and some of these include the text of rules and ethics opinions.

Judges are governed by a separate set of rules, in almost every jurisdiction based on the ABA's Model Code of Judicial Conduct. These rules are generally published in state court rules pamphlets with the rules of professional conduct. The Model Code is available on the ABA Center for Professional Responsibility's website <www.abanet.org/cpr/>, and Cornell's American Legal Ethics Library has links to state versions. The ABA has published an *Annotated Model Code of Judicial Conduct* (2004), and James J. Alfini et al., *Judicial Conduct and Ethics* (4th ed. 2007) analyzes issues in this area.

§ 7–4. Briefs and Other Court Documents

You can learn a great deal about the arguments and facts of a case by reviewing the materials submitted to the court by the parties. For appellate cases, two types of documents are particularly informative. *Briefs* are the written arguments and authorities cited by the attorneys for the parties. *Records* are documents from the lower court proceeding submitted as an appendix to the briefs, and include pleadings, motions, trial transcripts, and judgments. Some appellate cases also have petitions for review (such as the *petitions for certiorari* or *statements of probable jurisdiction* in the Supreme Court) and various motions. The progress of cases at the trial level is far less systematic, and the documents produced vary widely from case to case.

A case generally begins its journey in a court, whether trial or appellate, with an initial filing such as a complaint or appeal. The case is then assigned a *case number* or *docket number*, which is used to identify the case and its documents. A docket generally lists the parties, their attorneys, and each action in the case in chronological order. The docket number, the key to finding case documents, may be included at the beginning of a published decision or it may be cited in a secondary source. If you cannot identify the docket number for a case, you may have to ask the court clerk to consult an index by party name.

Supreme Court Briefs. As you might expect, the most widely available briefs are those filed in United States Supreme Court cases. Supreme Court case files are often quite voluminous, as many cases have not only the parties' briefs but also numerous filings by *amici curiae* ("friends of the court") supporting one side or the other.

Most Supreme Court briefs are now available online. The American Bar Association website has briefs in cases that have been decided on the merits since 2003 and in those that are scheduled for oral argument <www.abanet.org/publiced/preview/home.

html>. Its coverage of *amicus* briefs begins in 2007. Filings by parties and *amici* back to the 1930s (with selective coverage of older cases) are available through both Westlaw and Lexis. Retrospective electronic coverage is offered by Thomson Gale's *The Making of Modern Law: U.S. Supreme Court Records and Briefs, 1832–1978*.

Most large law libraries have records and briefs back to 1832 in microform, and a few libraries around the country even have printed collections. Briefs for hundreds of major cases, dating back to the 19th century, are reprinted in *Landmark Briefs and Arguments of the Supreme Court of the United States: Constitutional Law*. Cases through the 1973 term are covered in the first eighty volumes of this set, and about a dozen new cases are added each year.

Supreme Court Oral Arguments. Transcripts of Supreme Court oral arguments are also available in various formats. The Supreme Court website <www.supremecourtus.gov> has current PDF transcripts within hours of argument, as well as older arguments beginning with the 2000 term. Online coverage starts in 1979 (Lexis) or 1990 (Westlaw), and microform collections begin with the 1953 term. Arguments in major cases are available in *Landmark Briefs and Arguments of the Supreme Court of the United States: Constitutional Law*. The Oyez Project <www.oyez.org> has several thousand hours of recorded audio for arguments dating back to 1955.

If full argument transcripts are unavailable for a case, you may find excerpts in contemporary newspaper accounts. One of the most thorough sources for information on arguments since the 1930s is *The United States Law Week*, BNA's weekly newsletter on the Court's activities. It reports in detail on about two dozen arguments each term.

One way to determine the status of a Supreme Court case or to identify documents is through the Court's website <www.supremecourtus.gov>, which has information on cases pending on the docket, schedules of upcoming oral arguments, and other information. The docket has coverage back to 2001.

The United States Law Week also has information on the Supreme Court's docket, with a record of proceedings and summaries of cases filed. *Law Week*'s Supreme Court binder includes a Topical Index and Table of Cases, which lists docket numbers for cases before the Court, and a Case Status Report table listing cases by docket number with references to developments. *U.S. Law Week* is also available online by subscription <www.bna.com/products/lit/uslw.htm>. The Supreme Court Today section of the site provides several ways to track Supreme Court cases and is regularly updated with new decisions, filings, and other developments.

Other Appellate Courts. Records and briefs of the U.S. Courts of Appeals and state appellate courts are not as widely available as those from the U.S. Supreme Court. For federal courts, the fee-based information system PACER (Public Access to Court Electronic Records) has docket information and often includes briefs and other documents in recent cases. Cases are searchable by docket number or by parties' or attorneys' names. Registration is required, and there is a per-page charge to view docket sheets or documents other than opinions. Each court has its own PACER or CM/ECF (Case Management/Electronic Case Files) site, but the system has a centralized registration process <pacer.psc.uscourts.gov> and a nationwide U.S. Party/Case Index <pacer.uspci.uscourts.gov> that links directly to the docket sheets on individual courts' sites.

Online access to briefs in state appellate courts is less systematic than it is for federal courts, although a growing number of state court websites now include briefs. Sites for state briefs are listed, with links and search tips, in Michael Whiteman's regularly updated "Free and Fee Based Appellate Court Briefs Online" <www.llrx.com/features/briefs online.htm>.

Westlaw has nationwide coverage of federal and state appellate court briefs, back to the 1970s for some federal circuits and more recent for most state courts. (Click on the *i* icon to check the scope of coverage for a specific jurisdiction.) Lexis also has brief collections in its "Briefs, Motions, Pleadings & Verdicts" folder. Coverage for most courts begins around 2000.

Some briefs are available online from non-court websites. Parties or *amici curiae* may post their briefs on their own websites, and high profile documents are often available from news sites such as CNN <www.cnn.com>. Several organizations and government agencies provide access to briefs they have filed in the Supreme Court and in other appellate courts. The U.S. Department of Justice site has Supreme Court briefs filed by the Solicitor General since 1982 <www.justice.gov/osg/>. Whiteman's "Free and Fee Based Appellate Court Briefs Online" has links to several other potential sources.

For most courts, appellate records and briefs can also be found in local law libraries within the circuit or state. In some instances, however, you may need to contact the court or a judicial records center to obtain copies. Michael Whiteman & Peter Scott Campbell, *A Union List of Appellate Court Records and Briefs: Federal and State* (1999) has contact information for libraries and court clerks, with notes indicating the scope and format of each library's holdings and its lending policy.

Trial Courts. Appellate cases generally follow a standard path and produce specific documents such as the parties' briefs, the lower court record, and the court's opinion. Material from trial court litigation, on the other hand, is more varied and can be harder to identify and find. Some cases result in judges' opinions, such as a decision granting a motion for summary judgment, but many matters are decided without a written opinion. Cases can be decided by jury verdict, summary disposition, or settlement agreement. Some litigation produces dozens of memoranda or briefs submitted to support or oppose motions before, during and after trial, while other cases go to trial without any written submissions on points of law. Trial transcripts, if available, can be voluminous and expensive but may be essential sources of information.

Docket sheets for trial courts increasingly are available online, particularly for federal courts, with a growing number of courts providing online access to documents as well. The federal courts' PACER system covers recent cases in the federal district and bankruptcy courts. While docket sheets and court filings for some state courts are available online, for others this information may be more difficult to obtain. Most states have electronic docket systems, but means of access vary.

Docket sheets and trial documents are also available from fee-based online services. For cases since 2000, Westlaw has collections of dockets, pleadings, memoranda, and trial motions from both federal and state courts. Individual dockets can be tracked for e-mail notification of new developments. Other commercial subscription services, such as Legal Dockets Online <www.legaldockets.com> and LexisNexis CourtLink <courtlink.lexisnexis.com>, also provide access to docket information.

If electronic access is unavailable, you may need to contact the court directly to obtain a copy of a transcript or other documents. Some courts accept requests electronically or by telephone, while for others you will need to apply by mail or in person.

Access methods for both federal and state courts are explained in the annual *Sourcebook to Public Record Information: The Comprehensive Guide to County, State, & Federal Public Records Sources.* This book also explains how to obtain other public records, such as property and licensing information, much of which is now available through state and local government websites. You can find free public record sites through BRB's Free Resource Center <www.brbpub.com/pubrecsites.asp> or OnlineSearches.com's Free Public Records Search Directory <publicrecords.onlinesearches.com>. Public record databases are also available through subscription-based commercial services, including Westlaw and Lexis.

Information on trial verdicts and damage awards, primarily for various types of tort litigation, is available in services known as *verdict reporters.* These generally have a brief summary of the case's facts and claims, list attorneys and expert witnesses for each side, and report the resulting verdict. In the absence of any published opinions, this may be the best available record of a case's background and outcome. These reporters include several publications from Jury Verdict Research <www.juryverdict research.com> and the monthly newsletter *Verdicts, Settlements & Tactics.* Westlaw and Lexis both have several verdict reporter resources from around the country.

§ 7–5. Directories of Courts and Judges

Court directories serve a number of purposes. They provide contact information for clerks' offices, and some include judges' biographical data. This can be useful information for litigants appearing before a particular judge or panel, and for law students applying for clerkships after graduation.

Court websites, which usually include judges' contact data as well as some brief biographical information, are accessible through portals such as the Court Locator section of the federal judiciary homepage <www.uscourts.gov/courtlinks/> or the National Center for State Courts list of court websites <www.ncsconline.org/D_kis/>. Court sites, however, often have less information than is available through unofficial directories.

A number of directories focus on federal courts and judges. *Judicial Staff Directory* and *Judicial Yellow Book* include basic biographies of judges, as well as listings of court personnel such as clerks and staff attorneys. Like other volumes in the Staff Directories and Yellow Books series, these are available electronically and in print. *Almanac of the Federal Judiciary*, a two-volume looseleaf publication (also available on Westlaw), is the most thorough source for biographical information, and includes summaries of noteworthy rulings, media coverage, and lawyers' evaluations of judges' abilities and temperaments.

Several directions cover both federal and state courts. *Judicial Yellow Book* includes state appellate courts but not trial courts, and more thorough coverage is available in *BNA's Directory of State and Federal Courts, Judges, and Clerks* and CQ Press's *Directory of State Court Clerks & County Courthouses*. *The American Bench* is the most comprehensive biographical source for state judges, covering almost every judge in the United States and including an alphabetical name index. The National Tribal Justice Resource Center has a directory of tribal courts <www.ntjrc.org/tribalcourts/> (also available in print as *United States Tribal Courts Directory* (2d ed. 2006)). As noted in Chapter 3, *BNA's Directory of State and Federal Courts, Judges, and Clerks* and CQ Press's *Federal-State Court Directory* both include charts explaining the structure of each court's judicial system.

You may sometimes need information about judges involved in an older case or sitting on a particular court. If you know only the last names at the head of an opinion, your first step may be to determine the judges' full names. These can be found in tables in the front of most reporter volumes. For example, since 1882 the *Federal Reporter* has listed the sitting federal judges, with footnotes indicating any changes since the previous volume. Similar listings appear in each of West's regional reporters and in most official state reports. The Federal Judicial Center website <www.fjc.gov> has a database with biographical information about all life-tenured federal judges since 1789. Entries include links to information about manuscript sources and lists of other biographical sources, if available. Biographies of most appellate judges can also be found in standard sources such as *American National Biography* or *Who Was Who in America*.

§ 7–6. Formbooks and Jury Instructions

In the course of legal practice, many basic transactions and court filings occur with regularity. Rather than redraft these documents each time, attorneys frequently work from sample versions of standard legal documents and instruments. Model forms are available in both printed collections and electronic products. Some sets of forms are annotated with discussion of the underlying laws, checklists of procedural steps, and citations to relevant cases.

Several multivolume compilations of forms are published. Two of the major national sets are published as adjuncts to *American Jurisprudence 2d* and are linked to the encyclopedia by frequent cross-references. *American Jurisprudence Legal Forms 2d* has transactional instruments such as contracts, leases, and wills, and *American Jurisprudence Pleading and Practice Forms* focuses on litigation and other practice before courts and administrative agencies. Both sets are divided into several hundred topical chapters mirroring the organization of *Am. Jur. 2d*. Exhibit 7–2 on page 332 shows a page from *Am. Jur. Pleading and Practice Forms*, containing the beginning of a complaint for personal injuries caused by an animal falling through a defective ceiling.

Other comprehensive sets include *Current Legal Forms with Tax Analysis* and *West's Legal Forms*. Unlike the *Am. Jur.* sets, these are arranged by broad practice area such as estate planning or real estate. They may be better for understanding a wider range of related issues than for finding forms on very fact-specific topics.

Three major sets are devoted to forms used in federal practice, each with a different structure. *Bender's Federal Practice Forms* is arranged by court rule. *Federal Procedural Forms, Lawyers' Edition* is a companion to Thomson West's encyclopedic *Federal Procedure, Lawyers' Edition*, and is organized similarly, with several dozen subject chapters. *West's Federal Forms* is arranged by court, with separate volumes covering forms needed in the Supreme Court, Courts of Appeals, District Courts, Bankruptcy Courts, the Tax Court, and other specialized courts.

Sets of forms, varying in complexity and size, are also published for most states and for particular subject areas. Some sets, such as *Bender's Forms of Discovery*, are geared toward specific stages of litigation. Practice-oriented treatises and manuals frequently include appendices of sample forms, and in some states compilations of official forms are issued in conjunction with statutory codes. A source for a specific jurisdiction is usually the best place to start, as it is most likely to conform to the jurisdiction's laws and procedures.

Several sets of forms are available online, streamlining the drafting process by reducing the amount of text that needs to be keyboarded. Lexis has dozens of forms collections, including *Bender's Federal Practice Forms*, *Bender's Forms of Discovery*, and *Current Legal Forms*, as well as sets for several individual states. Westlaw has the two *Am. Jur.* form sets , *Federal Procedural Forms*, and numerous state-specific collections, as well as broad multi-jurisdictional resources combining the various published sets and providing official forms from federal and state courts and agencies. FORMFINDER, accessible from a link at the top of the Westlaw screen, offers a template on which you can choose one of four dozen topical areas and then specific subtopics, document types, and jurisdictions in which to search.

A more limited range of forms is available from free Internet sites, but these may be satisfactory for some transactions and court filings. LexisOne <www.lexisone.com> offers free access to more than 6,000 forms, listed topically and by jurisdiction. FindLaw <forms.lp.findlaw.com> has links to official sites for federal circuits and states, as well as a directory of sites with free and fee-based legal forms.

Most jurisdictions have published sets of *model* or *pattern jury instructions*, used by judges to explain the applicable law to jurors before they weigh the evidence and reach their decisions. Model jury instructions are useful in research because they provide a concise summary of a jurisdiction's ruling law on the issues covered, often accompanied by notes summarizing the leading cases. In a way, they can serve the same function as a *Restatement* or legal encyclopedia in outlining a state's basic legal doctrines.

Some court websites have model jury instructions, and both Westlaw and Lexis include instructions for federal courts and for several states. Some sets of jury instructions are published by state court systems and others by bar associations. The subject heading used by the Library of Congress and in most online catalogs for these sets is "Instructions to juries–[Jurisdiction]." Exhibit 7–3 on page 333 shows a page from a state set of jury instructions, with an instruction on the duties of owners of domestic animals.

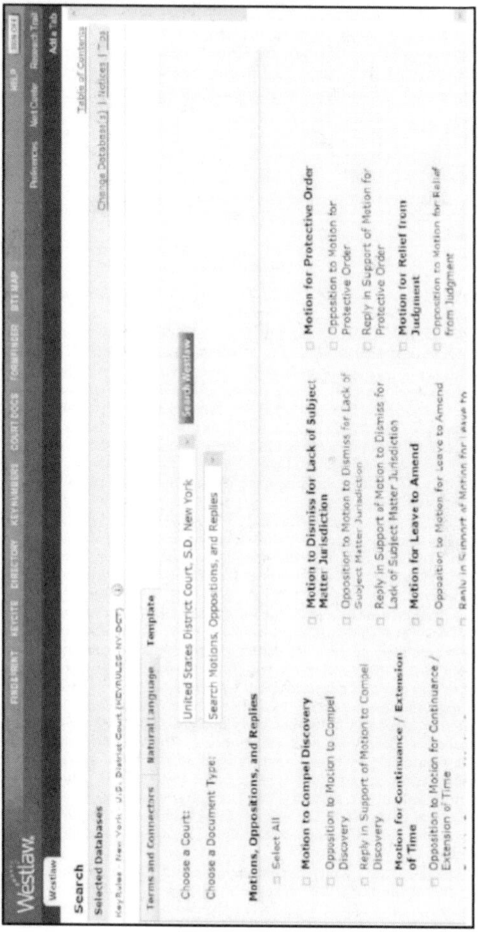

Exhibit 7–1. A KeyRules search screen in Westlaw

§ 2

§ 2 Complaint, petition, or declaration—By injured patron of livestock sales arena—Fall of animal through defective ceiling—Res ipsa loquitur

[Title of Court]

———————————,
[Plaintiff, Petitioner],   No. ————

v.
                                    ————————
                                    [Designate name of document]
———————————,
[Defendant, Respondent].

COMPLAINT

1. Plaintiff, ———— *[name]*, is now, and at all times mentioned was, a resident of ———— County, ———— *[state]*.

2. Defendants, ———— *[AB]* and ———— *[CD]*, are now, and at all times mentioned were, residents of ———— County, ———— *[state]*.

3. At all times mentioned, defendants were partners in and the proprietors of a business known as the ———— *[name of business]*, located at the ———— *[———— County Fair Grounds or as the same may be]* in or near the ———— edge of the city limits of ———— *[city]*, and were engaged in and operating what is generally known as a community livestock sales business, buying and selling for their own account and the account of various patrons and customers, various kinds of livestock, holding forth the premises as a place of public resort to all interested persons.

4. On ———— *[date]*, plaintiff and ———— *[her husband or his wife]* were on the premises of defendants' above-described business as customers and patrons at the sale held there on that day under the exclusive auspices, management, and control of defendants, and were legally on the premises as business invitees of defendants.

5. The premises used and occupied by defendants as a place of business consist of several frame buildings, livestock pens, and runaways; the principal building where most of the sales activities are conducted consists of ———— *[a large room at the south end of the building, in which patrons interested in buying and selling merchandise and inanimate personal property were congregated on that day, the business office of defendants, a lunch stand, and a livestock sales pavilion located on the second story and reached by way of a ramp leading up from the first floor of the principal building]*. The livestock sales pavilion is a recessed semicircle of board seats surrounding a pit or sales arena approximately ———— feet long and ———— feet wide in which livestock is exhibited for sale at the ground level. The arena is approximately ———— feet below the level of the lower tier of seats for spectators in the pavilion and is enclosed by a wooden railing approximately ———— feet in height from the first step level.

6. At about ———— *[time]* on that day, plaintiff was seated in a chair at the ———— end of the main floor engaged in visiting and conversing with friends and acquaintances, most of whom were spouses of patrons attending the sale. Suddenly, there was a loud commotion and noise overhead and simultaneously bits of plaster and debris began to fall from the ceiling onto plaintiff and others

Exhibit 7–2. A page from *Am. Jur. Pleading and Practice Forms*

Chapter 42

Animals

> **KeyCite®:** Cases and other legal materials listed in KeyCite Scope can be researched through the KeyCite service on Westlaw®. Use KeyCite to check citations for form, parallel references, prior and later history, and comprehensive citator information, including citations to other decisions and secondary materials.

§ 42:1   Domestic animals—Duties of owners⊘

It is the duty of the owner of domestic animals to exercise ordinary care to prevent them from running at large beyond the boundaries of his own land. If you believe from a preponderance of the evidence that the defendant violated the foregoing duty, then he was negligent. If you further believe from such evidence that any such negligence was a proximate cause of *[injury to the plaintiff] [damages to the plaintiff's property]* then, unless you further believe that the plaintiff was guilty of negligence that proximately contributed to cause his *[injuries] [damage]*, you shall return your verdict in favor of the plaintiff.

NOTES TO FORM

Commentary

Taken from the language in Rice v. Turner, 191 Va. 601, 605–606, 62 S.E.2d 24, 26 (1950) (rural area, cow on highway); Perlin v. Chappell, 198 Va. 861, 864, 96 S.E.2d 805, 808 (1957) (stockyard in city, escape of Brahma heifer). See Code § 55-316.

See also Page v. Arnold, 227 Va. 74, 80–81, 314 S.E.2d 57, 61 (1984) (rural area, pony on highway); Bradshaw v. Minter, 206 Va. 450, 455, 143 S.E.2d 827, 828–829 (1965) (spirited propensities of riding horse); Wilkins v. Sibley, 205 Va. 171, 173, 135 S.E.2d 765, 766 (1964) (rural area; mule on highway; negligent fastening of gate but no proof of proximate cause).

The duties set out in this section apply to such animals as livestock, but

Exhibit 7–3. A page from *Virginia Practice Series: Jury Instructions*

CHAPTER 8

SPECIALIZED AND NONLEGAL SOURCES

§ 8–1. Introduction

The resources many lawyers turn to most often are not the general codes, digests, and databases discussed in earlier chapters, but instead tools designed to help them in their specialized areas of law. Topical looseleaf and electronic services make lawyers' work easier by compiling related statutes, cases, and regulations in one location, along with explanations, forms, and other practice aids. These services and other resources such as newsletters and blogs provide the current awareness lawyers need to respond to and anticipate new legal developments, such as recently decided cases or proposed regulations.

This chapter also introduces more general sources for factual and interdisciplinary research. Law students sometimes focus so intently on legal literature that they neglect information from other disciplines. General reference sources, however, can give you essential background information, and scholarship in the sciences and social sciences can expand your perspectives and insights in analyzing legal issues. They can also help you prepare for litigation or understand issues such as standard of care or trade usage.

§ 8–2. Looseleaf and Electronic Services

A looseleaf service is a frequently updated resource that compiles the statutes, regulations, court decisions, administrative agency documents, and other materials in an area of law, and presents them in a cohesive manner accompanied by commentary or analysis.

The term "looseleaf" comes from the traditional manner of publication and supplementation in binders, but most modern looseleaf services are available online as well as in print. Printed services are more likely to be available to most law library patrons, but the electronic versions add the flexibility of keyword searching and the convenience of hypertext links between documents. Major looseleaf publishers such as BNA <www.bna.com>, CCH <www.cch.com>, and RIA <ria.thomsonreuters.com> all have platforms for Internet research. Exhibit 8–1 on page 365 shows an introductory screen of RIA Checkpoint, indicating the broad array of resources available, including editorial material, news/current awareness, and primary source materials.

A looseleaf service can be more efficient than more general sources because it integrates related legislative, regulatory and judicial primary sources and allows you to consider all of these together. It also summarizes and analyzes these primary sources. Exhibits 8–2 and 8–3 on pages 366–67 show sample pages from CCH's *Standard Federal Tax Reporter*. These pages follow the text of § 213 of the Internal Revenue Code governing deductibility of medical expenses. Exhibit 8–2 shows excerpts from committee reports for laws that amended this section, followed by the beginning of an Internal Revenue Service regulation with more specific information. Exhibit 8–3 shows a portion of CCH's explanation of the law, including a discussion of deductions for the costs of acquiring, training and maintaining service animals.

Another common feature of looseleaf services is that they classify and index the case law in their subject areas. Unlike West's key-number digest system, which is used only for judicial decisions, most looseleaf digest systems cover both court cases and administrative documents. Because they are designed for specific areas, these specialized systems may also offer a more sophisticated and detailed analysis of topics within their expertise. Exhibit 8–4 on page 368 shows annotations from the *Standard Federal Tax Reporter* of IRS rulings and Tax Court cases on service animal deductions and other topics.

Looseleaf and topical reporters often contain cases that are not published elsewhere, such as trial court decisions and rulings of state and federal administrative agencies. These decisions and rulings are generally published first in weekly looseleaf inserts. Some services then publish permanent bound volumes of decisions, while others issue transfer binders for storage of older material. Some online versions offer citators so that you can update your cases. KeyCite and Shepard's Citations cover most topical reporters, as do several specialized Shepard's print citators.

One of the most valuable features of looseleaf services is their current coverage of proposed legislation, pending litigation, and other legal developments. Many services include weekly or biweekly newsletters. *Standard Federal Tax Reporter* has several current awareness approaches, including a *Taxes on Parade* newsletter and extra issues with the text of important new documents such as tax reform bills and congressional committee reports. With online services, you can subscribe to e-mail newsletters or set up alerts for new content that matches your keyword searches.

Most looseleaf services are updated by replacing individual pages throughout the set so that the text is kept current without the need for separate supplements. Page numbering is designed to facilitate filing of new material and can be rather convoluted; pages 603–1 to 603–4 may be inserted, for example, between pages 603 and 604. To identify specific references as page numbers change, many services assign *paragraph numbers* to each section of material. A "paragraph" in this sense can vary in length from a few sentences to several pages. Each administrative decision, for example, is assigned one paragraph number and retains this number no matter how many new pages are added to the service. Paragraph numbers, not page numbers, are generally used in indexes and online versions, and are the designations by which most looseleaf services are cited. The page from the *Standard Federal Tax Reporter* shown in Exhibit 8–2, for example, includes both a page number at the top right (27,597) and a paragraph number at the bottom right (¶ 12,-541). It is easy to be misled by the page number, but remember that it is used only for filing purposes and that the paragraph number is the point of reference used in indexes and citations.

Whether in print or online, a typical service includes several types of indexes. The general or *topical index* provides detailed subject access. In many services, an additional index known as a

"Current Topical Index" or "Latest Additions to Topical Index" covers new material between the periodic recompilations of the main index. Exhibit 8–5 on page 369 shows a page from the topical index for the *Standard Federal Tax Reporter*, with references under "Dogs and other animals to aid handicapped persons, medical expenses" to the material shown in Exhibits 8–3 and 8–4. Note that the index includes very detailed references to annotations of court decisions and administrative rulings. The topical index is often the most effective place to begin your research, even in online services that offer full-text keyword searching.

Finding lists provide direct references to particular statutes, regulations, or cases by their citations. These can be particularly useful in searching for numerically designated agency materials, such as IRS rulings or SEC releases. Some of these lists also serve as citator services and include information on the current validity of materials listed.

Another device used in some services is the *cumulative index*. This is not a subject index but a list of cross-references from the main body of the service to current material. Under paragraph number listings, cumulative indexes update each topic with leads to new materials which have not yet been incorporated into the main discussion.

When you use a looseleaf service for the first time, you should take a moment to familiarize yourself with its features. You will find detailed instructions, with titles such as "How to Use This Reporter'' or ''About This Publication,'' at the beginning of the first volume. A particular service may include features that appear confusing at first but are very useful to the experienced researcher, and a few moments of orientation can save you considerable time and frustration.

There are several ways to determine whether a service is published in an area of interest. References to looseleaf services may appear in law review articles and cases, and lawyers or professors specializing in a field can provide advice. The annual directory *Legal Looseleafs in Print* includes regularly supplemented services, although it also lists numerous publications that are not updated very frequently. At the end of this volume, the list of resources in Appendix B includes selected looseleaf and electronic services in fields of major interest.

§ 8–3. Current Awareness

Lawyers must keep aware of developments in their areas of practice. They need to know about new court decisions, pending legislation, and agency announcements, as well as changes in the political, financial or business world. There are several approaches to keeping on top of current activities and new developments in the law, including legal and general-interest newspapers, newsletters, and blogs.

Regular current awareness reading serves another purpose as well. Individual research assignments can build your expertise on specific questions, but they won't give you a broad overview of an area of law. Only by reading about new developments on a regular basis will you develop the confidence that you're seeing the big picture and that your knowledge has no significant gaps. If you are new to a practice area, find out what senior attorneys are reading and sign up to see those publications.

Using features like Westlaw's WestClip, Lexis Alerts, and the alerting features of online services, you can set up automated searches that will run daily, weekly or monthly and notify you by e-mail when a search retrieves new documents matching your criteria. You can also use free features of major search engines like Google Alerts <www.google.com/alerts> and Yahoo! Alerts <alerts.yahoo.com> to automatically search the web for specific terms. Results can be delivered through e-mail or RSS ("Really Simple Syndication") feeds, with which you can bring together headlines from multiple news and blog sources to create your own custom news pages.

a. Legal Newspapers and Newsletters

News on developments in the legal profession is available from a number of daily and weekly newspapers. Legal newspapers often cover developing topics more rapidly than monthly or quarterly journals, and some also include lower court decisions that may not be reported elsewhere.

The articles and essays in legal newspapers can be hard to track down, but many newspaper websites have searchable archives available free or by subscription. LegalTrac and LRI, online periodical indexes discussed in Chapter 2, have coverage of several legal newspapers, including *Chicago Daily Law Bulletin*, *Legal Times*, *National Law Journal*, and *New York Law Journal*. Westlaw has several dozen daily and weekly newspapers, including all of the above titles. Lexis has the *Chicago Daily Law Bulletin* and several *Lawyers Weekly* newspapers for specific states.

One of the leading Internet sources for current legal news is law.com <www.law.com>, with stories from *Legal Times*, *National Law Journal*, and regional newspapers. Its website includes Quest, a legal search engine that covers legal newspapers, blogs, and publications from law firm websites. Other news sources include the *ABA Journal*'s Law News Now <www.abajournal.com/news> and the University of Pittsburgh School of Law's JURIST <jurist.law.pitt.edu>.

Legal newspapers across the country are listed by state in *Legal Researcher's Desk Reference* and *Legal Information Buyer's Guide & Reference Manual*. Both lists indicate frequency of publication and provide contact information and URLs.

Newsletters are another major source of current information in the legal world. Specialized newsletters often have a limited circulation and can be hard to find in academic or public law libraries, but they may be the best available sources for information about newly developing areas of law.

Newsletters are often the forum through which practitioners in specialized areas share information and documents. For example, a newsletter may include copies of pleadings or other trial court documents as well as articles on recent developments. Many newsletters are available both in print and online, with e-mail or RSS notification of new developments.

Several newsletters are available through Westlaw or Lexis. Westlaw has more than fifty Andrews Publications reporters, some on very specific topics such as repetitive stress injuries and others on broader areas such as antitrust litigation. Westlaw also has some 300 other newsletters, some focusing on specific states and others providing nationwide coverage. Lexis has dozens of Mealey's Litigation Reports files on topics from arthritis drugs to welding rods.

Looseleaf services, discussed in § 8–2, often include newsletters as part of the coverage of current developments. Some of these, such as the BNA publications *Antitrust & Trade Regulation Report*, *Criminal Law Reporter*, *Family Law Reporter*, and *Securities Regulation & Law Report*, are major current awareness tools in their fields. BNA also has about two dozen daily newsletters in specialized areas, some of which are electronic-only publications.

You can identify available newsletters for a subject area in *Legal Newsletters in Print*, which describes more than 2,200 newsletters with information about subscription prices and online access. This publication is available to subscribers, along with *Legal Looseleafs in Print*, as part of the Law-TRIO database <www.infosourcespub.com>.

b. Current Scholarship

Specialists need to know about scholarly as well as legal developments. A new article directly on a topic of concern may appear in any of the hundreds of law reviews and other legal journals published in this country, and may even be available online before or in lieu of publication.

Several resources have information about new issues of law reviews. The most extensive is Washington & Lee Law School's Current Law Journal Content (CJLC) <lawlib.wlu.edu/CLJC/>, which is available free and has searchable tables of contents for more than 1,500 law journals.

Current Index to Legal Periodicals (*CILP*) <lib.law.washington.edu/cilp/cilp.html>, published weekly by the University of Washington's Marian Gould Gallagher Law Library, is a subscription resource that combines tables of contents for new law review issues with the added value of subject indexing. It covers more than 600 law reviews, indexing articles under approximately 100 subject headings. Online access, limited to the most recent eight weeks, is available through Westlaw.

Many scholars rely on services such as the Social Science Research Network (SSRN) <www.ssrn.com> and the Berkeley Electronic Press <www.

bepress.com> to learn of new articles and working papers. Current abstracts are sent to subscribers by e-mail, and searchable Internet archives include free access to several thousand downloadable full-text documents.

c. Blogs and Other Online Resources

Blogs have become a major vehicle for timely dissemination of news and opinion. Law blogs (sometimes called "blawgs") are written on a wide range of topics, and some have become leading sources of current information. SCOTUSblog <www.scotusblog.com>, for example, often is the first source for breaking news about the Supreme Court.

Directories of legal blogs include the ABA Journal's Blawg Directory <www.abajournal.com/blawgs> and Justia BlawgSearch <blawgsearch.justia.com>. Both sites have samples of recent postings, links to blog sites, and search engines for searching blog postings. Exhibit 8–6 on page 370 shows a typical blog, in this instance on dog law issues.

Other forms of social media can also be used to monitor breaking news in the legal world. LexTweet <www.lextweet.com> provides a snapshot of Twitter posts by lawyers and other legal professionals, and its samples may suggest specific Twitterers worth following.

E-mail listservs and discussion groups are another way to keep on top of developments in a particular area, and can also be used to seek assistance with difficult research issues. Some lists disseminate information from organizations or government agencies to subscribers, while others are designed for communities of specialists to share news and ideas. Posing questions to this type of list often yields replies with leads that most researchers would otherwise miss. Another subscriber may offer help with a thorny legal issue or identify a source for an obscure document. Older messages, if available in a searchable archive, are a valuable repository of information. There are hundreds of listservs on legal issues. Resources such as CataList <www.lsoft.com/lists/listref.html> can help you find lists on topics of interest.

A number of courts and state legislatures offer automatic e-mail notification when a particular case or bill is acted upon, and several government agencies have mailing lists and RSS feeds summarizing new developments. The Food and Drug Administration <www.fda.gov>, for example, has dozens of update services for news on specific issues within its jurisdiction. Check agency websites for similar listservs and feeds in other fields.

§ 8–4. General News and Business Information

Legal newspapers focus on law-related activity, but for a broader picture of developments in business, politics and society it is necessary to monitor more general sources such as newspapers or news websites. In addition to their value for current awareness, news stories can also be rich sources for factual research or background information.

Two of the most convenient news sources for law students are Westlaw and Lexis. Each provides access to hundreds of newspapers, wire services, and business publications. The two systems have considerable overlap in coverage, but each has sources not found in the other; both, for example, have the *New York Times* and the *Washington Post*, while only Lexis has the full text of the *Wall Street Journal*.

Other online sources of news include websites for individual newspapers and multisource subscription databases such as Factiva <www.factiva.com>. Google News <news.google.com> has free and very current coverage of a wide range of newspapers, magazines, and wire services. Websites for specific newspapers and other news sources can be found through search engines or directory sites such as NewsVoyager <www.newsvoyager.com>.

Business developments are a major focus of research in news sources. You can also find company information through a number of other print and electronic directories and databases, several of which are available through either Westlaw or Lexis. The amount of available information on a company depends in part on whether it is publicly or privately held; because public companies must report to their shareholders and government regulators, they publish far more information. Basic data on public corporations can be found in sources such as *Standard & Poor's Register of Corporations, Directors & Executives* (Lexis), and you will find more extensive background and financial information in S & P's Corporate Descriptions Plus News (Lexis), or Hoover's Company Profiles (either Westlaw or Lexis). Parent and subsidiary companies can be identified in the *Directory of Corporate Affiliations* (Lexis).

Ward's Business Directory of U.S. Private and Public Companies <www.gale.cengage.com> includes information on more than 100,000 privately held companies. The broadest databases, such as American Business Directory and Dun's Electronic Business Directory (both available under some Westlaw subscriptions), cover millions of private businesses and have basic contact information and employment data.

Business entities generate voluminous public record filings. Publicly held corporations must file a number of documents with the Securities and Exchange Commission, including annual and quarterly financial reports, and these are available free through the SEC's EDGAR system <www.sec.gov/edgar.shtml>. SEC filings are also accessible through several subscription databases, including Westlaw and Lexis. Both public and private companies must register with secretaries of state or similar state offices. The National Association of Secretaries of State <www.nass.org> has links to state sites, most of which have searchable databases with basic information such as addresses, officers and registered agents.

§ 8–5. Statistics

Lawyers need demographic and statistical information for many purposes, from preparing for cross-examination of an expert witness to supporting a discrimination claim. Some statistical sources focus on legal matters, while others are more general.

Statistics on the federal courts, such as the number of cases commenced and terminated by district and by subject, can be found in the Administrative Office of the U.S. Courts' annual *Judicial Business of the United States Courts* and on its website <www.uscourts.gov/judbususc/judbus.html>. The National Center for State Courts site has a Court Statistics Project page <www.ncsconline.org/D_Research/csp/CSP_Main_Page.html> that offers several ways to query its statistical database and examine state court business. It includes PDF versions of two annual publications, *Examining the Work of State Courts* and *State Court Caseload Statistics*.

Criminal statistics are available from both federal and state governments, including two major sources from the U.S. Department of Justice. The Federal Bureau of Investigation issues *Uniform Crime Reports* (also known as *Crime in the United States*) in print and online <www.fbi.gov/ucr/ucr.htm>, focusing on criminal activities, and the Bureau of Justice

Statistics issues the online-only Sourcebook of Criminal Justice Statistics <www.albany.edu/source book/>, with a broader survey of the social and economic impacts of crime. The BJS website <bjs.ojp.usdoj.gov> has links to a variety of other statistics and publications.

The American Bar Foundation's *Lawyer Statistical Report* is the leading source on the composition of the U.S. legal profession. The most recent report, published in 2004, provides data as of 2000. The American Bar Association's Market Research Department <www.abanet.org/marketresearch/> has links to various websites with statistics on the legal profession, including demographics, salaries, and quality of life surveys.

The U.S. Census Bureau <www.census.gov> prepares the Census of Population and Housing every ten years, and all censuses since 1790 are available on its website <www.census.gov/prod/www/abs/decennial/>. The Bureau also undertakes an Economic Census on business and industry every five years <www.census.gov/econ/>. To find economic information about a particular industry, you will usually need to determine its North American Industry Classification System (NAICS) code <www.census.gov/eos/www/naics/>. The NAICS page also has information on the older Standard Industrial Classification (SIC) system which it replaced, but which is still used by some sources.

The *Statistical Abstract of the United States* is published annually by the Census Bureau in print and online <www.census.gov/compendia/statab/>. This basic reference source covers a wide range of economic and demographic statistics, and is particularly useful because it gives source information for each table. It thus serves as a convenient lead to agencies and publications with more thorough coverage of specific areas. Exhibit 8–7 on page 371 shows a table from the *Statistical Abstract* with information on the number of pets in U.S. households, including percentages of households with pets by income and size. Note that the table includes a source reference to the American Veterinary Medical Association publication *U.S. Pet Ownership and Demographics Sourcebook*, where more detailed information may be available.

The *Statistical Abstract* website has previous editions of the publication, all the way back to 1878. *Historical Statistics of the United States: Earliest Times to the Present* (Susan B. Carter et al. eds., 2006), available either in a five-volume printed set or online by subscription <hsus.cambridge.org>, is a comprehensive compendium of statistics from the *Statistical Abstract* and hundreds of other sources. Another source for statistics from government agencies is the FedStats website <www.fedstats.gov>, with links to numerous federal statistical sources by topic and by agency.

Annual reports and other publications of government agencies, trade associations, labor unions, and public interest groups generally contain statistical data relating to their work and interests. LexisNexis Statistical <web.lexis-nexis.com/statuniv/> provides access to much of this material, adding more than 100,000 tables each year. A companion product, LexisNexis Statistical DataSets, allows you to select subjects and variables to create your own customized data comparisons. You can also download free "raw" datasets from government agencies at Data.gov <www.data.gov>.

Most statistical sources focus on facts rather than opinions, but surveys can be important resources in many areas of the law from employment discrimination to trademark infringement. Polls and other sources of public opinion are available through a number of electronic sources. Gallup, Inc. <www.gallup.com> has free access to recent poll results and allows keyword searching of questionnaires and poll analyses on major topics. The subscription resources Polling the Nations <poll.orspub.com> and the Roper Center for Public Opinion Research <www.ropercenter.uconn.edu> have survey data from hundreds of organizations, accessible by keyword search or through subject indexes.

§ 8–6. Interdisciplinary Research

In either law school or legal practice, the use of secondary sources for background information and analysis is rarely limited to treatises and law review articles. Work from other disciplines can explain the policy bases for legal rules or add insights to buttress legal arguments. Practicing lawyers need nonlegal literature for several purposes, from investigating issues such as the standard of care to preparing for expert witness depositions.

General Periodical Indexes. Indexes to nonlegal periodical literature can supply valuable leads that might never be found through law reviews. Some of these are specialized indexes in particular disciplines, while others have comprehensive coverage of a wide range of sources (sometimes including legal journals). The online versions of many indexes link directly to full-text PDF versions of the articles listed.

Indexes from other disciplines such as ABI/INFORM (business and economics), America History & Life (U.S. and Canadian history), EconLit (economics), PAIS International (public policy), PsycINFO (psychology and related disciplines), or Sociological Abstracts may offer background information or interdisciplinary perspectives. A few indexes are available free on the Internet, such as the National Library of Medicine's PubMed version of MEDLINE, the comprehensive index of biomedical journals <www.pubmed.gov>. Most index databases, however, are accessible by subscription only. A few are available through Westlaw or Lexis, and researchers in university or law school libraries usually have access to many others. Most of these databases include searchable abstracts, which can be invaluable both in finding articles and in identifying whether they would be of value. Exhibit 8–8 on page 372 shows the PubMed abstract for an article in the *Journal of Forensic Sciences*, with references to other articles in journals such as *Interpersonal Violence* and *Behavioral Processes*.

ISI Web of Knowledge <www.isiwebofknowledge. com> is a very broad index covering more than 23,000 journals. You can also search for articles by author or title keyword, but it also functions like KeyCite or Shepard's in that you can run a "Cited Reference Search" to find articles citing a particular author or source.

Other major multidisciplinary indexes, one or more of which may be available by subscription at an academic library, include EBSCOhost Academic Search Complete <www.ebscohost.com>, InfoTrac OneFile <www.gale.cengage.com/onefile>, and Pro-Quest Central <www.proquest.com>. All of these databases serve as one-stop shops for a wide range of journal literature.

IngentaConnect <www.ingentaconnect.com> also has comprehensive coverage of current journal literature, with tables of contents information from more than 30,000 publications. One advantage of IngentaConnect is that searching is free to researchers unaffiliated with subscribing institutions. Most articles are available for fee-based download by nonsubscribers.

JSTOR <www.jstor.org> was mentioned in Chapter 2 as a source for retrospective coverage of several dozen legal journals; it also has full-text comprehensive coverage of hundreds of non-law scholarly journals. Two other subscription web services covering journal articles from as far back as

1665 are Periodicals Archive Online <pao.chadwyck.com> (full text of more than a thousand journals) and Periodicals Index Online <pio.chadwyck.com> (indexing of several thousand other journals).

Dissertations. Doctoral dissertations are valuable sources of scholarly research that are often overlooked by law students and lawyers. A dissertation is the product of several years of research, and it usually includes an introductory survey of the literature and an exhaustive bibliography of published and manuscript sources. These documents were once esoteric and hard-to-find, but digital access now makes them readily available as research tools. ProQuest Dissertations & Theses—Full Text <www.proquest.com> has most dissertations since 1997 as well as selected earlier works. (It also indexes older dissertations back to 1861.)

Online catalogs. No law library has every possible text, so if your research is limited to one library's holdings it may miss important works. WorldCat <www.worldcat.org> is a free resource with records for more than a billion items, in more than 10,000 libraries worldwide.

You can also search specific library catalogs, including the Library of Congress <catalog.loc.gov>. FindLaw's list of law schools by state <stu.findlaw.com/schools/usaschools/> includes direct links to library websites and online catalogs. Even more catalogs are accessible through lib-web-cats

<www.librarytechnology.org/libwebcats/>, which has links to libraries worldwide, geographically or by type of library (including law and other specialties).

Other reference sources. Most disciplines have various encyclopedias, dictionaries, bibliographies, research guides, directories, indexes, and other sources that may be valuable to you in a research project if you know where to look. One way to learn about available resources is through the American Library Association's subscription-based Guide to Reference <www.guidetoreference.org>, which covers hundreds of disciplines.

§ 8–7.　Legal History Resources

Most legal research involves determining the law now in effect, but you may at times need information on legal developments occurring decades or centuries ago. The background of a court decision, statute, or constitutional provision is of more than historical interest because it can continue to influence present day interpretation.

Many of the resources discussed in earlier chapters are invaluable in legal history research. Westlaw and Lexis have judicial opinions back to the 18th century, and access to older law review literature is available through the comprehensive backfiles of HeinOnline (from 1788) and Index to Legal Periodicals Retrospective (covering 1918–1981). Historical material from Congress is available in sources such as the digitized Serial Set publications from LexisNexis and Readex, and in the Library of Congress's "A Century of Lawmaking for a New Nation: U.S. Congressional Documents and Debates" <memory.loc.gov/ammem/amlaw>.

In addition there are other resources specifically designed for historical inquiry. Three of these resources focus on law books. The Making of Modern Law: Legal Treatises, 1800–1926 <www.gale.cengage.com/ModernLaw/> has more than 21,000 American and British works from the nineteenth and early twentieth centuries, searchable by author, title, or subject as well as full text. HeinOnline's Legal Classics Library <www.heinonline.org> has a more selective collection of about 1,500 titles, ranging in publication date from the early 17th century through the late 20th century, that can be searched or browsed by subject. West's Rise of American Law covers some 400 encyclopedias and treatises from 1820 to 1970, and is available through Westlaw as an additional subscription.

Legal materials are also integrated within more general online book collections. Early American Imprints <www.readex.com> focuses on American works and has more than 70,000 books, pamphlets and broadsides, in two sets: Series I: Evans, 1639–1800; and Series II: Shaw–Shoemaker, 1801–1819. English books from the 1700s are in Eighteenth Century Collections Online (ECCO) <www.gale.cengage.com/EighteenthCentury/>, and works published before 1700 can be found in Early English Books Online (EEBO) <eebo.chadwyck.com>.

Other more general digitization projects are also underway. Google Book Search <books.google. com> is digitizing millions of books from several major research libraries. The full text is searchable, and PDF copies of books in the public domain (generally those published before 1923) are available. Other projects include the Internet Archive's Text Archive <www.archive.org/detailstexts>, which has digitized almost two million books. Major works such as Sir William Blackstone's *Commentaries on the Laws of England* (4 vols., 1765–69) and Oliver Wendell Holmes's *The Common Law* (1881) are also available in modern facsimile printed editions, and some researchers may be able to use the original versions in rare book collections in libraries.

Other digitized resources have vastly increased access to contemporary accounts of major legal developments. Reports of the drafting and ratification of the U.S. Constitution, for example, can be found in America's Historical Newspapers <www.readex. com>, while the course of more modern developments such as the New Deal and civil rights litigation can be followed in ProQuest Historical Newspapers <www.proquest.com>, covering several major national newspapers including the *New York Times* and *Washington Post*. Google News Archive <news.google.com/archivesearch> allows you to search a variety of databases, including ProQuest, with a range of free, fee-based and subscription options for viewing the full text of articles.

Printed collections of historical legal documents are available on a variety of topics, and include such works as *The Documentary History of the Supreme Court of the United States, 1789–1800* (Maeva Marcus ed., 1985–2007) and *Judicial Cases Concerning American Slavery and the Negro* (Helen Tunnicliff Catterall ed., 1926–37). Library online catalogs and footnote references can lead to many others.

Legal history researchers have an array of scholarly monographs from which to choose, from wide-ranging sources such as Lawrence M. Friedman, *A History of American Law* (3d ed. 2005) to much more specific studies. One of the most significant works in American legal history is the multivolume Oliver Wendell Holmes Devise *History of the Supreme Court of the United States* (1971–date), which is perhaps the closest American counterpart to W. S. Holdsworth's monumental *A History of English Law* (1903–72).

Guides and bibliographies can be important resources in discovering historical materials. Works such as *Prestatehood Legal Materials: A Fifty–State Research Guide, Including New York City and the District of Columbia* (Michael G. Chiorazzi & Marguerite Most eds., 2005) have information on resources for specific jurisdictions. The predecessor to the *Index to Legal Periodicals*, entitled *Index to Legal Periodical Literature* (1888–1939), sometimes called the Jones–Chipman index after the names of its editors, covers articles as far back as 1770. Morris L. Cohen, *Bibliography of Early American*

Law (1998–2003) provides a comprehensive record of American legal publications up to 1860.

§ 8–8. Directories

Chapters 5 through 7 discussed directories covering federal and state governments, including legislatures, administrative agencies, and courts. Directories of lawyers and legal organizations can also be of value. Legal directories have background information about other lawyers and can help you establish contacts within the profession. Organizations interested in particular issues may be able to provide you with insights unavailable in any printed or electronic sources.

Numerous directories have contact and biographical information for lawyers. Most focus on individual states or particular specialties, but two comprehensive directories of the legal profession are published by divisions of the parent companies of Westlaw and Lexis. Each covers close to a million lawyers, but neither includes every lawyer in the country.

The *Martindale-Hubbell Law Directory* is the more established source, dating to the nineteenth century. Its online versions, through Lexis and on the Internet as the Martindale–Hubbell Lawyer Locator <www.martindale.com>, are the most inclusive. Basic listings have only mailing addresses, but many attorneys purchase more extensive entries with telephone numbers, e-mail addresses, and biographical information such as practice areas, education, bar admissions, and professional affiliations. Martindale–Hubbell has a Peer Review Rating system that evaluates lawyers who purchase biographical entries on legal ability and ethical standards. Legal ability ratings range from A (Very High to Preeminent) to C (Good to High), and these are published only if accompanied by an ethical standards rating of V (Very High). *Martindale-Hubbell* is also available in an annual printed edition of eight volumes listing lawyers and law firms by state and city, but it is limited to lawyers and law firms that have purchased listings.

West Legal Directory (WLD), the other nationwide directory of attorneys, is available on Westlaw. It has addresses and telephone numbers for practicing attorneys as well as lawyers working in areas such as business or legal education. For most attorneys included, you will also find biographical information such as education, professional affiliations, and areas of practice. The PROFILER feature is particularly useful for information on litigators, as it links the directory data with relevant cases, briefs, pleadings, other documents, and summaries of litigation history. Another version of WLD, the Thomson Legal Record <legalrecords.findlaw.com>, is available free online but omits biographical data for most attorneys.

Several other national directories of lawyers and law firms are available, although none is as comprehensive as *Martindale-Hubbell* or WLD. *Who's Who in American Law* has biographical information on prominent attorneys and legal scholars, and *The Best Lawyers in America* <www.bestlawyers.com> is a guide to highly respected practicing attorneys, listed by state and city under about seventy specialties. Two source for information on the management and recruiting personnel of major law firms are *Law Firms Yellow Book* and the National Association for Law Placement's *Directory of Legal Employers* <www.nalpdirectory.com>.

Other directories focus on attorneys working outside of law firms. *Directory of Corporate Counsel* has biographical information on lawyers working for companies and nonprofit organizations. Directories of public interest and government law offices include *Directory of Legal Aid and Defender Offices in the United States* and *National Directory of Prosecuting Attorneys*.

State and regional directories often provide more thorough listings of local lawyers than national directories. Legal Directories Publishing Co. publishes directories for about twenty states and offers a free online lawyer search <www.legaldirectories.com>. Many state and local bar associations also publish directories or offer attorney search features on their websites. Links to bar associations and other legal organizations are available from FindLaw <www.findlaw.com/06associations/> and WashLaw <www.washlaw.edu/bar/>.

Professional and trade organizations can provide a wealth of information in their areas of interest.

Two directories are notable for their broad coverage of both legal and nonlegal organizations. *Encyclopedia of Associations* (available online as Associations Unlimited <www.gale.cengage.com> and in Lexis) has descriptions and contact information for more than 25,000 national organizations. *National Trade and Professional Associations of the United States* (available online by subscription <www.association execs.com>) is less broad in scope but just as useful for basic information on major business-related organizations.

While most directories are somewhat specialized, a few try to provide answers to a wider range of inquiries. *Law and Legal Information Directory* covers legal organizations and bar associations as well as other resources such as law libraries, lawyer referral services, and a variety of federal and state government agencies. *The Legal Researcher's Desk Reference* is a handy paperback volume with an array of directory information including government offices, courts, and bar associations, and also includes other resources such as state court organization charts.

§ 8–9. Specialized Research Guides

Insights beyond those available from a general research guide such as this *Nutshell* are available in works focusing on specific topics. Specialized research guides (sometimes called "pathfinders") have been published as monographs and in legal bibliography journals such as *Law Library Journal*,

Legal Reference Services Quarterly, and LLRX.com <www.llrx.com>.

Specialized Legal Research (Penny A. Hazelton ed., 1987–date) covers more than a dozen topics, with chapters on admiralty, banking law, copyright, customs, environmental law, government contracts, immigration, income tax, labor and employment law, military and veterans law, patents and trademarks, securities regulation, and the Uniform Commercial Code. The volume also includes a bibliography of other specialized legal research sources. Tax research is the focus of several published works, including Joni Larson & Dan Sheaffer, *Federal Tax Research* (2007) and Gail Levin Richmond, *Federal Tax Research: Guide to Materials and Techniques* (7th ed. 2007).

Legal materials can vary greatly from state to state, and law library websites often have guidance on legal research issues in their home jurisdictions. Appendix A lists state-specific research guides, which can provide valuable details and information on sources.

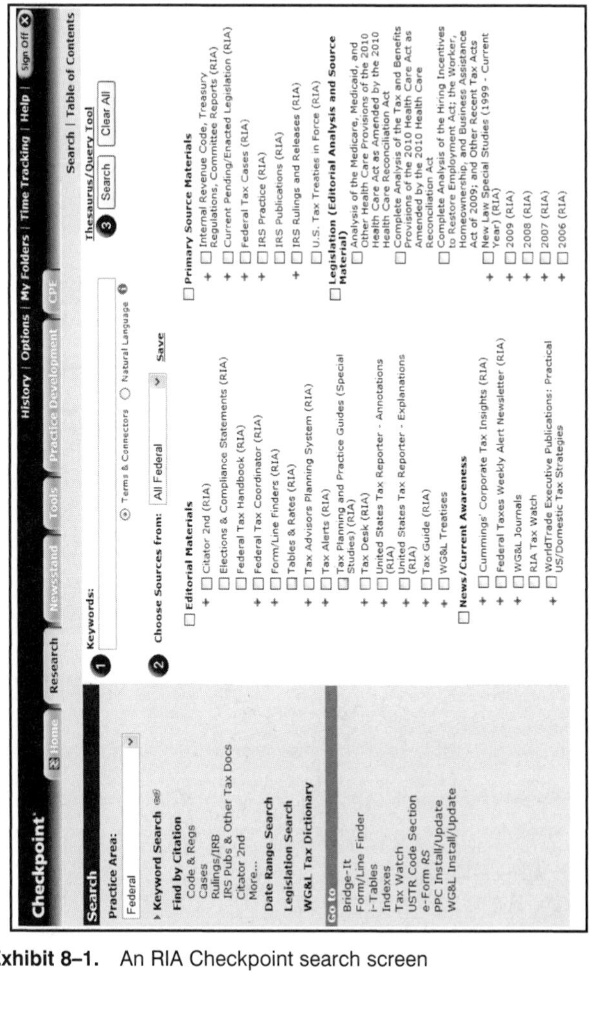

Exhibit 8–1.   An RIA Checkpoint search screen

MEDICAL AND DENTAL EXPENSES—§213 [¶ 12,540]   **27,597**

Effective Date. The provision applies to taxable years beginning after December 31, 1983.—**House Ways and Means Committee Report.**

The conference agreement follows the House bill. As in the case of other types of medical expenses eligible for deduction under section 213, the taxpayer must substantiate any deduction claimed for lodging expenses as prescribed by Treasury regulations (see Reg. sec. 1.213-1(h)).—**Conference Committee Report.**

See also ¶8007.014 for Committee Reports discussing the relationship between the dependency exemption and medical expenses.

Committee Reports on P.L. 97-248 (Tax Equity and Fiscal Responsibility Act of 1982)

.0129 *Senate amendment.*—The medical expense deduction is modified as follows:

(1) the $150 ceiling on the deduction for one-half of health insurance premiums is reduced to $100.

(2) the floor for deductible medical expenses is raised from 3 percent to 7 percent of adjusted gross income.

The provision is effective for taxable years beginning after December 31, 1982.

Conference agreement.—The conference agreement follows the Senate amendment, with several modifications. First, the separate $150 deduction for one-half of health insurance premiums is eliminated. Second, the floor for deductible medical expenses is raised from 3 percent to 5 percent of adjusted gross income. These first two provisions are effective for taxable years beginning after December 31, 1982. Third, effective for taxable years beginning after December 31, 1983, the one-percent floor under drug expenditures is eliminated, and the only drug expenditures which will be deductible will be expenditures for drugs which legally require a prescription or for insulin.—**Conference Committee Report.**

.013 Committee Reports on P.L. 89-97 (Social Security Amendments of 1965) are at 1965-2 CB 733 and 771.

.015 Committee Reports on P.L. 88-272 (Revenue Act of 1964) are at 1964-1 (Part 2) CB 125, 505, 700, 774.

.02 Committee Reports on P.L. 87-863 (1962) are at 1962-3 CB 1208 and 1213.

.03 Committee Reports on P.L. 86-470 (1960) are at 1960-1 CB 840, 843, 847.

.04 Committee Reports on P.L. 85-866 (Technical Amendments Act of 1958) are at 1958-3 CB 811, 922, and 1188.

.05 Committee Reports on 1954 Code Sec. 213 as originally enacted were reproduced at 562 CCH ¶ 2012.15.

• Regulations

➤➤➤ *Caution: Reg. §1.213-1 does not reflect recent law changes. For details, see ¶12,541.01.*

[¶ 12,541] § 1.213-1. **Medical, dental, etc., expenses.**—(a) *Allowance of deduction.*—(1) Section 213 permits a deduction of payments for certain medical expenses (including expenses for medicine and drugs). Except as provided in paragraph (d) of this section (relating to special rule for decedents) a deduction is allowable only to individuals and only with respect to medical expenses actually paid during the taxable year, regardless of when the incident or event which occasioned the expenses occurred and regardless of the method of accounting employed by the taxpayer in making his income tax return. Thus, if the medical expenses are incurred but not paid during the taxable year, no deduction for such expenses shall be allowed for such year.

(2) Except as provided in subparagraphs (4)(i) and (5)(i) of this paragraph, only such medical expenses (including the allowable expenses for medicine and drugs) are deductible as exceed 3 percent of the adjusted gross income for the taxable year. For taxable years beginning after December 31, 1966, the amounts paid during the taxable year for insurance that constitute expenses paid for medical care shall, for purposes of computing total medical expenses, be reduced by the amount determined under subparagraph (5)(i) of this paragraph. For the amounts paid during the taxable year for medicine and drugs which may be taken into account in computing total medical expenses, see paragraph (b) of this section. For the maximum deduction allowable under section 213 in the case of certain taxable years, see paragraph (c) of this section. As to what constitutes "adjusted gross income", see section 62 and the regulations thereunder.

(3)(i) For medical expenses paid (including expenses paid for medicine and drugs) to be deductible, they must be for medical care of the taxpayer, his spouse, or a dependent of the taxpayer and not be compensated for by insurance or otherwise.

2010(5) CCH—Standard Federal Tax Reports   **Reg. §1.213-1(a)(3)(i)   ¶ 12,541**

Exhibit 8–2. Committee reports and regulations in *Standard Federal Tax Reporter* (CCH)

MEDICAL AND DENTAL EXPENSES—§ 213 [¶ 12,540]   **27,617**

Medical and Dental Expenses

• • *CCH Explanation*

.029 Costs of service animals.—The costs to acquire, train and maintain a dog that assists a blind or deaf taxpayer are deductible medical expenses (Rev. Rul. 55-261 and Rev. Rul. 68-295, at ¶ 12,543.138). Similar costs attributable to a dog or other animal that assists individuals with other physical disabilities may also be deducted as medical expenses (Senate Finance Committee Report, P.L. 100-647).

.031 Change of climate.—The deductibility of expenses of moving to a different climate depends upon whether the change actually alleviates the illness and whether such alleviation is the primary purpose of the change. In one case, the taxpayer was allowed to deduct expenses incurred on behalf of a child whom he sent to an Arizona boarding school because of a bronchial condition. The deductible expenses included transportation but not those expenses which were attributable to the child's education. The court found that alleviation of the bronchial condition was the primary reason for sending the child to school in Arizona (*L.K. Stringham*, CA-6, 50-2 USTC ¶ 9367, at ¶ 12,543.82).

Lodging expenses that a taxpayer incurs after moving to a new location to alleviate a chronic ailment are deductible only where the taxpayer's lodging is primarily for and essential to medical care provided by a physician in a licensed hospital or related facility. (*A.L. Polyak*, 94 TC 337, Dec. 46,443 and *S.L. Bilder*, SCt, 62-1 USTC ¶ 9440, at ¶ 12,543.67).

.033 Transportation expenses.—Medical expenses include amounts paid for transportation "primarily for and essential to medical care." This includes taxi, bus, train, airplane, etc., fares to and from the point of treatment.

Transportation expenses primarily for and essential to medical care do not include the cost of meals and lodging while away from home receiving medical treatment (Reg. § 1.213-1(e)(1)(iv)). See ¶ 12,540.0125 and 12,543.012 regarding deduction of lodging expenses. However, the cost of meals and lodging while en route from a couple's home in Kentucky to the Mayo Clinic in Minnesota were deductible because transportation costs included the costs required to bring the patient to the place of treatment (see *M.C. Montgomery*, CA-6, 70-2 USTC ¶ 9466, at ¶ 12,543.81).

Medical expenses do not include a trip or vacation taken for a change in environment, improvement of morale, or general improvement of health, even if the trip is made on the advice of a doctor (see *L.W. Finlay*, 44 TCM 123, Dec. 39,106(M) at ¶ 12,543.82; see also IRS Pub. 502 "Medical and Dental Expenses" (for 2008 returns), p. 14). Expenses to travel to another city, such as a resort area, for an operation or other medical care prescribed by a doctor, do not qualify as medical expenses if the trip was made primarily for non-medical reasons (IRS Pub. 502, "Medical and Dental Expenses" (for 2008 returns)).

If it is necessary for someone to accompany an ill person in seeking medical aid or simply as a necessary companion, the deductibility of the other person's expenses depends upon the necessity of the accompanying person's presence (see *D.S.W. Kelly*, 28 TCM 1208, Dec. 29,811(M) at ¶ 12,543.82). Travel expenses incurred by a parent who is required to accompany a child because of the child's immaturity are deductible. Transportation expenses of a nurse or other person who can give injections, medications, or other treatment required by a patient who is unable to travel alone to obtain medical care are also deductible (see Rev. Rul. 58-110, ¶ 12,543.82).

Exhibit 8–3. Explanation in *Standard Federal Tax Reporter*

MEDICAL AND DENTAL EXPENSES—§ 213 [¶ 12,540]   **27,631**

of the accident. Loss of anticipated earnings was not deductible. Medical expenses were deductible only when incurred.

W.B. Andrews, 37 TCM 744, Dec. 35,144(M), TC Memo. 1978-174.

.138 Animals for handicapped individuals.— Medical expenses include the cost of a "seeing-eye" dog and its maintenance.

Rev. Rul. 55-261, 1955-1 CB 307, as modified by Rev. Rul. 58-8, 1958-1 CB 154, Rev. Rul. 58-280, 1958-1 CB 157, Rev. Rul. 63-91, 1963-1 CB 54 and Rev. Rul. 68-212, 1968-1 CB 91.

Amounts expended for the maintenance of a guide ("seeing-eye") dog which the taxpayer, who is blind, uses daily in the conduct of his business are medical expenses.

Rev. Rul. 57-461, 1957-2 CB 116.

Amounts paid for the acquisition, training, and maintenance of a dog for the purpose of assisting a dependent who is deaf are medical expenses.

Rev. Rul. 68-295, 1968-1 CB 92.

A taxpayer who suffered from a hearing impairment could deduct as a medical expense costs incurred in maintaining a cat that was registered as a hearing-aid animal and that would help to alleviate the effects of her handicap.

IRS Letter Ruling 8033038, May 20, 1980.

.139 Wheelchairs.—Where a sick or disabled person acquires a wheelchair, either manually operated or self-propelled, and uses it primarily for the alleviation of his sickness or disability and not merely to provide transportation between his residence and place of employment, purchase price and maintenance cost of the wheelchair are allowable medical expenses.

Rev. Rul. 58-8, 1958-1 CB 154, (modifying Rev. Rul. 55-261, 1955-1 CB 307) as amplified by Rev. Rul. 67-76, 1967-1 CB 70.

.140 Automobile medical insurance.—The taxpayers were not entitled to a medical expense deduction for premiums paid for automobile insurance because the premiums were not paid for medical care for either the taxpayers or their dependents.

G.K. Notter, 43 TCM 631, Dec. 38,815(M), TC Memo. 1982-96.

A taxpayer was not permitted to deduct the separately stated portion of an automobile insurance policy premium attributable to medical insurance. Although the amount was both reasonable and separately stated, the medical insurance portion of the policy covered all persons injured in or by the taxpayer's automobile. The deduction was not allowed because the portion of the medical insurance that covered the taxpayer, a spouse, and any dependents was not separately stated from the portion that covered other individuals.

Rev. Rul. 73-483, 1973-2 CB 75.

.142 Baby-sitter.—See ¶ 12,543.35.

.144 Blindness.—No deduction was allowed for tuition paid for a blind child who attended a privately operated college preparatory school that provided a regular coeducational program for its students.

A.P. Grunwald, 51 TC 108, Dec. 29,198.

Costs of special aids to assist in education of child becoming blind, such as tape recorder, special typewriter, projection lamp for enlarging written material, and special lenses, are to mitigate condition of losing sense of sight and are deductible as medical expenses.

Rev. Rul. 58-223, 1958-1 CB 156.

Amounts paid by a taxpayer to have someone accompany his blind child throughout the school day were deductible medical expenses.

Rev. Rul. 64-173, 1964-1 CB (Part 1) 121.

A taxpayer purchasing braille books and magazines for his blind child was allowed to deduct, as expenses for medical care, that portion of the purchase price that exceeded the price for regular printed editions.

Rev. Rul. 75-318, 1975-2 CB 88.

.146 Capital expenditures.—See the annotations discussing "Home modifications or improvements" at ¶ 12,543.48.

.148 Chemical dependency treatment.—See ¶ 12,543.355.

.150 Childbirth classes.—An allocable portion of a pregnant woman's expenses for a childbirth class qualified as "medical care" to the extent that the expenses were incurred for the purpose of preparing her for an active role in the process of childbirth. Such instructions are directly related to obstetrical care which is specifically included in the definition of medical care. A flat fee for each course allowed a "coach" to attend the class with the taxpayer, and, thus, the total fee had to be reduced by one-half prior to the allocation of the otherwise deductible expenses.

IRS Letter Ruling 8919009, February 6, 1989.

.151 Children, handicapped or retarded.—See ¶ 12,543.786.

.152 Chiropractors, osteopaths, etc.—A taxpayer was entitled to deduct as medical expenses amounts paid to a naturopathic doctor in connection with his wife's cancer. Code Sec. 213 does not bar deduction of expenses for nontraditional medical care, even where a medical doctor does not prescribe such care.

P.F. Dickie, 77 TCM 1916, Dec. 53,353(M), TC Memo. 1999-138.

Amounts paid for medical services rendered by practitioners, such as chiropractors and others rendering similar type services, constitute ex-

Exhibit 8–4.   Annotations in *Standard Federal Tax Reporter*

Exhibit 8–5. *Standard Federal Tax Reporter* topical index

Exhibit 8–6. A legal blog

Table 1204. Household Pet Ownership: 2006

[Based on a sample survey of 47,000 households in 2006. For definition of mean, see source]

Item	Unit	Dogs	Cats	Birds	Horses
Total companion pet population [1]	Million	72.1	81.7	11.2	7.3
Number of households owning pets	Million	43.0	37.5	4.5	2.1
Percent of households owning companion pets [1]	Percent	37.2	32.4	3.9	1.8
Average number owned per household	Number	1.7	2.2	2.5	3.5
PERCENT OF HOUSEHOLDS OWNING PETS					
Annual household income:					
Under $20,000	Percent	30.7	30.1	4.4	1.5
$20,000 to $34,999	Percent	37.3	33.6	4.2	1.7
$35,000 to $54,999	Percent	39.8	34.1	4.4	2.1
$55,000 to $84,999	Percent	42.8	35.5	3.7	1.9
$85,000 and over	Percent	42.1	33.3	3.7	2.3
Household size:[1]					
One person	Percent	21.9	24.7	2.1	0.8
Two persons	Percent	37.6	33.4	3.9	1.7
Three persons	Percent	47.5	39.1	5.1	2.3
Four persons	Percent	51.9	38.5	5.4	2.7
Five or more persons	Percent	54.3	40.0	6.6	3.6

[1] As of December 31, 2006.

Source: American Veterinary Medical Association, Schaumburg, IL, *U.S. Pet Ownership and Demographics Sourcebook, 2007* (copyright). See also <http://www.avma.org/>.

Exhibit 8–7. A table from the *Statistical Abstract*

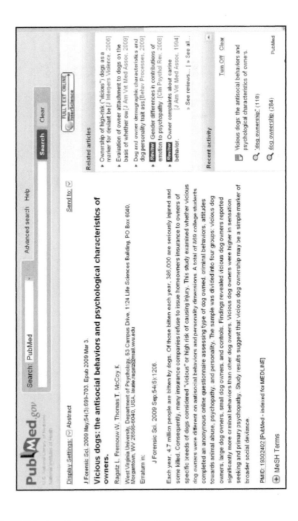

Exhibit 8–8.   An abstract from PubMed

CHAPTER 9

INTERNATIONAL LAW

---

§ 9–1. Introduction

Public international law is the body of rules and procedures intended to govern relations among nations. Although its primary historical functions have been the preservation of peace and regulation of war, international law now governs an ever

373

broader range of transnational activities. It regulates matters from copyright protection to the rights of refugees, and agreements such as the Convention on Contracts for the International Sale of Goods (CISG) have made international law an inherent aspect of commercial activity. *Public international law* is distinguished from *private international law* (or conflict of laws), which determines where, and by whose law, controversies involving more than one jurisdiction are resolved, as well as how foreign judgments are enforced.

A modern legal practice often requires knowledge of international law. If you are representing an American firm investing in another country, for example, you must be aware of treaties between the two nations as well as the investment and trade laws of both the United States and the other country. You may also need to examine jurisdictional issues in resolving disputes or in determining the application of one country's rules in the other's courts. This chapter focuses on international law, while research in the law of foreign countries is the subject of Chapter 10.

The classic statement of the sources of international law is Article 38 of the Statute of the International Court of Justice, identifying the bases on which it decides disputes:

(a) international conventions, whether general or particular, establishing rules expressly recognized by the contesting States;

(b) international custom, as evidence of a general practice accepted as law;

(c) the general principles of law recognized by civilized nations;

(d) ... judicial decisions and the teachings of the most highly qualified publicists of the various nations, as subsidiary means for the determination of rules of law.

International conventions (treaties) and *international custom* are generally considered the two most important sources. If a treaty is relevant to a problem involving its signatories, it is the primary legal authority. International custom is the actual conduct of nations, provided it is consistent with the rule of law. Custom is not defined in specific legal sources but is established by evidence of state practices. *General principles of law* are the most amorphous of the sources but are usually considered to be basic principles articulated in the classic texts of international law. *Judicial decisions* and *scholarly writings* are less important than treaties and international custom. Cases are generally not considered binding precedents in subsequent disputes, but they can aid in interpreting treaties and in defining custom.

§ 9–2. Preliminary Research

As in other areas, the first step in approaching most research problems in international law is to turn to a reference work, a treatise, or a law review article for general information and for help in analyzing the issues involved.

Encyclopedias and Treatises. The *Encyclopedia of Public International Law* (Rudolf Bernhardt ed., 1992–2000), published under the auspices of the Max Planck Institute for Comparative Public Law and International Law, is a five-volume work providing a comprehensive view of international law issues. Its articles are written by respected authorities and include brief bibliographies for further research. A revised edition is in progress, and completed articles are available electronically by subscription as the *Max Planck Encyclopedia of Public International Law* <www.mpepil.com>.

Edmund Jan Osmańczyk, *Encyclopedia of the United Nations and International Agreements* (Anthony Mango ed., 3d ed. 2003) is another multivolume encyclopedia with wide coverage of international law issues, as well as excerpts from treaties and other major documents. Shorter reference works include Anthony Aust, *Handbook of International Law* (2d ed. 2010) and *Routledge Handbook of International Law* (David Armstrong ed., 2009). The American Bar Association publishes *International Lawyer's Deskbook* (Lucinda A. Low et al. eds., 2d ed. 2002), designed as an introductory starting point for lawyers facing international law issues.

Several general treatises provide overviews of international law doctrine. *Oppenheim's International*

Law (Robert Jennings & Arthur Watts eds., 9th ed. 1992) is considered a classic work, and more modern treatises include Ian Brownlie, *Principles of Public International Law* (7th ed. 2008) and Malcolm N. Shaw, *International Law* (6th ed. 2008). The American Law Institute's *Restatement of the Law, Third, Foreign Relations Law of the United States* (1987) summarizes American law and practice in international law and foreign relations.

Journal Articles. International law has numerous scholarly periodicals, including more than seventy specialized journals published at U.S. law schools. Among the more prestigious professional journals are the *American Journal of International Law* and *International and Comparative Law Quarterly*. Many national societies of international law produce annual publications such as the *British Yearbook of International Law* or the *Annuaire Français de Droit International,* which usually contain scholarly articles as well as reprints of selected major documents. Many of these yearbooks and other sources are available by subscription in Hein-Online's Foreign and International Law Resources Database.

International law topics are well represented in the standard law review literature, and articles can be found through any of the full-text and index resources discussed in Chapter 2. *Index to Foreign Legal Periodicals* (1960–date, available through Westlaw and other database systems) principally covers journals published in countries outside the common law system, but it also indexes articles on international law in selected American law reviews. *Public International Law: A Current Bibliography of Books and Articles* (1975–date) is a comprehensive index of the literature in the field.

Dictionaries. International law has its own specialized terminology, and a dictionary can help you understand key concepts. The leading work is *Parry and Grant Encyclopaedic Dictionary of International Law* (John P. Grant & J. Craig Barker eds., 3d ed. 2009), which has descriptive entries with citations to major sources. James R. Fox, *Dictionary of International and Comparative Law* (3d ed. 2003) has more concise definitions of terms. You may also wish to consult more specialized works, such as H. Victor Condé, *A Handbook of International Human Rights Terminology* (2d ed. 2004), or Walter Goode, *Dictionary of Trade Policy Terms* (5th ed. 2007).

§ 9–3. U.S. Practice in International Law

For American lawyers and law students, materials on United States practice are the most frequently consulted research sources in international law. These include treaties and the materials needed to interpret them, as well as documents dealing with issues in U.S. foreign relations.

a. Treaties

Treaties are formal agreements between countries, and they have legal significance for both domestic and international purposes. Article VI of the U.S. Constitution provides that treaties are part of the supreme law of the land, giving them the same legal effect and status as federal statutes. Treaties and statutes can supersede each other as the controlling law within the United States, but a treaty that is no longer valid as U.S. law may still be binding in international law.

Treaty research generally involves several aspects: (1) finding its text in an authoritative source; (2) determining whether it is in force and with what parties and reservations; and (3) interpreting its provisions, with the aid of commentaries, judicial decisions, and legislative history. What resources to use may depend in large part on whether the United States is a party to a treaty or convention.

Treaty Process. Treaties between two governments are called *bilateral*, and those entered into by more than two governments are called *multilateral*. Parties' initial signatures to a treaty establish their agreement that its text is authentic and definitive, but nations are not bound until they approve the treaty through ratification (such as approval by two-thirds of the U.S. Senate) or some other procedure. Parties to multilateral treaties may add RUDs: *reservations* excluding certain provisions, or *understandings* or *declarations* providing their own interpretations of treaty terms. The texts of treaties usually identify the event that triggers their entry into force, often (in the case of multilateral conventions) when a specified number of nations have indicated their approval.

The President makes *executive agreements* with other countries under the Article II authority to conduct foreign affairs. These are similar in effect to treaties, but they do not require Senate approval and hence are often used to streamline the process and avoid controversy. The sources and research procedures discussed in this section generally apply to both treaties and executive agreements.

Sources. Treaties before 1950 were published in the *Statutes at Large* and have been reprinted in *Treaties and Other International Agreements of the United States of America 1776–1949* (Charles I. Bevans comp., 1968–75, available on HeinOnline), which contains four volumes of multilateral treaties (arranged chronologically), eight volumes of bilateral treaties (arranged alphabetically by country), and indexes by country and subject.

Beginning in 1950, *United States Treaties and Other International Agreements* (*UST*) became the official, permanent form of publication for treaties and executive agreements to which the United States is a party. *UST* was published through volume 35 (1983–84); the series has not officially ceased, but no further volumes have appeared. Exhibit 9–1 on page 406 shows the beginning of the Convention on International Trade in Endangered Species of Wild Flora and Fauna (CITES), as published in *UST*.

Before they appear in *UST*, treaties and agreements are issued in a numbered series of separately paginated pamphlets, *Treaties and Other International Acts Series* (*TIAS*). These are now available on the Department of State website <www.state.gov/s/l/treaty/>, but with a time lag of almost ten years. The site also has more recent treaties and agreements, within six months of the date they enter into force, under the heading "Reporting International Agreements to Congress under Case Act."

Because of the long delays in the publication of *TIAS* and *UST*, several commercial services are important sources for current treaties. Both Westlaw and Lexis have comprehensive treaty coverage from the 1770s through recent months. Another extensive online source, *Treaties and International Agreements Online*, is available as a subscription website <www.oceanalaw.com>. HeinOnline has a Treaties and Agreements Library with PDF versions of treaties in *Statutes at Large*, *UST*, and *TIAS*, as well as more recent treaties not yet published in these sources.

A citation to a treaty includes its name, the date of its signing, the parties (if there are three or fewer), and references to the main sources of publication. The *Bluebook* generally specifies citation of bilateral treaties to an official U.S. source (usually *Statutes at Large* or *UST*), if available, and of multilateral treaties to an official international source as well (usually the *United Nations Treaty*

Series). Because many recent treaties do not appear in these standard sources, they are often cited to versions appearing in journals, commercially published compilations, and electronic sources. The convention in Exhibit 9–1 is printed in the official sources and is cited as: Convention on International Trade in Endangered Species of Wild Fauna and Flora, Mar. 3, 1973, 27 U.S.T. 1087, 993 U.N.T.S. 243. The signing date is particularly important because it is used to identify treaties in most lists and indexes.

Indexes and Guides. Treaties are generally published chronologically rather than by subject, so you many need a guide or index to identify agreements with a specific country or on a particular topic. Many of these same resources also have information on treaty status.

Treaties in Force, an annual publication of the Department of State, is the official index to current United States treaties and agreements. It has citations to all of the major treaty publications, including *Bevans*, *UST*, *TIAS*, and the *United Nations Treaty Series*. The first section of *Treaties in Force* lists bilateral treaties by country and, under each country, by subject; and the second section lists multilateral treaties by subject. Exhibit 9–2 on page 407 shows a portion of the multilaterals section covering the convention seen in Exhibit 9–1. *Treaties in Force* is available online <www.state.gov/s/l/treaty/> along with background information and lists of recent treaty actions. Westlaw and Lexis have the current *Treaties in Force*, and HeinOnline has past editions back to 1929.

A commercially published *Kavass's Guide to the United States Treaties in Force* is also issued annually in print and on HeinOnline, and has subject and country indexes to both bilateral and multilateral treaties. These can be useful because the official *Treaties in Force* doesn't index bilateral treaties by subject or list multilateral conventions by country.

The major collections and series of U.S. treaties and international agreements are indexed by subject, date, and country in *United States Treaty Index: 1776–2000 Consolidation* (Igor I. Kavass ed., 2001–date), which is updated semiannually by *Kavass' Current Treaty Index*, available in print and on HeinOnline.

Sometimes one of the hardest steps in researching a treaty is identifying its *UST* and *UNTS* citations. Lists such as the University of Minnesota Law School's "Frequently–Cited Treaties and Other International Instruments" <library.law.umn.edu/researchguides/most-cited.html> can help. Searching the law reviews on Westlaw and LexisNexis for the title or subject of a treaty will often lead to numerous footnotes providing the necessary references.

Interpretation. Like statutes or constitutional provisions, most treaties contain ambiguities that can lead to controversies in interpretation and application. Several resources assist in understanding treaty terms, including court decisions and documents produced during a treaty's drafting and consideration. Neither KeyCite nor Shepard's covers citations to treaties, but you can learn of cases from law review articles and other secondary sources or use a treaty's name or citation in a full-text case law search.

The *United States Code Service* includes two volumes that can serve as starting points for finding cases. "International Agreements" contains the texts of about three dozen major conventions and treaties, accompanied by research references and case annotations, and "Annotations to Uncodified Laws and Treaties" has broader coverage of decisions interpreting U.S. treaties (but no treaty texts).

Records of Senate deliberation can illuminate the terms and meaning of U.S. treaties. *Treaty Documents* (until 1980, called *Senate Executive Documents*) contain treaties transmitted to the Senate for its consideration, and usually include messages from the President and the Secretary of State. The Senate Foreign Relations Committee analyzes treaties and issues *Senate Executive Reports* with its recommendations. Both Treaty Documents and Senate Executive Reports are issued in numbered series identifying the Congress and sequence in which they were issued. LexisNexis Congressional includes coverage of Senate treaty materials from 1817.

THOMAS <thomas.loc.gov> has legislative history summaries of treaty action since the 90th Congress (1967–68), with links to Treaty Documents (but not to reports). The looseleaf *Congressional Index* also includes a table of treaties pending before the Senate, with references to documents, reports, hearings, and ratifications.

b.   Foreign Relations Documents

State practice is the primary evidence of custom, one of the major sources of international law. To study state practice, you will need to turn to sources that explain how a particular nation has acted in the past.

Reference works such as *Encyclopedia of U.S. Foreign Relations* (Bruce W. Jentleson & Thomas G. Paterson eds., 1997) can provide a background understanding of U.S. practice. You will find more detailed discussion in a series prepared by the Department of State, *Digest of United States Practice in International Law*. This set compiles excerpts from treaties, decisions, diplomatic correspondence, and other documents reflecting the U.S. position on major issues of international law, accompanied by explanatory commentary. The Department of State website <www.state.gov/s/l/c8183.htm> has links to the full text of documents excerpted in the digests since 1989.

The Department of State also published earlier encyclopedic digests of U.S. practice that may be of value for historical research. These digests, commonly known by the names of their compilers (Wharton, Moore, Hackworth, and Whiteman), are all available in HeinOnline's Foreign and International Law Resources Database.

More extensive documentation of U.S. practice can be found in *Foreign Relations of the United States* (1861–date), a comprehensive record of material relating to such issues as treaty negotiation and international conflicts. There is a time lag of more than thirty years between the original (often confidential) issuance of these documents and their publication in this series. The set from 1861 to 1960 is available online through subscription databases and free from the University of Wisconsin <digicoll. library.wisc.edu/FRUS/>, and selected volumes for the Truman through Ford administrations are available from the Department of State website <history.state.gov/historicaldocuments>.

§ 9–4. General Treaty Research

The United States is not a party to every major multilateral treaty. The United Nations Convention on the Law of the Sea and the Vienna Convention on the Law of Treaties are just two of the many agreements that the U.S. has not ratified. Regional agreements in other parts of the world and bilateral treaties between other countries may also be important in your research. In addition to the U.S. treaty resources already discussed, more general resources are frequently needed as well.

Sources. The most comprehensive source for modern treaties is the *United Nations Treaty Series* (*UNTS*), containing more than 2,300 volumes and available free online as the United Nations Treaty Collection <treaties.un.org>. Since 1946 this series has published all treaties registered with the UN by member nations in their original languages, as well as in English and French translations. Exhibit 9–3 on page 408 shows the first page of the Agreement on the Conservation of Small Cetaceans of the Baltic and North Seas (ASCOBANS), as published in *UNTS*. Footnote 1 identifies the ratifications that caused the convention to enter into force in 1994.

The United Nations Treaty Collection website includes summaries and information on ratification status as well as treaty texts. It has several search options including popular name, title, and full text, but doesn't have a simple way to find documents by volume and page number. The *UNTS* is also available online by subscription in HeinOnline's United Nations Law Collection, which may be a more convenient source if you want to retrieve treaties by citation.

Treaties predating the creation of the United Nations can be found in two older series. The *League of Nations Treaty Series* (*LNTS*) (1920–46) is similar in scope to the *UNTS*, and is included in the online United Nations Treaty Collection. A retrospective collection, *Consolidated Treaty Series* (*CTS*), contains all treaties between nation states from 1648 to 1919.

Regional organizations also publish compilations of treaties among their members. The Council of Europe <conventions.coe.int> and the OAS <www.oas.org/DIL/> both have online collections of major treaties. The Hague Conference on Private International Law <www.hcch.net> has the text of several dozen conventions it has drafted on issues such as international civil procedure and recognition of judgments. Many countries publish current treaties in their official gazettes and on government websites, and new treaties are often printed in international law yearbooks and journals.

The American Society of International Law's Electronic Information System for International Law (EISIL) <www.eisil.org> has thousands of links to treaties and other documents in thirteen major subject areas. In addition to links to the primary sources, each record also includes a "More Information" button with citations, dates, and brief descriptions. Other free sources for the texts of major multilateral treaties and conventions include the Multilaterals Project at the Fletcher School <fletcher.tufts.edu/multilaterals/> and the University of Minnesota Human Rights Library <www.umn.edu/humanrts/>.

Indexes and Status Tables. The leading online index to multilateral conventions is the Flare Index to Treaties <ials.sas.ac.uk/treatyindex.htm>. It has basic information such as official titles and dates for more than 1,500 multilateral treaties, as well as citations to printed versions and links to online sources for the treaty text. The entry from the Flare Index for CITES, the convention in Exhibit 9–1, is shown in Exhibit 9–4 on page 409. Links are included to the CITES website and EISIL, as are citations of more than a dozen printed sources.

The World Treaty Index <depts.washington.edu/hrights/Treaty/trindex.html> is much broader in scope, covering more than 55,000 treaties of the 20th century. This is an updated version of a five-volume print publication (Peter H. Rohn comp., 2d ed. 1983–84). Christian L. Wiktor, *Multilateral Treaty Calendar, 1648–1995* (1998), is another major print resource, with information on more than 6,000 multilateral conventions.

Multilateral Treaties Deposited with the Secretary–General, published by the United Nations and available online <treaties.un.org>, is a leading source for determining the status of and identifying the parties to major conventions. This listing of several hundred treaties is arranged by subject, and provides citations, information on status, a list of parties with dates of signature and ratification, and the text of any reservations imposed by individual parties. Coverage is limited to treaties concluded under UN auspices or for which the Secretary–General acts as depository, so it excludes some major agreements such as CITES <www.cites.org> and the Geneva Conventions of 1949 <www.icrc.org/ihl>. Exhibit 9–5 on page 410 shows the entry for ASCOBANS, with ten countries now parties to the convention.

The *United Nations Treaty Series* has indexes for every 50 or 100 volumes, but no cumulative official index. This is less significant now that the United Nations Treaty Collection is available free online, but retrospective coverage back to 1946 is provided by a commercial publication, *United Nations Cumulative Treaty Index* (1999), and a regularly updated *United Nations Master Treaty Index on CD–ROM*.

Interpretation. Scholarly commentary and judicial decisions are the standard sources of treaty interpretation. An additional resource available for some multilateral conventions is the *travaux preparatoires* (documents created during the drafting process such as reports and debates). These are recognized under the 1969 Vienna Convention on the Law of Treaties as a source for clarifying ambiguous treaty terms. *Travaux* can be difficult to find, but they have been compiled and published for several conventions. For a guide to published sources and more information, see Jonathan Pratter, *À la Recherche des Travaux Préparatoires: An Approach to Researching the Drafting History of International Agreements*, GlobaLex (May/June 2008) <www.nyulawglobal.org/globalex/Travaux_Preparatoires1.htm>.

§ 9–5. Cases and Arbitrations

Although most disputes between nations are resolved by direct negotiation, some are submitted to international tribunals, arbitral bodies, or specially convened commissions. Courts established by regional organizations resolve cases between nations and their citizens, and are developing a growing body of international human rights law. Decisions of domestic courts on matters of international law can also be important sources, particularly as evidence of international legal custom.

a. International Court of Justice

The preeminent international tribunal is the International Court of Justice (ICJ), also known as the World Court, which settles legal disputes between nations. The ICJ was created in 1945 by the Charter of the United Nations as one of the organization's principal organs, succeeding the Permanent Court of International Justice (PCIJ) of the League of Nations. The Court meets at The Hague and consists of fifteen justices elected to nine-year terms.

The ICJ issues only a handful of decisions each year. These are published in *Reports of Judgments, Advisory Opinions and Orders* and are available on the ICJ website <www.icj-cij.org>. The site has material from every case the Court has heard since its inception and from cases heard by the PCIJ, as well as information on the current docket and basic documents such as the Statute of the Court and rules. Exhibit 9–6 on page 411 shows the opening page of the Court's decision in *Fisheries Jurisdiction (Spain v. Canada),* from the I.C.J. *Reports of Judgments.*

Decisions are also available through online databases such as HeinOnline and Westlaw. *International Law Reports* (1956–date) and its predecessor *Annual Digest and Reports of Public International Law Cases* (1932–55) contain all PCIJ and ICJ decisions, as well as English translations of selected decisions of regional and national courts on international law issues. The leading commentaries on the ICJ are Shabtai Rosenne, *The Law and Practice of the International Court, 1920–2005* (4th ed. 2006) and *The Statute of the International Court of Justice: A Commentary* (Andreas Zimmermann et al. eds., 2006).

b. Other Courts

The ICJ is not the only court of international scope. The Project on International Courts and Tribunals <www.pict-pcti.org> has information on dozens of global and regional tribunals, with links to basic documents and cases. The World Legal Information Institute's International Courts & Tribunals Library <www.worldlii.org/int/cases/> allows searching across more than 20,000 decisions from about twenty of these courts.

International Courts. An International Criminal Court <www.icc-cpi.int> with jurisdiction over war crimes, genocide, and crimes against humanity had its first session in March 2003. Its jurisdiction has been accepted by 110 countries, not including the United States. Cases, documents, and background information are available on the court's website, and *The Annotated Digest of the Interna-*

tional Criminal Court (2007–date) has abstracts of the ICC's developing case law, arranged by provisions of its statute, rules and regulations. Major secondary sources include William Schabas, *The International Criminal Court: A Commentary on the Rome Statute* (2010).

More focused courts address violations of international humanitarian law in specific countries. These include the International Criminal Tribunal for the former Yugoslavia (ICTY) <www.icty.org>, the International Criminal Tribunal for Rwanda (ICTR) <www.ictr.org>, and the Special Court for Sierra Leone <www.sc-sl.org>. Documents and judgments are available on the court websites, and major cases can be found in print in *Annotated Leading Cases of International Criminal Tribunals* (André Klip & Göran Sluiter eds., 1999–date). Their work is discussed in sources such as William Schabas, *The UN International Criminal Tribunals: The Former Yugoslavia, Rwanda, and Sierra Leone* (2006).

Another court of worldwide scope, the International Tribunal for the Law of the Sea (ITLOS) <www.itlos.org>, was created by the United Nations Convention on the Law of the Sea and established in 1996. ITLOS rules and cases are available on its website, and publications include P. Chandrasekhara Rao & Ph. Gautier, *The Rules of the International Tribunal for the Law of the Sea: A Commentary* (2006).

Regional Courts. The decisions of the courts of regional organizations have assumed growing importance in international law as the range of disputes over which they exercise jurisdiction grows. Among the most important of these regional courts are the European Court of Justice, the European Court of Human Rights, and the Inter–American Court of Human Rights.

The European Court of Justice <curia.europa.eu>, an organ of the European Union, resolves disputes between EU institutions and member states over the interpretation and application of EU treaties and legislation. A subordinate General Court (formerly the Court of First Instance) handles the initial hearing in most cases. All decisions since the Court of Justice's inception are available on its website, as well as through Westlaw and Lexis. Print sources include the official *Reports of Cases* (1959–date), *Common Market Law Reports* (1962–date), and CCH's *European Union Law Reporter* (1972–date). Commentaries include Anthony Arnull, *The European Union and Its Court of Justice* (2d ed. 2006) and L. Neville Brown & Tom Kennedy, *The Court of Justice of the European Communities* (5th ed. 2000).

The European Court of Human Rights <www.echr.coe.int> was created under the European Convention of Human Rights of 1950 for the international protection of the rights of individuals. The Court's website has basic texts and searchable case law. Decisions are published officially in *Reports of Judgments and Decisions*, and are also reported commercially in *European Human Rights Reports*

(1979–date, available on Westlaw). Cases are summarized in *Human Rights Case Digest* (1990–date, available on HeinOnline), and a variety of documents and decisions appear in the annual *Yearbook of the European Convention on Human Rights* (1958–date). *Human Rights Practice* (Jessica Simor ed., 2000–date) is a detailed guide to the Convention's articles and court procedures. Other secondary sources include Clare Ovey & Robin White, *Jacobs and White, The European Convention on Human Rights* (3d ed. 2002) and *Theory and Practice of the European Convention on Human Rights* (Pieter van Dijk et al. eds., 2006).

The Inter–American Commission on Human Rights <www.cidh.oas.org> hears complaints of individuals and institutions alleging violations of human rights in the American countries. The Commission, or a member state, can refer matters to the Inter–American Court of Human Rights <www.corteidh.or.cr>. Twenty-five countries (not including the United States) have accepted its jurisdiction. The Court's decisions are reported in print and on its website. The *Inter-American Yearbook on Human Rights* (1985–date) covers the work of both the Commission and the Court and includes selected decisions and other documents. Secondary sources include Jo M. Pasqualucci, *The Practice and Procedure of the Inter–American Court of Human Rights* (2003).

A third regional human rights court, the African Court on Human and Peoples' Rights <www.

african-court.org>, had its first meeting in 2006 and delivered its first judgment in December 2009. Its website has basic documents and information on its cases.

National Courts. Cases from domestic courts often address issues of international law, and their decisions can have both domestic and international significance. As mentioned earlier, *International Law Reports* contains decisions of national courts on international law issues. The Hague Justice Portal <www.haguejusticeportal.net> has a DomCLIC (Domestic Case Law on International Crimes) project with documents from courts in three dozen countries.

Cases from the U.S. and other countries under the Convention on Contracts for the International Sale of Goods (CISG) are available through UNI-LEX <www.unilex.info> and Pace University's Institute of International Commercial Law <www.cisg.law.pace.edu>. Case Law on UNCITRAL Texts (CLOUT) <www.uncitral.org/uncitral/en/case_law.html> has international trade law cases, and ECO-LEX <www.ecolex.org> is a gateway to environmental law decisions by national and international courts as well as treaties, legislation and other resources.

The American Society of International Law's i.lex: The Legal Research System for International Law in U.S. Courts <ilex.asil.org> is a searchable database of selected U.S. court cases on selected topics in international law. The site has summaries of the cases' backgrounds and significance as well as links to their full text.

c. Arbitrations

Many disputes, both between nations and between commercial partners, are settled by arbitration. Arbitrations between nations are published in the United Nations series, *Reports of International Arbitral Awards* (*RIAA*) (1948–date), which includes agreements reached by mediation or conciliation as well as awards resulting from contested arbitrations. RIAA is available online from the UN <www.un.org/law/riaa/> and from HeinOnline. Older arbitral decisions back to 1794 are reprinted in *Repertory of International Arbitral Jurisprudence* (1989–91).

Several sources cover international arbitrations between private parties, including *Mealey's International Arbitration Report* (1986–date, available in Lexis), *World Arbitration Reporter* (Hans Smit & Vratislav Pechota eds., 1986–date), and *Yearbook: Commercial Arbitration* (1975–date). Recent treatises in the area include Margaret L. Moses, *The Principles and Practice of International Commercial Arbitration* (2008) and *Redfern and Hunter on International Arbitration* (5th ed. 2009). The subscription site Kluwer Arbitration <www.kluwer arbitration.com> has access to a variety of major sources, including conventions, rules, and case law.

§ 9–6. International Organizations

National governments are the major parties in international law, but worldwide and regional intergovernmental organizations (IGOs) play a vital role by establishing norms, promoting multilateral conventions, and providing mechanisms for the peaceful resolution of conflicts. Even when not acting as lawmaking bodies, international organizations compile and publish many of the major research sources in international law.

a. United Nations and Related Agencies

The United Nations, founded in 1945 as a successor to the League of Nations, has greatly influenced the development of international law by providing an organizational forum and a center for the preparation and promotion of legislation and conventions. Its six principal organs are the General Assembly, Security Council, Economic and Social Council, Trusteeship Council, Secretariat, and International Court of Justice (ICJ).

The United Nations website <www.un.org> has a wealth of information about the organization, including news, descriptive overviews of its activities, and access to numerous documents. The best printed source for basic information is *United Nations Handbook*, published annually by the New Zealand Ministry of External Relations and Trade.

The *Yearbook of the United Nations* is a good starting point for historical research on UN activities. Although coverage is delayed three or four years, this publication summarizes major developments, reprints major documents, and provides references to other sources for the year covered. It is available free online <unyearbook.un.org>, with retrospective coverage from the first volume in 1946. The *Max Planck Yearbook of United Nations Law* (1997–date) is a major source for current scholarly commentary; older volumes are available free online <www.mpil.de/ww/en/pub/research/details/publications/institute/mpyunl.cfm>.

The *General Assembly Official Records* (GAOR) are important documents for UN research. The transcripts of the meetings of the assembly and its committees are accompanied by *Annexes* containing important documents produced during the session, and by *Supplements* containing annual reports submitted by the Secretary–General, Security Council, International Court of Justice, and various committees. The final supplement each year is a compilation of the resolutions passed by the General Assembly.

Resolutions are also reprinted in the *Yearbook of the United Nations* and are available online. The UN Documents site <www.un.org/documents/> has browsable access to General Assembly and Security Council resolutions since 1946, as well as recent meeting records and other major documents. The Official Document System of the United Nations <documents.un.org> is a search engine with the full text of all resolutions since 1946 and other documents beginning in 1993.

The UN produces a broad range of other publications, including numerous specialized yearbooks, statistical compilations, and conference proceedings. UN publications are indexed in UNBISNET <unbisnet.un.org>, the United Nations Bibliographic Information System. It covers materials since 1979, with older documents gradually being added. A commercial electronic service, *Access UN: Index to United Nations Documents and Publications* <www.readex.com>, has comprehensive retrospective coverage.

United Nations Documentation: Research Guide <www.un.org/Depts/dhl/resguide/> is a concise introduction to UN resources, including an explanation of its document symbols, discussion of the major organizational units, and more in-depth coverage of topics such as human rights and international law.

The United Nations also coordinates the work of several "specialized agencies" in particular subject fields, such as the Food and Agriculture Organization, the International Labour Organisation, and the World Health Organization, several of which have extensive law-related activities. The United Nations System website locator <www.unsystem. org> provides access to sites for more than eighty specialized organizations.

b.   World Trade Organization

The World Trade Organization <www.wto.org>, the successor to the General Agreement on Tariffs and Trade (GATT), was established in 1995 as the principal international body administering trade agreements among member states. The WTO acts as a forum for negotiations, seeks to resolve disputes, and oversees national trade policies. It is governed by a Ministerial Conference, which meets every two years, while most operations are handled by its General Council. Basic documents governing WTO operations are available on its website, and its *Annual Report* (1996–date) provides trade statistics and a commentary on the organization's work every year.

Controversies among WTO members are resolved by the Dispute Settlement Body. A three-member Panel is appointed to make findings of fact and conclusions, and its report is subject to review by the Appellate Body. Panel decisions and Appellate Body reports are available in the "Dispute Settlement" section of the organization's website as well as in several commercial series, including *International Trade Law Reports* (1996–date), *World Trade Organization Dispute Settlement Decisions: Bernan's Annotated Reporter* (1998–date), and Westlaw and Lexis. The subscription website WorldTrade-Law.net <www.worldtradelaw.net> has summaries and texts of decisions as well as other WTO documents.

Commentaries on the WTO include Mitsuo Matsushita et al., *The World Trade Organization: Law, Practice, and Policy* (2d ed. 2006) and *The World*

Trade Organization: Legal, Economic and Political Analysis (Patrick F. J. Macrory et al. eds., 2005).

c. European Union and Other Regional Organizations

For American lawyers, the European Union <europa.eu> is probably the most frequently encountered of the world's many regional organizations. The EU was established in 1993 by the Treaty on European Union (the Maastricht Treaty) as the more ambitious successor to the European Communities (European Atomic Energy Community, European Coal and Steel Community, and European Economic Community). As economic and social developments have led to increasing European integration and the Treaty on European Union has been amended by the Treaty of Lisbon (2007), the EU can be seen more as a supranational government than as a regional organization.

The major institutions of the EU are the European Commission, which proposes legislation, implements policies, and manages the Union; the European Parliament, a large elected body with legislative and advisory functions; the Council, which coordinates economic policies, concludes international agreements, and legislates in conjunction with the European Parliament; and the European Court of Justice (discussed in § 9–5 with other regional courts). The EU legislates through *regulations*, which are directly binding and don't require implementing legislation in member states, and *di-*

rectives, which must be implemented by member states to become effective.

Official sources of EU legal information include the *Official Journal of the European Union*, consisting of two series, *Legislation* (L) and *Information and Notices* (C), and the semiannual *Directory of Community Legislation in Force*, which provides subject access to treaties, regulations, directives and other legislative actions. Legislation and major documents are published in the EU's twenty official languages: Czech, Danish, Dutch, English, Estonian, Finnish, French, German, Greek, Hungarian, Italian, Latvian, Lithuanian, Maltese, Polish, Portuguese, Slovak, Slovene, Spanish and Swedish.

EUR–Lex <eur-lex.europa.eu> is a free website with access to the *Official Journal of the European Union* back to 1998, as well as the EU treaties, legislation, case law and legislative proposals. Westlaw and Lexis also have extensive EU databases. In addition to primary sources, Lexis has the four-volume treatise *Smit & Herzog on the Law of the European Union* (2d ed. 2005–date).

Several other reference sources on EU law are published. *Encyclopedia of European Union Law: Constitutional Texts* (Neville March Hunnings ed., 1996–date) has annotated versions of the treaties and other major texts. CCH's *European Union Law Reporter* (1972–date) is one of the most convenient starting points for many American lawyers because of its familiar format and broad coverage. One-volume works include Ralph H. Folsom, *Principles of European Union Law* (2d ed. 2009) and P.S.R.F. Mathijsen, *A Guide to European Union Law* (9th ed. 2007).

Other important regional organizations include the Organization of American States (OAS) <www. oas.org> and the Council of Europe <www.coe. int>, both of which draft and promote multilateral treaties among their member states. As discussed in § 9–5, they both have judicial systems designed to protect human rights in their regions.

Information on about two dozen major intergovernmental organizations can be found in *International Encyclopaedia of Laws: Intergovernmental Organizations* (1997–date). The biennial *Yearbook of International Organizations*, also available online by subscription <www.uia.be>, is a six-volume directory with profiles and contact information for thousands of international groups and associations.

§ 9–7. Sources for Further Information

International law has a wide range of print and electronic resources, and you will find that bibliographies and research guides are invaluable sources of leads and research tips. The American Society of International Law's *ASIL Electronic Resource Guide* <www.asil.org/erghome.cfm> is a useful and frequently updated guide. It has narrative descriptions of and links to resources on treaties, international organizations (with separate chapters on the European Union and the United Nations), and several topical areas such as human rights, environmental law, and intellectual property. Another major Internet source for international law information is GlobaLex <www.nyulawglobal.org/globalex/>, which publishes several dozen research guides on specific topics, each containing numerous links to resources.

Marci Hoffman & Mary Rumsey, *International and Foreign Legal Research: A Coursebook* (2008) is a thorough examination of research methods in print and online, covering public international law, international organizations, and several specialized topics including human rights, international environmental law, and international trade law. *Guide to International Legal Research*, published annually by the George Washington International Law Review, has annotated listings of published and online resources.

CONVENTION ON INTERNATIONAL TRADE IN ENDANGERED SPECIES
OF WILD FAUNA AND FLORA

The Contracting States,

RECOGNIZING that wild fauna and flora in their many beautiful and varied forms are an irreplaceable part of the natural systems of the earth which must be protected for this and the generations to come;

CONSCIOUS of the ever-growing value of wild fauna and flora from aesthetic, scientific, cultural, recreational and economic points of view;

RECOGNIZING that peoples and States are and should be the best protectors of their own wild fauna and flora;

RECOGNIZING, in addition, that international cooperation is essential for the protection of certain species of wild fauna and flora against over-exploitation through international trade;

CONVINCED of the urgency of taking appropriate measures to this end;

HAVE AGREED as follows:

ARTICLE I

Definitions

For the purpose of the present Convention, unless the context otherwise requires:

(a) "Species" means any species, subspecies, or geographically separate population thereof;

(b) "Specimen" means:

    (i) any animal or plant, whether alive or dead;

    (ii) in the case of an animal. for species included in Appendices I and II, any readily recognizable part or

Exhibit 9–1. A page from *United States Treaties and Other International Agreements*

CONSERVATION

Convention on nature protection and wildlife preservation in the Western Hemisphere, with annex.

Done at the Pan American Union, Washington, October 12, 1940.
Entered into force April 30, 1942.
56 Stat. 1354; TS 981; 3 Bevans 630; 161 UNTS 193.

Depositary: <u>Organization of American States</u>
Status:
<u>http://www.oas.org/DIL/treaties_signatories_ratifications_subject.htm</u>

Parties

Argentina [1]
Brazil
Chile
Costa Rica
Dominican Republic
Ecuador
El Salvador
Guatemala
Haiti
Mexico
Nicaragua
Panama
Paraguay
Peru
Suriname
Trinidad and Tobago
United States
Uruguay
Venezuela

NOTE

1 With reservation.

Convention on international trade in endangered species of wild fauna and flora, with appendices.

Done at Washington March 3, 1973.
Entered into force July 1, 1975.
27 UST 1087; TIAS 8249; 993 UNTS 243.

Depositary: <u>Switzerland</u>
Status: <u>http://www.cites.org/</u>

Parties

Afghanistan
Albania
Algeria
Antigua and Barbuda
Argentina [1]
Australia
Austria [2]
Azerbaijan
Bahamas, The
Bangladesh
Barbados
Belarus
Belgium
Belize
Benin
Bhutan
Bolivia
Botswana

Exhibit 9–2. An excerpt from *Treaties in Force*

218 United Nations — Treaty Series • Nations Unies — Recueil des Traités 1994

AGREEMENT[1] ON THE CONSERVATION OF SMALL CETACEANS OF THE BALTIC AND NORTH SEAS

The Parties,

Recalling the general principles of conservation and sustainable use of natural resources, as reflected in the World Conservation Strategy of the International Union for the Conservation of Nature and Natural Resources, the United Nations Environment Programme, and the World Wide Fund for Nature, and in the report of the World Commission on Environment and Development,

Recognizing that small cetaceans are and should remain an integral part of marine ecosystems,

Aware that the population of harbour porpoises of the Baltic Sea has drastically decreased,

Concerned about the status of small cetaceans in the Baltic and North Seas,

Recognizing that by-catches, habitat deterioration and disturbance may adversely affect these populations,

Convinced that their vulnerable and largely unclear status merits immediate attention in order to improve it and to gather information as a basis for sound decisions on management and conservation,

Confident that activities for that purpose are best coordinated between the States concerned in order to increase efficiency and avoid duplicate work,

Aware of the importance of maintaining maritime activities such as fishing,

Recalling that under the Convention on the Conservation of Migratory Species of Wild Animals (Bonn 1979),[2] Parties are encouraged to

---

[1] Came into force on 29 March 1994, i.e., 90 days after six Range States had expressed their consent to be bound by signature, not subject to ratification, acceptance or approval, or by deposit of an instrument of ratification, acceptance or approval with the Secretary-General of the United Nations, in accordance with article 8.5:

Participant	Date of definitive signature (s) or of deposit of the instrument of ratification or approval (AA)
Belgium	14 May 1993
Denmark	29 December 1993 AA
Germany	6 October 1993
Netherlands	29 December 1992 AA
Sweden	31 March 1992 s
United Kingdom of Great Britain and Northern Ireland	13 July 1993

[2] United Nations, *Treaty Series*, vol. 1651, No. I-28395.

Exhibit 9–3. A page from the *United Nations Treaty Series*

Flare Index to Treaties: Treaty details

Title
International convention on international trade in endangered species of wild fauna and flora

Other titles
CITES

Additional keywords
Threatened species, extinction, over-exploitation

Date concluded
03/03/1973

Place concluded
Washington

Published in
UKTS 101 (1976), Cmnd 6647; 27 UST 1087, TIAS 8249; JOF 17 Sep 1978; 1978 RTAF 63; 30 Vert A 684; 12 ILM 1085; 5 Ruster 2228; 4 Churchill 218; Kiss 259. Amendments to Annexes, 1976: 22 Ruster 399. Amendments to text, 1979: no details. Amendments to Annexes, 1979: UKTS 33 (1980), Cmnd 7857; 22 Ruster 402. Amendments to Annexes, 1981: UKTS 77 (1981), Cmnd 8395. Amendments to text, 1983: Misc 2 (1984), Cmnd 9129

Check abbreviation
Check abbreviation for Treaty source

Web version1
http://www.cites.org/eng/disc/text.shtml

IALS accepts no responsibility for the accuracy of the information included in the web sites to which the Index links. Web sites are listed in no particular order but efforts have been made to include only those that appear to be more authoritative.

Indexed in
Bowman & Harris Treaty 613

EISIL link
http://www.eisil.org/index.php?sid=505333232&id=564&t=link_details&cat=449

Authentic texts
Chinese
English
French
Russian
Spanish

Depository
Switzerland

Exhibit 9–4. An entry from the Flare Index to Treaties

9. AGREEMENT ON THE CONSERVATION OF SMALL CETACEANS OF THE BALTIC AND NORTH SEAS

New York, 17 March 1992

ENTRY INTO FORCE:	29 March 1994, in accordance with article 8(5).
REGISTRATION:	29 March 1994, No. 30865.
STATUS:	Signatories: 6. Parties: 10.
TEXT:	United Nations, *Treaty Series*, vol. 1772, p. 217; and C.N.338.1995.TREATIES-2 of 22 November 1995 (procès-verbal of rectification of the French authentic text).

Note: The Agreement was approved at Geneva on 13 September 1991, during the Third Meeting of the Conference of the Parties to the Convention on the Conservation of Migratory Species of Wild Animals pursuant to article IV (4) of the said Convention, which was done at Bonn on 23 June 1979 ("Bonn Convention"). The Agreement was open for signature at United Nations Headquarters in New York on 17 March 1992 and will remain open for signature at United Nations Headquarters until its entry into force.

Participant	Signature		Definitive signature(s), Ratification, Accession(a), Acceptance(A), Approval(AA)		Participant	Signature		Definitive signature(s), Ratification, Accession(a), Acceptance(A), Approval(AA)	
Belgium	6 Nov	1992	14 May	1993	Netherlands[1]	29 Jul	1992	29 Dec	1992 AA
Denmark	19 Aug	1992	29 Dec	1993 AA	Poland			18 Jan	1996 a
European Union	7 Oct	1992			Sweden			31 Mar	1992 s
Finland			13 Sep	1999 a	United Kingdom of Great Britain and Northern Ireland[2]	16 Apr	1992	13 Jul	1993
France			3 Oct	2005 a					
Germany	9 Apr	1992	6 Oct	1993					
Lithuania			27 Jun	2005 a					

Notes:

[1] For the Kingdom in Europe.

[2] For the United Kingdom of Great Britain and the

Bailiwick of Guernsey. For the Bailiwick of Jersey (notification received on 26 September 2002).

Exhibit 9–5. A page from *Multilateral Treaties Deposited with the Secretary–General*

432

INTERNATIONAL COURT OF JUSTICE

1998
4 December
General List
No. 96

YEAR 1998

4 December 1998

FISHERIES JURISDICTION CASE

(SPAIN *v.* CANADA)

JURISDICTION OF THE COURT

Subject of the dispute — Role of the Application with regard to the determination of the questions on which the Court must adjudicate — Definition of the dispute by the Court — Specific acts taken by Canada on the basis of certain enactments and regulations, and legal consequences of those acts.

Jurisdiction of the Court — Question to be determined by the Court itself — No burden of proof.

Declarations of acceptance of the Court's compulsory jurisdiction — Conditions and reservations as elements serving to determine the scope of acceptance of the Court's jurisdiction and not as derogations from a wider acceptance already given — Interpretation of the various elements of a declaration as forming a single whole — Successive declarations — Régime applicable to the interpretation of declarations as unilateral acts, and that established for the interpretation of treaties — Interpretation of the relevant terms of a declaration, including reservations, in a natural and reasonable manner, due regard being had to the intention of the declarant State — Ascertaining the intention — Contra proferentem rule — Effectiveness principle — Legality of the acts covered by a reservation not relevant for purposes of interpretation of that reservation — Article 33 of the Charter.

Subparagraph 2 (d) of the Canadian declaration of 10 May 1994 — Intention at the time of the subparagraph's adoption — Links between Canada's new declaration and its new coastal fisheries protection legislation — Parliamentary debates.

Interpretation of the text of the reservation:

"Disputes arising out of" — Broad and comprehensive character of the phrase — Disputes having as their "subject-matter" the measures referred to in the reservation, "concerning" such measures or having their "origin" therein.

"Conservation and management measures" — "Measure" as an act, step or proceeding — "Measure" of a "legislative" nature — Relationship between a stat-

4

Exhibit 9–6. The first page of an International Court of Justice decision

CHAPTER 10

THE LAW OF OTHER COUNTRIES

---

§ 10–1. Introduction

Globalization has made the laws of other countries increasingly significant to American social, economic and legal life. The law of a foreign country may be relevant in U.S. court proceedings involving international trade or family law, and scholars and lawmakers study other legal systems to better understand and improve our own. A serious legal problem involving a foreign legal system requires consultation with a lawyer who is trained and licensed in that jurisdiction, but any American lawyer dealing with a transnational matter must know how to develop a basic understanding of the other country's law.

Foreign law sources are also essential to the study of comparative law, in which differences among national legal systems are analyzed. The extent to which American courts should cite precedent from other countries is the subject of vigorous debate, but there is no question that decisions from common law countries have had persuasive value in the development of American tort and contract doctrine.

§ 10–2. Legal Systems of the World

The legal systems of most countries are classified as either *common law* or *civil law*. Each system has its own history, fundamental principles, procedures, and forms of publication for legal sources. As explained in Chapter 1, legal doctrine under the common law is traditionally developed over time through specific cases decided by judges rather than from broad, abstract codifications. Judicial decisions are among the most important sources of new legal rules in a common law system.

Civil law is derived from Roman law, and forms the basis for the legal systems of the countries of continental Europe, Latin America, and parts of Africa and Asia. The civil law system has several distinctive characteristics, including the predominance of comprehensive and systematic codes governing large fields of law (civil, criminal, commercial, civil procedure, and criminal procedure), little weight allocated to judicial decisions as legal authority, and great influence of legal scholars who interpret, criticize and develop the law through commentaries on the codes.

Some jurisdictions do not fit clearly into either major system. A few countries, such as Scotland and South Africa, have aspects of both civil law and common law. Others are strongly influenced by customary law or traditional religious systems, particularly Islamic or Talmudic law. The law of these countries may be a mixture of civil *or* common law and the customary or religious legal system. Some countries even combine elements of three or more legal systems.

JuriGlobe <www.juriglobe.ca> is an online guide with maps, descriptions of the major systems, and lists of countries in each category. Texts discussing the history and concepts of the world's legal systems include René David & John E.C. Brierly, *Major Legal Systems in the World Today: An Introduction to the Comparative Study of Law* (3d ed. 1985), and H. Patrick Glenn, *Legal Traditions of the World: Sustainable Diversity in Law* (3d ed. 2007).

The differences between the common law and civil law systems have become less marked in recent years, as each system adopts features of the other. American jurisdictions have increasingly adopted comprehensive subject codifications, such as the Uniform Commercial Code, while some civil law countries are giving greater weight to judicial decisions. Nonetheless, basic differences remain in how legal issues are perceived and research is conducted.

§ 10–3. Reference Sources in Foreign and Comparative Law

While thorough research on a foreign law issue will require you to read the original primary sources, you can develop a working knowledge of major legal issues through print and online reference materials. You will usually want to begin with an encyclopedia or treatise for a general introduction to a national legal system or a specific subject, and then find translations or summaries of the primary sources. Foreign law research guides describing and linking to sources can help you discover the available resources.

a. Encyclopedias and Legal System Guides

Several encyclopedic works discuss national legal systems and specific legal topics within those systems.

Legal Systems of the World: A Political, Social, and Cultural Encyclopedia (Herbert M. Kritzer ed., 2002) is a four-volume work providing an introductory overview by jurisdiction and subject. Articles on countries discuss history, major legal concepts, and the structure of the legal system, with references for further reading. Subject articles generally compare civil law and common law approaches.

Modern Legal Systems Cyclopedia (Kenneth Robert Redden & Linda L. Schlueter eds., 1984–date) has surveys of the legal systems of more than 170 jurisdictions, but many of its chapters are quite outdated. The set has not officially ceased publication, but it has not been updated in several years. *Law and Judicial Systems of Nations* (4th ed. 2002) has a concise overview of bar organization, legal education, and court systems of 193 countries, with a brief explanation of each legal system.

The United States government publishes several guides to legal issues in foreign countries. The International Trade Administration's Export.gov site <www.export.gov/mrktresearch/> has legal and commercial guides for specific countries and industries, and the State Department's International Judicial Assistance site <travel.state.gov/law/info/judicial/judicial_702.html> covers topics such as enforcement of judgments and obtaining evidence abroad.

The Central Intelligence Agency's World Factbook <https://www.cia.gov/library/publications/the-world-factbook/> has demographic and economic information about the countries of the world. Basic country information, such as economic conditions, political developments, and statistics, can also be found in annual reference sources such as *Europa Year Book: A World Survey* and *The Statesman's Yearbook*. Both of these are available in subscription online editions, as Europa World Plus <www. europaworld.com> and Statesman's Yearbook Online <www.statesmansyearbook.com>.

A number of guides to the legal systems of specific countries are published in English. These generally explain legal institutions, summarize major doctrines, and provide leads to research resources. Recently published titles include Daniel C.K. Chow, *The Legal System of the People's Republic of China in a Nutshell* (2d ed. 2009) and Howard D. Fisher, *The German Legal System and Legal Language* (4th ed. 2009). Some works cover the legal systems of a region, such as Rose–Marie Belle Antoine, *Commonwealth Caribbean Law and Legal Systems* (2d ed. 2008) or Chibli Mallat, *Introduction to Middle Eastern Law* (2007).

The most comprehensive treatment of comparative law is the *International Encyclopedia of Comparative Law* (1971–date). Of seventeen planned volumes, only five (Persons and Family, Contracts in General, Restitution/Unjust Enrichment, Torts, and Business and Private Organizations) have been published in their final bound format. Pamphlets on specific topics have been issued in other areas, including a series of "National Reports" pamphlets on individual countries.

Two recent one-volume reference works have more current coverage of comparative law issues. *Elgar Encyclopedia of Comparative Law* (Jan Smits ed., 2006) and *The Oxford Handbook of Comparative Law* (Mathia Reimann & Reinhard Zimmermann eds., 2006) both contain chapters by leading scholars analyzing the legal systems of specific countries or regions as well as studies of particular topics and subject areas.

International Encyclopaedia of Laws (IEL) consists of several sets focusing on specific subjects with separate monographic pamphlets for individual countries. The largest of these works, *International Encyclopaedia for Labour Law and Industrial Relations* (1977–date), covers more than sixty countries. Newer, less extensive sets are available in almost two dozen other subject areas, but the chances of finding a specific country covered for a particular subject are not always promising. The IEL website <www.ielaws.com> includes lists of which countries are covered in each set, under the heading "Published Monographs," and the full text is available online by subscription through Kluwer Law Online <www.kluwerlawonline.com>.

b. Research Guides and Indexes

When starting research in the law of another country, you need a sense of its major primary sources and the places where you can find answers and analysis. A research guide can point the way and make you a knowledgeable traveler in a foreign land.

The subscription site Foreign Law Guide <www. foreignlawguide.com> is one of the best starting points, covering almost every country in the world. It discusses each national legal system and its history, describes the major codifications and gazettes, notes sources for legislation and court decisions (including those available in English), and lists codes and laws covering specific subject areas. If available, links are provided to online sources. Exhibit 10–1 on page 436 shows an excerpt from the Paraguay section of Foreign Law Guide with information about basic primary sources, including references to translations and online sources.

GlobaLex <www.nyulawglobal.org/globalex/> is a free website with research guides for more than 130 countries. These guides generally summarize the legal system and describe available documentation, with links to numerous web resources.

Other guides to research in foreign legal systems include Marci Hoffman & Mary Rumsey, *International and Foreign Legal Research: A Coursebook* (2008), and Claire M. Germain, *Germain's Transnational Law Research: A Guide for Attorneys* (1991–date). English legal research is discussed in Guy Holborn, *Butterworths Legal Research Guide* (2d ed. 2001), and John Knowles, *Effective Legal Research* (2d ed. 2009); and similar treatment for Canada is offered by works such as Douglass T. MacEllven et al., *Legal Research Handbook* (5th ed. 2003).

Articles on foreign legal issues can be found in the legal periodical databases and indexes discussed in Chapter 2. Deeper coverage is available from specialized resources. *Index to Foreign Legal Periodicals* (1960–date), available through various database systems including Westlaw commercial subscriptions, covers more than 500 journals from seventy-five countries, as well as commemorative *festschriften* and other collections of essays. It indexes journals published outside the United States, the United Kingdom, and the Commonwealth, and articles in selected American and Commonwealth journals on international law, comparative law, or the domestic law of other countries. Westlaw offers *Index to Canadian Legal Literature* and *Legal Journals Index*, which covers more than four hundred British and European publications.

c. Summaries and Translations of Laws

If you are relying on English-language sources in your research, you can find many multinational summaries and digests on specific subjects in addition to translations of some actual laws. While summaries and translations cannot substitute for the original sources, they can provide some familiarity with the basic concepts and issues of a foreign law problem.

The basic laws of government structure and individual liberties are found in national constitutions. Two works with introductory overviews are *Encyclopedia of World Constitutions* (Gerhard Robbers ed., 2007) and Robert L. Maddex, *Constitutions of the World* (3d ed. 2008). Each summarizes the constitutional histories, governmental structures, and approaches to fundamental rights of more than 100 countries.

The most comprehensive printed collection of current constitutions in English translation is the looseleaf set *Constitutions of the Countries of the World* (1971–date), online by subscription <www.oceanalaw.com>. For some foreign-language countries, the original text of the constitution is included as well. The University of Bern's International Constitutional Law <www.oefre.unibe.ch/law/icl/> has about ninety constitutions in English, with introductory pages providing constitutional background and history. The University of Richmond's Constitution Finder <confinder.richmond.edu> has links to constitutions from more than 200 nations and territories, some in more than one language.

Extensive collections of historic constitutions have been assembled by Horst Dippel of the University of Kassel. *Constitutions of the World, 1850 to the Present* (2002–date) is a microfiche set, and *Constitutions of the World from the Late 18th Century to the Middle of the 19th Century* (2005–date) is a print compilation with a companion website, The Rise of Modern Constitutionalism, 1776–1849 <www.modernconstitutions.de>.

Basic laws and procedures for about eighty countries are summarized in the Martindale–Hubbell International Law Digests, available either in Lexis or at Martindale.com <www.martindale.com> as part of the "Legal Library" section. Subjects covered include business regulation, foreign trade, family law, property, and taxation. Most national digests are prepared by lawyers in that country and include references to codes, laws, and other sources.

Laws affecting international business are the most likely sources to be available in English. Several collections covering specific topics are published, including *Digest of Commercial Laws of the World* (rev. ed. 1998–date), *Investment Laws of the World* (1973–date), and *International Securities Regulation* (1986–date).

Online collections of national laws in specific subject areas are available from several international organizations. These include the International Labour Organization's NATLEX <natlex.ilo.org>, UNESCO's Collection of National Copyright Laws <www.unesco.org/culture/copyrightlaws/>, and the World Intellectual Property Organization's Collection of Laws for Electronic Access (CLEA) <clea.wipo.int>.

Commercial laws of some countries are available through Westlaw, Lexis, and other databases, but online access to other civil law sources in English is far less common. The official French site Legifrance <www.legifrance.gouv.fr> has searchable English translations of major French codes, and the German Law Archive <www.iuscomp.org/gla/> has numerous sources in English including statutes, court decisions, and secondary sources.

Relatively few judicial decisions in foreign languages are translated into English, but several resources have some case law. *International Law Reports* (1919–date) contains cases from national courts on international law and human rights topics, and the University of Texas's Foreign Law Translations site <www.utexas.edu/law/academics/centers/transnational/work_new/> has decisions from Austria, France, Germany, and Israel. Specialized sources include *Bulletin on Constitutional Case–Law* (1993–date), in print and online <www.codices.coe.int>; *East European Case Reporter on Constitutional Law* (1994–date); and *International Labour Law Reports* (1978–date).

While it cannot substitute for professional translation, an automated translation system such as Google Translate <translate.google.com> can give you at least a sense of the scope and subject of a document. This may help you determine whether a more accurate translation would be needed.

d. Dictionaries

Language differences can be a major hurdle to understanding legal sources from a foreign legal system. Even legal systems sharing the same language can have different meanings for the same terms. Legal dictionaries can give you at least a superficial sense of the differences in meaning and usage.

The major British legal dictionary is *Jowitt's Dictionary of English Law* (Daniel Greenberg ed., 2d ed. 2010); two shorter paperback works are *The Law Student's Dictionary* (2008) and *Osborn's Concise Law Dictionary* (11th ed. 2009). Daphne A.

Dukelow, *The Dictionary of Canadian Law* (3d ed. 2004) is the most substantial treatment of Canadian legal definitions.

Numerous bilingual dictionaries translate foreign terms into English, although many of these simply translate words without explaining the underlying legal concepts. Two recommended works by Henry Saint Dahl, with definitions derived from statutes and other primary sources, are *Dahl's Law Dictionary: Spanish–English/English–Spanish* (4th ed. 2006) and *Dahl's Law Dictionary: French to English/English to French* (3d ed. 2007); both are available (in older editions) in Lexis. Other respected Spanish–English dictionaries include Cuauhtémoc Gallegos, *Merl Bilingual Law Dictionary* (2005), and Jorge A. Vargas, *Mexican Legal Dictionary* (2d ed. 2009).

Citation forms for foreign legal materials are often confusing for American lawyers. The *Bluebook* includes information for more than thirty countries, covering statutory, judicial, and other frequently cited sources. Broader coverage is provided by *Guide to Foreign and International Legal Citations* (2006), available free online <www.law.nyu.edu/journals/jilp/>. Guides to citation format in other countries include *OSCOLA: The Oxford Standard for Citation Of Legal Authorities* (2006) <denning.law.ox.ac.uk/published/oscola.shtml> and the McGill Law Journal's *Canadian Guide to Uniform Legal Citation* (6th ed. 2006). *World Dictionary of Legal Abbreviations* (Igor I. Kavass & Mary

Miles Prince eds., 1991–date) has lists of foreign abbreviations, with separate sections for some two dozen countries, languages, regions, and subjects.

§ 10–4. Original Sources

Your next step after consulting available reference materials is to investigate primary legal sources from the country. Many of these sources are now available online, although understanding them still requires knowledge of a foreign legal system and its language. Many countries have both free and subscription-based legal databases similar to those available in the United States. This section focuses on resources available to most American researchers.

a. Links to Country Websites

Several resources have directories of law-related websites in countries around the world. These include sites discussed earlier, including Foreign Law Guide <www.foreignlawguide.com> and GlobaLex <www.nyuglobalaw.org/globalex/>, both of which combine descriptive summaries with links to sources.

Other resources also have collections of links to websites. Major sites with country pages and links to constitutions, legislation, government sites, and other resources include the Harvard Law Library's Foreign & International Law Resources: An Annotated Guide to Web Sites Around the World <www.law.harvard.edu/library/research/guides/int_foreign/

web-resources/>, the Library of Congress's Guide to Law Online <www.loc.gov/law/help/guide.php> and the World Legal Information Institute (WorldLII) <www.worldlii.org>.

The World Bank's Doing Business site <www.doingbusiness.org/lawlibrary/> has links to national laws on business-related topics, including civil codes and constitutions, for over 180 countries. You select the countries and the topics you'd like to see, click on "Create Report," and retrieve a list of specific acts and regulations linked to government website sources. Many of the documents are translated into English.

b. Common Law Jurisdictions

The resources and research methods for other common law countries are similar to those of the United States, making them the most accessible of foreign legal systems. This section looks briefly at two of our most closely related common law jurisdictions: England (which is part of the United Kingdom but has a separate body of law from Northern Ireland and Scotland) and Canada. Similar resources are available for other common law countries such as Australia and New Zealand.

The United Kingdom has an "unwritten" constitution, meaning that its basic constitutional principles are not found in one specific document. One major difference between British and U.S. law is that the U.K. Parliament has unlimited power, and its acts cannot be held unconstitutional. Canada's

Constitution, dating to 1867, is the source of powers for both the federal Parliament and the provincial legislatures. Areas such as criminal law and family law are matters of Canadian federal law rather than provincial law, and in general any powers not specifically delegated to the provinces are reserved to the federal government.

Judicial decisions from other common law countries can have persuasive value in U.S. courts and are thus the most important primary sources for American lawyers. Even more significant are the historical cases predating U.S. independence that were expressly accepted as part of American common law by state reception statutes.

English law reporting dates back to the fragmentary reports in the *Plea Rolls*, beginning with the reign of Richard I in 1189. The *Year Books*, covering 1285 to 1537, contain notes of debates between judges and counsel on the points in issue in cases. Following the *Year Books* for several centuries came the *nominate* or *nominative* reports, that is, court reports named for the person who recorded or edited them.

More than 270 series of nominative reports were cumulated into *The English Reports* (1900–32), covering cases from 1220 to 1865 in 176 volumes. *The English Reports* is available online from several subscription sources, including Westlaw and HeinOnline, and free from the Commonwealth Legal Information Institute <www.commonlii.org/int/cases/EngR/>. Another compilation of older cases, the *Revised Reports*, includes some decisions not found in *The English Reports*. The leading source for accounts of major trials for treason and related offenses is *A Complete Collection of State Trials* (William Cobbett & Thomas Bayly Howell eds., 1809–28).

Exhibit 10–2 on page 437 shows a decision of the Court of King's Bench in *M'Kone v. Wood*, a dog bite case from 1831, as published in *The English Reports*. Note the bracketed star paging references to pages 1 and 2 of the original nominative reporter, Carrington & Payne's *Nisi Prius Reports* (cited as C. & P.). The references to Trinity Term and Hilary Term are to divisions of the English legal year, a calendar that dates back to the 1200s and is still used today <www.judiciary.gov.uk/keyfacts/legal_year/term_dates.htm>.

England now has one system of trial and appellate courts, with the new Supreme Court of the United Kingdom replacing the House of Lords as the court of last resort in 2009. Civil actions are tried in one of the divisions of the High Court (Queen's Bench, Chancery, or Family) or in lower courts of limited jurisdiction, with review by the Court of Appeal and from there by the Supreme Court. Criminal trials are conducted in a Crown Court, with the same two-tier appeal system.

The Canadian court system is similar to that of the United States, with federal and provincial courts, although the Supreme Court of Canada is the final arbiter on both federal and provincial issues. Most matters are first heard in provincial court, but the Federal Court of Canada has trial jurisdiction over matters such as intellectual property, maritime law, and claims against the government.

As in the United States, new British and Canadian decisions are published in official or authorized series of reports and in unofficial commercial reporters and online services. Westlaw and Lexis both have broad coverage of judicial decisions from the United Kingdom and Canada. Free Internet access to decisions is provided by the British and Irish Legal Information Institute (BAILII) <www.bailii.org> and the Canadian Legal Information Institute (CanLII) <www.canlii.org>.

The standard source for modern English decisions is the semi-official *Law Reports* (1865–date), which now consists of four series: *Appeal Cases* (Supreme Court, European Court of Justice, and Judicial Committee of the Privy Council), *Queen's Bench Division*; *Chancery Division*; and *Family Division*. Before appearing in these four separate series, new cases are published in *Weekly Law Reports*, which also has some decisions that are unreported in the four *Law Reports* series. *All England Law Reports* (1936–date) is a commercially published reporter and includes some decisions not published in the *Weekly Law Reports*. Numerous specialized subject reporters such as *Criminal Appeal Reports* and *Family Law Reports* are also available. Westlaw and

Lexis both have access to the *Law Reports* from 1865 along with several other reporters.

Canada has authorized reports for its federal courts (*Canada Supreme Court Reports* and *Federal Court Reports*), as well as reports for provincial and territorial courts, unofficial series such as *Dominion Law Reports*, and a variety of specialized topical reporters. Westlaw and Lexis have Canada Supreme Court decisions back to 1876, with more recent coverage of other courts.

Much case research in other common law countries is done by keyword through free and commercial database systems, but online research is supplemented by many of the same types of resources found in the United States, including treatises, encyclopedias, and digests. *Halsbury's Laws of England* (4th & 5th eds. 1973–date) is the standard English encyclopedia, encompassing statutes and administrative sources as well as case law. Two regional encyclopedias include coverage of Canadian federal law: *Canadian Encyclopedic Digest (Ontario)* (3d/4th eds. 1973–date), and *Canadian Encyclopedic Digest (Western)* (3d/4th eds. 1979–date). Westlaw provides access to both works. A new series, *Halsbury's Laws of Canada* (2006–date), is about halfway to its projected completion in seventy volumes.

Both England and Canada have major national digests, somewhat similar to the West digest system: *The Digest: Annotated British, Commonwealth and European Cases* (3d ed. 1971–date), and the *Canadian Abridgment* (3d ed. 2003–date, available on Westlaw). Each country also has tools for finding later cases that have considered an earlier decision, such as *Current Law Case Citator* in England and *Canadian Case Citations*. KeyCite is available for Canadian cases on Westlaw.

Statutes in other common law jurisdictions are published both in session laws and in compilations of statutes in force, and are available from government and commercial websites. One major difference from the U.S. model is that statutes are generally compiled alphabetically by name or chronologically, rather than by subject as in the *United States Code.* Statutes are not assigned code titles and sections, but instead are usually identified by their original name and date of enactment.

The most frequently used printed source for English statutes is the unofficial compilation *Halsbury's Statutes of England and Wales* (4th ed. 1985– date). This is somewhat similar to U.S. annotated codes in that sections are followed by footnote annotations to judicial decisions. Current English statutes are also available free from the UK Statute Law Database <www.statutelaw.gov.uk>, as well as through Westlaw and Lexis. Session laws, known as *Public General Acts*, are available online <www. opsi.gov.uk/acts.htm> with comprehensive coverage beginning with 1988.

For Canadian statutes there is no annotated, regularly updated publication similar to *Halsbury's Statutes.* Consolidated Statutes of Canada are available from the Department of Justice Canada <laws.justice.gc.ca>, and CanLII <www.canlii. org> has links to provincial sources. Much of this material is also available from Westlaw, Lexis, and other commercial databases.

The standard historical collection of English statutes is the *Statutes of the Realm* (1810–28), covering 1235 to 1714. This set is part of HeinOnline's English Reports Library, and some volumes are available free through British History Online <www.british-history.ac.uk>. Several other chronological collections were published during the 19th century under the title *Statutes at Large*, extending coverage to the beginning of the modern *Public General Acts* in 1866. Justis <www.justis.com> has subscription online coverage of statutes from 1235 to date.

The first step in identifying and finding an older English statute is deciphering its citation. Acts before 1963 are generally cited not by calendar year but by regnal year (the year of a monarch's rule). The act that changed the citation system, for example, was passed during the session of Parliament that spanned the tenth and eleventh years of the reign of Elizabeth II, and is cited as Acts of Parliament Numbering and Citation Act, 10 & 11 Eliz. 2, ch. 34 (1962). Tables to convert regnal years to calendar years are printed in reference works such as *Black's Law Dictionary*, and a regnal year calculator is available online <www.albion.edu/english/ calendar/Regnal_Years.html>.

c. Civil Law Jurisdictions

An American lawyer or law student researching the law of a civil law country must be cognizant of the major differences between the civil and common law systems, and the effect of these differences on how legal problems are evaluated and researched. In theory, a code in the civil law tradition is designed to cover all legal situations that might occur. Instead of searching for precedents in factually similar judicial decisions, as a civil law researcher you would look first to the abstract provisions of the code for a logical and appropriate legal principle.

Secondary sources are invaluable in civil law research. Scholarly commentary is given great weight by civil lawyers, and leading treatises are essential resources. Some legal encyclopedias, particularly the French *répertoires* published by Dalloz, are also highly esteemed, with articles by leading legal scholars. Civil law countries also have a multitude of legal periodicals commenting on legal developments and often printing legislative texts and judicial decisions. In France, for example, the leading legal periodicals, *Recueil Dalloz* (1808–date) and *La Semaine Juridique* (1927–date), provide both primary sources and scholarly articles.

After introductory study in an encyclopedia, treatise, or journal article, your next step is to consult the relevant code or other statutes applicable to the problem. Most civil law countries have several separately published codes. These include the traditional major codes (civil, criminal, commercial, civil procedure and criminal procedure), and more recent codifications compiling statutes on specific subjects such as taxation, labor law, and family law.

Some civil law countries, such as France, rely primarily on annotated editions of the codes. In others, particularly Germany, exhaustive article-by-article commentaries on the major codes are among the most important legal sources. The most scholarly and reputable of these commentaries, such as the one-volume *Palandt* and the multivolume *Staudinger*, have considerable persuasive authority, often greater than judicial decisions.

Official websites in many countries provide access to their codes, although these versions rarely include annotations or commentary. Westlaw and Lexis have primary sources from very few jurisdictions in their original language, but foreign subscription databases (if available) offer more extensive coverage.

After studying the code and commentary, you should then find administrative orders and judicial decisions implementing or interpreting the legislative norms. Legislation, regulations, and decrees are most often found in official gazettes, comparable to but usually broader in scope than the *Federal Register*. Foreign Law Guide lists these sources and provides links where available. The free website Government Gazettes Online <www-personal. umich.edu/~graceyor/doctemp/gazettes/> has links to gazettes from about sixty countries, with information about their contents and searchability.

Court decisions are published in most civil law countries, even though they are generally of secondary importance. Their status is gradually changing, if only because civil lawyers now study precedent from supranational bodies such as the European Court of Justice and the World Trade Organization. Most civil law jurisdictions, however, continue to have fewer court reports and less developed tools for finding cases by subject. In many countries, you may need to search legal periodicals for relevant court decisions. Sources such as the Foreign Law Guide and Globalex articles list appropriate sources.

MAJOR PUBLICATIONS

MAJOR CODIFICATIONS

1. Civil Code

Código civil de la República del Paraguay. Ley 1,183 of 18 Dec 1985 in *Registro oficial* 23 Dec 1985. In force 1 Jan 1987 (replacing Paraguayan version of the Argentine Civil code in force 1871–1986). Sections 669–1,201 (contracts and obligations). Translated at http://checkpoint.ring.com/ ‡

2. Code of Civil Procedure

Código de procedimientos de la República de Paraguay (Código procesal civil). Ley 1,337 of 20 Oct 1998 in *Registro oficial* 4 Nov 1998.

3. Commercial Code

Código de comercio of 1903. Modified by Ley 154 of 13 Dec 1969 and Ley 1,034 of 15 Dec 1983. This code was effectively abrogated by the new Civil code which includes a codification of commercial law. The commercial aspects of the Civil Code are supplemented by separate pieces of legislation.

4. Criminal Code

Código penal Ley 1,160 of 16 Oct 1997 in *Registro oficial* 26 Nov 1997. Official text at http://www.itacom.com.py/ministerio_publico/codigo_penal. In force 26 Nov 1998. Replacing the 1914 codification.

5. Code of Criminal Procedure

Código de procedimientos penales. Ley 1,286 of 8 Jul 1998 in *Registro oficial* 14 Jul 1998. Full text available in Spanish, with English summary, at http://www.pln.gov/ ‡ Replacing 1980 code over a transitional period that concluded 28 Feb 2003. Compare with Ley 1,444 of 25 Jan 1999. Full text available in Spanish, with English summary, at http://www.pln.gov/ ‡

OFFICIAL GAZETTE

Registro oficial de la República del Paraguay. [Vol 1]– . 1869/70– . Asunción, 1887– . (cited herein as *Registro oficial*). This is actually a separate section of the Gaceta oficial containing laws, decrees, resolutions and regulatory legislation. The other section is titled "Avisos y anuncios" and is of little legal interest.

Exhibit 10–1. An excerpt from Foreign Law Guide

REPORTS of CASES Argued and Ruled at NISI
PRIUS, in the Courts of KING'S BENCH,
COMMON PLEAS, and EXCHEQUER, together
with Cases tried on the CIRCUITS and at the
OLD BAILEY. From the Sittings after Trinity
Term, 1831, to the Sittings after Hilary Term, 1833.
By F. A. CARRINGTON and J. PAYNE, Esqrs.,
of Lincoln's Inn, Barristers-at-Law. Volume V.
London, 1833.

[1] PROMOTIONS.
1831.

In Trinity Vacation, Philip Williams, Henry William Tancred, Francis Ludlow
Holt, and Charles Butler, Esqrs., were appointed his Majesty's Counsel learned in the
law.

COURT OF KING'S BENCH.
Sittings at Westminster, after Trinity Term, 1831, before
Lord Tenterden, C. J.
June 14th, 1831.
M'KONE *v.* WOOD.

(In an action against a party, for keeping a dog accustomed to bite mankind, it is
not essential that the dog should be his; if he harbours the dog, or allows it to
be at, and resort to, his premises, that is sufficient.)

[Referred to, *North* v. *Wood*, [1914] 1 K. B. 629.]

Case for keeping a dog accustomed to bite mankind. Plea—General issue.

On the part of the plaintiff, it was proved, that the dog had bitten the plaintiff,
and that it had bitten two other persons before; but one of the witnesses, who proved
that he had made a complaint to the defendant respecting the dog, stated, that the
defendant had told him that the dog belonged to a person who had been his servant,
but who had left him.

It was also proved, on the part of the plaintiff, that the dog was seen about the
defendant's premises, both before and after the time when the plaintiff was bitten.

[2] Campbell, for the defendant, submitted that there was not sufficient evidence
to shew that this was the defendant's dog; but, on the contrary, it was shewn that
it was not. He therefore contended that the defendant was not liable in this action.

Lord Tenterden, C. J.—It is not material whether the defendant was the owner of
the dog or not; if he kept it, that is sufficient; and the harbouring a dog about one's
premises, or allowing him to be or resort there, is a sufficient keeping of the dog to
support this form of action. It was the defendant's duty, either to have destroyed
the dog, or to have sent him away, as soon as he found that he was mischievous.

Verdict for the plaintiff.—Damages £5.

Follett and S. Martin, for the plaintiff.

Campbell, for the defendant.

[Attornies—J. Humphreys, and E. Young.]
850

Exhibit 10–2.   A page from the *English Reports*

APPENDIX A

STATE LEGAL RESEARCH GUIDES

These guides are suggested for further information on the materials and research methods in individual states. The list, which is limited to works published since 1990, includes several journal articles discussing state practice materials and research methods, as well as chapters in a two-volume loose-leaf set edited by Frank G. Houdek, *State Practice Materials: Annotated Bibliographies* (2002–date). The American Association of Law Libraries has issued a series of brief guides to state materials or government documents, but these titles are generally listed here only if no other recent guide is available for that state. Websites for law libraries within a state are also good sources for guides listing and describing the state's major printed and online legal resources.

Alabama   Gary Orlando Lewis, *Legal Research in Alabama: How to Find and Understand the Law in Alabama* (2001).

Scott DeLeve, "Alabama Practice Materials: A Selec-

	tive Annotated Bibliography" (2005), in *State Practice Materials: Annotated Bibliographies*.
Alaska	Catherine Lemann & Susan Falk, "Alaska Practice Materials: A Selective Annotated Bibliography" (2008), in *State Practice Materials: Annotated Bibliographies*.
Arizona	Tamara S. Herrera, *Arizona Legal Research* (2008).
	Jacquelyne Gayle Kasper, "Arizona Practice Materials: A Selective Annotated Bibliography" (2009), in *State Practice Materials: Annotated Bibliographies*.
	Kathy Shimpock–Vieweg & Marianne Sidorski Alcorn, *Arizona Legal Research Guide* (1992).
Arkansas	Coleen M. Barger, *Arkansas Legal Research* (2007).
	Kathryn C. Fitzhugh, "Arkansas Practice Materials II: A Selective Annotated Bibliography," 21 *U. Ark. Little Rock L.J.* 363 (1999).

California

Larry D. Dershem, *California Legal Research Handbook* (2d ed. 2008).

John K. Hanft, *Legal Research in California* (6th ed. 2007).

Henke's California Law Guide (Daniel W. Martin ed., 8th ed. 2006).

Judy C. Janes, "California Practice Materials: A Selective Annotated Bibliography" (2005), in *State Practice Materials: Annotated Bibliographies*.

Hether C. Macfarlane & Suzanne E. Rowe, *California Legal Research* (2008).

Colorado

Mitch Fontenot, "Colorado Practice Materials: A Selective Annotated Bibliography" (2004), in *State Practice Materials: Annotated Bibliographies*.

Robert M. Linz, *Colorado Legal Research* (forthcoming 2010).

Connecticut

Lawrence G. Cheeseman & Arlene C. Bielefeld, *The Connecticut Legal Research Handbook* (1992).

Jessica G. Hynes, *Connecticut Legal Research* (2009).

Jonathan Saxon, "Connecticut Practice Materials: A Selective Annotated Bibliography," 91 *Law Libr. J.* 139 (1999).

Delaware

Patrick J. Charles & David K. King, "Delaware Practice Materials: A Selective Annotated Bibliography," 89 *Law Libr. J.* 349 (1997).

Peter J. Engler, *Selective Annotated Bibliography of Delaware State Documents and Other Resources Used in Delaware Legal Research* (2008).

District of Columbia

Leah F. Chanin, "Legal Research in the District of Columbia," in *Legal Research in the District of Columbia, Maryland and Virginia* (2d ed. 2000).

Michelle Wu, "District of Columbia Practice Materials: A Selective Annotated Bibliography" (2002), in *State Practice Materials: Annotated Bibliographies*.

Florida

Barbara J. Busharis & Suzanne E. Rowe, *Florida Legal Research: Sources, Pro-*

cess, and Analysis (3d ed. 2007).

Nancy L. Strohmeyer, "Florida Practice Materials: A Selective Annotated Bibliography" (2007), in *State Practice Materials: Annotated Bibliographies*.

Betsy L. Stupski, *Guide to Florida Legal Research* (7th ed. 2008).

Georgia

Leah F. Chanin & Suzanne L. Cassidy, *Guide to Georgia Legal Research and Legal History* (1990).

Nancy P. Johnson, Elizabeth G. Adelman & Nancy J. Adams, *Georgia Legal Research* (2007).

Nancy P. Johnson, Kreig L. Kitts & Ronald E. Wheeler, Jr., "Georgia Practice Materials: A Selective Annotated Bibliography" (2007), in *State Practice Materials: Annotated Bibliographies*.

Hawaii

Leina'ala R. Seeger, "Hawaii Practice Materials: A Selective Annotated Bibliography" (2004), in *State Practice Materials: Annotated Bibliographies*.

Idaho

Tenielle Fordyce–Ruff & Suzanne E. Rowe, *Idaho Legal Research* (2008).

Jean Mattimoe, "Idaho Practice Materials: A Selective Annotated Bibliography" (2009), in *State Practice Materials: Annotated Bibliographies*.

Illinois

Phill W. Johnson, "Illinois Practice Materials: A Selective Annotated Bibliography" (2006), in *State Practice Materials: Annotated Bibliographies*.

Laurel Wendt, *Illinois Legal Research Guide* (2d ed. 2006).

Mark E. Wojcik, *Illinois Legal Research* (2d ed. 2009).

Indiana

Richard E. Humphrey, "Indiana Practice Materials: A Selective Annotated Bibliography" (2004), in *State Practice Materials: Annotated Bibliographies*.

Iowa

John D. Edwards, *Iowa Legal Research Guide* (2003).

Kansas

Joseph A. Custer & Christopher L. Steadham, *Kansas Legal Research* (2008).

Joseph A. Custer et al., *Kansas Legal Research and Reference Guide* (3d ed. 2003).

Joseph A. Custer, "Kansas Practice Materials: A Selective Annotated Bibliography" (2002), in *State Practice Materials: Annotated Bibliographies*.

Kentucky

Helane E. Davis, "Kentucky Practice Materials: A Selective Annotated Bibliography" (2009), in *State Practice Materials: Annotated Bibliographies*.

Kurt X. Metzmeier et al., *Kentucky Legal Research Manual* (3d ed. 2005).

Louisiana

Mary Garvey Algero, *Louisiana Legal Research* (2009).

Win–Shin S. Chiang, *Louisiana Legal Research* (2d ed. 1990).

Catherine Lemann, "Louisiana Practice Materials: A Selective Annotated Bibliography" (2006), in *State Practice Materials: Annotated Bibliographies*.

Maine

Christine I. Hepler & Maureen P. Quinlan, *MaineS-*

John Tessner et al., *Minnesota Legal Research Guide* (2d ed. 2002).

Suzanne Thorpe, *Minnesota Legal Research* (forthcoming 2010).

Mississippi   Anne M. Klingen, "Mississippi Practice Materials: A Selective Annotated Bibliography" (2002), in *State Practice Materials: Annotated Bibliographies*.

Missouri   Wanda M. Temm & Julie M. Cheslik, *Missouri Legal Research* (2007).

Montana   Robert K. Whelan et al., *A Guide to Montana Legal Research* (8th ed. 2003) <courts.mt.gov/content/library/guides/guide.pdf>.

Nebraska   Kay L. Andrus et al., *Research Guide to Nebraska Law* (2008 ed.).

Beth Smith, "Nebraska Practice Materials: A Selective Annotated Bibliography" (2004), in *State Practice Materials: Annotated Bibliographies*.

Nevada

G. LeGrande Fletcher, "Nevada Practice Materials: A Selective Annotated Bibliography," 91 *Law Libr. J.* 313 (1999).

Jennifer Larraguibel Gross et al., *Nevada Legal Research Guide* (2005).

New Jersey

Paul Axel–Lute, *New Jersey Legal Research Handbook* (5th ed. 2008), with online supplement <law-library.rutgers. edu/ilg/njlrhb5.php>.

David A. Hollander, "New Jersey Practice Materials: A Selective Annotated Bibliography" (2008), in *State Practice Materials: Annotated Bibliographies*.

New Mexico

Theresa Strike, *Guide to New Mexico State Publications* (3d ed. 2009).

Mary A. Woodward, "New Mexico Practice Materials: A Selective Annotated Bibliography," 84 *Law Libr. J.* 93 (1992).

New York

Elizabeth G. Adelman & Suzanne E. Rowe, *New York Legal Research* (2008).

William H. Manz, *Gibson's New York Legal Research Guide* (3d ed. 2004).

William Manz, "New York Practice Materials: A Selective Annotated Bibliography" (2009), in *State Practice Materials: Annotated Bibliographies*.

North Carolina

Miriam J. Baer & James C. Ray, *Legal Research in North Carolina* (2006).

Scott Childs, *North Carolina Legal Research* (2010).

Scott Childs & Nick Sexton, *North Carolina Legal Research Guide* (2d ed. 2009).

Julie L. Kimbrough, "North Carolina Practice Materials: A Selective Annotated Bibliography" (2009), in *State Practice Materials: Annotated Bibliographies*.

North Dakota

Rhonda R. Schwartz, "North Dakota Practice Materials: A Selective Annotated Bibliography" (2008), in *State Practice Materials: Annotated Bibliographies*.

Ohio

Katherine L. Hall & Sara A. Sampson, *Ohio Legal Research* (2009).

Kenneth S. Kozlowski & Susan N. Elliott, "Ohio Practice Materials: A Selective Annotated Bibliography" (2005), in *State Practice Materials: Annotated Bibliographies*.

Melanie K. Putnam & Susan Schaefgen, *Ohio Legal Research Guide* (1997).

Oklahoma

Ann Walsh Long, "Oklahoma Practice Materials: A Selective Annotated Bibliography" (2007), in *State Practice Materials: Annotated Bibliographies*.

Oregon

Mary Clayton & Stephanie Midkiff, "Oregon Practice Materials: A Selective Annotated Bibliography" (2005), in *State Practice Materials: Annotated Bibliographies*.

Suzanne E. Rowe, *Oregon Legal Research* (2d ed. 2007).

Pennsylvania

Barbara J. Busharis & Bonny L. Tavares, *Pennsylvania Legal Research* (2007).

Joel Fishman & Marc Silverman, "Pennsylvania Practice Materials: A Selective Annotated Bibliography"

(2003), in *State Practice
Materials: Annotated Bibliographies.*

Frank Y. Liu et al., *Pennsylvania Legal Research
Handbook* (2008 ed.).

Puerto Rico

Luis Muñiz Argüelles & Mig-
dalia Fraticelli Torres, *La
Investigación Jurídica en el
Derecho Puertorriqueño:
Fuentes Puertorriqueñas,
Norteamericanas y Españo-
las* (4th ed. 2006).

Rhode Island

Daniel J. Donovan, *Legal Research in Rhode Island (including Federal and State
Research Materials)* (4th
ed. 2004).

South Carolina

Paula Gail Benson, *A Guide
to South Carolina Legal
Research and Citation* (2d
ed. 2009).

Pamela Rogers Melton &
Christine Sellers, "South
Carolina Practice Materi-
als: A Selective Annotated
Bibliography" (2008), in
*State Practice Materials:
Annotated Bibliographies.*

South Dakota

Matthew E. Braun & Kasia
Solon, "South Dakota
Practice Materials: A Selec-

tive Annotated Bibliography" (2008), in *State Practice Materials: Annotated Bibliographies*.

Delores A. Jorgensen, *South Dakota Legal Research Guide* (2d ed. 1999).

Tennessee

Toof Brown, III, "Tennessee Practice Materials: A Selective Annotated Bibliography" (2004), in *State Practice Materials: Annotated Bibliographies*.

Sibyl Marshall & Carol McCrehan Parker, *Tennessee Legal Research* (2007).

Texas

Matthew C. Cordon & Brandon D. Quarles, *Specialized Topics in Texas Legal Research* (2005).

Brandon D. Quarles & Matthew C. Cordon, *Researching Texas Law* (2d ed. 2008).

Brandon D. Quarles & Matthew C. Cordon, "Texas Practice Materials: A Selective Annotated Bibliography" (2006), in *State Practice Materials: Annotated Bibliographies*.

Spencer L. Simons, *Texas Legal Research* (2009).

Utah   Jessica Van Buren et al.,
                        Utah Legal Research Guide
                        (forthcoming 2010).

                        Kory D. Staheli, "Utah Prac-
                        tice Materials: A Selective
                        Annotated Bibliography,"
                        87 *Law Libr. J.* 28 (1995).

                        Mari Cheney, *Utah Legal Re-*
                        sources Bibliography
                        (2009).

Vermont   Virginia Wise, *A Bibliograph-*
                        ical Guide to the Vermont
                        Legal System (2d ed. 1991).

Virginia   *A Guide to Legal Research in*
                        Virginia (John D. Eure &
                        Gail F. Zwirner eds., 6th
                        ed. 2008).

                        Leslie A. Lee, "Virginia Prac-
                        tice Materials: A Selective
                        Annotated Bibliography"
                        (2002), in *State Practice*
                        Materials: Annotated Bibli-
                        ographies.

                        Sarah K. Wiant, "Legal Re-
                        search in Virginia," in *Le-*
                        gal Research in the District
                        of Columbia, Maryland and
                        Virginia (2d ed. 2000).

Washington   Penny A. Hazelton et al.,
                        Washington Legal Re-

searcher's Deskbook 3d
(2002).

Julie Heintz–Cho et al.,
Washington Legal Research
(2d ed. 2009).

West Virginia   Ann Walsh Long, "West Virginia Practice Materials: A
Selective Annotated Bibliography" (2004), in *State
Practice Materials: Anno-
tated Bibliographies.*

Wisconsin   *Legal Research in Wisconsin*
(Theodore A. Potter ed., 2d
ed. 2008).

Ellen J. Platt & Mary J.
Koshollek, "Wisconsin
Practice Materials: A Selective, Annotated Bibliography," 90 *Law Libr. J.* 219
(1998).

Wyoming   Debora A. Person, *Wyoming
State Documents: A Bibli-
ography of State Publica-
tions and Related Materials*
(2006).

APPENDIX B

MAJOR TREATISES AND SERVICES BY SUBJECT

Note: Availability in Lexis and Westlaw is noted if the material is included in standard academic subscriptions. Some resources (such as BNA services) are available at additional cost, and others (such as West hornbooks) are offered to practitioners but not to law schools.

ADMINISTRATIVE LAW (KF5401–KF5425)

Alfred C. Aman & William T. Mayton, *Administrative Law* (2d ed. 2001)

Charles H. Koch, Jr., *Administrative Law and Practice* (2d ed. 1997–date) [Westlaw]

Richard J. Pierce, Jr., *Administrative Law Treatise* (5th ed. 2010–date)

Jacob A. Stein et al., *Administrative Law* (1977–date) [Lexis]

ADMIRALTY AND MARITIME LAW (KF1096–KF1137)

Elijah E. Jhirad et al., *Benedict on Admiralty* (7th ed. 1958–date) [Lexis]

Thomas J. Schoenbaum, *Admiralty and Maritime Law* (4th ed. 2004–date) [Westlaw]

ANTITRUST & TRADE REGULATION (KF1601–KF1668)

Louis Altman, *Callmann on Unfair Competition, Trademarks and Monopolies* (4th ed. 1981–date) [Westlaw]

Philip Areeda & Herbert Hovenkamp, *Antitrust Law: An Analysis of Antitrust Principles and Their Application* (2d & 3d eds. 2000–date)

Herbert Hovenkamp, *Federal Antitrust Policy: The Law of Competition and Its Practice* (3d ed. 2005)

Earl W. Kintner, *Federal Antitrust Law* (1980–date) [Lexis]

Lawrence A. Sullivan & Warren S. Grimes, *The Law of Antitrust: An Integrated Handbook* (2d ed. 2006)

Julian O. Von Kalinowski et al., *Antitrust Laws and Trade Regulation* (2d ed. 1996–date) [Lexis]

Services: *Antitrust & Trade Regulation Report* (BNA), *Trade Regulation Reporter* (CCH)

ART AND ENTERTAINMENT LAW (KF4288–KF4305)

Leonard D. DuBoff & Sally Holt Caplin, *The Deskbook of Art Law* (2d ed. 1993–date)

Ralph E. Lerner & Judith Bresler, *Art Law* (3d ed. 2005) [Westlaw]

Alexander Lindey & Michael Landau, *Lindey on Entertainment, Publishing, and the Arts* (3d ed. 2004–date) [Westlaw]

BANKING LAW (KF966–KF1040)

Barkley Clark & Barbara Clark, *The Law of Bank Deposits, Collections, and Credit Cards* (rev. ed. 1999–date)

Michael P. Malloy, *Banking Law and Regulation* (1994–date)

Fred H. Miller & Alvin C. Harrell, *The Law of Modern Payment Systems* (2003)

William H. Schlichting et al., *Banking Law* (1981–date) [Lexis]

Services: *Banking Report* (BNA), *Federal Banking Law Reporter* (CCH)

BANKRUPTCY (KF1501–KF1548)

Collier on Bankruptcy (Alan N. Resnick & Henry J. Sommer eds., 15th & 16th eds. 1985–date) [Lexis]

Daniel R. Cowans, *Bankruptcy Law and Practice* (7th ed. 1998–date)

David G. Epstein et al., *Bankruptcy* (2d ed. 1993)

Norton Bankruptcy Law and Practice (William L. Norton, Jr. ed., 3d ed. 2008–date) [Lexis, Westlaw]

Services: *Bankruptcy Law Reporter* (BNA), *Bankruptcy Law Reporter* (CCH), *Bankruptcy Service* (West) [Westlaw]

CIVIL RIGHTS (KF1325, KF4741–KF4786)

Joseph G. Cook & John L. Sobieski, *Civil Rights Actions* (1983–date) [Lexis]

Harold S. Lewis & Elizabeth J. Norman, *Civil Rights Law and Practice* (2d ed. 2004)

Sheldon H. Nahmod, *Civil Rights and Civil Liberties Litigation: The Law of Section 1983* (4th ed. 1997–date)

Martin A. Schwartz & John E. Kirklin, *Section 1983 Litigation* (3d/4th eds. 1997–date)

COMMERCIAL LAW (KF871–KF890)

Larry E. Edmondson, *Domke on Commercial Arbitration* (3d ed. 2003–date) [Westlaw]

William D. Hawkland, *Uniform Commercial Code Series* (1982–date) [Westlaw]

Lary Lawrence, *Lawrence's Anderson on the Uniform Commercial Code* (3d ed. 1981–date) [Westlaw]

Deborah L. Nelson & Jennifer L. Howicz, *Williston on Sales* (5th ed. 1994–date)

James J. White & Robert S. Summers, *Uniform Commercial Code* (5th/6th eds. 2002–date)

COMMUNICATIONS LAW (KF2761–KF2849)

Peter W. Huber et al. *Federal Telecommunications Law* (2d ed. 1999–date)

Harvey L. Zuckman et al., *Modern Communications Law* (1999–date)

CONFLICT OF LAWS (KF410–KF418)

Eugene F. Scoles et al. *Conflict of Laws* (4th ed. 2004)

Russell J. Weintraub, *Commentary on the Conflict of Laws* (5th ed. 2006–date)

CONSTITUTIONAL LAW (KF4501–KF4558)

Erwin Chemerinsky, *Constitutional Law: Principles and Policies* (3d ed. 2006)

Jennifer Friesen, *State Constitutional Law: Litigating Individual Rights, Claims, and Defenses* (4th ed. 2006–date)

Ronald D. Rotunda & John E. Nowak, *Treatise on Constitutional Law: Substance and Procedure* (4th ed. 2007–date)

Laurence H. Tribe, *American Constitutional Law* (2d/3d eds. 1988–2000)

CONSTRUCTION LAW (KF901–KF902)

Philip L. Bruner & Patrick J. O'Connor, *Bruner & O'Connor on Construction Law* (2002–date) [Westlaw]

Construction Law (Steven G. M. Stein ed. 1986–date) [Lexis]

CONTRACTS (KF801–KF839)

Corbin on Contracts (Joseph M. Perillo ed., rev. ed.1993–date) [Lexis]

E.   Allan Farnsworth, *Farnsworth on Contracts* (3d ed. 2004–date)

Richard A. Lord, *Williston on Contracts* (4th ed. 1990–date) [Westlaw]

John Edward Murray, Jr., *Murray on Contracts* (4th ed. 2001) [Lexis]

Joseph M. Perillo, *Calamari and Perillo on Contracts* (6th ed. 2009)

CORPORATIONS (KF1384–KF1480, KFD213)

James D. Cox & Thomas Lee Hazen, *Cox and Hazen on Corporations* (2d ed. 2003–date)

Fletcher Cyclopedia of the Law of Private Corporations (1931–date) [Westlaw]

Franklin A. Gevurtz, *Corporation Law* (2000)

Martin D. Ginsburg & Jack S. Levin, *Mergers, Acquisitions, and Buyouts* (semiannual)

F.   Hodge O'Neal & Robert B. Thompson, *O'Neal and Thompson's Close Corporations and LLCs: Law and Practice* (rev. 3d ed. 1997–date) [Westlaw]

Services: *Corporate Practice Series* (BNA), *Corporate Governance Guide* (CCH), *Corporation* (Aspen Publishers)

CRIMINAL LAW AND PROCEDURE (KF9201–KF9479, KF9601–KF9763)

Sara Sun Beale et al., *Grand Jury Law and Practice* (2d ed. 1997–date) [Westlaw]

Randy Hertz & James S. Liebman, *Federal Habeas Corpus Practice and Procedure* (5th ed. 2005–date) [Lexis]

Wayne R. LaFave, *Search and Seizure: A Treatise on the Fourth Amendment* (4th ed. 2004–date) [Westlaw]

Wayne R. LaFave, *Substantive Criminal Law* (2d ed. 2003–date) [Westlaw]

Wayne R. LaFave et al., *Criminal Procedure* (3d ed. 2007–date) [Westlaw]

Paul H. Robinson, *Criminal Law Defenses* (1984–date) [Westlaw]

Service: *Criminal Law Reporter* (BNA)

DISABILITIES (KF480, KF3469)

Peter Blanck et al., *Disability, Civil Rights Law, and Policy* (2004)

Michael L. Perlin, *Mental Disability Law: Civil and Criminal* (2d ed. 1998–date)

Henry H. Perritt, Jr., *Americans with Disabilities Act Handbook* (4th ed. 2003–date)

Laura F. Rothstein & Julia Rothstein, *Disabilities and the Law* (4th ed. 2009–date)

EDUCATION LAW (KF4101–KF4257)

Education Law (James A. Rapp ed., 1984–date) [Lexis]

William A. Kaplin & Barbara A. Lee, *The Law of Higher Education* (4th ed. 2006)

Service: *Individuals with Disabilities Education Law Report* (LRP Publications)

EMPLOYMENT AND LABOR LAW (KF3301–KF3580)

The Developing Labor Law: The Boards, the Courts, and the National Labor Relations Act (John C. Higgins ed., 5th ed. 2006–date)

Frank Elkouri & Edna Asper Elkouri, *How Arbitration Works* (6th ed. 2003)

Robert A. Gorman & Matthew W. Finkin, *Basic Text on Labor Law: Unionization and Collective Bargaining* (2d ed. 2004)

Arthur Larson & Lex K. Larson, *Larson's Workers' Compensation Law* (1952–date) [Lexis]

Lex K. Larson, *Employment Discrimination* (2d ed. 1994–date) [Lexis]

Barbara Lindemann & Paul Grossman, *Employment Discrimination Law* (4th ed. 2007–date)

Mark A. Rothstein et al., *Employment Law* (4th ed. 2009–date)

Charles A. Sullivan & Lauren M. Walter, *Employment Discrimination: Law and Practice* (4th ed. 2009–date) [Loislaw]

Services: *Collective Bargaining Negotiations and Contracts* (BNA), *Employment Coordinator* (West), *Labor Law Reporter* (CCH), *Labor Relations Reporter* (BNA), *Occupational Safety &*

Health Reporter *(BNA),* Pension & Benefits Reporter *(BNA),* Pension Plan Guide *(CCH)*

ENVIRONMENTAL LAW (KF3775–KF3816)

Frank P. Grad, *Treatise on Environmental Law* (1973–date) [Lexis]

Law of Environmental Protection (Sheldon M. Novick et al. eds., 1987–date)

William H. Rodgers, Jr., *Environmental Law* (1986–date)

A.   Dan Tarlock, *Law of Water Rights and Resources* (1988–date) [Westlaw]

Water and Water Rights (Robert E. Beck ed., 1991–date)

Services: *Environment Reporter* (BNA), *Environmental Law Reporter* (Environmental Law Institute) [Lexis, Westlaw]

EVIDENCE (KF8931–KF8969, KF9660–KF9678)

Paul C. Giannelli & Edward J. Imwinkelried, *Scientific Evidence* (4th ed. 2007–date) [Lexis]

Michael H. Graham, *Handbook of Federal Evidence* (6th ed. 2006–date) [Westlaw]

McCormick on Evidence (Kenneth S. Broun ed., 6th ed. 2006)

Stephen A. Saltzburg et al., *Federal Rules of Evidence Manual* (9th ed. 2006–date) [Lexis]

Weinstein's Federal Evidence (Joseph M. McLaughlin ed., 1997–date) [Lexis]

John Henry Wigmore et al., *Evidence in Trials at Common Law* (4th ed. 1961–date) [Loislaw]

FAMILY LAW (KF501–KF553)

Adoption Law and Practice (Joan H. Hollinger ed., 1988–date) [Lexis]

Homer H. Clark, Jr., *The Law of Domestic Relations in the United States* (2d ed. 1987)

Donald T. Kramer, *Legal Rights of Children* (2d ed. 2005–date)

Service: *Family Law Reporter* (BNA)

FEDERAL PRACTICE (KF8820–KF9058, KF9650)

Erwin Chemerinsky, *Federal Jurisdiction* (5th ed. 2007)

Alba Conte & Herbert B. Newberg, *Newberg on Class Actions* (4th ed. 2002–date) [Westlaw]

Eugene Gressman et al., *Supreme Court Practice* (9th ed. 2007)

Moore's Federal Practice (Daniel R. Coquillette et al. eds., 3d ed. 1997–date) [Lexis]

Charles Alan Wright & Mary Kay Kane, *Law of Federal Courts* (6th ed. 2002)

Charles Alan Wright et al., *Federal Practice and Procedure* (1st–4th eds. 1969–date) [Westlaw]

Service: *The United States Law Week* (BNA)

HEALTH CARE (KF3821–KF3838)

Barry R. Furrow et al., *Health Law* (2000)

David W. Louisell et al., *Medical Malpractice* (1960–date) [Lexis]

Services: *Health Law Reporter* (BNA), *Medicare–Medicaid Guide* (CCH)

IMMIGRATION (KF4800–KF4848)

Austin T. Fragomen, Jr. & Steven C. Bell, *Immigration Fundamentals: A Guide to Law and Practice* (4th ed. 1996–date) [Westlaw]

Austin T. Fragomen, Jr. et al., *Immigration Procedures Handbook* (annual) [Westlaw]

Charles Gordon et al., *Immigration Law and Procedure* (rev. ed. 1966–date) [Lexis]

Dan Kesselbrenner & Lory D. Rosenberg, *Immigration Law and Crimes* (1984–date) [Westlaw]

INSURANCE (KF1146–KF1238)

Rowland H. Long & Mark S. Rhodes, *The Law of Liability Insurance* (1966–date) [Lexis]

New Appleman on Insurance [gradually replacing *Holmes's Appleman on Insurance, 2d*] (Jeffrey E. Thomas ed., 2009–date) [Lexis]

Lee R. Russ & Thomas F. Segalla, *Couch on Insurance 3d* (1995–date) [Westlaw]

INTELLECTUAL PROPERTY (KF2971–KF3193)

Donald S. Chisum, *Chisum on Patents* (1978–date) [Lexis]

Paul Goldstein, *Goldstein on Copyright* (3d ed. 2005–date)

J.   Thomas McCarthy, *McCarthy on Trademarks and Unfair Competition* (4th ed. 1996–date) [Westlaw]

Roger M. Milgrim, *Milgrim on Trade Secrets* (1967–date) [Lexis]

R.   Carl Moy, *Moy's Walker on Patents* (4th ed. 2003–date) [Westlaw]

Melville B. Nimmer & David Nimmer, *Nimmer on Copyright* (1963–date) [Lexis]

LEGAL ETHICS (KF305–KF314)

James J. Alfini et al., *Judicial Conduct and Ethics* (4th ed. 2007–date)

Geoffrey C. Hazard, Jr. & W. William Hodes, *The Law of Lawyering* (3d ed. 2001–date)

Ronald E. Mallen & Jeffrey M. Smith, *Legal Malpractice* (annual) [Westlaw]

Service: *ABA/BNA Lawyer's Manual on Professional Conduct* (BNA)

LOCAL GOVERNMENT (KF5300–KF5332)

John Martinez et al., *Local Government Law* (1981–date)

Eugene McQuillin et al., *The Law of Municipal Corporations* (3d ed. 1949–date) [Westlaw]

PARTNERSHIPS AND LIMITED LIABILITY COMPANIES (KF1371–KF1381)

Alan R. Bromberg & Larry E. Ribstein, *Bromberg and Ribstein on Partnership* (1988–date)

William A. Gregory, *The Law of Agency and Partnership* (3d ed. 2001)

Larry E. Ribstein & Robert R. Keatinge, *Ribstein and Keatinge on Limited Liability Companies* (2d ed. 2004–date)

PRODUCTS LIABILITY (KF1296–KF1297)

Louis R. Frumer & Melvin I. Friedman, *Products Liability* (1960–date) [Lexis]

David G. Owen, *Products Liability Law* (2d ed. 2008)

Services: *Product Safety & Liability Reporter* (BNA), *Products Liability Reports* (CCH)

PROPERTY (KF560–KF720)

Friedman on Leases (Patrick A. Randolph, Jr. ed., 5th ed. 2004–date) [Westlaw]

Grant S. Nelson & Dale A. Whitman, *Real Estate Finance Law* (5th ed. 2007) [Westlaw]

Powell on Real Property (Patrick J. Rohan ed., 1949–date) [Lexis]

William B. Stoebuck & Dale A. Whitman, *The Law of Property* (3d ed. 2000)

Thompson on Real Property (David A. Thomas ed., 1st/2d eds. 1994–date) [Lexis]

REMEDIES (KF9010–KF9039)

Dan B. Dobbs, *Dobbs Law of Remedies: Damages, Equity, Restitution* (2d ed. 1993)

George E. Palmer, *The Law of Restitution* (1978–date)

Linda L. Schlueter, *Punitive Damages* (5th ed. 2005–date) [Lexis]

SECURITIES (KF1066–KF1084, KF1428–KF1457)

Harold S. Bloomenthal, *Securities Law Handbook* (annual) [Westlaw]

Thomas Lee Hazen, *Treatise on the Law of Securities Regulation* (6th ed. 2009–date) [Westlaw]

Joseph C. Long, *Blue Sky Law* (1985–date) [Westlaw]

Louis Loss & Joel Seligman, *Fundamentals of Securities Regulation* (5th ed. 2004–date)

Louis Loss et al., *Securities Regulation* (3d/4th eds. 1989–date)

Services: *Blue Sky Law Reports* (CCH), *Federal Securities Law Reports* (CCH), *Securities Regulation & Law Report* (BNA)

TAXATION (KF6271–KF6645)

Boris I. Bittker & Lawrence Lokken, *Federal Taxation of Income, Estates, and Gifts* (2d/3d eds. 1989–date) [Westlaw]

Boris I. Bittker et al., *Federal Income Taxation of Individuals* (3d ed. 2002–date) [Westlaw]

Jerome R. Hellerstein & Walter Hellerstein, *State Taxation* (3d ed. 1998–date) [Westlaw]

William S. McKee et al., *Federal Taxation of Partnerships and Partners* (4th ed. 2007–date) [Westlaw]

Jacob Mertens, Jr., *The Law of Federal Income Taxation* (1942–date) [Westlaw]

Richard B. Stephens et al., *Federal Estate and Gift Taxation* (8th ed. 2002–date) [Westlaw]

Arthur B. Willis et al., *Partnership Taxation* (6th ed. 1997–date) [Westlaw]

Services: *Federal Estate and Gift Tax Reports* (CCH), *Federal Tax Coordinator 2d* (RIA), *Standard Federal Tax Reports* (CCH), *State Tax Guide* (CCH), *United States Tax Reporter* (RIA)

TORTS (KF1246–KF1327)

Dan B. Dobbs, *The Law of Torts* (2001–date)

Oscar S. Gray, *Harper, James and Gray on Torts* (3d rev. ed. 2006–date)

Rodney A. Smolla, *Law of Defamation* (2d ed. 1999–date) [Westlaw]

Stuart M. Speiser et al., *The American Law of Torts* (1983–date)

TRUSTS AND ESTATES (KF726–KF780)

George G. Bogert & George T. Bogert, *The Law of Trusts and Trustees* (2d/3d eds. 1977–date) [Westlaw]

William J. Bowe & Douglas H. Parker, *Page on the Law of Wills* (1960–date) [Lexis]

A. James Casner & Jeffrey N. Pennell, *Estate Planning* (6th ed. 1995–date)

William M. McGovern & Sheldon F. Kurtz, *Wills, Trusts and Estates* (3d ed. 2004)

Austin Wakeman Scott et al., *Scott and Ascher on Trusts* (5th eds. 2006–date)

ZONING AND LAND USE (KF5599–KF5710)

Daniel R. Mandelker, *Land Use Law* (5th ed. 2003–date) [Lexis]

Arden H. Rathkopf & Daren A. Rathkopf, *Rathkopf's The Law of Zoning and Planning* (1975–date) [Westlaw]

Julius L. Sackman et al., *Nichols on Eminent Domain* (3d ed. 1964–date) [Lexis]

Patricia E. Salkin, *American Law of Zoning* (5th ed. 2008–date) [Westlaw]

RESOURCE INDEX

References are to Pages

Boldface references are to illustrations

Note: Entries in plain type are online resources, available either for free or by subscription. Entries in italics are print publications, many of which are also available online. See the *Nutshell*'s companion website <www.law.virginia.edu/nutshell> for a regularly updated collection of links to all websites mentioned in the book.

SUBJECT INDEX

References are to Pages

Boldface references are to exhibits

†